Soul and Psyche

The Bible in Psychological Perspective

Wayne G. Rollins

Fortress Press

Minneapolis

To Donnalou
sine qua non

SOUL AND PSYCHE
The Bible in Psychological Perspective

Copyright © 1999 Augsburg Fortress. All rights reserved. Except for brief quotations in critical articles or reviews, no part of this book may be reproduced in any manner without prior written permission from the publisher. Write to: Permissions, Augsburg Fortress, Box 1209, Minneapolis, MN 55440.

Cover design by Marti Naughton
Book design by Julie Odland

Rollins, Wayne G.
    Soul and Psyche : the Bible in psychological perspective / Wayne
    Rollins
        p.   cm.
    Includes bibliographical references and indexes.
    ISBN 0-8006-2716-4 (alk. paper)
    1. Bible — Psychology.   I. Title.
    BS645.R65   1999
    220.6'o1'9 — dc21   99-39508
                                                            CIP

The paper used in this publication meets the minimum requirements for American National Standard for Information Sciences — Permanence of Paper for Printed Library Materials, ANSI Z329.48–1984.   ∞™

Manufactured in the U.S.A.   AF 1-2716

03   02   01   00   99   1   2   3   4   5   6   7   8   9   10

Contents

Preface

Everything to do with religion, everything it is and asserts, touches the human soul so closely that psychology least of all can afford to overlook it.

C. G. Jung[1]

We do not yet grasp what historical forces brought forth and determined early Christianity. But beside and within this external history there is an inner history. . . . Anyone who thinks that this religion can be illumined historically and factually without psychological reflection is just as much in error as one who pretends that everything about this religion can be said in this fashion.

Gerd Theissen[2]

The psychological and psychoanalytical analyses of human experience have proven their worth in the area of religion and enable one to detect multidimensional aspects of the biblical message. . . . The aid that can come from this approach to . . . [the historical-critical] method cannot be underestimated.

Joseph A. Fitzmyer, S.J.[3]

In the last third of the twentieth century a discipline has resurfaced within biblical studies that applies psychological and psychoanalytic insight to the study of the Bible, its origins, its content, its interpretation, and the history of its effects. The discipline is called psychological biblical criticism,[4] keeping with the scholarly tradition of using the term *criticism* to refer to strategies for studying newly appreciated aspects of the Bible. The purpose of this volume is to present a history of the discipline, a definition of the field, and an agenda for its application to biblical exegesis and hermeneutics (the analysis and interpretation of the Bible).

Psychological biblical criticism is one of many new approaches to Scripture that have developed since the 1960s. Prior to that time, the approach most commonly taken by biblical scholars was that of historical-literary criticism. Since then, new angles of vision have developed that bring attention to previously unnoticed aspects of Scripture. These include, for example, ideological, feminist, rhetorical, social-scientific, canonical, contextual, structuralist, narrative, reader-response, and psychological criticism.

What psychological biblical criticism brings to the study of the Bible is a renewed appreciation of the role of the human psyche or soul in the history of the Bible and its interpretation.

The present volume aims at telling the story of psychological criticism, from both a retrospective and prospective view. Chapters 1–3 are retrospective, chapters 4–6 are prospective.

Chapter 1 traces the history of biblical psychologies—the earliest attempt to approach Scripture with a psychological question in mind—from the early church to the beginning of the twentieth century. Throughout, I use modern categorizations of psychology although those terms were not used at the time. The chapter ends with the landmark work of Franz Delitzsch, *A System of Biblical Psychology* (1855), penned shortly before the birth of modern psychology, and M. Scott Fletcher's, *The Psychology of the New Testament* (1912).

Chapter 2 documents the early twentieth century shift within psychological biblical studies away from biblical psychology (biblical ideas about the human soul or psyche) to the new psychoanalytic insights of Sigmund Freud and Carl Gustav Jung, with their emphasis on unconscious as well as conscious activities of the human soul.

Chapter 3 traces psychological criticism through the twentieth century, from the negative reaction to psychology within mainline biblical scholarship during the first seven decades, to the change in attitude signaled in F. C. Grant's call to a "Psychological Study of the Bible" in 1968. The chapter analyzes the reasons for this change, documents its results, and provides a comprehensive survey of psychological approaches to the Bible and its interpretation since the 1960s. Writing in the 1990s, Joseph Fitzmyer, S. J., comments on this research:

> The psychological and psychoanalytical analyses of human experience have proven their worth in the area of religion and enable one to detect multidimensional aspects of the biblical message. In particular, this approach has been invaluable in the analytical explanation of biblical symbols, cultic rituals, sacrifice, legal prohibitions, and biblical tabus. Yet once again, there is no one psychological or psychoanalytic exegesis that can substitute for the properly oriented historical-critical method, whereas the aid that can come from this approach to that method cannot be underestimated.[5]

Chapter 4, the beginning of the prospective section, proposes a definition and research agenda for the field. It provides a history of the terms, *psyche, soul*, and *self*, and suggests a working model of the self as presuppositional for the field. It also outlines the special "revisioning" that a psychological critical approach brings to the Bible, its origins, its interpretation, its history, and its purpose.

Chapter 5 proposes the exegetical agenda (the analysis of the Bible's content), suggesting the application of psychological insight to seven aspects of the text: biblical symbols, archetypal images, and myths; unconscious factors at work in the history of biblical motifs and cultic practices; the psychodynamics within biblical narratives and texts; the psychology of biblical personality portraits; the psychology of biblical religious experience, ranging from dreams and exorcisms to glossolalia and conversion; the psychology of biblical ethics; and biblical psychology.

Chapter 6 discusses the hermeneutical agenda (the interpretation of the Bible's meaning). This involves the application of psychological insight to four aspects of the transaction that takes place between text and reader: the effects of texts on readers; the effects of readers on texts; the extratextual methods to which readers resort for the performance of texts (for example, homilies, stained glass windows, miracle plays, liturgies, and creeds); and the history of biblical effects—both pathogenic and therapeutic—on individuals and communities.

In the end, the goal of psychological biblical criticism is to look at the Bible and its interpretation with an eye to what James Dittes has called the "habits of the soul."[6] In the context of thinking about the Bible and its interpretation, the following "habits" would be of special interest: the ways in which the human soul experiences lostness and sickness; the ways the soul finds healing and revelation of meaning; the words, images, symbols, and literary genres it devises to convey that meaning; the richly different forms of expression it finds to celebrate that meaning; and the ways it applies that meaning to its own life or the lives of others, aimed at effects that can be helpful, but sometimes destructive. These "habits" would also include the psychic baggage the soul brings to all its tasks and situations, drawn from its own experience, but also from a larger reservoir of revelation and insight that can lift the soul beyond the ordinary. From a psychological biblical-critical perspective the Bible is preeminently a demonstration of the "habits of the soul." It is a book of the soul, written to the soul, about the soul, for the soul's care and cure.

It is my hope that this volume and the growing number of works in this field may further the rapprochement between two perspectives that have long been at loggerheads in the field of biblical studies: the historical and the psychological. It is time for biblical scholarship to take seriously the psychological aspects of biblical studies as matters of fact, and therefore as part of the agenda of critical biblical scholarship. To be sure, the historical approach has served well in protecting against a mindless reading of the Bible. But a psychological approach is needed to protect against a reading that is soulless. As Carl Jung observed, "Everything to do with religion, everything it is and asserts, touches the human soul so closely that psychology least of all can afford to overlook it."[7] Nor can biblical scholarship.

I would like to thank many friends and colleagues who have contributed to the project this volume represents: James E. Dittes, for his long-standing interest in and support of this project; Margaret Alter, D. Andrew Kille, and J. Harold Ellens for reviewing sections of the manuscript; and Wilhelm Wuellner for compiling one of the early bibliographic lists of works in the field. I am also indebted to various members of the steering committee and participants in the Society of Biblical Literature program unit on Psychology and Biblical Studies for collaborative input, critical judgment, and support in the development of the SBL unit. These include: Paul N. Anderson, Matthias Beier, Kamila Blessing, Schuyler Brown, Martin J. Buss, Marcus Borg, Donald Capps, Adela Yarbro Collins, Charles T. Davis, III, David J. Halperin, Bernhard Lang, André Lacocque, Dan Merkur, David L. Miller, Michael Willett Newheart, Ilona N. Rashkow, Ralph L. Underwood, and Walter Wink.

I am grateful to Assumption College colleagues, Roger Corriveau, A.A., Ellen Guerin, R.S.M., and Gerald McCarthy in theology; Arlene Vadum, Edmund O'Reilly, and Leonard Doerfler in psychology; George Aubin in linguistics for assistance on technical points; and André Dargis, A.A., Nuala Cotter, R.A., Thérèse Duross, R.A., Marc LePain, and Diane McGuire for collegial interest and encouragement in the project. I am also indebted to Assumption College for the award of a full year sabbatical leave in 1996–97 for research on this project, to the Graduate Theological Union in Berkeley, California, for the use of its library and for its cordiality to visiting scholars, and to the Berkeley Presbyterian Mission Homes for ecumenical and international hospitality during that sabbatical year. I would like to express appreciation as well to Marshall D. Johnson, J. Michael West, K. C. Hanson, Cynthia Thompson, Charles B. Puskas, and Julie Odland of Fortress Press for their commitment to the project, expert help, and ability to make the rough places plain.

Finally, my thanks to my sons and their wives, who were always interested in the state of the project, and to my wife Donnalou, constant collaborator and soul mate.

Part One
Retrospect

1

Biblical Psychology

The Early Church
to the Early Twentieth Century

> Biblical psychology is no science of yesterday. It is one of the oldest sciences of the church.
>
> Franz Delitzsch, 1861[1]

> Philosophers and physicians can tell us what to call these faculties, how they are to be distinctly classified, and in what portions of the body they are to be exercised.
>
> Tertullian, ca. 200 C.E.[2]

> Pity poor psychology. First it lost its soul, then its mind, then consciousness, and now it's having trouble with behavior.
>
> Anonymous[3]

In 1855, Franz Julius Delitzsch, one of the premier biblical scholars of the nineteenth century, published the first edition of *A System of Biblical Psychology*.[4] Sigmund Freud was born one year later; Carl Jung was not to be born for another twenty years; and Wilhelm Wundt, often called the "principal founder of modern psychology," was not to establish his first psychological laboratory for another twenty-three years.[5] Delitzsch opens his work with the pronouncement that "biblical psychology is no science of yesterday. It is one of the oldest sciences of the church." Surveying Western theology from Justin Martyr and Tertullian, Augustine and Gregory the Great, through Aquinas and the Reformation up to his own time in the nineteenth century, Delitzsch concludes "that the ancient church had a psychological literature that claims respect no less for its extent than for its substance."[6]

Biblical psychology can be defined as the study of the biblical perspective on the origin, nature, pathology, health, and destiny of the human psyche or soul.[7] A theological and philosophical discipline, biblical psychology represents the longest phase in the story of a psychological critical approach to the Bible. The present chapter will recount its history, focusing on three dimensions: 1. the origination of the term *psychology* (by biblical theologians) in the sixteenth century and its gradual metamorphosis in meaning in the nineteenth and twentieth centuries; 2. the emergence of biblical psychological reflection in the second century—with roots in the "psychology" of Aristotle, Plato, and the Stoics—and its development in dialogue with the Greek tradition in the patristic, medieval, Reformation, and Enlightenment periods, visiting Tertullian and Augustine en route as case studies; and 3. the content and significance of Delitzsch's *A System of Biblical Psychology* (1855) along with M. Scott Fletcher's, *The Psychology of the New Testament* (1912), as two prime examples of biblical psychology in the late nineteenth and early twentieth centuries.

The Origin and Metamorphosis of the Term *Psychology*

Psychology was studied and practiced long before it was named. The term was coined in the sixteenth century to designate the venerable discipline of research and reflection by philosophers and biblical scholars on the nature, habits, and powers of the human psyche, anima, or soul. It makes its first documented appearance at the onset of the Reformation: a latinized form of the word, *psichologia*, occurs in an obscure reference to the work of an obscure Serbo-Croatian, Marco Marulic (1524). Shortly after, in 1530, Philipp Melanchton, Luther's protégé, a theologian and biblical scholar, introduced the term in his *Commentarius de Anima* ("Commentary on the Soul"), to differentiate *psychology*, the study of the human soul (*anima/psyche*), from *pneumatology*, the study of the spirit (*spiritus/pneuma*), which at the time denoted not only humans, but classes of angels, demons, and gods as well.[8]

By 1583 the term appeared in its French form, *psychologie*, and in 1590, Marburg scholar, Rudolf Goeckel (1547–1628) employed the Greek form in the title of a book, *Psychologia, hoc est, de hominis perfectione* ("Psychology — That Is, Concerning Human Improvement"), a volume that went through three printings before the end of the century.[9] By 1653, psychology was seen as one of three subdivisions of anthropology: psychology (the soul), somatology (the body), and hematology (the blood).

By the 1700s psychology was a legitimate field of inquiry. Christian von Wolff (1679–1754) produced two volumes that defined the two fields into which it would be divided for the next two hundred years, *Psychologia*

Empirica (1732) and *Psychologia Rationalis* (1734). *Empirical psychology* rests on what is immediately observable to sense experience. *Rational psychology*, also known as *philosophical* or *metaphysical* psychology (von Wolff's preference), rests on "reason and innate ideas in the search for truth," in the traditions of Plato and the Stoics.[10]

By the 1800s, when Franz Delitzsch wrote *A System of Biblical Psychology*, the term *psychology* enjoyed currency in German and French philosophical circles, and began to appear in cognate form in other languages: Italian (*psicologia*), Scandinavian (*psykologi*, *psychologi*), and English (*psychology*).[11] At the same time, however, it also began undergoing a shift in meaning, edging away from "the study of the soul" or "psyche" to the more empirically defensible study of the mind. Already in the mid-1600s, British Empiricist Thomas Hobbes had dismissed the notion of soul as at best a metaphor for life and at worst "pernicious Aristotelian nonsense," tracing all psychological events to material causes in the nervous system and brain.[12] In 1836, William Hamilton, professor of logic and metaphysics at Edinburgh, testified to the term's shift in meaning as well as its growing popularity: "The term psychology is now, and has long been the ordinary expression for the doctrine of the mind [no longer psyche] in the philosophical language of every other European nation."[13]

By mid-nineteenth century, psychology had come of age professionally, as evidenced in its widening acceptance in academic, medical, scientific, legal, educational, and theological circles, and its gradual institutionalization in professional journals, societies, and university departments. The first issue of *The Journal of Psychological Medicine and Mental Pathology* appeared in 1848; Herbert Spenser published a textbook, *Principles of Psychology*, in 1855. Psychology as a discipline in its own right was professionally differentiated from anthropology and the biological sciences (as well as from biblical psychology), and was appreciated increasingly for its relevance to the work of other disciplines, such as educational theory, law, and language. By the end of the century, in the United States alone, over two dozen universities offered instruction in psychology, and three psychological journals were published.[14] In 1892, G. Stanley Hall of Clark University founded the American Psychological Association with thirty-one charter members. Two years later, his optimism about the discipline was plain:

> "Psychology" is already represented in two score of the best institutions. It has already a voluminous literature; . . . it studies the instincts of animals from the highest to the lowest . . . it studies the myths, customs and beliefs of primitive man . . . it devotes itself to the study of sanity and nervous diseases. . . [and] is slowly rewriting the whole history of philosophy and, in the opinion of many of its more sanguine devotees, is showing itself not only to be the long hoped

for, long delayed science of man, to which all other sciences are bringing their ripest and best thoughts, but is introducing a period that will be known hereafter as the psychological era of scientific thought even more than a few recent decades have been marked by evolution.[15]

What does the term *psychology* come to mean in the first half of the twentieth century? Something quite different from its sixteenth century origins. As François Lapointe observes, "Psychology gained currency precisely at the time when psychology was about to become anything but the 'study of the soul,'"[16] or, one might add, "anything but the study of the psyche." The nineteenth century founders of the American Psychological Association would have been astonished to discover that by mid-twentieth century, the term *psyche* had dropped out of psychology in many quarters. It had first been conceived of in English as *soul*, then *mind*, then *consciousness*, then *behavior*; finally the word itself became conspicuous for its absence from most psychology texts.[17] As one wag observed: "Pity poor psychology. First it lost its soul, then its mind, then consciousness, and now it's having trouble with behavior."[18] By the end of the twentieth century, however, the tide turns, and the words *soul* and *psyche* begin to resurface in popular and professional use:

> As neurologists, psychologists and biologists have zeroed in more and more precisely on the physical causes of mental disorders, they have found themselves addressing a much deeper mystery, a set of interrelated conundrums probably as old as humanity: What, precisely, is the mind, the elusive entity where intelligence, decision making, perception, awareness and sense of self reside? Where is it located? How does it work? Does it arise from purely physical processes. . . ? Or is it something beyond the merely physical—something ethereal that might be close to the spiritual concept of the soul?[19]

In the 1990s, the American Psychological Association reported fifty-eight different fields within the discipline of psychology, ranging from physiological psychology, psychobiology, and psychometrics, to behavioral, social, and cognitive psychology, to pastoral psychology, learning theory, and psychoanalysis, to name a few.[20] At the same time it evidenced signs of a growing split between the academic scientists and the mushrooming number of clinical-practitioners. For some, the psyche (not to mention soul) is a bogus concept, beyond empirical demonstration. But for an increasing number of others, the concept of psyche has inched back into psychology with some of its original sixteenth-century meaning; it designates a field of study devoted to the *psyche* (Greek), *soul* (English), or *Seele* (German)—each a semantic cue for the centered unity that appears to constitute the self and its interrelated faculties of perception, sensation, mind, memory, emotion, will, and imagination, among others.

Biblical psychology plays a significant role in the history of this enterprise, as a specialized way of thinking about the psyche in dialogue with the great psychological tradition in Greco-Roman philosophy. Originating in the second century, biblical psychology continues in the nineteenth and twentieth centuries as one of the voices in the mélange of psychological schools that define the field today.

Biblical Psychology within the Context of the History of Psychology

As Delitzsch noted, "Biblical psychology is no science of yesterday."[21] But neither is psychology itself. According to most contemporary historians of the field, psychology "is as old as the inquiring self-conscious mind of man."[22] R. S. Peters and C. A. Mace identify three stages in the history of psychology: a "presystematic," "systematic but prescientific," and "scientific."[23] In all three periods biblical psychology plays a role.

Stage 1, presystematic psychology, is "by far the longest of the three phases."[24] It is found universally in the form of folk wisdom that offers observations and reflections on the nature, structure, habits, foibles, powers, and purpose of the human soul, mediating this wisdom in stories, fables, legends, myths, proverbs, riddles, exhortations, homilies, admonitions, and laws. The wisdom tradition of the Judeo-Christian Bible finds itself especially at home in this category, along with elements from the myths and legends of Genesis, the legal codes, the prophetic literature, the psalms, the sayings of Jesus, and Pauline parenesis. The Bible regularly offers psychological observations on the human condition, ranging from recommendations for probing the hidden depths of the self (Prov. 20:5), to comments on the eye as an instrument of projection (Matt. 7:23).

Stage 2, systematic but prescientific psychology, is better known as *philosophical* psychology. It has flourished in the West for over two thousand years, from the dawn of classical Greek psychology in the fourth century B.C.E., through the birth of British empirical psychology in the seventeenth century and the new scientific psychology in the nineteenth, and continuing on its own into the twentieth century in a parallel but uneasy relationship with those two movements. Its key characteristic is reliance on rational thought and philosophic reasoning as the source of its thinking about the human psyche/soul.

Philosophical psychology developed in three phases. The first phase originates with classical Greek and Roman philosophical and physiological reflection on the nature of the psyche. It extends from Plato (428–348 B.C.E.) and Aristotle (385–322 B.C.E.), to the physician Galen (130–200 C.E.) and the neo-Platonic philosopher, Plotinus (205–270 C.E.). Their work, especially Aristotle's three-volume work on the psyche/soul, sets the terms and ground rules for psychology over the next two millennia. The second phase can be called *theological psychology* or *biblical psychology*. It originates in the second century C.E. when Christianity became an increasingly dominant cultural voice and sought to revise classical philosophical psychology with insights from the psychology of Christian Scripture and tradition. It extends through the medieval, renaissance, Reformation, and Enlightenment periods into the nineteenth and twentieth centuries, culminating with works such as Delitzsch's *A System of Biblical Psychology* (1855) and Fletcher's *The Psychology of the New Testament* (1912). It then disappears for most of the twentieth century. The third phase, emerging in the seventeenth century, represents a new brand of rationalist philosophical psychology, inaugurated by René Descartes (1596–1650), who has been called "the first great psychologist of the modern age."[25] His psychology is marked by two assumptions. First, it considers rational reflection, rather than the senses, to be the most faithful guide to truth:

> The first was never to accept anything as true if I did not have evident knowledge of its truth: that is, carefully to avoid precipitate conclusions and preconceptions, and to include nothing more in my judgments than what presented itself to my mind so clearly and so distinctly that I had no occasion to doubt it.[26]

Second, it regards the "I" or the human mind/psyche as a unique endowment of humans, "subject to its own rules and principles," and worthy of independent study, "separate from the body":

> I observe . . . this truth—I think, therefore I am. . . . I concluded that I was a thing or substance whose whole essence or nature was only to think, and which . . . has no need of space or of any material thing or body. Thus it follows that this ego, this mind, this soul, by which I am what I am, is entirely distinct from the body. . . . Even if the body did not exist, the soul would not cease to be all that it now is.[27]

As opposed to the body—which for Descartes was a hydraulic machine with a clockwork mechanism—the mind is free, endowed with ideas, memory, and passions. This focus on the mind and its capacity to understand itself through ratiocination will provide the foundation for a school of psychological thinking up through the twentieth century, from Thomas Hobbes (1588–1679), Benedict Spinoza (1632–77), and Wilhelm Leibniz (1645–1716), to Immanuel Kant (1724–1804) and beyond. It will be resolutely challenged, however, by the experimentally based scientific psychology that comes to flower in the last quarter of the nineteenth century.

Stage 3, scientific psychology, marks the emergence of psychology as an empirical science. "Psychological thinkers of the seventeenth and eighteenth centuries [had] considered themselves to be tending the vineyards of philosophy; those of the nineteenth century saw themselves as part of the newly triumphant enterprise known as natural science."[28] This stage opens with the work of British Empiricists, beginning with John Locke (1632–1704) and his "Essay Concerning Human Understanding," William Berkeley (1685–1753), David Hume (1711–76), James Mill (1773–1836), John Stuart Mill (1806–73), and Alexander Bain (1818–1903). They write against a background of prolific scientific discoveries. In the seventeenth century, these discoveries produce the decimal system, logarithms, analytic geometry, calculus, the air pump, the microscope, the barometer, the thermometer, and the telescope. In the eighteenth century, they produce physiology, electricity, atomic theory, mathematics, astronomy, botany, preventive medicine, evolutionary theory, and the discovery of hydrogen, oxygen, and nitrogen.

The figure who emerges as the encyclopedist and systematist of scientific psychology and who "drew the intellectual map of the territory and defined it as a new domain of science" is Wilhelm Wundt (1832–1920).[29] The laboratory he established in Leipzig in 1879, conducting scientific psychological experiments for the first time outside the classroom, set the standard for experimental psychology. However it also became the academic breeding ground for hundreds of psychologists who would staff psychological laboratories or departments of psychology in Europe and the United States. In 1940, there were 4,000 psychologists in America; by the last decade of the twentieth century, there were 149,000.[30]

With this historical map in mind, we return to the second stage in the history of psychology, the systematic but prescientific era, in which philosophical psychology and its offspring, biblical psychology, emerge.

Classical Greco-Roman Psychology

What we now call systematic psychology begins with the landmark work of Aristotle, *Peri Psyches* ("Concerning the Psyche"), more commonly referred to in its Latin version, *De Anima*. It explores the nature and reaches of the soul (*psyche*), identifying its parts and properties in relationship to the body (*soma*), namely, reason (*nous*), spirit/will (*thymos*), and desire (*epithymia*), along with memory, sensation, learning, perception, motivation, emotion, socialization, personality, and imagination. In providing the first systematic psychology Aristotle "laid down the lines along which the relationship between various manifestations of soul and mind were conceived" for two millennia. "Nothing of any great importance [in psychology] happened after the death of Aristotle in 322 B.C.E. until the seventeenth century, when new systems were inspired by the rise of the physical sciences."[31]

The period is also marked by the contributions of Plato as well as Empedocles, Anaxagoras, Hippocrates, Pythagoras, Epicurus, Democritus, the Stoics, Galen, and Plotinus. Collectively the Greco-Roman psychological tradition succeeded in identifying "nearly all the significant problems of psychology that have concerned scholars and scientists ever since."[32]

They raise the question of *how the psyche relates to the body*. Plato located the rational, immortal part of the psyche in the brain; Aristotle in the heart.

They develop parallel *psychological research strategies* that will be normative for two millennia. Plato's method of psychological research is rational and philosophical, echoing the contention of Parmenides that true knowledge comes from the striving of inward reason and innate ideas toward the truth. Aristotle, like Empedocles, adds an empirical dimension that turns to sensory data as the source of truth about things. Anticipating modern laboratory psychology, he researches animal and insect behavior, exploring the eating, mating, nest-building, migration, hibernation, escape behavior and social collaboration, courtship, and breeding habits of hundreds of species.

The Greeks write extensively on *epistemology and perception*: how humans know what they know; whether reason or the senses are more reliable as sources of knowledge; how sensation is relative to the state of the observer; and whether humans are born with innate knowledge waiting to be recalled to memory (Plato) or with a *tabula rasa* (Aristotle) filled up in time by experience and perception.

They study the *relation of stimulus and sensation*, discovering that a sensation can perdure long after the stimulus has ceased.

They enumerate the *four passions* (grief, fear, desire, and pleasure) and *five senses*, and they theorize on the "four humours" or personality types (sanguine, phlegmatic, choleric, and melancholic). They attribute these humours respectively to fluids in various bodily organs: blood in the heart, phlegm in the brain, yellow bile in the liver, and black bile in the spleen.

They examine the phenomenon of *memory* with an eye to improving its operation, anticipating the work of eighteenth century "associationists" in noting how mental images are awakened in memory through a chain of associations. Plato notes, for example, that a lyre or garment of the beloved can evoke an image of the beloved in the mind's eye.

In proto-Freudian fashion they stress *the primacy of reason over instinctual drives*, and the preferability of long-term gain over against the immediate dictates of the animallike drive toward sheer physical pleasure.

Like Freud and Jung they speak of *dreams* as the expression of suppressed desire, and sleep as a time when the rational soul attains truths not otherwise attainable.

In *The Art of Poetry* Aristotle anticipates the psychoanalytic concept of *catharsis* in observing the purgative effect drama can exercise on the emotions of an audience.

In *The Art of Healing*, Greek physician Hippocrates (460 B.C.E.), provides a prescientific *glossary of psychological maladies*, ranging from melancholia, mania, and postpartum depression, to phobias, paranoia, and hysteria—assigning them to imbalance among the four "humours." He writes, "Men ought to know that from the brain, and the brain only, arise our pleasures, joys, laughter, and jests, as well as our sorrows, pains, grief, and tears . . . . These things that we suffer all come from the brain when it is not healthy."[33]

Six hundred years later, Galen (130–200 C.E.)—the physician and anatomist in Alexandria whose writing will dominate medicine until the Renaissance and who is our primary informant on Hippocrates—prescribes a cure for diseases of the soul that involves *a process of self-examination and counseling*, anticipating the "talking cure" of Freud:

> If [a person] wishes to become good and noble, let him seek out someone who will help him by disclosing his every action which is wrong. . . . For we must not leave the diagnosis of these passions to ourselves but we must entrust it to others. . . . This mature person who can see these vices must reveal with frankness all our errors. Next, when he tells us some fault, let us first be immediately grateful to him; then let us go aside and consider the matter by ourselves; let us censure ourselves and try to cut away the disease not only to the point where it is not apparent to others, but so completely as to remove its roots from our soul.[34]

How does classical psychology relate to biblical psychology? It is no accident that a third-century tractate by Tertullian, a sixth-century treatise by Cassiodorus, a thirteenth-century commentary by Aquinas, and a sixteenth-century commentary by Philipp Melanchton all adopt the title of Aristotle's *De Anima*, "Concerning the Soul."[35] They typify the dual vocation of Christian "psychologists" up to the Reformation: to elaborate the biblical doctrine of the origin, life, purpose, and destiny of the self; and to defend this doctrine vis-à-vis classical philosophy, in ongoing dialogue with Aristotle, Plato, the Neoplatonists, and the Stoics. This dialogue proceeded in four distinct phases: the Patristic period, the Scholastic period, and the Renaissance/Reformation periods, and late nineteenth and early twentieth century in works on biblical psychology.

Biblical Psychology in the Patristic Period

The premier commentators on the psyche during this period are two North Africans, Tertullian of Carthage (150–220 C.E.), who has been called author of "the first Christian psychology,"[36] and Augustine of Hippo (354–430 C.E.), the latter designated by some as the "father of modern psychology" or as "the first modern psychologist."[37]

The list includes many others: Melito of Sardis[38] (d. ca. 190 C.E.), Gregory Thaumaturgus[39] (ca. 213–270 C.E.), the African apologist Arnobius of Sicca[40] (275–311 C.E.) and his student Lactantius[41] (240–332 C.E.). It includes the Cappadocian Gregory of Nyssa[42] (330–395 C.E.), who created a counterpart to Plato's *Phaedo* in his "dialogue" with his dying sister Makrina on the psyche and on resurrection; Nemesius,[43] Bishop of Emesa in Syria (ca. 390 C.E.), whose treatise "On Human Nature," with its ample reflections on human physiology and psychology, was cited nearly a millennium later by Albertus Magnus, Peter Lombard, and Thomas Aquinas. It also includes the French Claudianus Mamertus[44] (425–474 C.E.), author of the three-volume *De Statu Animae* ("On the Nature of the Soul"); the Roman senator and monk, Flavius Magnus Aurelius Cassiodorus[45] (485–580 C.E.); the Alexandrian philosopher and sometime Christian, Joannes Philiponus[46] (ca. 500 C.E.); the Christian philosopher Aeneas of Gaza[47] (d. 518 C.E.), author of the dialogue on the immortality of the soul in the *Theophrastus*; and Gregory the Great (540–604 C.E.) in the fourth book of his *Dialogues* on *De Aeternitate Animarum*.[48] But the great luminaries remain Tertullian and Augustine.

Tertullian (150–220 C.E.). Tertullian developed his concept of the soul in four treatises: *De Anima* ("Concerning the Soul"), *Apologeticum* ("The Apology"), *De Testimonium Animae* ("Concerning the Testimony of the Soul"), and *De Censu Animae"* ("Concerning the Citizenship of the Soul"), a work cited in *De Anima* but not preserved.

The *De Anima*, the largest of Tertullian's works, has been called "the first Christian psychology."[49] In it Tertullian takes up the argument of his earlier (lost) work, *De Censu Animae*, launching an attack on psychological theories in classical psychology that are at variance with the Christian biblical perspective. Franz Delitzsch describes it as the first ecclesiastical attempt to supersede the two great classical statements on the psyche, Plato's *Phaedo* and Aristotle's three-volume *De Anima*. Part 1 of Tertullian's *De Anima* (chap. 4–22) sketches the basic qualities of the soul; Part 2 (chap. 23–37.4) discusses the origin of the soul and its relation to spirit, mind, and body; Part 3 (chap. 37.5–58) advances a developmental psychology of the soul, discussing its growth and its various states of puberty, sin, sleep, dreaming, death, and after-death.

This first developed example of biblical psychology in the Christian tradition provides an illustration of acerbic Christian dialogue with the classical tradition. On the one hand, Tertullian appears to be irreconcilably opposed to Greek philosophy:

> What indeed has Athens to do with Jerusalem? What concord is there between the Academy and the Church? What between heretics and Christians? Our instruction comes from the porch of Solomon, who himself taught that the Lord should be sought in simplicity of heart. Away with all attempts to produce a mottled Christianity of Stoic, Platonic and dialectic composition. We want no curious disputation after possessing Christ Jesus, no research after enjoying the gospel![50]

On the other hand, Tertullian is unmistakably dependent on Greek philosophy. He acknowledges that "philosophers have sometimes thought the same things as ourselves" (*De Anima* 2), and he frequently shores up his own position with citations from Poseidonius, Philo, Chrysippus, Seneca, Aristotle, Plato, the Stoics, Heraclitus, Democritus, and Didymus of Alexandria, the court-philosopher of Augustus.[51] His *De Anima* depends heavily on the four-volume work, *Peri Psyches* ("On the Soul") by Soranus of Ephesus, an early second-century physician from Rome.

In his analysis of the soul/anima Tertullian replicates the menu of inquiry established in classical psychological tradition. He identifies the *faculties of the soul* as "immortality, reason, sensation, intelligence, and free will" (*De Anima* 38.6), noting how *sense perception and mind cooperate to produce knowledge* (6.5; 17.2–6). Sense perception governs "corporeal, visible, and tangible things," and the mind governs "spiritual, visible and secret things" (18.6). Following Plato, he notes also that *senses can deceive us*, as when an oar under water appears bent or broken, when we "mistake thunder for the rumble of a cart or vice versa," or when "the same pavement which scratches our hands is smooth to our feet" (17.3). Over against Aristotle he holds that *functions of mind, emotion, sensation, and perception are not separate but unified systems* (12.5), whereas some philosophers have proposed dividing psychic activity into two (Plato), three (Zeno), five (Aristotle), six (Panaetius), seven (Soranus), eight (Chrysippus), nine (Apollophanes), twelve (some Stoics), or seventeen (Posidonius) parts (14.1–2).

Tertullian postulates a *directing or governing principle* in the self, namely the heart (15.3), using biblical passages in support of this theory.[52] He reports, however, that other philosophers locate the governing principle in other body parts: the head (Plato), the crown of the head (Xenocrates), the brain (Hippocrates), the base of the brain (Herophilus), the outer membranes of the brain (Strato and Erasistratus), between the eyebrows (Strato the physician), or in the breast (Epicurus) (15.5). He affirms Plato's differentiation of *two irrational factors* in the self, the "irascible" and "concupiscible," the first of which we share "with lions, the second with flies" (16.3). He discerns the difference between *normal and abnormal functioning of the senses*, noting that mental illness skews sense perception, as when "Orestes looks at his sister and thinks she is his mother" (17.9).

The physiology and psychology of sleeping and dreaming are also explored by Tertullian. Dreams provide evidence that the anima is "always in motion, always active, and . . . never succumbs to rest" (43.5), a point of view affirmed in modern psychoanalytic theory.[53] Though some classical philosophers regard dreams as vain, false, or meaningless (Homer, Aristotle, Epicurus), Tertullian casts his lot with those who find truth in dreams (Artemon, Antiphon, Strato, Philochorus, Epicharmus, Serapion, Cratippus, and Dionysius of Rhodes), citing a five-volume history of dreams by Hermippus of Berytus (46.11), and theorizing a typology of dreams, reminiscent of contemporary dream theory, that includes, anticipatory dreams (46.2–9), dreams suggested to the psyche by everyday events, dreams that inexplicably arise in consciousness "from ecstasy and its attendant circumstances," as well as delusive dreams from the devil, and dreams from God (47.2–4).

One of the more important psychological theories of Tertullian is his contention that the soul comes equipped from birth with God-given built-in predilections and gifts, whereby "the baby knows its mother, recognizes its nurse, . . . refuses the breast of another and the bed that is unfamiliar" (19.8). Echoing Seneca's theory, he states that "the seeds of all arts and ages are implanted in us [from birth] and God, our Master, secretly produces the qualities of our mind" (20.1). In the *Apology* Tertullian expands this notion with his celebrated statement, "*anima naturaliter Christiana,*" "the soul is natively Christian," making the point that the human soul, even though "weakened by lust and concupiscence," intuitively seeks God (*Apol.* 17.5–6)—a passage cited by C. G. Jung, making the same point.[54] Tertullian anticipates the German "nativist" psychology of Leibniz and Kant—echoed in psychological systems ranging from Plato to Jung—that holds the human psyche to be something more than a *tabula rasa* (Aristotle). Rather, it arrives with a structured set of predilections, propensities, and "gifts" that inform and guide the life of the individual along that higher trajectory for which the soul is intrinsically intended. Tertullian composes a soliloquy to the soul:

> I call you not as when, fashioned in schools, trained in libraries, fed in Attic academics and porticoes, you belch wisdom. I address you simple, rude, uncultured and untaught. . . . I want your inexperience. . . . I demand of you the things you bring with you into man, which you know either from yourself or from your author, whoever he may be (*De Test. Animae*, 1).

Augustine (354–430 C.E.). The study of psychology is quintessential for the theological agenda of Augustine, the premier theologian of the Patristic era. Next to the knowledge of God, which is the primary objective for Augustine, the most important undertaking is the knowledge of the human soul/anima/psyche. For Augustine, insight into the first requires careful examination of the second, since the second is made in the image of the first. His dialogue with "reason" in the "Soliloquies" makes the point:

> Reason: What, then do you want to know?
> Augustine: The very things for which I have prayed.
> R: Summarize them concisely.
> A: I want to know God and the soul.
> R: Nothing else?
> A: Nothing else at all.[55]

As Ernest Fortin has observed, the study of the soul is central for Aristotle's "whole philosophical enterprise." Fortin explains:

> The reason is simple. Anyone who would seek the truth must know something about the instrument with which he seeks. . . . He owes it to himself to gain an insight into the nature of the soul . . . and the many factors which, unless one is aware of them, are liable to interfere with its operations, such as inveterate habits, unexamined opinions, and the promptings of a disordered appetite. . . . Augustine held the study of the soul to be the pivot on which the whole of the intellectual life turns and the key to our understanding of everything else.[56]

Augustine's study of the soul (anima/psyche) is scattered throughout his writing, but focused in his works relating to psychology, including *De anima et eius origine* ("Concerning the Soul and its Origin"), *De duabus animabus* ("Concerning the Two Souls"), *De Immortalitate Animae* ("Concerning the Immortality of the Soul"), an unfinished complement to the *Soliloquies*, and above all, *The Confessions*, and *De Quantitate Animae* ("Concerning the Greatness of the Soul"),[57] a work he recommends to his readers twenty-five years after its publication. His method throughout is to integrate classical and biblical thought, creating an unprecedented synthesis of Christianity and classical culture, a by-product of which is a model of biblical psychology that will serve the Scholastics and Reformers centuries later.[58]

Augustine's most distinctive contribution to Western psychological tradition is found in the method he adopts for probing the human soul. Earlier patristic psychologists had employed one of two methods, rational hypothesis (Plato) or empirical observation (Aristotle). Augustine, offers a third: Return into yourself. With the *Confessions*, Augustine inaugurates a tradition in West-ern psychology of coming to the truth about oneself through introspection and private experience. Introspection is a process of "self-searching, self-question-ing, self-discovery, self-description, and self-assessment," involving an analysis of the inner person, memory, human motives, and will.[59] With this shift, Augustine sets the stage for a tradition of interior self-examination that will extend from Descartes to modern psychoanalytic and cognitive psychology. Augustine accordingly has been described as the "the first modern spirit, one of the founders of modern Western consciousness."[60]

What does Augustine discover about the anima through his introspection? Like Tertullian he tours the agenda of psychological issues developed by the classical and earlier patristic "psychologists." He identifies five broad levels of the soul/psyche: the vegetative (self-nourishing), the sensible, the discursively rational, the ethical, and the intellectual. He also finds that the soul is both rational and irrational. The irrational soul (*anima irrationalis*) is marked by appetite, sense-perception, memory, anger (*ira*), and desire (*libido*), all of which are common to humans and animals. The rational soul is the seat of the mind and will.[61]

Augustine's theory of the process of sense-perception mirrors modern physiological psychology. Adopting a model of the nervous system elaborated by the Alexandrian physicians Herophilus and Erasistratus, Augustine pro-poses that sense stimuli move to the brain via fine, pipelike passages (*tenues fis-tulae*), called "roads," "streets," or paths." These terminate in the "foremost of the three ventricles in the cerebrum," the other two ventricles serving as the seat of memory and the source of motor nerves. He also nicely differentiates between the senses that actually absorb part of the object (smell, taste) and those that do not (touch, sight, and hearing).[62]

Augustine analyzes the emotions of joy (*laetitia*), sadness (*tristitia*), desire (*cupiditas*), and fear (*timor*), postulating that "joy is the extending of the soul; sadness the contraction of the soul; desire the soul's going forward; fear the soul's flight" (Io. ev. tr. 46.8). He speculates on psychosomatic illness, noting that "the soul is not only affected by the flesh, so that it desires, fears, rejoices and grieves, but . . . it can also be agitated by these emotions from within itself" (*Civ.* 14.5). In addition he notes that distortions can take place in the imagi-native faculty when disease is present, when the link between brain and the senses is blocked, or when the mind is overworked.[63]

One of Augustine's most innovative contributions to what we might call the psychology of his time was his proposal that the three most powerful fac-ulties of the soul are memory (*memoria*), understanding (*intelligentia*), and will (*voluntas*)—as opposed to the Platonic triad of reason (*nous*), spirit/vitality (*thymos*), and desire (*epithymia*). For Augustine, this "trinity" of human faculties, like all other "trinities" he finds in the structure of life, is to be seen as a reflection of the triune Godhead.[64]

Memory for Augustine is a supreme function of the anima/psyche/soul. One might almost equate it with consciousness. In animals it makes habit possible; in humans it makes spatial and temporal continuity possible as well as creative imagination. It is called "the stomach of the mind" or more felicitously, the "roomy chamber" that holds "the treasures of countless images." With the power to recall at will, memory can recollect something seen, heard, or thought with a sharpness and vividness that almost matches the original sensation. For Augustine, memory is virtually the totality of the conscious self: "Great is the power of memory . . . a deep and endless multiplicity; and this thing is my mind, and this thing am I myself."[65]

Understanding for Augustine is the faculty that distinguishes humans from animals. It is constituted by two powers: reason and an inner sense. Reason is the governing faculty of the self that helps us reason from things seen to things unseen, from sense data to the concept of number, to wisdom, to truth, and finally to God. But reason is assisted by another factor which Augustine identifies as "inner light" or "inner truth": "But when things are spoken of which we perceive through the mind, that is through intellect and reason, we are talking about things which, being present, we see in that inner light, by which he himself who is called the inner man is illuminated, and in which he delights." This "inner man" or "inner light" is comparable to C. G. Jung's concept of the Self, which functions as a guiding psychic factor compensatory to human consciousness.[66]

Will is fundamental to Augustine's psychology and theology because it provides a clue to understanding the psychodynamics of evil, sin, and human culpability. He writes, "God has created me with free will; if I have sinned, I have sinned . . . I, not fate, not chance, nor the devil." At the same time Augustine will make the daunting psychological proposal that the human will, having gotten us into sin and evil, is incapable of getting us out. What is required is divine grace breaking into our lives and souls from outside, an insight that will speak to Calvin and Luther, and that will inform Christian theology and what we now call psychology for a thousand years.[67]

Beyond Tertullian and Augustine. The psychologies of Tertullian and Augustine demonstrate that psychological thinkers during the patristic period were wrestling with a slate of four questions that David Hothersall, in his *History of Psychology*, identifies as the defining issues for psychology throughout its history: "Is a science of the mind possible?" "What is the nature and locus of the mind?" "What is the relation of mind and body?" "What is the relative role of nature or nurture in the formation and development of the mind?"[68]

One of the most ambitious demonstrations of patristic interest in the *science of the mind* comes from Nemesius of Emesa (ca. 390 C.E.). Widely read in philosophy and medicine, he constructed a systematic catalogue of psychological and physiological issues of the period in his *Peri Physeos Anthropou* ("Concerning the Nature of Man"). Using the theories of the non-Christian philosophers as his point of departure, he moved toward a "Christian" position, discoursing on the following topics: the soul; the union of soul and body; the faculties of imagination, feeling, intellect, memory, thought, and expression; the nature of the will and voluntary and involuntary acts; the senses of touch, taste, hearing, smell, and sight; and the irrational part of the soul, or "passions" (concupiscence, pleasures, grief, fear, and anger).[69]

The second question, on *the nature and locus of the mind*, was debated vigorously at the time. People took sides either with Aristotle, who locates the mind in the heart, or with Plato, who locates it in the brain, or with the Stoics who locate it in the breast. Nemesius of Emesa and John of Damascus (675–749 C.E.), following the Greek physician Galen, foreshadowed modern brain physiology by localizing various psychic functions in separate portions of the brain: the imagination in the front part, the intellect in the middle, and memory in the hindmost.[70]

On the third question, concerning *the relation of mind and body*, the early church writers focus on three issues of continuing interest in the history of psychology. The first is the issue of psychosomatics, the mystifying and sometimes pathological interplay between body and mind/soul, as Augustine observed.[71] The second is the metaphysical question of whether the psyche/soul/mind is to be regarded simply as an epiphenomenon of the body, coming in and out of existence with the body (or brain), or somehow manifests an intelligence, imagination, moral passion, creativity, and autonomy that are not reducible simply to physical factors but may precede or succeed the life of the body. The third question concerns the basic constitution of the self, whether it is a dichotomous (body and soul) or trichotomous (body, soul, and spirit) entity. In general the early church writers adopt the trichotomous position, reflecting their experience of a "spirit" that intrudes into conscious life in a way that vivifies, directs, inspires, and heals.

This third question has particular significance since the early Christian movement cannot be comprehended psychologically without taking into account its self-understanding as a spirit-filled people. The canonical Gospels and the Pauline writings attest to this, as does also Irenaeus, who makes the following psychological observation, remotely reminiscent of psychoanalytic anthropology:

> There are three things out of which . . . the complete man is composed—
> flesh, soul, and spirit. One of these does indeed save and form—this is the
> spirit [*pneuma*]; while as to another it is united and formed—that is the flesh
> [*sarx*]; that which is between those two—that is the soul [*psyche*], which
> sometimes indeed, when it follows the spirit, is raised up by it, but sometimes
> it sympathizes with the flesh and falls into carnal lusts.[72]

The fourth question on *the relative role of nature or nurture in the formation and development of the mind* finds its expression in the early church debate over whether infants are born, as Plato contended, with preprogrammed, innate, "self-taught" images of truth, beauty, and goodness, or whether they arrive with a mental blank slate (*tabula rasa*) that knows and aspires to nothing until it is filled and shaped by experience and education, as Aristotle proposed. The issue was widely debated; Arnobius of Sicca (275–311 C.E.) endorsed both points of view.

From the Platonic perspective, Arnobius argued that "knowledge is simply recollection (*anamnesis*)." He asks: "Is there any human being who has not entered the day of his nativity with a knowledge of that beginning? To whom is it not an innate idea; in whom has it not been impressed, indeed, almost stamped into him in his mother's womb; in whom is it not deeply planted that there is a King and Lord and Regulator of all things which are?"[73]

From the Aristotelian perspective, Arnobius argued that our mind from infancy is a *tabula rasa*. To demonstrate the point, he proposes a "psychological experiment," first suggested by Herodotus, of raising a newborn from birth to adulthood in a "quiet cave with controlled temperature and with a constant cycle of light and darkness" but with "no contact with other humans," receiving little sensory input and fed with the same food. Arnobius maintains that such a person would have no knowledge of language, custom, or fashion, and would "stand speechless, with less wit and sense than any beast, block or stone." [74]

The nature vs. nurture debate continues into the present in two major schools of psychology: the *empiricists*, from John Locke to the modern behaviorist, B. F. Skinner, who tend to favor nurture and environment as the definitive formative factor of mind and the psychic self; and the *nativists*, from Descartes and Kant to G. Stanley Hall, Lewis Terman, Carl Jung, Sigmund Freud, Abraham Maslow, and cognitive psychologists, who emphasize inborn qualities of mind and the psychic life, a point of view widely confirmed both in biblical and patristic thought.

Biblical Psychology in the Scholastic Period

Though the psychology of Augustine dominated Christian thinking from the sixth to the tenth centuries, a shift occurred in the eleventh and twelfth

centuries with the rediscovery of Aristotle and the development of a "naturalistic faculty psychology" grounded in Aristotle's *De Anima*.

During the Scholastic period the doctrine of the soul/anima/psyche
came to be regarded as necessary to any *summa*, or "complete doctrine." It is
addressed by scholastics, natural philosophers, and mystics: the Irish lumi-
nary, John Scotus Erigena (ca. 810–ca. 877), Hugh of St. Victor (d. 1142),
Albertus Magnus (1193–1280), Thomas Aquinas (1225–74), Duns Scotus
(1266–1308), and Bonaventure (1217–74).[75] Bonaventure alone preserves
the Augustinian tradition; the rest are drawn to the new wave of interest in
Aristotle.

The new psychology of this period can be called "biblical" only by a
stretch; it cites biblical passages in support of its conclusions, but derives its
fundamental portrait of the psyche from Arabic psychological models (based
on Aristotle), preeminently those devised by Avicenna (Abu Ali al-Husayn Ibn
Sina, 980–1037) and a century later, Averroes (Ibn Rushd, 1126–98).[76]

Avicenna, to whom Aquinas acknowledges his debt, had memorized the
Metaphysics of Aristotle by the age of seventeen. Born in Boukhara, he
became a court physician whose *Canon of Medicine* achieved new heights in
Arabic medicine. His most important work related to psychology is *Kitab al-
Najat* ("The Book of Salvation"). In it he combines Aristotelian philosophical psychology with the Roman medical tradition of Galen and Hippocrates.
He offers a range of psychological observations, for example, identifying the
four human temperaments, observing how they vary with age, race, and climate, and assigning the gamut of human faculties to various ventricles of the
brain. He exercises his greatest influence on the West through his theory of
the "seven faculties" of the human psyche, a model that Aquinas will adopt
almost *in toto*. (Aquinas will object, however, to Avicenna's attributing certain
"divine" functions to humans, a perspective he will correct in the *Summa
Theologica*.)[77]

Aquinas, the "Angelic Doctor," was introduced to Avicenna (and thus Aristotle) through his mentor at the University of Paris, Albertus Magnus. His
work constitutes the "summit of the medieval synthesis," reconciling Christian thought and Aristotelian philosophy. Though in general Aquinas
acknowledges reason and revelation as the twin sources of human knowledge, his treatment of human psychology is based largely on reason, that is
to say, on Aristotle and bits of Galen, Augustine, and others. Only occasionally does he revise this philosophical psychology with a theological nugget
from standard biblical or traditional Christian "psychology," for example,
body-soul dualism.[78]

Aquinas's treatment of psychology is concentrated in the opening sections of the *Summa Theologica* that deal with God and humanity, specifically the "Treatise on Man," "Treatise on Human Acts," and "Treatise on Habits." Using his characteristic question-and-answer method, he advances an Avicennian portrait of the psyche with three facets: the *vegetative soul*, the *sensitive soul*, and the *rational soul*. The *vegetative soul* is pre- "psychological," officiating over the three bodily functions of nutrition (to sustain the body), augmentation (to seek the body's proper size), and generation (to reproduce).

The *sensitive soul* is constituted by three elements. The first is the *exterior senses* of sight, hearing, smell, taste, and touch. The second is the *interior senses* of imagination (that apprehends absent objects), memory (that preserves the image of an object), intuition or estimation (that assesses the possible harm or benefit of an object), and "common sense" (Aristotle's notion of a "unifying" sense that integrates the data produced by the other senses and traces them to a "common" object). The third element is the *sensitive appetites*, namely, the "concupiscable" and the "irascible." The concupiscable appetite teaches us to desire or avoid appropriate objects, leading to the emotions of love, desire, and joy (when aroused by a good thing), or hatred, aversion, and sorrow (when repulsed by an evil thing). The irascible appetite provides the appropriate psychological response to difficulty or threat, producing hope or despair (when confronted with a good that is difficult to obtain), or courage, fear, or anger (when faced with evil). This catalogue of emotions is more systematic and thorough than that of any previous philosopher.

The highest function of the anima/psyche/soul is the *rational soul*, consisting of memory, imagination, and intellect. Expanding on the theory of "the philosopher" (his nickname for Aristotle), Aquinas postulates two types of intellect. One, named the "possible intellect," consists of understanding, judgment, and reasoning as it applies to perception. The second is Avicenna's "agent intellect." For Avicenna, the agent intellect is the highest element in our psychic makeup, a faculty that actualizes our knowledge of universals, leads us to knowledge of the ideal forms, and provides divine illumination. For Aquinas, the function of the agent intellect is not purely natural. Rather, it is to "abstract *ideas* or concepts from our perceptions, and to know, through faith, those other truths, such as the mystery of the Trinity, that cannot be known through reason."[79]

Biblical Psychology in the Renaissance and Reformation

The age of the Renaissance (1350–1600) marks the transition from the religious milieu of the medieval-scholastic world to the secular milieu of the emerging modern world. Three features of the Renaissance bear on the history of psychology. First is the printing press, invented in 1450. The device made thirteenth and fourteenth century biblical, theological, and classical works more broadly accessible than ever before, not only in the original Greek, Latin, and Hebrew, but in vernacular translations of French, German, English and Italian. By 1500, Europe had over a thousand printing houses with a total production of over two million volumes. Non-Christian classics of pagan antiquity were widely circulated, so that the plays, rhetoric, poetry, and history of the Greeks and Romans were pitted against the literature of Christian piety. Second, a new humanism emerged with the notion that "being human" is more important than being Christian, as Christianity was conceived in late medieval piety. Third, the political and intellectual power of the Church was challenged by the new science of astronomy (Copernicus, Galileo, Bruno, Tycho, and Kepler), of biology (Harvey), of geography (Columbus and Magellan), of mapmaking (Mercator), of art, anatomy, and experimental design (da Vinci), and of a new thrust of independent thinking from within the walls of Christendom itself (Luther, Calvin, Huss, Wycliffe), insistent on, among other things, relating the religion of the hierarchy to the life and language of the masses.[80]

Psychology during this period assumed two forms, that of ongoing classical philosophical psychology in the tradition of Augustine and Aristotle, and that of an emergent explicitly biblical psychology in the post-Reformation period.

Classical philosophical psychology flourished in the Renaissance. Forty-six new commentaries on the *De Anima* were published, in addition to reprints of earlier commentaries. Sixty-nine new works dealing with the "immortality of the soul" and forty-eight with "freedom of the will" were also produced. In addition, a landmark three-volume work, frequently cited by historians of psychology, appeared from the pen of Juan Luis Vives (1492–1540), entitled *De Anima et Vita*. Book One, treats the Aristotelian notion of psyche and, following Galen, locates the five internal senses in the ventricles of the brain. Book Two reduplicates the Augustinian schema of the mind's threefold faculties (memory, understanding and will), adding notes on the powers of reason and the phenomenon of sleep. Book Three, observes the effect of emotions on physiological change. In 1915, behaviorist John Watson (1878–1958) designated Vives as "father of modern psychology," possibly oblivious to the classical and biblical/theological psychological tradition on which Vives's work stood.[81]

In addition to these familiar forms of continuing philosophical psychology, two other developments emerged with a past in classical antiquity and a spotty future in the history of psychology. The first is *physiognomy*, the art of detecting personal qualities, and sometimes intelligence, through cues in facial features, bodily build, and gait. Physiognomy traces its roots in ancient times to a book *Physiognomika* (incorrectly attributed to Aristotle). This "science" was the driving power behind a widely circulated handbook called *Secreta Secretorum* ("Secrets of Secrets"), a manual of "secret" cues for the use of government officials and clerical administrators in selecting and screening staff. A Spanish physician, Juan Huarte, familiar with the work of Aristotle, Galen, and Nemesius, published a best seller, *Examen de Ingenios para las Ciencias* ("The Examination of Men's Wits"), in 1575, as an early volume on educational psychology, linking bodily signs and behavior patterns to types of intellectual ability. He found the faculty of memory especially germane to the professions of linguistics, law, divinity, cosmology, and arithmetic, and the faculty of imagination as fundamental to the work of the physicist, musician, astrologer, artist, and "man of letters."

A second development in the field of practical psychology is the revival of interest in *mnemonics*, the theory and science of memory retention. This was developed by rhetoricians in Greco-Roman times (for example, Aristotle's *De Memoria*) and recovered by Albertus Magnus and Aquinas in the Scholastic period. Giordano Bruno (1548–1600), burned at the stake during the Inquisition for his heliocentrism, was renowned for the vast mnemonic scheme he had devised.[82]

Beyond these developments, the air was filled with an unprecedented spirit of free inquiry that will lead to the "first formal philosophical and scientific antecedents of psychology," as it has come to be known in the twentieth century.[83] By the 1600s, groundwork is in place for the two major camps: rational psychology, beginning with René Descartes (1596–1650), and empirical psychology, beginning with John Locke (1632–1704).

Post-Reformation biblical psychology is exemplified in the lectures and publications of Luther's protégé, Philipp Melanchton, the virtual father of the term *psychology* for the world of church and university. As noted earlier, *psichologia* makes its first appearance with the Croato-Serbian Marco Marulic (1524), known only by name. But Melanchton is the first to use the term in an academic setting, employing it in his lectures (1530) and his *Commentarius De Anima* (1540), the first compendium of psychology published in Germany. Melanchton gave lectures on the theme before immense audiences, and republished his commentary in 1552 under the title, *Liber de Anima*. Unlike his mentor Luther, an Augustinian monk who was more inclined to build his psychology around a Platonic-Augustinian model, Melanchton favored Aristotle, whom he read in the original. Despite his attraction to the Greeks, Melanchton, like Tertullian, measured the truth of classical psychology by the light and standard of biblical revelation. His work sparked a flurry of disputation on psychology at Wittenberg and other German universities in the 1500s and 1600s, establishing a tradition of biblical psychology as a formally accepted subdivision of theological anthropology.[84]

One of the first books to use the term *psychology* in its title was a work on biblical psychology published in 1619 by Caspar Bartholinus, teacher of medicine and theology at the University of Copenhagen. In *Manuductio ad veram Psychologiam e sacris literis* ("Guide to a True Psychology from the Sacred Writings"), Bartholinus states that his objective is a biblical *psychologia*, that is a "true doctrine of the human soul," acknowledging, however, that this is not always an exact science. He identifies Genesis 2:7 as the foundation of a true biblical psychology, with its portrait of man, formed from the dust of the ground by the Lord God, who breathes life into his nostrils, making him a living being. Bartholinus quotes the passage in Latin, then proceeds to provide an exegesis of the Hebrew original. At one point, in the mode of Philo of Alexandria, he comments that Moses (the presumed author) knows of the four (Aristotelian) causes. The efficient cause of man is the Lord God; the material cause is the earth; the formal cause, the breath of life; and the objective or teleological cause, that "he might become a living soul." Writing before the onset of biblical criticism in the early 1700s, Bartholinus demonstrates the commitment of Reformation psychology to a biblically based doctrine over against the natural anthropology and psychology of Aristotle and Plato.[85]

Several other works bear mentioning, such as the 1769 volume by Magnus Friedrich Roos, *Fundamenta psychologiae ex sacra Scriptura sic collecta* ("Fundamentals of Psychology Gathered from Sacred Scripture"), which treats the subject lexicographically, analyzing key psychological terms (for example, *psyche, pneuma, kardia*), and the later definitive work in 1843 by J. T. Beck, *Umriss der biblischen Seelenlehre* ("Outlines of Biblical Teaching on the Soul"). Delitzsch describes the latter as the first attempt to reduce biblical psychology to a scientific form, and to promote the claim that biblical psychology has "an independent existence in the organism of entire theology."[86]

Delitzsch also cites three "veterans" who have both added greatly to "experimental psychology and its history" and supplied "abounding materials for biblical psychology." They are: Christoph. Ad. von Eschenmauer (d. 1852), Jos. Ennemoser (d. 1854), and above all, G. H. von Schubert (d. 1860), author of *Symbolik des Traums* ("Dream Symbolism") in 1840, *Ueber die Krankheiten und Störungen der Menschlichen Seele* ("Concerning the Illnesses and Disturbances of the Human Soul") in 1845, and *Geschichte der Seele* ("History of the Soul") in 1850. Finally, Delitzsch commends J. G. F. Haussmann's, *Die biblische Lehre vom Menschen* ("Biblical Teaching on Man," 1848), for the "living manner" in which it incorporates a discussion of biblical psychology under the rubric of Biblical anthropology.[87]

Biblical Psychology from the Mid-Nineteenth to the Early Twentieth Centuries: Two Case Studies

Franz Delitzsch and M. Scott Fletcher published their work against a background of growth and change in the field of psychology. The psychology Delitzsch knew in 1855 was becoming a *Naturwissenschaft*, a natural science, culminating in 1879 with Wundt's establishment of the first independent experimental laboratory. By 1912, Fletcher was seeing a proliferation of departments of psychology in universities across Europe and the United States. Both writers show a willingness to learn what they can from the "new psychology" to illumine the biblical text and its understanding of the self, but they also take a stance, instructive for contemporary biblical critics, of asking what the new psychology can learn from biblical psychology and its vision of the self.

Franz Julius Delitzsch, A System of Biblical Psychology (1855)

Hermann Gunkel, in a 1927 biographical article on Franz Julius Delitzsch (1813–90), acknowledges his "comprehensive learning, his sparkling spirit, his honest piety" and the fact that he was a "beloved teacher."[88] A professor of Hebrew and Old Testament at the University of Leipzig, and a master of Hebrew, Arabic, Syriac, Samaritan, Persian, Greek, and Latin texts, Delitzsch produced numerous commentaries on both Old and New Testament works, along with a prodigious mix of other writings, including a history of postbiblical Jewish poetry, a history of the Complutensian Polyglot, and a book on the iris, born of his lifelong love of flowers. He was a devout Lutheran with a social conscience. He spoke out against anti-Semitism, and in 1886 established the Institutum Iudaicum Delitzschianum in honor of Levy Hirsch, a man who had befriended and housed Delitzsch's family when Delitzsch was a young boy.[89]

Always adapting to new ideas, he accommodated the new biblical criticism that was developing in the second half of the nineteenth century. Thus he came to accept that the Bible "is a book just as much human as divine," and to repudiate the mindlessness of a fundamentalism that might "declare even the punctuation of the OT to be inspired and the NT Greek to be free from all offences against classicality of form." At the same time, faithful to his pietistic, even mystical sentiment, he maintained his focus on the text's timeless meaning for the soul.[90]

Delitzsch wrote *A System of Biblical Psychology* between the second (1853) and third editions (1860) of *The Commentary on Genesis*. His objective was to answer a question of personal importance to him, namely how the human soul relates to the phenomena of "spirit" and matter. With his interest piqued by the earlier biblical psychologies of Roos and Beck, he set out to answer the question with a program of research on Plato, the Indian Vedanta, "anthropologic researches," and the "immensely wide range of [current] psychological literature" (vii–ix).

Delitzsch understands biblical psychology to be "a scientific representation of the doctrine of Scripture on the psychical constitution of man as it was created, and the ways in which this constitution has been affected by sin and redemption. There is such a doctrine in Scripture" (16). Over against detractors who argue that Scripture no more provides an objective *psychology* than it does a *cosmology*, Delitzsch replies that Scripture says "infinitely more about man's soul and spirit than about Orion and the Pleiades" (15). He acknowledges, consonant with the new biblical criticism of his time, that there are indeed varieties of authors and points of view in Scripture, but contends that nevertheless we can still find a generally harmonized anthropology and psychology presupposed in all of Scripture, aimed at providing a picture of the "psychical constitution" of the human soul, of the illnesses and sins that beset it, and of ways to a cure it (salvation, redemption) (16).

Delitzsch's method and procedure cast a wide net. He places equal emphasis on both the "Book of nature" (the sciences) and the "Book of scripture" (23). Delitzsch is convinced of the need "to see clearly and without prejudice the rays of truth" which shine "outside the range of . . . confessions of faith" (7). He praises contemporaries who have added to "experimental psychology" supplying "abounding materials for biblical psychology" (9–12). Though he himself avoids using current "physiologic notices" that are patently foreign to Scripture (for example, the cerebral system or circulation of the blood), he does find occasion to apply contemporary psychological diagnostic concepts to biblical stories, for example, acknowledging that Saul's being among the prophets might be an instance of "pathologic irritation" (423). In discussing human anatomy he demonstrates extensive knowledge of medical vocabulary, referring to the ganglionic nervous system, vaso-motor nervous system, the abdominal and pelvic cavity, and the lumbar vertebrae (318). He introduces recent research on somnambulism and magnetism (310–12), at the same time repudiating the "human quackery" associated with clairvoyance (25). Delitzsch also adverts favorably to the wisdom of Graeco-Roman psychology, on occasion siding with the classics over against Scripture. At one point he expresses preference for Plato's dualism vs. the "falsely" called trichotomy of Scripture, defending his position with the rhetorical retort, "Is what Plato or what Plotinus teach to be absolutely branded, because Plato and Plotinus teach it?" (118).

The table of contents in Delitzsch's work provides a paradigm of topics typical of "biblical psychologies" of the period, reminiscent of issues debated in classical thought and the Patristics:

1. the question of preexistence of the soul

2. creation, "the origin of the psyche," "the difference of sex," "traducianism and creationism," and the trichotomous constitution of persons as a unity of spirit, soul, and body

3. the fall and the emergence of sin, shame, and conscience

4. the "natural condition" of the "I" (ego) as characterized by freedom, reason, spirit; the "seven powers of the soul"; the threefold developmental stages of the self; heart and head; the phenomena of sleeping, waking, dreaming, somnambulism, health and sickness, and psychosomatic illness

5. "the divine-human archetype"; regeneration of the self and the phenomena of conscious and unconscious processes of grace, new life in the spirit, ecstasy, and *theopneustia* (being filled with the spirit)

6. death

7. resurrection (as opposed to the extrabiblical doctrine of metempsychosis or "transmigration" of souls).

Six features of Delitzsch's approach merit special attention for their relevance to issues and terms that will characterize subsequent work on psychology and biblical studies. First, he insists that biblical psychology is to be seen as an independent science discreet from—though closely related to and important for—biblical theology and dogmatics. The purpose of biblical theology and dogmatics is to analyze and systematize biblical doctrine; the purpose of biblical psychology "has to do with the human soul" and "with the constitution of human nature" as affected by the new humanity exemplified in the life of Jesus of Nazareth (18–19, 384).

Second, he offers a helpful distinction between biblical psychology and general psychology. General psychology consists of two major schools from the seventeenth to the nineteenth century: "physical empirical" psychology (in the tradition of Locke, Wundt, and experimental psychology) based on empirical research; and "philosophic-rational" psychology (in the tradition of Descartes and Spinoza) based on philosophic speculation. Delitzsch advocates that biblical psychology has "to adopt a different method from that of the empirical or rational psychology" (198). Whereas the latter takes empirical analysis of the human psyche as its starting point, the former begins with the "revealed" biblical postulates about human nature as its point of departure.

Third, he acknowledges that he is making a trial use of "newly-coined words and daring ideas" (vi). These words and ideas in retrospect prove to be harbingers of late nineteenth and early twentieth century psychological issues and terminology: for example, he refers to archetypes (*Urbilder*) (381–92), to the personality and the "I" (ego as distinct from spirit, soul, and body [179–80]), and to conscious and unconscious (*bewusste, unbewusste*) dimensions of experience (402–5). He advocates taking the reality of the unconscious seriously: "It has been a fundamental error of most psychologists hitherto, to make the soul only extend so far as its consciousness extends; it embraces, as is now always acknowledged, a far greater abundance of powers and relations than can commonly appear in its consciousness" (330).

Fourth, he develops a biblical psychological model of human development, or what he calls "changeful history" of the human soul (459), anticipating patterns of modern developmental theory. Part of the developmental process is organic, and therefore unconscious, taking place "without our knowledge and will" (323). But the goal of the developmental process is to move from a *natural*, unconscious state to a *personal*, conscious, and free *pneumatico-psychical* state (189). Though the personal state, to be sure, is present "in every stage of his growth, . . . even in the embryonic state," a truly conscious sense of personal life becomes real for him only when he apprehends himself as ego and comes out of the bondage of unconsciousness (188).

Fifth, Delitzsch examines dream theory with a range of considerations that to some extent parallels the work of C. G. Jung (324–37). Acknowledging that the Bible can issue "emphatic warning" against reliance on dreams (Eccles. 5:7), especially "deceitful dreams" (Jer. 23:26), Delitzsch proceeds to survey the biblical evidence on dreams. He also reviews the insights of classical antiquity, citing Aeschylus, the Talmud, Tertullian, and Philo, noting the threefold classification of dream types offered by Synesius—the dream of foreboding, of conscience, and of revelation—as well as the instances of "waking visions" referred to in the Bible (Ezek. 8:1; Dan. 10:7; Acts 7:55).

Sixth, with an eye to his profession as theologian, scholar, and churchman, he defends the inclusion of psychology within the ranks of critical biblical research as a God-given capacity "granted to the human soul . . . of raising itself above itself by self-investigation" (xiv).

The bottom line for Delitzsch's biblical psychology is not that the Bible advances a model of the psyche and its constituent faculties, but that it informs the reader of the "natural condition" of the self and proffers a vision of the new humanity to which it is called. In this vein, Delitzsch asks, "What is biblical psychology?" and answers: "It is psychology which has to offer to dogmatics the knowledge that is required for the understanding of the human essential constitution of the God-man" (384); it is "the restoration of the true human nature" (18). The goal of a biblical psychology thus involves not only description and analysis, but diagnosis and a protocol of treatment—a perspective not foreign to some modern psychological and psychotherapeutic approaches.

M. Scott Fletcher, The Psychology of the New Testament *(1912)*

In 1912, fifty-seven years after Delitzsch wrote *A System of Biblical Psychology*, M. Scott Fletcher, a recent graduate of Oxford University, published *The Psychology of the New Testament*. Professor H. Rashdall of New College, Oxford, urged its publication as a "serious effort to appropriate and utilize all the resources which modern Philosophy, Psychology, and Criticism have placed at the disposal of the theologian for understanding the true and permanent meaning of the New Testament of Christianity itself." Written under the direction of B. H. Streeter, the book sought "to interpret the psychological language and spiritual experiences of the New Testament in terms of modern thought."[91]

Like Delitzsch, Fletcher advances both a descriptive and prescriptive goal. The descriptive goal is to arrive inductively "at a knowledge of the psychological conceptions of the New Testament writers, . . . looked at from their standpoint, but interpreted in terms of present-day psychology" (6). Biblical psychology for Fletcher is "the description and explanation which the Scriptural writers give of the mental and spiritual constitution of man" (7). The prescriptive goal is to uncover "the conception of human personality which the New Testament reflects" as "both an actuality and an ideal of manhood" (250). Following Höffding's dictum that "the concept of personality must always constitute the central thought of psychology" (249), Fletcher sets out to extrapolate from the New Testament a picture of what "man is and might become" (146), "what the human personality may attain to" (165), with the historical assumption that the "New Testament affords us psychological material of the highest value" in understanding a new and "fuller view of the nature of human personality" (10).

The table of contents shows a relatively unrestrained use of explicit psychological terminology in comparison with Delitzsch. Following an opening chapter on "The Relation of Biblical to Modern Psychology," the book divides into three parts with a total of fifteen chapters. Part 1, "The Psychological Terminology of the New Testament," follows the Patristic agenda of analyzing the key conceptual components of biblical psychology, namely soul, spirit, heart, and flesh. Part 2, "The Psychological Experiences of the New Testament," includes chapters on "Jesus and Man in the Synoptic Gospels," focusing on the effect of the personality of Jesus on those around him, on "The Conversion of Paul" and the psychology of the consciousness of sin and grace, on "The Psychology of Repentance and Faith," and finally on "The Regenerate Man," exploring the psychology of rebirth, renewal, and sanctification. Part 3 examines "Comparative Conceptions of Personality," with separate chapters on "The Christian Personality," "The Jewish Conception of Personality," "Greek and Christian Views," and "The Relation of the Christian Idea to Modern

Theories." In this final chapter Fletcher states that his overall objective has been to demonstrate that the "teaching about God and man [in the New Testament] enlarged all hitherto existing conceptions about each and their relation to one another" (301).

Fletcher's method is to combine the best of historical criticism with the best of modern scientific psychology. He uses the historical critical method "to study the Biblical teaching about man from the standpoint of the biblical writers themselves" and he uses modern psychology to understand its meaning. Fletcher defines modern psychology as "the science of the 'soul' or 'mind' [that]. . . considers all possible states of consciousness." It "treats of all sensations, feelings, modes of thought, and acts of will. It seeks to find out the nature of emotion, intellect, memory, imagination, instinct, and volition." Furthermore it sees the self as a unified, psychological being. The three conscious states identified by Kant, namely, "Cognition, Feeling and Conation," are not to be seen as separate faculties but as "modes of consciousness" of a unified ego or self, "often called the 'soul' in philosophical language." Fletcher acknowledges that although psychology proper cannot answer questions on metaphysics, it is not fundamentally hostile to philosophy or religion. In fact, Fletcher finds that it often leads to new insight into religion, as has been shown "by writers like James, Starbuck, and others, who are but the pathfinders in the new subject of religious psychology." "Modern scientific psychology has furnished the biblical student with a new instrument of wonderful precision with which to analyse and seek to understand the Scriptural terms which describe the mental and moral nature of man."[92]

Fletcher suggests four contributions that derive from an approach to Scripture that focuses on "the psychological language and spiritual experiences of the New Testament in terms of modern [psychological] thought."[93] First, it will enrich our understanding of religious phenomena, such as "demon possession" or "conversion." On Paul's conversion, for example, Fletcher tells us:

> [H]istorical criticism fails to reveal the deepest springs of Paul's convictions and missionary activities. . . . Paul's inward state was really one of great complexity psychologically. . . . There is every ground to suppose that his ideas, his conscience, and his sensitive nature were all alike stirred . . . by what he heard and saw in Jerusalem of the Christians, and also that these psychical elements came into conflict with one another. . . . The conversion followed on the interaction of all the elements of Paul's consciousness—intellectual, emotional, and moral. . . . Impulses and inhibitions, reason and passion, old traditions and new truths, produced a state of such inner discord and doubt that at last he raged forth a persecutor. . . . Fanaticism is often the expression

of inward doubt. . . . But Saul of Tarsus carried in the depths of his mind an idea and an image. . . . Ideas and images may be suppressed, but they live and work in the sub-conscious realm of personality until some crisis or experience brings them into the light of full consciousness.[94]

Second, a biblical psychological approach can help recover the psychodynamic value that terms like *spirit* and *flesh* conveyed for biblical authors. It does this by "purging our minds from later [dogmatic] ideas that have attached themselves to the word."[95]

Third, personality theory will be of interest to a biblical psychological approach. "The personality of Jesus and the immediate influences which he exerted on other personalities are psychological facts to be examined in the interests of human personality generally."[96]

Fourth, a biblical psychological approach will have an interest in the phenomenon of the psychic effect of early Christianity. Fletcher reminds us, somewhat hyperbolically, that "it must be remembered that the Gospel preached by Jesus Christ and his apostles stirred the ancient world to its depths." The psychic effect of this event will be evidenced in several ways. Citing Pentecost as a paradigm of the mind-set that emerged in early Christianity, Fletcher points to three aspects of what the disciples experienced: "enlarged self-consciousness"; "possession of unexpected powers" that reinforced their "self-determination"; and new insight into the social significance of human personality, recognizing that the "human personality only reaches its highest development in a social environment "in mutual fellowship with one another and with God." He also speaks of a "profound modification of ideas concerning man" and a "transformation of human nature itself." Finally, he notes that the postpentecostal experience requires new, "enriched psychological terminology . . . to express the fuller life that followed," as evidenced in the language of "new being," "sanctification," being "in Christ," "the renewal of one's mind," being "born from above," "justification," "salvation," "transformation," "liberation," "regeneration," and a "new, second man."[97]

Fletcher's assessment of the value of biblical psychology in 1912 bears remarkable resemblance to aspects of the approach taken by Gerd Theissen seventy-one years later in his 1983 work, *Psychological Aspects of Pauline Theology*. Theissen speaks of "psychological exegesis" as an arm of historical criticism, whose special objective is to clarify the "psychic factors and aspects" at work in the text of the New Testament, in the lives of its writers, and in the experience of the early Christian community that produced it, focusing specifically on the "new patterns of experience and behavior that appeared with ancient Christianity."[98]

A Look Ahead

Biblical psychology is the first and longest phase of psychological biblical criticism. We have seen that it has four objectives. The first is *descriptive*, namely to identify the biblical understanding of the nature, origin, powers, and destiny of the psyche/soul. The second is *analytic*, to identify psychodynamic factors at work in biblical personalities (like Paul), in biblical religious phenomena (like dreams, prophetic inspiration, and speaking in tongues), and in biblical effects (such as the enlarged consciousness produced by the earliest Christian preaching of which Fletcher speaks). The third is *diagnostic*, to identify and assess what has gone wrong in the human condition from a biblical standpoint. The fourth objective is *prescriptive*, to learn what the Bible teaches about the highest reaches of human personality and what methods of nurture, care, healing, and formation it prescribes for the attainment of that higher nature—a process classically described as the *cura animarum*, the care and cure of souls.

In the next two chapters we will continue the history of psychological biblical criticism, adding to it the monumental analytical contributions of Freud and Jung (chapter 2), then the increasingly diverse contributions since the 1960s by biblical scholars and biblically oriented psychologists (chapter 3).

2
Freud and Jung

Psychoanalysis and the Bible Since 1900

My deep engrossment in the Bible story (almost as soon as I had learned the art of reading) had, as I recognized much later, an enduring effect upon the direction of my interest.

Sigmund Freud[1]

We must read our Bible or we shall not understand psychology. Our psychology, whole lives, our language and imagery are built upon the Bible.

Carl Gustav Jung[2]

The psychological study of the Bible moves in a new direction with the appearance of Sigmund Freud (1856–1939) and Carl Jung (1875–1961). Whereas biblical psychology from Tertullian to Delitzsch had focused on the psyche/soul as conceived by the biblical authors, Freud and Jung turned their powerful observational skills to the study of the psyche/soul as manifested in the lives of individuals and cultures, including religious institutions and religious texts.

The work of Freud and Jung, based on decades of clinical observation and research, left a significant mark on Western culture. Even though university departments of psychology often excluded consideration of Freud and Jung, Freudian theory became the dominating influence in psychology by the 1950s, with a proven record of applicability of his thought and method to the human and social sciences.[3] A couplet of W. H. Auden proposed in midcentury that "to us he [Freud] is no more a person; now but a whole climate of opinion."[4] By the 1970s Carl Jung's work on symbol, dream, archetype, and myth was widely known and his notion of psychological types had even slipped into the marketplace through the Myers-Briggs Personality Type Indicator test. The combined impact of Freud and Jung on individual and cultural self-understanding in the West resulted in a set of terms, phrases, and concepts that made their way into everyday speech: the unconscious, psychological complexes, introversion and extraversion, the id-ego-superego triad, the concepts of repression, projection, sublimation, and transference, the pleasure principle, the reality principle, and Freudian slips.

Though Freud and Jung enjoyed a six-year period of cordial and even intense correspondence after their initial meeting in 1907, they parted ways in 1913 over the issue of Jung's interest in religious symbols of transformation. Freud denounced that interest as a venture into the "black tide of mud . . . of occultism."[5] The vehemence of Freud's objection was in part a function of the psychoanalytic agenda he had carved out for himself. Ludwig Binswanger, a friend of Freud's, reports that in reply to the complaint that he paid too little attention to the spiritual side of life, Freud answered that "he was too busy with the lower, basic structure of our minds to have the time to dedicate to those loftier levels."[6] Freud, by his own admission, approached religion from the "lower floors" perspective, from which he came to see religion as a "universal obsessional neurosis" (though in later life he modified this position). Jung, on the other hand, though no less a critic of conventional religiosity, was beginning to take a look at the "higher" end of the psyche, and saw in the best of religion and religious texts the traces of an impressive "therapeutic system in the truest sense of the word," displaying a side of religion that Jung believed had been long eclipsed by preoccupation with creeds and dogmas whose link with life had been forgotten.[7]

Despite striking differences, Freud and Jung displayed a remarkably similar approach to culture, religion, and the Bible. Both had a lifelong personal and professional psychological interest in the Judeo-Christian Scriptures. Both were past-masters of suspicion, hunting for unconscious factors lurking unrecognized in religious beliefs, practices, rituals, and texts. Both deplored mindless bibliolatry and blind subscription to religious authority. Both began life with an interest in Scripture and toward the end of their careers felt an inner need to work on biblical themes. Both were interested in the beguiling and mysterious qualities of classical literature, especially literature that wrestled with the great human themes that were also at the heart of biblical thought. Both were skilled linguists: equal to the Greek of the New Testament, with some working knowledge of Hebrew (and in Freud's case, Yiddish), and thoroughly at home in English, French, German, and Latin. Both were shaped by the religious and scriptural traditions of home and culture; Freud came from a Moravian and Austrian Jewish family with faint ties to cabalistic Judaism, Jung from a Swiss Reformed Protestant parsonage. Above all, both were driven by a commitment to alleviate human psychic suffering and to factor in the role of religion and Scripture in that suffering—a turn of mind that itself might be traceable to religious and biblical sources.

Both voices are important to hear on the Bible. Though their theories were amplified and even superseded by emerging schools of psychology and psychoanalysis later in the twentieth century, the questions they raised in the first half of the century lay the groundwork for most psychological approaches to Scripture in the second half.

Sigmund Freud and the Bible

Sigmund Freud's familiarity with the Bible, its effect on his life, and his interest in the text in later life are greater than commonly supposed. In his autobiography, Freud reports, "My deep engrossment in the Bible story (almost as soon as I had learnt the art of reading) had, as I recognized much later, an enduring effect upon the direction of my interest."[8] Freud's biographer, Ernest Jones, found this admission "incomprehensible"; some editors expunged it from later editions of "An Autobiographical Study."[9] But the testimony and facts of Freud's life, beginning in Freiberg, Moravia (eastern Czechoslovakia) in 1856, and ending in England in 1939, indicate that the Bible played a significant role in Freud's consciousness, culminating with his *Moses and Monotheism* (1939) but evident throughout his writing.

Théo Pfrimmer's thesis, *Sigmund Freud, Lecteur de la Bible* ("Sigmund Freud, Reader of the Bible"), notes at least 488 biblical references in Freud's correspondence and writing. He cited twenty-one of the thirty-nine books of the Hebrew Bible; he cited the Gospel of Matthew forty-eight times. In addition, Pfrimmer lists 111 allusions to biblical texts, from Genesis to the First Epistle of John. The biblical figures Freud was most attracted to are Joseph, Abraham, Moses, Jesus, and Paul. Pfrimmer also notes that Freud was given to the use of biblical paraphrase, such as "casting out the devil with Beelzebub," or in a letter to a friend, "No one can help in what oppresses me, it is my cross, which I must bear, and heaven knows my back is getting noticeably bent under it."[10]

In what follows we will explore Freud's use of the Bible and biblical themes, his major writings on the Bible, and elements in his perspective that contribute to the development of a psychological critical approach to the Bible.

The Bible and Biblical Themes in Freud's Life and Work

The Bible and its themes appear prominently in five areas of Freud's life: in his early use of a family Bible; in the literature he read; in his encounters with Christians; in his travels and visits to churches and museums, especially in Rome; and in his relationship to his Judaic roots.

When Freud was thirty-five years old, his father presented him with the old family Phillipson Bible. The Hebrew inscription, written by his father, indicates that Freud had begun reading the Bible when he was seven years old.

Pfrimmer finds allusions to this Bible and its rich illustrative materials scattered throughout Freud's works, with references to its illustrations of biblical and ancient near eastern weapons, insignia, sacred images, temples, sculpture, costumes, funerary rites, commerce, money, jewelry, and ruins. One Freud biographer contends that "it was the Bible as literature, as psychology, as cultural history, and as religion that formed the mind" of the young Freud far more than the physical or biological sciences, and that it informed his writing and his psychological theory from beginning to end.[11]

Freud always had a prodigious literary appetite and was drawn especially to books that dealt with the great themes common to religious traditions. In an interview late in life, he reported, "I am a scientist by necessity, and not by vocation. I am really by nature an artist. Ever since childhood, my secret hero has been Goethe. I would like to have become a poet, and my whole life long I've wanted to write novels."[12] Goethe's *Faust* is the text Freud cites most frequently, fascinated with its depiction of the soul's struggle with evil, its emphasis on the theme of redemption, and its portrait of the simple faith of the peasant heroine Margaret.[13]

Freud reports that in 1907 he was asked to name "ten good books," and comments that if the question had instead asked for the "ten greatest books" he would have included Goethe's *Faust* at the top of the list, along with the tragedies of Sophocles and Shakespeare's *Hamlet*. He adds that had he been asked to name favorites, he would have mentioned Milton's *Paradise Lost* and Heine's *Lazarus*, a collection of twenty short poems focusing on the two Lazarus figures in the New Testament.[14] He tells us that at the age of thirteen he "repeatedly feasted" on Cervantes's *Don Quixote*.[15] He acknowledges that in his later work he derived his ideas of free association and the talking cure from Goethe, Victor Hugo, and the Roman Catholic confessionals, which had tutored him in the power of catharsis, a phenomenon "the Catholics knew . . . for centuries."[16]

Freud's stance toward Christianity was ambivalent.[17] He was profoundly aware of the anti-Semitism permeating the culture of his time, as is evidenced in his account of a youthful conversation with his father:

> He told me a story to show me how much better things are now than they had been in his days. "When I was a young man," he said, "I went for a walk one Saturday in the streets of your birthplace [Freiberg]; I was well dressed, and had a new fur cap on my head. A Christian came up to me and with a single blow knocked off my cap into the mud and shouted: 'Jew! get off the pavement!'" "And what did you do?" I asked. "I went into the roadway and picked up my cap," was his quiet reply. This struck me as unheroic on the part of the big, strong man who was holding the little boy by the hand.[18]

Anti-Semitism forced Freud to leave university research early in his career. On June 3, 1938, a year before his death, it drove him from Vienna to England.[19] But his attitude toward institutional Christianity, oddly, remained mixed. He was aware, on the one hand, of the historical role of the Church in providing a breeding place for anti-Semitism, but on the other, that "only this Catholicism protects us against Nazism."[20]

Freud's attitude toward individual Christians had a positive side, attributable no doubt to his congenial relationship with a number of Christians who played important roles in his life. One of these was his Moravian nanny, Resi (Theresa) Wittek, who raised Freud for his first three years. A pious Catholic from Freud's birthplace of Freiberg in Moravia (150 miles northwest of Vienna), she had initiated Freud into the piety of this largely Catholic area, marked by its devotion to Mary. Freud's mother would later tell him, "She was always taking you to church. When you came home you used to preach and tell us all about how the loving God conducted his affairs." Freud's biographers suspect that Freud's fascination with churches and cathedrals, heaven, hell, the Devil, and the themes of salvation and resurrection derived from this childhood experience.[21]

A second Christian friend was Oskar Pfister, a Swiss Protestant minister, who established a lifelong cordial relationship with the Freud family. Pfister's father, also a pastor, had become so anguished at his inability to help a young parishioner who was dying that he took up the study of medicine to equip himself to be a "physician to the body and the soul at the same time." The younger Pfister, in a similar frame of mind, had rejected a chair in systematic and practical theology in 1908, disillusioned with his theological pursuits, only to discover Freud's writing a few weeks later, a discovery that struck him with the "force of revelation," disclosing a strategy for the cure of souls that none of his previous study had been able to supply. Pfister undertook training in psychoanalysis with Freud and became a lifelong champion of Freud's approach, pointing to parallels between Freud's thought and his own on love as the foundation of a healthy life, and finding analogies between Freud's psychoanalytic therapy and biblical descriptions of healing.[22] Freud called Pfister a "remarkable man, . . . a true servant of God, a man in the very idea of whom I should have had difficulty believing, in that he feels the need to do spiritual good to everyone he meets." He congratulated Pfister for his article on St. Paul, noting that he himself had "always had a special sympathy [for Paul] . . . as a genuinely Jewish character."[23]

Freud's reports on his travels to European museums, cathedrals, and religious sites attest to his fascination with biblical and Christian religious themes. He writes after a visit to Notre Dame Cathedral in Paris, "My first impression on entering was a sensation I have never had before: 'This is a church.'. . . I have never seen anything so movingly serious and somber, quite unadorned and very narrow." He made trips to St. Mark's in Venice and to Assisi, as well as to Milan to see Da Vinci's "The Last Supper." Following a trip to Dresden, he wrote admiringly of three paintings, Holbein's *Madonna*, Raphael's *Madonna*, and Titian's *Maundy Money*, and undertook a psychoanalytic essay on Da Vinci's *Virgin and Child with St. Anne*. A reproduction of *The Healing of Aeneas and the Raising of Tabitha* by Masaccio and Masolino, a composite painting depicting healing themes from the New Testament (Acts 9:32–42), hung on a wall near his desk in Vienna. The city of Rome, above all, fascinated Freud. His personal correspondence speaks enthusiastically of the catacombs and the treasures of the Vatican. Having postponed a trip there for years, he wrote a friend, Karl Abraham, in 1913, "I have quickly recovered my spirits and zest for work in the incomparably beautiful Rome, and in the free hours between visits to museums, churches, and the Campagna I have managed to write."[24]

Freud's relationship to his Jewish cultural and religious heritage is equally ambivalent. Though he never officially identifies himself with Jewish institutional religion, his life and work are clearly formed by his religious and biblical past. The Hebrew name given him by his Reform Jewish parents was Schlomo (Solomon). Though the Friday sabbath meals and Jewish dietary laws were not consistently observed in his childhood home, Freud does recount at the age of eighteen the foods that his "modestly pious family" ate on the holidays of Passover, the Jewish New Year, and the Day of Atonement.[25] The family's use of the Phillipson Bible, combined with Freud's memory of his father's Talmud study and ability to recite the Passover Haggadah by memory, attests to his exposure to the tradition, even though he made a conscious decision not to be observant. Freud married a woman from an Orthodox Jewish family, Martha Bernays, who in time decided to go along with his repudiation of religious observance in the household. In the end, Freud reported that even though the Judaism of his childhood no longer provided a home for them, something of the essence of the meaning and joy of Judaism would not leave their house.[26]

Though Freud distanced himself from observant Judaism, his personality, his psychoanalytic theory, and his interest in religion toward the end of his career show its abiding effect. The effect on his personality is evident in a letter to the B'nai B'rith Lodge in 1926, in which he states that his Jewishness is not a matter of faith or national pride, but of "inner identity" and "psychological structure" characterized by "independence of mind, iconoclasm, and the capacity to stand against the 'compact majority.'"[27] In 1886 Freud wrote his fiancée, "I have often felt as though I had inherited all the defiance and all the passion with which our ancestors defended their temple. . . ."[28] Judaism's effect on his psychoanalytic theory is evident in Freud's techniques of textual interpretation and his theory of the importance of human sexuality, which can be traced to his interest in cabalistic Jewish mysticism. Freud's library contained a large collection of Judaica that included books on the mystic tradition, with a copy in French of its most important literary expression, the *Zohar*.[29]

Finally, the effect of Freud's cultural and religious heritage in Judaism is evident in the point of view he develops in his later years. Freud notes in his autobiography that the bulk of his career, devoted to the natural sciences, medicine, and psychotherapy, was a "lifelong detour." He describes his later years as an opportunity to return to "the cultural problems which had fascinated me long before, when I was a youth scarcely old enough for thinking, namely the investigation of the origins of religion and morality." A specific manifestation of this return is his fascination with Michelangelo's statue of Moses, found in the church of St. Peter in Chains in Rome. In 1912 he visited the statue repeatedly over the course of three weeks. The effect of these visits is reflected in his essay *The Moses of Michelangelo* (1914) and in his last great work, *Moses and Monotheism* (1939), a work, according to one commentator, that Freud regarded as the first of a "vast work which would apply psychoanalytical theories to the whole of the Bible."[30]

Freud on the Bible

Freud wrote two books directly bearing on biblical issues, *Totem and Taboo* (1913) and *Moses and Monotheism* (1939), and a third, bearing on issues related to psychological biblical criticism, *The Future of an Illusion* (1927). We will consider them in the order they were written.

Totem and Taboo appeared during the period (1900–20) when Freud, between the ages of 44 and 64, was defining psychoanalysis. This period is marked by three definitive works: *The Interpretation of Dreams* (1900), commonly referred to as marking the birth of the psychoanalytic movement, *Three Essays on the Theory of Sexuality* (1905), and *Beyond the Pleasure Principle* (1920).

The thesis of *Totem and Taboo* is that tribal totem meals are cultic repetitions, unconsciously perpetuated, of a ritual of propitiation for a primordial slaying of a jealous tribal "father" who had kept all the females to himself and driven away his sons. The result of the slaying by this "primal horde" of sons was tribal guilt. The mechanism for mitigating that guilt is the ritual slaughter of a totem animal with whom the tribe has experienced the same sort of love/fear relationship as it did with the father, and a totem meal in which the flesh of the sacrificial victim is shared by the group. The totem animal is regarded as a reincarnation of the father; its slaughter achieves expiation for the guilt of patricide. A corollary to the ritual is the promulgation of taboos in the form of laws against patricide and against sexual relations within one's own tribe. These forestall the repetition of the primordial event.

Freud maintains that all religions, including Christianity, attempt to solve the problem of guilt felt in regard to a primordial father. He finds a hint of the theme of primordial rebellion in the Christian notion of original sin. He notes that in the Christian theological scenario of the atonement, the son, slain in expiation for the sins of the "rebellious sons" against the father, represents the requisite "totem substitute" to regain rapport with that father. The cultic meals commemorating this event, Freud notes, involve the act of consuming the body and blood of the son, establishing cultic identification with him, and by so doing, also with the father.

Totem and Taboo was dismissed by many ethnologists and historians of religion on grounds that the evidence is far slimmer than suggested by Freud's sources.[31] But the considerations Freud introduces in this book continue to bear on studies in the psychology of religion and are relevant for the work of psychological biblical criticism—for example, the question of the psychocultural roots of rituals and moral codes and the mystery of the irresistible power and authority with which they emerge in religions and cultures, or the "psychological archaeological" question of the ancient cultural trauma, the vestigial cultural memory, or the universal pattern of human psychic reckoning (such as the structural tendency toward the Oedipal complex) that might inform a text or a cultic tradition. Robert Paul, in his *Moses and Civilization: Freud and the Judeo-Christian Master Narrative*, argues that Freud's myth of the primal horde, though not taken very seriously even in the field of psychoanalysis, nevertheless provides an

> almost perfectly accurate model of the myth that we already know to be the central organizing master narrative of the Judeo-Christian tradition, namely the Bible. The mythic paradigm of the primal horde is not, then, something that hovers in the air structuring the zeitgeist or a ghostly skeleton hidden away in the unconscious collective memory of the West. It is, on the contrary, the most widely known, read, and performed sacred story we have, whose influence on the West, and through it on life on this planet, has been incalculable.[32]

The Future of an Illusion (1927) is a penetrating critique of institutional religion as Freud saw it from his late nineteenth and early twentieth century European vantage point.[33] Its daring quality exemplifies a defining aspect of Freud's persona as one who has a "passion for the truth," determined "not to be deceived." No doubt fired by his reading of Ludwig Feuerbach's critique of Christianity, Freud resolved "to become independent of fettering authorities," "to dispense with illusions," and to measure institutional religion and the culture of his time against the "reality principle."[34] He had warned his friend, the Reverend Oskar Pfister, that the book was on its way; to Freud's amazement, Pfister took the book as an honest statement from a friend and published a review in the psychoanalytic journal *Imago* under the title, "The Illusion of a Future." Pfister made the telling point—echoed in later reviews, and in time conceded by Freud himself—that "one difference [between Pfister and Freud] derives chiefly from the fact that you [Freud] grew up in proximity to pathological forms of religion and regard these as 'religion.'"[35]

The pathology of religion is the subject of *The Future of an Illusion*. Freud advances his well-known thesis that religion is a "universal obsessional neurosis," originating in the infantile stage of mankind, deriving from the child's helplessness and its longing for a protective, cosmic father to defend it against nature and fate. Motivated by the pleasure principle, the infantile mind resorts to wish fulfillment by projecting a friendly face onto a hostile world, providing for a more secure existence. In time, the mind generates the myths, laws, stories, and rituals that it then compulsively rehearses to sustain this illusory world and to stave off misfortune or punishment. In the process, religion creates a false preoccupation with eschatology that effectively dehistoricizes its practitioners by focusing attention on a future life that will compensate for the sufferings and deprivation of the present. Though Freud recognizes some benefit in religion, he believes that in the end it denies reality, it contradicts science ("the only road which can lead us to a knowledge of reality outside ourselves"), and it diverts us from this-worldly responsibility, keeping us in a state of childlike ignorance, intellectually and morally.

Eventually the limitations of Freud's tour de force against religion became apparent, even to Freud. Long after the publication of *The Future of an Illusion*, Freud wrote to his psychoanalytic colleague, Sandor Ferenczi, that the book seemed inadequate. "Now it seems childish to me already; basically I think something else. Analytically I consider it weak, and as a confession of faith, inappropriate." He later stated that he had created a phantom of religion for the purpose of "getting it out of the way."[36] But as radical, provincial, and unrestrained as it is, *The Future of an Illusion* contributes importantly to the task of a psychological critical approach to religion, religious texts, and their interpretations, by inviting consideration of the unconscious elements perennially at work in what humans think, do, and write.

Moses and Monotheism (1939) appears as the last great work of Freud's third and final phase (1920–39), from his sixty-fourth to eighty-third year. His biographers refer to *Moses and Monotheism* as a "return of the repressed," since Freud turns to a subject matter he had earlier dismissed. Freud tells us that the idea of *Moses and Monotheism* would not let go of his imagination and that it tormented him "like an unredeemed spirit," comparable to Jung's experience in writing his sole biblical work, *Answer to Job*.[37]

Freud's fervor in writing *Moses and Monotheism* is an effect of his fascination in later life with the Moses of Michelangelo in the Chapel of Saint Peter in Chains in Rome. He could not understand the powerful effect of the statue on his psyche; he writes, "A rationalist or perhaps analytic disposition within me struggles against my being deeply moved and not knowing why I am and what has moved me . . ." and "why I am subject to so powerful an impression."[38]

What did Freud find in the statue? First he found a new, inspiring portrait of Moses that bears remarkable resemblance to the homeostatic or balanced self of Freud's psychoanalytic theory. This statue is not the conventional image of the patriarchal figure who breaks the sacred tablets in a rage. The Moses of Michelangelo has "assimilated his anger," has "overcome his passion," and is the "bodily expression of the highest psychic achievement that is possible for a human being, the overpowering of one's passions in favor of and in fulfillment of a destiny to which one has committed oneself." He is a man who no longer remains "under the spell of sensuality." Freud was also fascinated by the audience he imagined this Moses was looking at: "the riffraff," the unintegrated, sensual selves who "hold to no [religious] conviction," figures with whom Freud had no difficulty identifying.[39]

The book advances the astonishing thesis that there were two Moses figures. The first, and more admirable one, is not a Jew but an Egyptian, probably the illegitimate son of Pharaoh's daughter. He is a convert to the monotheism of the earlier Pharaoh Ikhnaton. After Ikhnaton's death, when monotheism is quashed, the first Moses undertakes a freedom movement for the Israelite slaves, tutoring them in Ikhnaton's monotheism. At first they respond favorably to Moses, repudiating their earlier religion of magic, mysticism, and sensuality in favor of the higher spirituality Moses advocated. In time, however, they rebel against Moses and put him to death. Two generations later a second Moses appears, an advocate of "the fire demon Yahweh," who picks up on the monotheism of the first Moses and interpolates it into the worship of Yahweh, thus establishing the Mosaic religion known in Scripture.[40]

In time Freud was to refer to *Moses and Monotheism* as a "novel," and well he might, since it seems to be more a work of projection than historical analysis. It is no small wonder that passionate objections came from both Christians and Jews, clergy and scholars. William Foxwell Albright, the dean of biblical archaeological research at the time, characterized the book as a "futile but widely read example of psychological determinism . . . totally devoid of serious historical method." Biblical scholar Abraham Shalom Yahuda denounced Freud's work as an expression of "fanatical . . . hatred of

Israel."[41] For Freud, however, the value of the book was its recognition of two types of religion, the type he had described in *The Future of an Illusion*, and a nobler more spiritual type that he felt was latent in contemporary Judaism in partially repressed form. As such—and despite its limitations from a historical-critical standpoint—the book provides a psychological critical precedent for undertaking a comparative assessment of the psycho-spiritual aspects, strengths, and deficiencies of different types of religions, religious systems, and texts.

Freud's Contribution to Psychological Biblical Criticism

Joachim Scharfenberg makes the comment in *Sigmund Freud and His Critique of Religion* (1988) that " If Rudolf Bultmann has . . . shown that they [biblical scholars] cannot get along without philosophy, then the same is certainly also true for psychology."[42] Though much of Freud's work on religion and the Bible has since been refined, corrected, or dismissed, it nevertheless leaves a legacy of psychological-critical hermeneutical questions that get at dimensions of the text to which classical historical criticism has been professionally oblivious. Freud's work lays the groundwork for considering five dimensions of the text largely ignored in earlier exegesis: the unconscious as a factor at work in the text and reader; psychodynamic factors at work in textual narratives and interpretive approaches; psychological aspects of biblical religious phenomena; comparative assessment of biblical psychology; and psychological assessment of the effects of religious systems and texts.

The unconscious as a factor at work in text and reader. When he departed from his medical colleagues Josef Breuer and Wilhelm Fliess by offering a psychological rather than physiological explanation of hysteria and sexual aberrancy, Freud spoke of a "division of labor: you the biological, I the psychological; you at the end of the stars, I at the end of the soul; you with the brightness of the sun, I with the darkness of the unconscious." Freud has been rightfully called a "master of interpretation,"[43] probing human behavior to detect the ubiquitous manifestations of the unconscious. He did not invent the idea of the unconscious or the term itself, which most likely originated in the early 1700s.[44] His contribution was to transform the concept of the unconscious from a hypothesis about "unconscious ideas" that break into consciousness, to a hypothesis about a "mental place" where power-laden memories, ideas, dreams, fears, and anticipations are stored and generated, and where intrapsychic conflicts are at work, manifesting themselves unconsciously in what we say, do, read, and write.[45] Freud provides the groundwork for studying the Bible and its interpretation with an eye to the unconscious factors at work in writer and reader and in the communities and cultures of which they are part.

Psychodynamic factors at work in textual narratives and interpretive approaches. Freudian theory suggests the possibility of detecting psychological dynamics and strategies at work in the biblical text or its interpretation—for example, manifestations of repression, denial, sublimation, projection, regression, displacement, transference, and reaction formation.[46] It also suggests a line of research that would undertake analysis and commentary on the psychodynamic difference between law-oriented and conscience-oriented moral codes, on taboos and the psychology of ritual repetition, on the role of projection in the promulgation of God images, on the intrapsychic struggle between the instinctual and the ideal in stories of biblical figures, and on the dynamics of transference and counter-transference in the process of biblical reading and interpretation. It further suggests developing exegetical strategies that would foster the "unconcealing"[47] of factors in the biblical text or reader that tend to engender repression, compulsive behavior, neurotic guilt, or obsessive fixation either with the text or with prescribed methods for interpreting it.

Psychological aspects of biblical religious phenomena. Though Freud's only extensive commentary on biblical/religious phenomena is in the anthropologically faulted *Totem and Taboo*, his collected works provide hints of other possible lines of research on more solid ground. These would include inquiries into "demon possession" and hysteria,[48] sexual laws and practices, dreams, glossolalia, and speech as therapy. In an essay entitled, "Great is Diana of the Ephesians" (a phrase from Acts 19:28, but also the title of a poem by Goethe), Freud suggests that when the cult of Diana was displaced by the cult of Mary in Ephesus, values of the former were preserved in the latter. He sees this as suggesting the psychological principle that "important people are apt to be 'revenants' of still earlier figures,"[49] an observation with possible application to the interpretation of key biblical figures.

Comparative assessment of biblical psychology. One task of psychological biblical criticism (noted in the previous chapter) is to construct a biblical psychology, that is, to spell out the portrait(s) of the human soul/psyche/self articulated in the Bible. As the early church writers demonstrated, that task has a comparative aspect: to evaluate the biblical model of the psyche in light of other models, ancient or modern. The purpose of such a comparison is to assess the capacity of each model to encompass the full range of psychological qualities that characterize the human condition, and to portray these qualities adequately. When, for example, Freud's view of the psyche is compared with that of the Bible, we find they share special interest in two aspects of the self, namely human depravity and human suffering. A task of biblical psychology will be to compare the Freudian and the biblical models for differences but also for possible mutual illumination.[50]

Psychological assessment of the effects of religious systems and texts.
Implicit in Freud's work is a question, rarely voiced by biblical critics, that
inquires into the pathogenic and therapeutic effects of religions and religious
texts on individuals and cultures. The question lies at the heart of Freud's psy-
chotherapeutically oriented agenda, and as such recommends itself for consideration as one of the objectives of psychological biblical criticism.

The notion of pathogenic and therapeutic effects presupposes a vision of
what constitutes health and illness. For Freud, health is a function of those
qualities that enable the self to cope with *ananke*, the classical Greek term for
"necessity," connoting the natural constraints, limits, burdens, and suffering
that characterize human existence. Freud writes, "I have tried to show that
religious ideas have sprung from the same need as all the other achievements
of culture: from the necessity for defending itself against the crushing
supremacy of nature."[51] A healthy response to *ananke* for Freud is epitomized
in two mottoes, *Logos* and *ananke* ("reason and reality") and *eros* and *ananke*
("love and reality").[52] Though the earlier Freud had proposed reason and science as the antidote to human suffering, the later Freud added love: "that
direction of life that takes love as its center and expects all satisfaction to come
from loving and being loved."[53]

Freud's hermeneutical legacy challenges the psychological critic to go
beyond psychological description to psychological value judgments. This
involves establishing psychological criteria, either on biblical or extrabiblical
grounds, in light of which the possible pathogenic or therapeutic content and
effects of the Bible and its interpretation on generations of readers can be
assessed.[54]

Freudian Approaches in Contemporary Biblical Scholarship

The power of Freud's insights into the nature and habits of the human psyche
has had its effect on art and literary critics for decades, but more recently on
biblical criticism. Though few biblical scholars would think of themselves as
thoroughly Freudian, many are indebted to Freud for new insight into the
Bible and its history of interpretation. In his 1978 article on "The Heuristic
Value of a Psychoanalytic Model in the Interpretation of Pauline Theology,"
New Testament scholar Robin Scroggs writes:

> I believe that Paul shares with the psychoanalytic vision the same deep
> insights into human reality and dynamic, despite the apparent enormity sep-
> arating the language systems. . . . Freud himself suggested that Paul made an
> important step toward bringing the repressed to consciousness. I believe this
> is true far beyond what Freud believed."[55]

Other biblical scholars who have utilized Freudian-based models for biblical interpretation in the past two decades include David Halperin, Daniel Merkur, Stephen Moore, Ilona Rashkow, Richard Rubenstein, Gerd Theissen, Mary Ann Tolbert, and Wilhelm Wuellner. To their number should be added psychologists and theologians who have applied a Freudian approach to biblical understanding, such as Françoise Dolto, Gérard Séverin, Stanley Leavy, Robert A. Paul, Oskar Pfister, H. L. Philp, Paul Ricoeur, Anna-Maria Rizzuto, Joachim Scharfenberg, Antoine Vergote, Paul Vitz, and Dorothy Zeligs.[56]

From Freud to Jung

The differences between the approaches of Sigmund Freud and Carl Gustav Jung are more a matter of focus than of theory. In a 1929 essay entitled "Freud and Jung: Contrasts," Carl Jung cited several differences between himself and Freud. First, Jung faulted Freud for "overemphasizing the pathological aspect of life and for interpreting man too exclusively in the light of his defects." Jung continues: "I prefer to look at man in the light of what in him is healthy and sound" as opposed to Freud's emphasis on a "psychology of neurotic states of mind." Second, Jung criticized Freud for "taking sexuality as the only psychic driving force," noting it was only after their break in 1913 that Freud began to take other factors into account. What Jung finds missing is "the necessity of rediscovering the life of the spirit." At the risk of being "accused of mysticism" Jung holds that "man has, always and everywhere, spontaneously developed a religious function, and . . . the human psyche from time immemorial has been shot through with religious feelings and ideas." Freud, he maintains, has forgotten that through "ceremonial ritual, initiation, rites, and ascetic practices," humankind has aimed at reconciling itself to the "forces of psychic life" and at finding an "equal balance of the flesh and the spirit."[57]

Jung's concentration on the healthier aspects of the human psyche rather than the pathological, and his developed interest in the religious function as expressed in symbol, story, ritual, and myth, offer a corrective to Freud. In addition, Jung's life and work manifest a familiarity with the Bible and the biblical worldview that is unmatched among his psychological and psychoanalytic peers.

Carl Gustav Jung and the Bible

A most striking fact about Swiss analytical psychologist, Carl Gustav Jung (1875–1961), is the ubiquitous presence of the Bible in his life and thought, literally from cradle to grave. No document is cited by Jung more often. No cast of characters from any tradition is summoned to the stage of his discourse with greater regularity than biblical figures such as Adam and Abraham, Melchizedek and Moses, Peter and Paul. The degree of Jung's critical interest in the Bible, its worldview, its images and symbols, and its interpretation in the modern world is unparalleled in the life and work of any twentieth-century psychologist. In this section we will turn to three aspects of the role of the Bible and biblical interpretation in Jung's life and work: the Bible as problem and project in Jung's life; Jung's use of the Bible; Jung's contribution to the agenda of psychological biblical criticism. We will then look at Jungian effects in biblical scholarship.

The Bible as Problem and Project in Jung's Life

Raised in a Swiss Reformed Protestant parsonage and engaged as a youth in active dialogue with six clergy on his mother's side and two clergy uncles on his father's, Jung was initiated into a lifelong relationship and dialogue with the Bible. He writes in a 1957 letter, "You can rest assured that having studied the Gospels for a life-time (I am nearly 83!) I am pretty well acquainted with the foundations of our Christianity."[58] But it was precisely this nineteenth-century biblical context in tension with Jung's emerging thought and experience that framed the problem for the lifelong project the Bible would constitute for him.

The problem and promise of the Bible for Jung are associated with four experiences: the biblicism of the Reformed Protestant piety and theology of Jung's youth; its polar opposite, the rationalistic historicism of the new biblical criticism at the end of the nineteenth century; the faith crisis of his preacher father; and his personal experience of the archetypal power of biblical images.

The Biblicism of Reformed Protestant Piety. Jung's early experience with Reformed piety spurred him to find a new way to understand the Bible. The theological language of Reformed Protestantism seemed so unrelated to his experience. As a youth he found this language "stale and hollow, like a tale told by someone who knows it only by hearsay and cannot quite believe it in himself." Jung describes the Reformed mindset as that of a Christian who "puts his Church and his Bible between himself and his unconscious," mindlessly reciting catechetical slogans and offering praise to a God "out there," totally oblivious of the "God within" which Jung had read about in Paul, John, and the tradition of the mystics. Jung censured his Reformed contemporaries for being "more interested in protecting their institutions than in understanding the mystery that symbols present," having "stripped all things of their mystery and numinosity," including the Bible.[59]

Rationalistic Biblical Criticism. At the opposite end of the theological spectrum, Jung attacked the new historical-critical biblical scholarship, freighted with "the garish conceits of the enlightenment." Jung found this type of "rationalistic historicism" guilty on three counts: it sacrificed the numinous aspect of the Bible on the altar of rationalistic positivism; it severed Scripture from its roots in a "living religious process"; and it defused the powerful symbols and stories of the Bible through a process of "demythologization." In his Terry lectures at Yale Jung commented:

> Nor has scientific criticism . . . been very helpful in enhancing belief in the divine character of the holy scriptures. It is also a fact that under the influence of a so-called scientific enlightenment great masses of educated people have either left the church or have become profoundly indifferent to it. If they were all dull rationalists or neurotic intellectuals, the loss would not be regrettable. But many of them are religious people. . . .[60]

Jung was neither ignorant of nor opposed to biblical scholarship. In response to a request from American writer, Upton Sinclair, for Jung's opinion on his new novel, A *Personal Jesus*, Jung offers ample evidence of his familiarity with biblical Greek, ancient near Eastern literature, and the history of biblical scholarship. Recalling the "Life of Jesus research" of Ernest Renan, David Strauss, and Albert Schweitzer, Jung criticized Sinclair for excluding certain portions of the text as "later interpolations" in order to create a portrait of Jesus that would be "convincing to a modern American mind. . . . You give an excellent picture of a possible religious teacher," he wrote Sinclair, "but you give us no understanding of what the New Testament tries to tell, namely the life, fate, and effect of a God-Man. . . ." Jung concluded with the injunction, "Sure enough, we must believe in Reason. But it should not prevent us from recognizing a mystery when we meet one. It seems to me that no rational biography could explain one of the most 'irrational' effects ever observed in the history of man. I believe that this problem can only be approached through his history and comparative psychology of symbols." Jung likened his critical approach to the Bible to that of Wilhelm de Wette (1780–1849), initiator of the historical-critical approach to the Pentateuch and friend of Jung's grandfather, whose hermeneutical method was to "mythize" or extract the "symbolic value" of "marvelous" Bible stories rather than concentrate exclusively on their literal meaning.[61]

The Faith Crisis of Jung's Father. Up to the day he died in 1896, Jung's pastor-father was caught in the conflict between the demand for unquestioning faith stemming from his roots in traditional piety, and the intellectual doubt that "rationalistic historicism" had planted in his mind. Jung had been admonished by his father at an early age, "You always want to think. One ought not to think, but believe." The tragedy of this "sacrifice of the intellect" was heightened by the fact that Jung's father had once had an active intellectual life, having "studied Oriental languages in Göttingen and done his dissertation on the Arabic version of the Song of Songs."[62]

Jung took his father's death as a sign of unfinished business that he was destined to assume. He wrote, "I feel very strongly that I am under the influence of things or questions which were left incomplete and unanswered by my parents and grandparents and more distant ancestors. . . . It has always seemed to me that I had to answer questions which fate had posed to my forefathers, and which had not yet been answered, or as if I had to complete, or perhaps continue, things which previous ages had left unfinished."[63] His father's death marked the beginning of a project for Jung, namely, to vindicate his father's life, his father's religion, and his father's commitment to the Bible, albeit from a psychological perspective that his father at best was only beginning to understand.

Jung's Experience of Archetypal Biblical Images. The role biblical archetypal images played in Jung's personal life colored his attitude toward the Bible. One example from among many is his recounting how the image of Paul came to his rescue at the time of his father's death:

> Always Paul's experience on the road to Damascus hovered before me, and I asked myself how his fate would have fallen out but for his visions. Yet this experience came upon him while he was blindly pursuing his own way. As a young man I drew the conclusion that you must obviously fulfill your destiny in order to get to the point where a donum gratiae might happen along. . . . I have remained true to this attitude all my life. From this you can easily see the origin of my psychology: only by going my own way, integrating my capacities headlong (like Paul), and thus creating a foundation for myself, could something be vouchsafed to me. . . .[64]

The passage casts light on a comment of Jung made in his *Visions Seminar* (1930–34): "We must read the Bible or we shall not understand psychology. Our psychology, whole lives, our language and imagery are built upon the Bible."[65]

Jung's Use of the Bible

The monumental role of the Bible in Jung's life and work is seldom acknowledged by Jungian commentators or biographers. For example, Vincent Brome's *Jung: Man and Myth* includes an appendix on "Jung's Sources," in which he cites philosophers, psychologists, novelists, poets, and history of religions texts—from Plato, to Freud, to Rider Haggard, Goethe, and the Tibetan *Book of the Dead*. Not once does Brome mention the Bible, though it is cited more often than any other document in the Jungian corpus, as illustrated in these four examples.

While a medical student, Jung delivered a lecture in January 1899 to the "Basel section of the color-wearing Zofingia" society that he had joined four years earlier. The title, unlikely for a medical student, was: "Thoughts on the Interpretation of Christianity, with Reference to the Theory of Albrecht Ritschl."[66] Ritschl (1822–89) was a systematic theologian; Jung had recently been introduced to his thought as one of the "new aspects of Protestant theology . . . much in fashion in those days." Jung found the "historicism" of Ritschl's theology "irritating,"[67] and in his lecture flew into Ritschl's antimystical interpretation of Christian origins. A remarkable feature of the lecture is the list of fifty-five biblical passages that Jung had mustered for the disquisition.[68]

A second example of the importance of the Bible in Jung's life is his *Answer to Job* (1951), his only essay on an explicitly biblical theme. According to Jungian analyst, Nathan Schwartz-Salant, Jung found *Answer to Job* the only work of his that proved "totally satisfying."[69] Reminiscent of Freud's sense of "psychological compulsion" in writing *Moses and Monotheism*, Jung writes that "the Book 'came to me' . . . as if accompanied by the great music of a Bach or Handel." He later reports: "If there is anything like the spirit seizing one by the scruff of the neck, it was the way this book came into being."[70]

The title, *Answer to Job*, does not suggest the variety of issues addressed. Topics range from Ezekiel to the Apocalypse, from John to Paul, from the Wisdom literature to the Johannine epistles; Jung also devotes unexpected attention to the 1950 Papal Dogma on the Assumption of Mary and the meaning such a dogma might signify in the mid-twentieth century.

Above all, the book begins to lay some of the theoretical groundwork for a psychological critical approach to the Bible. At the outset Jung announces his hermeneutical stance, stating that he writes not as a biblical scholar, but as a "layman and physician who has been privileged to see deeply into the psychic life of many people." Jung's purpose is to examine religious statements, not with respect to the physical facts they report but with respect to the "psychic facts" they attest to:

> Religious statements are psychic confessions, which in the last resort are based on unconscious, i.e., on transcendental processes. These processes are not accessible to physical perception but demonstrate their existence through the confessions of the psyche. The resultant statements are filtered through the medium of human consciousness. . . . Whenever we speak of religious contents we move in a world of images that point to something ineffable. We do not know how clear or unclear these images, metaphors, and concepts are in respect of their transcendental object. . . . I am also too well aware of how limited are our powers of conception. . . . But, although our whole world of religious ideas consists of anthropomorphic images that could never stand up to rational criticism, we should never forget that they are based on numinous archetypes, i.e. on . . . [a] foundation which is unassailable by reason. We are dealing with psychic facts which logic can overlook but not eliminate.[71]

Jung's observations about the origin and nature of religious statements and biblical texts are instructive for psychological biblical criticism. Jung contends that religious statements, whether in or out of Scripture, originate in the psyche, and as such are psychic facts, that is they exist as autonomous and powerful entities in the psychic life of the individual who entertains them.

A third indication of the role the Bible plays in Jung's life and work is the *General Index* to his collected works. Under "Bible" it lists twenty columns of citations, more columns than those devoted to any other single text.[72] They include reference to fifty-three of the sixty-six books of the Old and New Testaments, as well as apocryphal and pseudepigraphic writings of the Old Testament (Life of Adam and Eve, Syrian Apocalypse of Baruch, Ecclesiasticus, Book of Enoch, 2 Esdras, Tobit, and Wisdom of Solomon) and the apocryphal writings of the New Testament (Book of the Apostle Bartholomew, Gospel of the Egyptians, *Epistolae Apostolorum*, Ascension of Isaiah, Acts of John, Acts of Peter, Gospel of Peter, Gospel of Philip, Apocalypse of Zephaniah, and Acts of Thomas). There are references to the critical volumes by R. H. Charles on the apocrypha and pseudepigrapha of the Old Testament, and to the works on the New Testament apocrypha by Edgar Hennecke and by M. R. James.

In addition to the listings under the word *Bible*, the index has separate headings for biblical names, terms, stories, themes, and phrases, along with references to theologians and biblical interpreters. These include 185 biblical names, many cited more than a dozen times. Entries under the letter "A," for example, include Aaron, Abel, Abraham, Adah (wife of Esau), Adoni-Bezek (a Canaanite king), Ahasuerus, Ahijah, Andrew, Azazel (the scapegoat), and Augustus. Also listed are biblical topics and themes—for example, abyss, Amorites, Antichrist, Annunciation, Antiochus, Apostle, Ark of the Covenant, Areopagus, Ascension. The "A" listing also includes Greek terms—*anthropos* (man) and *agnoia* (ignorance)—the Latin phrase *agnata fides* (consanguine faith), and the Hebrew terms *adamah* (earth), and *aleph* (the letter "A"). Finally, ancient writers and biblical commentators are also included: Abelard, Albertus Magnus, Ambrose, Anselm, and Augustine.

In addition to this glossary of biblical names are 230 biblical phrases and themes, many appearing more than once. We find Jung picking up on the Pauline phrase, "inner man," central to Jungian anthropology; he alludes to the "mote in your brother's eye" as an illustration of projection; and he recurrently cites the Markan question, "Why callest Thou me good?" to demonstrate the Christological complexity of the Gospels. Jung also shares some of the Biblical images that have archetypal power for him: the pearl of great price, the house built on sand, the grain of mustard seed, the journey of Adam out of the garden, and the buried treasure in the field.

A fourth and final demonstration of Jung's use of the Bible and of its role as a conscious project for him is the vertical marker in the family graveyard plot at Küsnacht. It contains the family crest and, on the side, two Latin inscriptions. The first is, *Vocatus atque non vocatus, Deus aderit* ("Summoned or not summoned, God will be present"), the oracular Delphic utterance that Jung found in Erasmus and that he subsequently inscribed over the doorway through which patients entered his home at Küsnacht. The second is the citation of 1 Corinthians 15:47, *Primus homo terrenus de terra, secundus homo coelestis de coelo* ("The first man is of the earth, a man of dust: the second is celestial man, with roots in heaven"). Thus the Bible is part of Jung's conscious project from beginning to end.

Jung's Contribution to Psychological Biblical Criticism

Peter Homans observes in his essay, "Psychology and Hermeneutics: Jung's Contribution," that Jung does not provide a full-blown hermeneutical system nor does he delineate "the full range of problems involved in a theory of interpretation of religious forms."[73] But the corpus does leave two resources for attempting the construction of a Jungian hermeneutical model. The first is a scattering of essays in which Jung addresses the problem of the hermeneutics of literature and art directly. These include *Answer to Job*, "Commentary on 'The Secret of the Golden Flower,'" "On the Relation of Analytical Psychology to Poetry," and above all, "Psychology and Literature."[74] The second is the myriad of interpretive comments Jung makes on biblical texts throughout the Jungian corpus. From these two sources, one can extract eleven topics that recommend themselves as fundamental to the construction of a psychological-critical approach to the Bible: texts as a function of the psychological structure of human personality; the unconscious as a factor at work in text and reader; the compensatory function of archetypal images, symbols, and myths; the nature and function of dreams; psychological aspects of biblical personality portraits; the psychology of biblical religious phenomena; therapeutic elements and effects of the biblical text; psychological analysis of biblical ethics; the psychology of biblical interpretation; revisiting biblical psychology; "amplification" and "active imagination" as hermeneutical models.

Texts as a function of the psychological structure of human personality. The first and fundamental proposition of a Jungian hermeneutic is that religion and religious texts are "not only a sociological and historical phenomenon" but also a function of the "psychological structure of human personality." As Jung notes in the introduction to his essay on "Psychology and Literature," although literary imagination "constitutes the proper province of literary science and of aesthetics . . . it is also a psychic phenomenon, and as such it probably must be taken into account by the psychologist." For Jung "the human psyche is the womb of all the arts and sciences," which means that all human expression, including religion, art, and literature, has been processed through the human psyche and bears evidence of the psychic habits, processes, dispositions, truths, and visions that gave it birth.[75]

It should be noted that Jung is eager to distance his "psychological approach" from the "psychologizing" approach he identifies with Freud, which can employ psychological analysis to reduce a psychic artifact (for example, a poem, work of art, piece of literature, an image of God, or a dogma) either to an illusion or to a symptom of neurosis. The result of this approach in the popular mind, Jung claims, has been that "every attempt at adequate psychological understanding is immediately suspected of psychologism." Jung argues that this need not be the case if psychological inquiry focuses on the content of symbolic expression rather than on the psychological state of the author that produced it:

> The personal life of the artist is at most a help or a hindrance, but is never essential to his creative task; . . . his personal career may be interesting and inevitable, but it does not explain his art. . . . The essence of a work of art is not to be bound in the personal idiosyncrasies that creep into it . . . but in its rising above the personal and speaking from the mind and heart of the artists to the mind and heart of mankind.[76]

The unconscious as a factor at work in text and reader. For Jung as for Freud, a fundamental postulate of the psycho-hermeneutical approach is the *recognition of the unconscious* as a factor at work in all human expression, including religious texts. Jung concurs with Freud on two of the dimensions of the unconscious, the personal and the historical (possible psychic remnants of an earlier tribal consciousness), but adds a third dimension, namely, the collective or objective unconscious.

With respect to the *personal unconscious* of the author of a text, Jung assumes two primary factors at work in the text: the psychological-type orientation of the writer (sensing, thinking, feeling, intuiting), which will manifest itself in the treatment and choice of materials in the text; and the psychological history of the author—complexes, projections, sublimations, urges, passions, and so forth—that will be at work in the text as a psycho-hermeneutical factor. The latter is difficult to identify with any degree of accuracy, but is nonetheless present as a psycho-hermeneutical fact.

With respect to a *historical unconscious*—remnants of the pre-Christian or pre-Israelite consciousness that might reside unconsciously in Christian and Hebrew sacred texts—Jung writes, "Everything has its history, everything has 'grown,' and Christianity, which is supposed to have appeared suddenly as a unique revelation from heaven, undoubtedly also has its history. . . . It is exactly as if we had built a cathedral over a pagan temple and no longer knew that it is still there underneath." Jung adds that the presence of pre-Christian factors in Christian texts, unconscious as they are, continue to have their effect, and that as contemporary Western culture has the unconscious stamp of Judaeo-Christianity upon it, so "we are also stamped by what existed before Christianity."[77]

With respect to the *collective unconscious*, or as Jung also refers to it, the *objective unconscious*, this too is at work in religious texts. Jung describes it as "a sphere of unconscious mythology whose primordial images are the common heritage of mankind." Though the objective unconscious "will forever elude our attempts at understanding," its traces can be detected in the images that recur transculturally in slightly different guises in symbols, dream narratives, stories, myths, epic narratives, apocalypses, and tales of heroic figures.[78] The contemplation and amplification of such images constitute a major part of a psycho-hermeneutical agenda. It includes examining their function and effect in the biblical text and in Bible-reading communities, comparing their form and content with commensurate images in other cultural traditions, and inquiring into their meaning for the human condition.

The compensatory function of archetypal images, symbols, and myths. Recognizing the unconscious compensatory function of archetypal images, symbols, and myths is a prime objective for a Jungian psycho-hermeneutic. As noted above, these images seem to be the primary point of access to the great themes indigenous to the collective unconscious.

A keystone of Jung's psychology is that the unconscious spontaneously produces images of direction or integration for individuals and cultures. Classical religions characteristically traffic in such images, which in the end have to do, not just with history "back then" or "out there" but with the "now" and the "within." From Jung's perspective, the purpose of these images within the economy of the psyche is to correct the "course" of the psyche when it has become "one-sided or adopts false attitudes." This serves as a corrective not only to the individual psyche, but to the psychic attitude of an entire culture or age when it has become sidetracked or when it forgets its *raison d'être*.

In the case of the individual these images often manifest themselves in dreams; in the case of an entire culture they are mediated in the forms of great literature, music, or art. Jung writes:

> Therein lies the social significance of art: It is constantly at work educating the spirit of the age, conjuring up the forms in which the age is most lacking. The unsatisfied yearning of the artist reaches back to the primordial image in the unconscious which is best fitted to compensate the inadequacy and one-sidedness of the present.[79]

More often than not, the artist of which Jung speaks is an analogue to the Old Testament prophet, who by virtue of his lack of adaptation to the culture around him, is psychologically equipped to detect "the [missing] psychic elements that are waiting to play their part in the life of the collective." In this instance, "the lack of adaptation turns out to his advantage" and to the advantage of the collective psyche of the community he addresses.[80]

The nature and function of dreams. Comparative research into the self-regulatory function of dreams in contemporary and biblical perspective is a fourth line of inquiry recommended by a Jungian hermeneutic. Although Jung agreed with much of Freud's theory about dreams as the "royal road to the unconscious," he also parted company. Freud's psychopathological approach regarded the dream as an intentionally disguised expression of repressed instinctual urges. Thus he focused not on the dream itself but on its latent content, using free association to tease out that content for conscious recognition. Jung saw the dream as part of the self-regulating system of the psyche which provided images compensatory to consciousness—a concept not foreign to the Bible (Job 33: 15–17).

A Jungian psycho-hermeneutic approach can make at least four contributions to the study of biblical dreams. (Note, however, that Jungian dream theory would not presume to interpret a biblical dream from the standpoint of the dreamer, since the dreamer is not available for comment.) First, it can offer a classification of a given biblical dream from the standpoint of a Jungian typology of dreams (such as initial dreams, "big dreams," recurrent dreams), locating the biblical dream in the broader context of general dream theory. Second, it can contribute to a history of dream interpretation, comparing the oneiro-interpretive approach of the Bible with that of Greco-Roman culture, Rabbinic Judaism, and later Christian writers such as Clement, John Chrysostom, and Augustine. Third, it can offer comparative observations from a contemporary psychological perspective on biblical dreams and their biblical interpretations, for example, Peter's recurrent "universalistic" dream and its interpretation (Acts 10:9–16). Fourth, it can provide possible insight into the archetypal dimensions of certain biblical dream images that occur in other cultural contexts.

Psychological aspects of biblical personality portraits. Psychological analysis of biblical portraits of personalities and personality types is another possible function of a psychological hermeneutic; it suggests two, possibly three, new lines of exegetical inquiry. The first is simply *character analysis*. This would include, for example, analyzing the psychic habits, strategies, and defenses implicit in the textual portrait of a biblical figure, and commenting on the conscious and unconscious factors that are possibly operative within the psycho-dynamics of the narrative. Such analysis adds a psychological dimension to the interpretive work of literary and narrative critics.

A second line of inquiry focuses on portraits of biblical personalities as *models of individuation.* Freud clearly saw Moses as such a model. Jung found such models in the figures of Adam, Abraham, Paul, and preeminently of Christ as the exemplification of the archetype of the Self.[81]

A third possible contribution of a psychological approach to biblical personalities is *psychoanalytic.* Though Jung objected strongly to the Freudian focus on the psychopathology of authors, the biblical interpreter would benefit from psychoanalytic observations on literary portraits. In the strictest sense, of course, psychoanalysis of biblical figures is ruled out by the absence of the analysand. But a number of recent studies, especially from a Freudian perspective, have suggested that psychoanalytic observations in the hands of seasoned analysts can provide meaningful and compelling insight into the psychodynamic factors at work in author and text.[82]

The psychology of Biblical religious phenomena. Like Freud, Jung did not specify the full range of religious phenomena to be found in the Bible. But he frequently offered psychological commentary on specific instances: for example, ritual practice (footwashing, eucharist, burnt offering, purification rites), mystical experience (visions, dreams, prophecy, photisms, auditions, inspiration, revelation, the inner light, *enthousiasmos*), religious states ("twice-born religion," *metanoia, kenosis,* martyrdom, the phenomena of sin, guilt, forgiveness, grace, sanctification), religious practices (prayer, glossolalia), and religious experiences (miracles, transfiguration, resurrection). These demonstrate the light that psychological and psychoanalytic commentary can shed on such phenomena, and point to the need for a more systematic and cross-culturally sensitive approach that enlists aid from sister disciplines, such as social and anthropological psychology.[83]

Therapeutic elements and effects of the biblical text. As Freud's work underlined the need for a psychologically oriented hermeneutic to identify pathogenic elements in religious systems, Jung's research underlined the need for psychological exploration of the therapeutic elements. The therapeutic potential of the text is not ordinary fare in biblical scholarship, but it is inherent to a psychological critical approach that sees itself in the service of a psychotherapeutic agenda. For Jung, the goal of religious texts in specific and religion in general is the *cura animarum,* the care and cure of souls. In his essay, "The State of Psychotherapy Today," he writes that "religions are psychotherapeutic systems in the truest sense of the word. . . . They express the whole range of the psychic problem in mighty images; they are the avowal and recognition of the soul, and at the same time the revelation of the soul's nature."[84] (As noted earlier, they also provide models of individuation.) In taking note of the therapeutic elements and effects of the Bible, a psychological hermeneutic can both learn from and be of service to the work of pastoral counselors who have long observed the therapeutic and pathogenic dynamic between the Bible and its readers.[85]

Psychological analysis of biblical ethics. Another area of inquiry to which a psychological hermeneutic can contribute is biblical ethics. A definitive work has yet to be written on the "ethics of consciousness" suggested in Jung's work, but it is clear that Jung finds analogues to such an ethic in the life of Paul, as he indicates in his introduction to Erich Neumann's, *Depth Psychology and a New Ethic*. Commenting on a variant logion of Jesus from the fifth century Codex Bezae at Luke 6:4 ("Man, if indeed thou knowest what thou doest, thou art blessed; but if thou knowest not, thou art cursed, and a transgressor of the law"), Jung says, "here the moral criterion is *consciousness*, and not law or convention."[86] The spectrum of ethical postures in the Bible—from the deontological ethics of the law codes, to the love-ethic of the Johannine Christ, to the ethics of the spirit in Paul—would benefit from an approach that seeks to understand the psychological factors at work in the propagation, adoption, and application of the various types of moral codes and ethical systems in the Bible and biblical culture.

The psychology of biblical interpretation. In a sense, Jung predated reader-response criticism, with its focus on the role of the reader in the construction of a text, when he acknowledged the effect of readers in shaping what is to be seen and heard in texts. In his more cynical moments, he admits that readers get whatever they want out of the Bible: "anything can be authorized out of the Bible."[87] More constructively he advances the theory of psychological types to account for the diverse renderings that different readers bring to and derive from the Bible. The work of both Freud and Jung calls for fuller exploration of the psychic factors at work in biblical interpretation.[88]

Revisiting biblical psychology. Though Jung does not develop a biblical psychology, his work articulates one. Defined by Delitzsch as the discipline devoted to articulating the biblical view(s) of the origin, nature, and destiny of the psyche/soul/self, biblical psychology is important not only as a matter of record, but also as a possible source of insight for contemporary, psychological self-understanding. The effect biblical psychology can exercise on one's *Weltbild* is evident throughout the Jungian corpus: its perennial concern with the soul; its sense of destiny or call; its openness to the wisdom of dreams, revelations, and visions; its appreciation of the interplay between good and evil; its appreciation of the sequence of sin and grace in human experience; and its sense of the numinous.[89] Jung's work accordingly finds in biblical psychology a model that has the capacity to inspire its readers with a new vision of the self.

"Amplification" and "active imagination" as hermeneutical models. In *The Bible and the Psyche*, Jungian analyst Edward Edinger writes, "The events of the Bible, although presented as history, psychologically understood are archetypal images. . . . As we read these stories with an openness to their unconscious reverberations we recognize them to be relevant to our own most private experience."[90] This statement summarizes Jung's primary hermeneutical goal, to bring the "metaphysical" "within the range of experience," taking the "thought-forms that have become historically fixed" and trying "to melt them down again and pour them into moulds of immediate experience."[91] A psychohermeneutical approach to the Bible from a Jungian perspective presupposes that the purpose of the text is to relate to the experience of the reader and the reading community at some level (for example, the conceptual, cognitive, conative, affective, moral, or intuitive level), and at that level to "heal," change, transform, or illumine.

The two methods Jung developed for this "final" hermeneutical step of relating the text to the life of the reader are the processes of amplification and active imagination.

"Amplification" proceeds at two levels: subjective (personal) and objective (collective). At the personal level the process of amplification aims at aiding the reader in articulating the personal meanings the text has awakened for him/her. At the collective level the process of amplification aims at providing the reader with a broader frame of reference within which to understand a given biblical image or figure, interpreting it in the context of the glossary of archetypal images that recur in the art, literature, and religions of the world. It also aims at drawing out untapped meanings in the text. Jung insists that a Goethe or a Blake, an Isaiah or a Paul is never fully conscious of all that they have said.[92] The interpreter gives birth to those meanings not yet consciously noted and articulated. This benefits the author, the reader, and the broader humanity for whom, according to Jung, the image has emerged and "been revealed" from the depths of the objective unconscious in the first place.

The second method, "active imagination," takes the interpretive process one step further by translating the amplified message into new forms. These can range from painting, dancing, storytelling and clay, to stained glass window, liturgy, musical cantatas, mystery plays, and religious pageants, or even new translations or versions of the text.[93]

This method presupposes that because "a living symbol expresses some-thing that is not fully conscious, or able yet to become fully conscious," the imagination, catalyzed by a text, is enlisted to search for the unconscious con-tent the symbol may have evoked in the self. To do that, conscious thinking is not enough.[94] For the wisdom of the unconscious to come into play requires fantasy (regarded by Peter Homans as the primary psychological activity in Jung's psychological hermeneutic) and reduced ego functioning. As Jung observes, "often the hands know how to solve a riddle with which the intellect has wrestled in vain."[95] From a psychological standpoint, something is "gained in translation" rather than lost, since each interpretive technique presupposes a discrete angle of vision that perceives things in the text that other faculties and modes of expression cannot catch. The potter, the dancer, the story-teller, the musician, the playwright, and the preacher all come to the text with sui generis aptitudes and appetites that render specific dimensions of the text sus-ceptible to their vision and interpretation.

The goal of a psycho-hermeneutical approach will be to integrate these psychological considerations with the battery of other critical approaches and methods available in the field, but at the same time seek to bend the hermeneutical effort as a whole into the service of the ultimate goal, which from a Jungian perspective is to "create more and more consciousness. As far as we can discern," Jung writes," the sole purpose of human existence is to kin-dle a light in the darkness of mere being."[96]

Jungian Approaches in Contemporary Biblical Scholarship

Carl Jung is reported to have commented to friends, " I do not want anybody to be a Jungian. I want people above all to be themselves."[97] Though full-fledged Jungians or Freudians are rare among scholars, an increasing number of them in the field of psychology and/or theology have found in Jung's life and work a framework for understanding self and text that brings new ques-tions and fresh insight to their work. Among the key books are Eugen Drewer-mann's monumental *Tiefenpsychologie und Exegese*, published in 1984 (which Ulrich Luz characterized as "the most exciting event in the field of hermeneutics in the last decade"); David Cox's 1959 *Jung and St. Paul: A Study of the Doctrine of Justification by Faith and Its Relation to the Concept of Individuation*; and Edward Edinger's 1986 *The Bible and the Psyche: Indi-viduation Symbolism in the Old Testament*.[98]

To these should be added the following: Peter Homans, for his extensive work on Jungian hermeneutics; Elizabeth Boyden Howes and Sheila Moon of the Guild for Psychological Studies; and Morton Kelsey, John Sanford, David L. Miller, Antonio Moreno, Murray Stein, Trevor Watt, and Heinz Westman, for the wide range of research reflected in their work. Others on this list include a growing number of biblical scholars: Schuyler Brown, Adela Yarbro Collins, James Goss, Maria Kassel, D. Andrew Kille, Diarmuid McGann, Gerd Theissen, Michael Willett Newheart, Walter Wink, Wilhelm Wuellner, and the present author. What these and others have written in the field of psychology and biblical studies will be the subject of the next chapter, tracing the broad spectrum of developments in the field of psychological biblical criticism beginning in the 1960s.

3
Psychological Biblical Criticism in the Twentieth Century

This is a new kind of Biblical criticism. The earlier disciplines are all necessary and important, . . . but psychological
criticism opens up a wholly new and vast, far-reaching
scene. . . . Beyond the historical and exegetical interpretation of the Bible lies the whole new field of depth psychology and psychoanalysis.

F. C. Grant (1968)[1]

Can the life context of religious texts be clarified without
consideration of psychic factors and aspects?

Gerd Theissen (1983)[2]

If Rudolf Bultmann has impressively shown that they cannot
get along without philosophy, then the same is certainly also
true for psychology.

Joachim Scharfenberg (1988)[3]

For the first three quarters of the twentieth century, psychology did not enjoy
a favorable press in biblical circles, popular or scholarly. Carl Jung noted a
certain "wrinkling of the nose" among some clergy at the mention of the word.
Robin Scroggs found a guild-wide resistance to the term among biblical scholars; his attempt to discuss the use of psychoanalytic models with a European
elder statesman met with the response: "Bultmann taught us years ago to be
suspicious of psychology." Gerd Theissen corroborates this impression in the
opening line of *Psychological Aspects of Pauline Theology*: "Every exegete has
learned that psychological exegesis is poor exegesis."[4] How this antipathy
toward psychology developed among biblical scholars in the early twentieth
century and how psychological criticism began to be reinstated in the 1960s is
the subject of this chapter.

Psychology and Biblical Studies Up to the 1960s: An Uneasy Relationship

In the first decade of the twentieth century psychologists and biblical scholars had little difficulty with one another. In 1901, psychology was described irenically as "the halfway house between biology with the whole range of the objective sciences, on the one hand, and the moral sciences with philosophy, on the other hand."[5] The half that biblical studies dealt with was philosophical psychology in the form of biblical psychology, à la Franz Delitzsch (1855) and M. Scott Fletcher (1912).[6] The tradition continued into midcentury, with Emil Brunner's 1936 essay on biblical psychology in his volume, *God and Man: Four Essays on the Nature of Personality*,[7] and into the 1950s with Rudolf Bultmann's biblical anthropology, which acknowledged his debt to the "biblical psychologies" of the past.[8]

Turn-of-the-century biblical scholarship, in the tradition of Augustine, Meister Eckhardt, Calvin, Schleiermacher, and Kierkegaard, had no compunction against offering observations, either in biblical commentaries or in sermons, on psychological aspects of the text or on the characters or events it described.[9] Franz Delitzsch, as noted earlier, diagnosed the behavior of King Saul as "pathologic irritation." M. Scott Fletcher commented on the psychological effect of Jesus and his personality, on the "enlarged self-consciousness" of the participants in the first Pentecost, and on the "impulses," "inhibitions," "fanaticism," and "subconscious" dimensions of the "great complexity" that Paul is "psychologically."[10]

Antipathy to psychology emerges, however, in reaction to what is perceived as psychological excess, namely, the interpretations of the person of Jesus undertaken by Karl Hase (1829), Christian Hermann Weisse (1838), and Heinrich Julius Holtzmann (1863), who (among others) insisted that a valid historical reconstruction of the life of Jesus must include a "psychological analysis" of his developing messianic self-consciousness. The most enduring blows came from Wilhelm Wrede and Albert Schweitzer. Wrede, in *Das Messiasgeheimnis in den Evangelien* (1901), denounced the methodology of D. F. Strauss as a psychologizing depiction of the life of Jesus that could not be supported from the text of Mark's Gospel: "The study of the life of Jesus suffers from psychological conjecture, and this is a kind of historical guesswork." Schweitzer, in *Skizze des Lebens Jesu* (1901), repudiated these developmental psychological reconstructions as a "patchwork of opinions" produced by "mediocre minds" who "with much else that is modern, . . . transferred to him [Jesus] our modern psychology, without always recognizing clearly that it is not applicable to him and necessarily belittles him." Schweitzer reinforced his attack in 1913 with the publication of *The Psychiatric Study of Jesus: Exposition and Criticism*, in which he took objection to four medical treatises that concluded, on the basis of psychopathological analysis of the Gospel records, that Jesus of Nazareth was "mentally diseased." This conclusion, Schweitzer thought, should "be rated as exactly zero" on both medical and historical-critical grounds.[11]

Schweitzer did not intend to condemn psychology as a whole, only "faulty" and "amateurish" instances of it. The effect of his critique on biblical scholars, however, was amplified by three features of early nineteenth-century psychology: excessive psychoanalytic reductionism; the biological reductionism and materialism of behavioral psychology; and the systematic exclusion of references to religion and the psychology of religion in professional psychological journals after 1930. The result was a virtual ban on things psychological among professional biblical scholars for the better part of the century.[12] For example, Werner Kümmel's 1972 survey of New Testament scholarship, *The New Testament: The History of the Investigation of Its Problems*, makes no mention of the names or publications of biblical psychologists like Delitzsch and Fletcher, resorting simply to issuing caveats against the dangers of psychologizing.[13]

One of the scholars caught in the cross fire was William Sanday (1843–1920), Lady Margaret Professor of New Testament and Canon of Christ Church, Oxford. In 1910 and 1911 Sanday produced two volumes, "Christologies Ancient and Modern" and *Personality in Christ and in Ourselves*, professing his interest in the "new psychology." Sanday insisted with William James (1842–1910) that psychology dare not be limited to the consideration of conscious states alone, citing the following from James's *Varieties of Religious Experience* (1902):

> I cannot but think that the most important step forward that has occurred in psychology since I have been a student of that science is the discovery, first made in 1886, that, in certain subjects at least, there is not only the consciousness of the ordinary field, . . . but an addition thereto in the shape of a set of memories, thoughts and feelings which are extra-marginal and outside of the primary consciousness altogether, but yet must be classed as conscious facts of some sort, able to reveal their presence by unmistakable signs. I call this the most important step forward, because, unlike the other advances which psychology has made, this discovery has revealed to us an entirely unsuspected peculiarity in the constitution of human nature.[14]

Sanday focuses on this "peculiarity" and enlists the concepts of "subliminal consciousness" or "unconscious cerebration" to interpret biblical phenomena such as the "superconsciousness" of prophetic inspiration and the divine personality of the historical Jesus.[15]

Vincent Taylor, writing forty years later, reports that these two volumes of Sanday were "rejected on all sides" within the circles of "learned opinion."

A. E. Garvie denounced Sanday in an article entitled "The Danger of Mares' Nests in Theology." Others dismissed the books "as an aberration which might decently be interred." But Taylor adds, "This tendency, I think, is to be regretted for there is much to be learned from theories which prove to be wanting." In a chapter entitled "Christology and Psychology" in his 1958 work, *The Person of Christ in New Testament Teaching*, Taylor writes:

> One can fully understand the point of view of those who think that psychology has very little to contribute to the discussion of Christological problems. Nevertheless, it does not seem right to refuse to make a psychological approach to Christology. In the early Christian centuries psychological elements entered into the philosophical aspects of Christological discussions and helped to shape the doctrine of the Trinity. We ought not, therefore, to neglect the better understanding of human personality made possible by the psychology of today.[16]

Taylor demonstrated that resistance to the new psychology, though comprehensive, was not universal. Other scholars during this period provided numerous hints of the conviction that psychological considerations were indispensable for understanding writers, readers, and texts. In the field of Old Testament studies, for example, a tradition of psychological analysis of prophecy and prophetic inspiration went virtually unchallenged.[17] Within the history of religions school, Hermann Gunkel (1888) suggested that biblical reference to the workings of the Holy Spirit is a "matter of real psychological events, not of phrases or of superstition."[18] Johannes Weiss (1913) raised the question whether in dealing with religious experience

> we are obliged to ask whether or not in addition to the supernatural factors . . . there were other factors . . . which may be much more readily understood by us. We must ask about the human and historical antecedents of this inspiration, and its psychological conditionings.[19]

Wilhelm Bousset (1913) in his widely read, *Kyrios Christos*, insisted that the New Testament notion of "preexistence" is not only a "history of religions" concept, but a psychological one, that occurs "in the unconscious, in the uncontrollable depth of the overall psyche of the human community." Adolf Deissman criticized the "doctrinaire students" of his time "who are more interested in the theories of Primitive Christianity than in its psychic forces, namely the conviction of being in Christ." He also proposed that the concepts of reconciliation and redemption in Paul are "psychically synonymous." B. H. Streeter in *The Four Gospels* (1936) defended his theory that the Fourth Gospel is the product of mystical imagination by adverting to psychological research on dreams and visions. E. Hoskyns (1947) in his commentary, *The Fourth Gospel*, spoke of the "unconscious symbolism" by which the author relates the story of Christ to the experience of the Johannine community.[20] Henry J. Cadbury, in his 1953 review of "Current Issues in New Testament Studies," issued this appeal for psychological research:

> Over against the somewhat sterile-seeming subjects of language and litera-
> ture may be set the more popular attractive problems of the New Testament
> thought. . . . More important than the immediate problems of origins, even
> those of exact date and authorship, are those of culture or Weltanschuung.
> To put it bluntly, I find myself much more intrigued with curiosity about how
> the writers got that way than with knowing who they were. These problems
> are psychological rather than literary. Even the larger questions of language
> are psychological; how much more so are the developments of such individ-
> uals as Jesus and of Paul and of the unknown religious personalities behind
> Revelation, and Hebrews, and the Fourth Gospel! It is regrettable that so lit-
> tle has been done and is being done to match the study of expression with a
> study of mind and experience. Here is perhaps a relatively neglected area of
> New Testament research.[21]

C. A. Simpson, in his presidential address to the Society for Old Testament Study in 1960, urged looking at "biblical theology" not only as a "systematized statement of what the Bible has to say," but also as a "statement of the meaning of the biblical ideas . . . in the light of the subsequent experience of the church—historical, psychological, conscious and subconscious."[22] But it is not until 1968 that a mandate is issued by New Testament scholar F. C. Grant to dismantle the wall that has divided psychology and biblical studies for the greater part of the century and to develop a full scale, psychological-critical study of the Bible.

An Attitudinal Change within Biblical Scholarship Toward Psychology: F. C. Grant, "Psychological Study of the Bible" (1968)

In a 1968 *Festschrift* for Erwin R. Goodenough, F. C. Grant states:

> Dr. Goodenough pointed out the value and importance, even the necessity, of
> the psychological interpretation of the Bible. This is a new kind of Biblical
> criticism. The earlier disciplines are all necessary and important, . . . but psy-
> chological criticism opens up a wholly new and vast, far-reaching scene. . . .
> [B]eyond the historical and exegetical interpretation of the Bible lies the
> whole new field of depth psychology and psychoanalysis.[23]

Though Grant's essay went virtually unnoticed, it signaled the beginnings of an across-the-board shift in attitude toward psychology within the guild of biblical scholarship.

Reasons for the Change

Three factors account for the change. The first is *the sudden surge of new research paradigms in biblical scholarship in the late 1960s and early 1970s* that developed with the realization that the classical disciplines of historical-literary criticism lacked the tools to address new types of hermeneutical and exegetical questions. Walter Wink's hyperbolic statement in 1973 that "historical biblical criticism is bankrupt" signaled the shift. But Wink was not alone. The year before, Helmut Harsch and Gerhard Voss published *Versuche mehrdimensionaler Schriftauslegung* (*Experiment in Multidimensional Scriptural Interpretation*), arguing that the historical-critical method needed to be supplemented by other approaches, such as the new literary, patristic, art historical, and psychological criticism. Three years later Pierre Grelot proposed in "L'exegese Biblique au Carrefour" ("Biblical Exegesis at a Crossroads") that exegesis can no longer ignore the potential contributions of the human sciences (ethnology, sociology, linguistics, and psychology).

In the 1960s and 1970s Paul Ricoeur was urging that hermeneutics be conducted in full conversation with the "counterdisciplines" of historical philosophy (Aristotle, Kant, Spinoza), contemporary philosophy (Jaspers, Marcel, Heidegger), phenomenology (Husserl), history of religions (Eliade), anthropology (Lévi-Strauss), and psychoanalysis (Freud).[24] Accordingly, in 1977, John Dominic Crossan undertook to forecast that "Biblical study will no longer be conducted under the exclusive or even dominant hegemony" of one or two disciplines, but rather "through a multitude of disciplines interacting mutually as a field criticism."[25] By the 1990s these anticipations of the 1970s were realized in a proliferation of new critical strategies, including structuralist, rhetorical, social scientific, feminist, ideological, narrative, deconstructionist, materialist, audience, reader-response, personal/autobiographical, contextual, and psychological criticism.

A second factor leading to the change of attitude among biblical scholars toward psychology was the *psychologization of the Western mind*, largely the product of the ubiquitous influence of the new psychoanalytic thought. This cultural development made it virtually impossible for biblical scholars to deny the relevance of psychology for their life and work.

This realization was heightened through the work of theologians and pastoral counselors who had seen the relevance of psychological research for theological and pastoral self-understanding. Paul Tillich was one of the primary apologists for this perspective.[26] In addition, three books appeared in the 1950s that were widely read by theologians, clergy, and biblical scholars: David E. Roberts's *Psychotherapy and the Christian View of Man* (1950), Albert E. Outler's *Psychotherapy and the Christian Message* (1954), and Carroll A. Wise's *Psychiatry and the Bible* (1956).

Specific applications of psychological insight to biblical interpretation began to appear from the late forties to the mid sixties. They include: Fritz Kunkel's *Creation Continues: A Psychological Interpretation of the First Gospel* (1947); Sidney Tarachow's "St. Paul and Early Christianity: A Psychoanalytic Study" (1947); Theodor Reik's "Psychoanalytic Studies of Biblical Exegesis" (1951); David Cox's *Jung and St. Paul* (1959); Heinz Westman's *The Springs of Creativity: The Bible and the Creative Process of the Psyche* (1961); and Robert Leslie's *Jesus and Logotherapy* (1965), in which he applied the thought of Viktor Frankl to an understanding of the psychodynamics at work in the teaching and healings of Jesus. The result was that mainline biblical scholars began to introduce psychological language into their writing—for example, noting the problem of "cognitive dissonance" in apocalyptic literature, or speaking of the "function of the gospels" as having "both conscious and unconscious dimensions," or citing the character of Ezekiel as grist for "a fascinating psychological study."[27]

A third factor accounting for the shift in the attitude of biblical scholars toward psychology is *change within the field of psychology itself.* In the 1970s new voices in psychology—particularly humanistic, cognitive, and developmental psychologies—were challenging the reductionism of Freudian psychoanalysis and the materialistic determinism and positivism of behaviorism. This provided new openings for the application of psychology to religion.[28] Also, both old and new names of psychologists "friendly" to religion were gaining recognition at both the academic and popular levels. This was evident in the renewed interest in the work of William James,[29] Carl Jung,[30] Viktor Frankl, Theodor Reik, Erich Fromm, and Gordon Allport, and in the appearance of new work by Robert Coles, Anna-Maria Rizzuto, Stanley Leavy, and Dorothy Zeligs, as well as in the sectional programming of the American Psychological Association.[31]

Evidence of the Change

The change in biblical scholarship's attitude toward psychology is evident in four areas: the development of new journals committed to research in the field; articles and books since the late 1960s; the establishment of a program unit on Psychology and Biblical Studies in the Society of Biblical Literature, the flagship biblical scholarly association in the United States; and notices of the field in encyclopedias, dictionaries, and surveys of contemporary biblical scholarship.

1. New journals. One of the first signs of the shift was the appearance of the *Journal of Psychology and Theology* in 1973, the *Journal of Psychology and Christianity* in 1982, and *Biblical Interpretation: A Journal of Contemporary Approaches* in 1993 (the first two originated in the evangelical and conservative traditions). In the initial number of the *Journal of Psychology and Theology*, editor Bruce Narramore defined its objective as providing "an interdisciplinary forum for the integration of biblical and psychological truth." He added:

> In many quarters the whole process of 'curing sick souls' is moving from the church to the doorsteps of psychologists and other mental health professionals. Increasingly our society is looking to psychology to shed new light on the basic issues of human existence. . . . The evangelical church has a great opportunity to combine the special revelation of God's word with the general revelation studied by the psychological sciences and professions. The end result of this integration can be a broader (and deeper) view of human life. Historically we have failed to have sufficient dialogue and interaction. Currently we are in a position to gather relevant objective data, seek well constructed theoretical views and find improved techniques for applying our biblical and psychological data.[32]

In similar fashion the *Journal of Psychology and Christianity* identified its goal as exploring "how the insights we have about the dynamics of human health and illness illumine the messages in the text of the Bible."[33] The third journal, *Biblical Interpretation: A Journal of Contemporary Approaches*, announced in its 1993 inaugural issue the "need for the field of biblical studies to become more public and more pluralistic," inviting the submission of "articles that discuss specific biblical texts in the light of fresh insights that derive from the diversity of relevant disciplines," including sociology, anthropology, archaeology, philosophy, history, linguistics, literary theory, and psychology.[34]

2. Articles and books since the late 1960s. Between 1968 and 1972, almost on signal, a sheaf of articles and books appeared from within the orbit of biblical scholarship (as opposed to the work of psychologists, popular and academic, writing without benefit of biblical scholarship). These called for a fresh look at the contributions psychological and psychoanalytic research might bring to the task of biblical interpretation.

The period began with F. C. Grant's essay on "Psychological Study of the Bible" and Helmut Harsch's article on "Psychologische Interpretationen biblischer Texte?" ("Psychological Interpretation of Biblical texts?"), both of which appeared in 1968. Three years later Antoine Vergote published his study of Romans 7, "Apport des données psychanalytique à l'exégese: vie, loi et clivage du moi dans l'epître aux Romains 7" ("The Contribution of Psychoanalytic Principles to Exegesis: Life, Law, and the Split Ego in Romans 7"). In 1969 and 1970 two landmark essays introduced Jungian and Freudian considerations into the hermeneutical circle that would eventually include biblical studies: Peter Homans's "Psychology and Hermeneutics: Jung's Contribution" (1969) and Paul Ricoeur's *Freud and Philosophy: An Essay on Interpretation* (1970). In 1972 Richard Rubenstein produced his strikingly bold Freudian study, *My Brother Paul*, and Yorick Spiegel published a milestone collection of essays under the title, *Psychoanalytische Interpretationen biblischer Texte* (*Psychoanalytic Interpretations of Biblical Texte*). Spiegel organized the essays into six categories: psychoanalytic hermeneutics, sexual and dream symbolism, father and son motifs (including essays on sacrifice and the sacrificial victims), the search for the "mother" (with psychological interpretations of the fall, the sabbath, and the Holy Spirit), repression and projection (including studies of King David and Judas), and biblical narration and ethnology (with an essay on the passage through the Red Sea).

The succeeding generation of research, from the late 1970s through the 1990s, approached the biblical material from one of four perspectives: Freudian-oriented, Jungian-oriented, composite/comparative, and theoretical. Those who adopted a Freudian-oriented model of biblical interpretation include Robin Scroggs, *Paul for a New Day* (1977), Mary Ann Tolbert, *Perspectives on the Parables: An Approach to Multiple Interpretations* (1978), David Halperin, *Seeking Ezekiel: Text and Psychology* (1993), and Ilona Rashkow, *The Phallacy of Genesis: A Feminist-Psychoanalytic Approach* (1993). In *The Postmodern Bible* (1995), written by members of the Bible and Culture Collective, Stephen Moore's essay, "Psychoanalytic Criticism," elucidated the biblical hermeneutics of Freud, Jacques Lacan, and the post-Freudians Julia Kristeva and Luce Irigaray.[35] Mention should also be made of psychoanalyst Dorothy Zeligs, whose *Psychoanalysis and the Bible: A Study in Depth of Seven Leaders* (1974) is a balanced historical-, literary-, and psychological-critical reading of the biblical accounts of Abraham, Jacob, Joseph, Samuel, Saul, David, and Solomon. Her *Moses: A Psychodynamic Study* (1986) was also written from a Freudian perspective.

Works coming out of a Jungian-oriented hermeneutic include Dan O. Via's early study, "The Prodigal Son: A Jungian Reading" (1975) and Walter Wink's "On Wrestling with God: Using Psychological Insights in Biblical Study" (1978). Wink also applied the Jungian hermeneutical strategy of active imagination to the interpretation of Biblical texts in his *Transforming Bible Study: A Leader's Guide* (1989). Further works include Adela Yarbro Collins's interpretation of apocalyptic symbol in her *Crisis and Catharsis: The Power of the Apocalypse* (1984) and my own *Jung and the Bible* (1983) and two interpretive essays, "Jung on Scripture and Hermeneutics: Retrospect and Prospect" (1985) and "Jung's Challenge to Biblical Hermeneutics" (1987).

In 1984–85, Eugen Drewermann published his massive two-volume work, *Tiefenpsychologie und Exegese* (*Depth Psychology and Exegesis*), applying archetypal analysis to biblical images and themes. This same focus on archetypal images characterized Maria Kassel's 1982 *Biblische Urbilder Tiefenpsychologische Auslegung nach C. G. Jung* (*Primordial Biblical Images: Depth-psychological Interpretation according to C. G. Jung*), as well as her series of publications in the 1970s and 1980s.

Jung and the Interpretation of the Bible (1995) was the first collection of essays by biblical scholars using a Jungian approach to Scripture. Edited by David L. Miller, it included among others, Schuyler Brown (who had also written "The Beloved Disciple: A Jungian View" in 1990), Michael Willett Newheart, and myself. Another contributor, D. Andrew Kille, is one of the first doctoral candidates in the United States to work on a degree in the joint fields of psychology and biblical studies.

Mention should also be made of John Sanford, a Jungian analyst and Episcopal priest. Though technically not a biblical scholar, he has combined serious biblical critical work with psychological analysis. Sanford produced a string of biblical psychological interpretive works, beginning in 1970 with *The Kingdom Within*, a psychological study of the Jesus-sayings tradition. In 1974 he published *The Man Who Wrestled with God: Light from the Old Testament on the Psychology of Individuation*, highlighting the patterns of individuation at work in the narratives on Adam and Eve, Jacob, Joseph, and Moses. The same approach characterizes his *King Saul, the Tragic Hero: A Study in Individuation* (1985). In 1993 Sanford produced *Mystical Christianity: A Psychological Commentary on the Gospel of John*, his most ambitious project from an exegetical standpoint.

A third perspective, composite/comparative, recognizes the variety of psychological models that can be applied to the task of biblical interpretation. In 1978, Yorick Spiegel's second edited collection, *Doppeldeutlich: Tiefendimensionen biblischer Texte* (*Double Meanings: Depth Dimensions of Biblical Texts*) includes Jungian psychology, Fritz Perls's Gestalt therapy, transactional analysis, and psychoanalytic *Rollendrama*. Patrick Henry's chapter on "Water, Bread, Wine: Patterns in Religion" in his *New Directions in New Testament Study* (1979) considers "the potential impact of psychology on New Testament study," with comparisons of Jung and Richard Rubenstein's Freudian approach to Baptism, Eucharist, and Christology.

Gerd Theissen's major work, *Psychological Aspects of Pauline Theology*, first published in German in 1983, attempts to integrate and apply the insights of three major psychological schools—learning theory, psychody-namics (Freud/Jung), and cognitive psychology—to the exegesis of specific Pauline texts. John W. Miller's "Psychoanalytic Approaches to Biblical Religion" (1983) compares the approaches of Sigmund Freud, Theodor Reik, David Bakan, and Dorothy Zeligs. The volume by Wilhelm Wuellner and Robert C. Leslie, *The Surprising Gospel: Intriguing Psychological Insights from the New Testament* (1984), compares the application of a variety of psychological approaches—for example, Jung, Frankl, Henry Stack Sullivan, Rollo May, Virginia Satir—to specific biblical texts. In *Jonah: A Psycho-Religious Approach to the Prophet* (1990), André LaCocque and Pierre-Emmanuel Lacocque take Jung's archetypal psychology as their point of departure, but add the interpretive contributions of Sigmund Freud, Melanie Klein, Donald Winnicott, Harold Searles, and the Jungians Jolande Jacobi and Erich Neumann.

The fourth perspective, theoretical, attempts to define the goals and methods of psychological exegesis, to defend its use within the canons of research in both biblical studies and psychology, and to establish the ground rules for its application to texts. Though demonstrated in introductory fashion in the opening section of Gerd Theissen's *Psychological Aspects of Pauline Theology* (1987), it is the raison d'être for the entirety of Martin Leiner's imposing study, *Psychologie und Exegese: Grundfragen einer textpsychologischen Exegese des Neuen Testaments* (1995). This work was presented initially to the Evangelical Theological Faculty of Ruprecht-Karls University in Heidelberg as a dissertation under Theissen's supervision. It begins with a survey of the degree to which various forms of psychological interpretation are present in contemporary culture, both in religion and in the arts and sciences, and includes a sketch of the history of recent psychological biblical interpretations, with special emphasis on European literature. Its aim is to establish a foundation of sound methodological and theoretical principles for relating the methods and goals of the two disciplines, psychology and biblical studies.

The work concludes with an apologia for cooperation between the two disciplines, citing the criteria of coherence, correspondence, and consensus as the litmus test for evaluating any psychological-exegetical project. It proposes three contributions psychological exegesis can make to biblical scholarship: to help recognize the implicit psychology in all interpretations, whether classical historical or psychological; to formulate new kinds of questions that, when addressed to the text, lay bare the psychological factors at work in the early Christian ethos; and to bring to exegetical discussion a psychological method of textual evaluation.

Hundreds of additional articles and books have been published by pastoral counselors, theologians, psychologists, clergy, and popular writers. They approach the material from a variety of psychological perspectives and with varying degrees of familiarity with scholarly biblical methods. Many of them are cited in the survey below and listed in the bibliography.

3. The SBL Program Unit on Psychology and Biblical Studies. By 1991, interest in psychological biblical criticism had reached a point where the Society of Biblical Literature approved a proposal to establish a program session unit on "Psychology and Biblical Studies." The unit had a threefold stated purpose. First, it would present a historical-critical overview of psychological approaches to Scripture. Second, it would assess the significance of these approaches for ongoing biblical research, exegesis, and interpretation. Third, it would provide a forum for considering and developing the future agenda of psychological criticism as a subdiscipline within biblical studies. In the first six years, the papers presented in the Psychology and Biblical Studies Group represented approaches from Freudian, Jungian, cognitive, and developmental psychological perspectives, along with the application of self psychology, the psychodynamic theories of Murray Bowens and Milton Erickson, psychodynamics, pastoral counseling, and object relations theory.[36]

4. Notices in surveys of contemporary biblical scholarship. A final class of evidence for the recognition of psychology as an adjunct discipline for biblical research is its citation in standard surveys of biblical studies, encyclopedias, and dictionaries. The earliest encyclopedia entry is Antoine Vergote's "Psychanalyse et interprétation biblique" ("Psychoanalysis and Biblical Interpretation") in the *Supplément au Dictionnaire de la Bible* (1973–75). It provides a sketch of the contributions of psychoanalysis in the Freudian mode, with a bibliography of approximately sixty titles. In 1979, surveys appeared from two additional authors, Michel Sales and Daniel Harrington. In his article, "Possibilités et limites d'une lecture psychanalytique de la Bible" ("Possibilities and Limits of a Psychoanalytic Reading of the Bible"), Sales offered an extended portrait of psychoanalysis from both a Freudian and a Jungian perspective, plus an annotated review of sixteen articles available in French. He concluded that the extant literature, though sparse, shows promise in limited but important ways (for example, biblical anthropology). In *Interpreting the New Testament*, Daniel Harrington described psychological interpretation as one of several "new methods" of exegesis, citing the Freudian and Jungian readings, one aim of which is to help explain why certain texts, such as the Parable of the Prodigal Son, are attractive to so many people. He also noted the importance of acknowledging the psychological predispositions of biblical interpreters.

In 1990, David K. Miell's "Psychological Interpretation" appeared in the British publication, *A Dictionary of Biblical Interpretation*. He reviewed the progress in the field, noting that since the fifties and sixties psychoanalytic interpretations, exemplified in the work of Richard Rubeinstein and Gerd Theissen, proceeded "with a more sophisticated awareness of the problems of reductionism and of cultural distance." Miell also noted that the range of psychological disciplines appropriated in biblical interpretation is growing to include "insights drawn from across the wide range of cognitive, social, clinical and developmental aspects of modern empirical psychology." He faulted Theissen for employing "psychological concepts pragmatically, eclectically and piecemeal" and for attempting to create a false integration of different psychological methods that fails to recognize the "inherent contradictions between the theoretical paradigms." Miell concludes that all of this points to the ongoing need for biblical scholars to "become better acquainted with the vast corpus of existing psychological theory and research . . . as psychology and theology continue to grow as partners in dialogue."[37]

In her survey of contemporary hermeneutics, *The Revelatory Text: Interpreting the New Testament as Sacred Scripture* (1991), Sandra M. Schneiders includes "psychological or psychoanalytic approaches." She writes: "The attraction of psychological methods lies in the relevance of such methods to contemporary interests in personal transformation and in the depth comprehension of personal agents." According to Schneiders, "the fact that the human and personality sciences are modern developments that were unknown to the biblical authors does not invalidate their use in interpretation," provided the interpreter respects the cultural distance between the biblical authors and themselves. She maintains that "psychological types of interpretation," though not without problems, "have produced some interesting results by highlighting dimensions of some texts that other methods have overlooked and by engaging readers with the biblical material in a way that more traditional academic approaches have sometimes been unable to do." She believes they have also provided ammunition for challenging the myth of "neutrality and objectivity in textual interpretation." In the end, Schneiders advances a sturdy set of criteria for evaluating psychological as well as other new approaches:

> The criteria for judging the results of both psychological and sociological approaches to the text will be those of effectiveness. If these new methods produce explanations that are as good as or better than those derived from more traditional methods, if the explanations are self-consistent and comprehensive in explaining the whole of texts rather than isolated fragments, if they reveal aspects of the text that have heretofore been invisible or answer questions that have heretofore resisted solution, if the data they produce accord with the solidly established data of previous investigation, they will have validated themselves. If the personality and social sciences prove effective for biblical

research, and they seem well on the way to doing so, other types of inquiry into human reality may very well also be applied to the biblical texts.[38]

One of the first "introductions to the New Testament" that mentions psychological biblical criticism is Russell Pregeant's *Engaging the New Testament: An Interdisciplinary Introduction* (1995), which cites two separate instances of "psychological approaches." The first, labeled "Psychological Approaches to the Bible," is described as one of the ways of reading the Bible that focuses on "the use of the psychological theories of Sigmund Freud and C. G. Jung" with special attention to the unconscious factors at work in writer and reader and to the power of archetypal patterns in textual narratives (such as the death and resurrection accounts). Though Pregeant proposes a number of questions that psychological criticism will have to address, he notes that "psychological approaches have an immediate point of contact in almost every reader's experience and therefore great potential for awakening interest in biblical studies." His second reference to psychological criticism reviews "A Freudian Interpretation of Paul," citing Robin Scroggs's *Paul for a New Day*, which draws on "Freudian theory" for psychodynamic insight into Paul's understanding of humanity under the law."[39]

The growing acceptance of psychology as a legitimate subdiscipline within biblical studies is evident in a 1993 document of the Pontifical Biblical Commission on "The Interpretation of the Bible in the Church." In the preface, Joseph Cardinal Ratzinger notes how the "methodological spectrum of exegetical work has broadened in a way which could not have been envisioned thirty years ago. New methods and new approaches have appeared, from structuralism to materialistic, psychoanalytic and liberation exegesis," as well as "new attempts to recover patristic exegesis and to include renewed forms of a spiritual interpretation of scripture." In his 1994 volume, *Scripture, the Soul of Theology*, Joseph A. Fitzmyer offers the following comment in his explication of the Pontifical Biblical Commission's presentation on a "Psychological Approach":

> The psychological and psychoanalytical analyses of human experience have proven their worth in the area of religion and enable one to detect multidimensional aspects of the biblical message. In particular, this approach has been invaluable in the analytical explanation of biblical symbols, cultic rituals, sacrifice, legal prohibitions, and biblical tabus. Yet once again, there is no one psychological or psychoanalytic exegesis that can substitute for the properly oriented historical-critical method, whereas the aid that can come from this approach to that method cannot be underestimated.[40]

Psychological Biblical Criticism Since the 1960s: Representative Problems, Approaches, and Applications

This section provides a field report on five aspects of development within the emerging field of psychological biblical criticism: naming the field; definitions of the field in theory and practice; questions, caveats, and concerns; representative psychological approaches; and representative applications.

Naming the Field

Researchers in this field have wrestled with a name or title for what they are about. An American group has settled on "psychological biblical criticism," adding the word *biblical* to the phrase *psychological criticism* used by F. C. Grant in 1968 (and coined by G. Stanley Hall in 1904). Gerd Theissen (1983) experimented with two other titles, "psychological exegesis" and the more ornate "a hermeneutically oriented psychology of religion," but the first is too sparse (since the discipline is not limited to exegesis) and the latter too general and imprecise. French scholars have suggested "une lecture psychanalytique de la Bible" ("psychoanalytic reading of the Bible"). This has two drawbacks: it limits the field to psychoanalysis; and it limits the focus to the written text, whereas the discipline to date has also dealt with authors, readers, and communities, past, present, and future. Others have used "psychological or psychoanalytic approach," which may suggest that the discipline represents a single approach rather than a diversity of approaches.

My own preference is "psychological biblical criticism" (suggested by D. Andrew Kille). The word *criticism* connotes the complexity of method and content and the rigor of critical analysis that the field represents. Adding the word *biblical* mitigates the possible reductionist connotation of the phrase "psychological criticism," while highlighting the larger "biblical critical" tradition from which the discipline has emerged and to which it is committed.[41]

Defining the Field

Though a comprehensive definition of the field of psychological biblical criticism is still in the making, a number of attempts are noteworthy.

Gerd Theissen offers a partial definition in *Psychological Aspects of Pauline Theology*, where he describes the objective of "psychological exegesis"—coterminous with that of historical-critical exegesis—as "to make texts intelligible on the basis of their context in life" with special attention to "psychic factors and aspects." Theissen earmarks for research two dimensions of that life context: the "new patterns of experience and behavior that appeared with ancient Christianity" as evidenced in the text of the New Testament, and the "inner history of humanity" that was at work in the emergence of Christianity. He explains:

> We do not yet grasp what historical forces brought forth and determined early Christianity. . . . But beside and within this external history there is an inner history of humanity. . . . This internal history is no less important than the external. . . . Anyone who thinks that this religion can be illumined historically and factually without psychological reflection is just as much in error as one who pretends that everything about this religion can be said in this fashion.[42]

Eugen Drewermann, though technically not a biblical scholar, has produced a torrent of work that emphasizes the importance of reclaiming the "timeless meaning" to be found in biblical myths, stories, sagas, dreams, legends, miracle stories, visions, wisdom sayings, apocalypses, parables, and even historical narratives. His method does not address the entire project of psychological biblical criticism, but provides a compendious demonstration of a Jungian-oriented approach which focuses on three dimensions of the biblical text: the historical milieu, the mythic dimension (the manifest stories or accounts in the text), and above all, the "elemental experiences" that have come to expression in the text as they are shared by all humans.[43]

A number of scholars have attempted a generic definition of the field and its objectives. They include J. Cheryl Exum and David J. A. Clines in *The New Literary Criticism* (1993); Ilona N. Rashkow in *The Phallacy of Genesis: A Feminist-Psychoanalytic Approach* (1993); members of the Bible and Culture Collective in their essay on "Psychoanalytic Criticism" in *The Postmodern Bible* (1995); the present author in "Rationale and Agenda for a Psychological-Critical Approach to the Bible and Its Interpretation" (1996); and J. Harold Ellens in "The Bible and Psychology, an Interdisciplinary Pilgrimage" (1997).

Exum and Clines, as well as Rashkow, speak specifically of a "psychoanalytic" approach. All five aim at a comprehensive understanding of psychology and/or psychoanalysis as a modality for understanding the Bible, seeing its production, content, and interpretation as a function, in part, of the habits of the psyche/soul/self. (The ramifications of their thought will be explored in chapter 4.)

Exum and Clines, in their introductory editorial essay, offer a précis of psychoanalytic criticism, seeing it as one of five new literary critical approaches (along with feminist, materialist or political, reader-response critical, and deconstructionist). They write:

> A psychoanalytic criticism can take as its focus the authors of texts, the texts themselves, or the readers of the texts. Since authors serve their own psychological needs and drives in writing texts, their own psyches are legitimate subjects of study. It is not often we have access to the psyche of a dead author, but even if little can be said about the interior life of real authors, there is plenty to be inferred about the psyches of the authors implied by the texts. Just as

psychoanalytic theory has shown the power of the unconscious in human beings, so literary critics search for the unconscious drives embedded within texts. We can view texts as symptoms of narrative neuroses, treat them as overdetermined [responding to multiple motives], and speak of their repressions, displacements, conflicts and desires. Alternatively, we can uncover the psychology of characters and their relationships within the texts, and ask what it is about the human condition in general that these texts reflect, psychologically speaking. Or we can turn our focus upon empirical readers, and examine the non-cognitive effects that reading our texts have upon them, and construct theoretical models of the nature of the reading process.[44]

Ilona Rashkow, whose book combines reader-response and psychoanalytic theory, proposes that psychoanalysis contributes to biblical interpretation a model for understanding what transpires in the process of reading. She maintains that reading is a "replication of the psychoanalytic process itself," and draws our attention to four parallels. First, in both reading and psychoanalysis, a "switching between two ways of seeing" takes place: in the reader and the analyst, at the level of the unconscious and the self-conscious. Second, in reading and in doing analysis one focuses not only on "what" is said, but on "how" it is said. Third, the process of "identification" and "catharsis" can occur both in reading and in psychoanalysis, "which opens one to change, the kind of change which breaks old schemata or the way we see them, and ultimately the way we see the world." Fourth, both the reader and the analyst find themselves making value judgments of the text and the events it narrates, in an ineluctable tendency to "try to shape the text until it is the kind of setting in which we can gratify our wishes and defeat our fears."[45]

In a similar vein, the authors of "Psychoanalytic Criticism" sees psychoanalysis not as "a tool or instrument that can simply be applied to the Bible so much as a para-religious discourse in its own right, deeply engaged in many of the same issues that pervade the biblical texts," for example, its preoccupation with the ineffable—"the father as God, God as Father, and God as (m)Other"—with guilt, with the "prescription (and subversion) of human gender roles," with "generational inheritance and conflict," and with "remembering and reconfiguring the past."[46]

The present writer has also sketched an agenda for psychological biblical criticism in "Rationale and Agenda for a Psychological-Critical Approach to the Bible and Its Interpretation" (1996):

The goal of a psychological-critical approach is to examine texts (including their origination, authorship, and modes of expression, their construction, transmission, translation, reading, and interpretation, their transposition into kindred and alien art forms, and the history of their personal and cultural effect) as expressions of the structure, processes, and habits of the human psyche, both in individual and collective manifestations, past and present.[47]

J. Harold Ellens—who is the founding editor of the *Journal of Psychology and Christianity*—characterizes the field thus:

> It is possible today to bring the insights and models of psychology to bear upon a biblical text, assessing the nature and function of the author, of the implied or stated intended audience, of the real audiences in the church's history which interpreted the text, together with their interpretations, and thus assess the reasons, healthy or pathological, for the constructs that were expressed in the text and in subsequent uses of it. That is to say, in addition to all the other . . . critical paradigms which are legitimately applied to the text of scripture, surely we must apply the paradigms for understanding how humans function, what they tend to say, why they say what they say the way they say it, and what messages mean as seen through standardized psychological paradigms when applied in a given context. Psychology is another lens through which it is possible to see any text and understand dimensions of it and the way it reflects the living human documents behind it which could not be understood if one did not employ this lens.[48]

Perhaps Antoine Vergote offers the most apt expression of this theoretical perspective, certainly the most succinct. For him, the purpose of psychological biblical criticism is "to understand the mental universe of the biblical tradition."[49] A fuller discussion of the description of the field will follow in chapter 4.

Concerns, Questions, and Caveats

Six important concerns need to be addressed as the discipline of a psychological-critical approach to the Bible develops. First, what is its place within the larger framework of the historical-critical enterprise? When G. Stanley Hall proposed in 1914 that a psychological approach suggests "something *above* textual or historical criticism and shows that these cannot be finalities," he was anticipating the substance of Walter Wink's dictum that "historical biblical criticism is bankrupt." Neither Hall nor Wink saw psychological biblical criticism displacing historical criticism, but rather amplifying it with new critical models aimed at highlighting dimensions of the text that the historical-critical method was neither equipped nor disposed to address. One of these dimensions for Wink is the capacity of Scripture to illumine "our present with new possibilities for personal and social transformation," which is one aspect of the text that psychological biblical criticism will want to examine.[50]

A second concern with psychological approaches is the perennial problem of "psychologism" and "reductionism." This is the tendency that Albert

Schweitzer had discredited earlier: to reduce the text to nothing more than a psychological phenomenon, often pathological. David Miell faults the "naive psychologism"—and the unsystematic and poorly articulated psychological theories—of earlier treatments of "the *personality* of Job, the *consciousness* of Jesus, the *conversion* of Paul, as (essentially abnormal) phenomena requiring (and legitimating) *ad hoc* psychoanalytic explanations." He states further that "while freely speculating about these 'inner lives,' scholars rarely reflected at all critically upon their own implicit psychological assumptions."[51] In 1922 Carl Jung addressed the problem of psychological reductionism as it raised its head in art, literature, and religion:

> In the realm of religion . . . a psychological approach is permissible only in regard to the emotions and symbols which constitute the phenomenology of religion, but which do not touch upon its essential nature. If the essence of religion and art could be explained, then both of them would become mere subdivisions of psychology. . . . If a work of art is explained in the same way as a neurosis, then either the work of art is a neurosis or a neurosis is a work of art."[52]

A third concern is the question of psychological models. Though research in the 1970s tended to operate out of either a Freudian or a Jungian model, it has since become clear that no single model is adequate to the whole. Accordingly, work in the eighties and nineties has experimented with a spectrum of models, ranging from object relations and behavioral psychology to post-Freudian approaches of Jacques Lacan, Julia Kristeva, and Luce Irigary. With such a mélange of models, a continuing concern will be to avoid an eclectic and piecemeal mixing "without regard to the inherent contradictions between the theoretical paradigms from which those concepts properly derive." David Miell finds this problem brewing in Theissen's occasional indiscriminate mixing of three different psychological models in his interpretation of Pauline texts.[53]

A fourth concern about psychological biblical criticism is the cultural distance between the first century and the modern "mind." In 1963, Krister Stendahl broached this issue in his essay "The Apostle Paul and the Introspective Conscience of the West," suggesting that those who find Paul caught in an internal, "psychological" struggle in Romans 7 are reading through the lens of modern introspective psychology. Klaus Berger, in a major work on the "historical psychology" of the New Testament, *Historische Psychologie des Neuen Testaments* (1991), faults Rudolf Bultmann, Gerd Theissen, and Eugen Drewermann for alleged importation of twentieth-century philosophical and psychological presuppositions into the New Testament. Berger accordingly advocates a "historical psychology" that takes as presuppositional the "strangeness" and "foreignness" of the first-century text and its "historical distance" from modern self-understanding. Russell Pregeant in 1995 asks whether we might not "misread an ancient text if we try to correlate it with our own psychological patterns?" Social-science critic John Pilch, in his 1997 article "Psychological and Psychoanalytical Approaches to Interpreting the Bible in Social-Scientific Context," raised similar caveats about assuming psychological constants across cultural lines (albeit affirming in the same breath his confidence that psychological anthropology is equipped to bridge the gap).[54]

Continuing reflection, research, and debate must focus on key questions raised by this concern. Has, for instance, the "inner spiritual life of humanity" and its conceptualization experienced the "far-reaching historical change" between the first and the twentieth centuries that Berger presumes? Can any modern apparatus be culturally free of presuppositions when approaching antiquity? Is any conversation possible between ancient texts and modern readers without assuming some common psychological ground? Certainly the historical survey in chapter 1 of the present work indicates a surprising conceptual continuity between the earliest psychological systems in Greco-Roman culture, biblical thought, and contemporary self-understanding.[55]

A fifth concern, originating in the religious community, is the tendency among psychological biblical critics to stress the symbolic, mythic, and archetypal depths of the Bible at the expense of its faith-propositional and historical character. Russell Pregeant maintains that theological and religious critics "will contend that the Bible not only expresses unconscious processes but also makes truth claims."[56] Though this concern merits further theological and psychological reflection, psychological biblical criticism will leave questions of the historical, theological, or metaphysical validity of truth claims to the historian and theologian. Instead it will focus on the meaning of these claims, on the conscious and unconscious factors in the life of the biblical author that affect their promulgation, and on the conscious or unconscious factors that affect their capacity to have an impact on the mind and life of the original readers and of generations of readers to follow.

A sixth concern is whether a psychological approach focuses on individual psychology at the expense of social psychology, ignoring the social context and sociopolitical thrust of the biblical writings. Though it is true that a good deal of Freudian and Jungian theory focused on the psychodynamics of the individual, many of its concepts and concerns are fundamentally social—for example, Freud's concern with civilization, Jung's concern with the Self as an ego-transcending reality, along with the ideas of the collective unconscious, the superego, and cognitive dissonance. From its inception, psychological biblical criticism has included research in the field of social psychology.[57]

Representative Psychological Approaches

As noted earlier, the two systems adopted by most psychological biblical critics in the early 1970s were those of Freud and Jung. Yorick Spiegel, however, branched out in his second volume (1978) by adding Gestalt psychology and transactional analysis. In 1983, John W. Miller included the work of Theodor Reik and David Bakan; in 1990 André and Pierre-Emmanuel LaCocque included object relations psychologists Melanie Klein and Donald Winnicott. To date the repertory encompasses more than fifteen types or schools of psychological or psychoanalytic thought. The following brief survey lists these psychological schools somewhat in order of their frequency of deployment, beginning with learning theory and cognitive psychology, two models that Theissen includes in his study of Paul, moving onto developmental psychology, existential psychotherapy, object relations psychology, and "Wir" ("we") psychology, and ending with other, lesser used psychological approaches.

Learning theory, or "religion as socially learned experience and behavior," directs exegesis to consider "the new stimuli, . . . new reinforcers, and new models that occur in the symbolic world of ancient Christianity." Rooted in behavioral psychology, learning theory draws attention to the fact that the Bible is, as Theissen maintains, "one of the most important textbooks of human behavior and experience" and that it describes, attests to, and advocates behavioral change through its pages. Accordingly, learning theory's goal is to note behavioral change as a dominant feature and theme of the text, and to attempt to understand the psychological dynamics that inform such change. These dynamics include the stimuli ("associative learning"), new reinforcers ("operant learning"), and new models ("imitative learning") that occur in the symbolic world of biblical culture, with special attention to how the Christ figure generates new models of human behavior.[58] Other applications of behavioral psychology are found in the work of Bufford (1977, 1982), Reynierse (1975), Bolin (1979), Reed (1985), Gruber (1986), and Atkinson (1993).

Cognitive psychology seeks to illumine the cognitive restructuring or revisioning of reality, along with the cognitive processes by which this revisioning takes place and "cognitively dissonant" elements are transcended. The revisioning is documented, expressed, and advocated in the New Testament (in response to the "Christ event"). The processes include new causal attribution, new anticipations, new self-assessment, and new role options; cognitively dissonant elements include sin, lostness, meaningless suffering, and despair. A cognitive approach to New Testament Christology would emphasize the shift in self-perception that the Christ symbol generates—for example, in Pauline theology, from identification with Adam to identification with Christ; in

Johannine theology, from a self-perception of "slave" to "friend."[59] Other applications of cognitive psychology are found in the work of Reed (1985) and Tan (1987).

Developmental psychology deals with the characteristics and processes of human behavior that change from one age or stage to another, focusing on personality, moral, and faith development, as well as cognitive and social behavioral development. Relying on the work of Erik Erikson, Jean Piaget, and James Fowler, a number of studies have adopted a developmental psychology approach to the Bible, commenting both on examples and models of human development. For example: Lyn Bechtel on the processes of maturation evident in the Adam and Eve myth (1994); Paul N. Anderson on stages of Christology in the Fourth Gospel (1996); John W. Miller on evidence of cognitive development in the life of Jesus as portrayed in the Gospels (1987; 1997); and W. Vogels on the inner development of Job (1983). Related research, enlisting Lawrence Kohlberg's stages of moral development (pre-conventional, conventional, post-conventional) to analyze ethical codes and moral perspectives of Scripture, appears in the work of Motet (1978) and Shepard (1994).

Existential psychotherapy, also called *logotherapy*, was developed by Viktor Frankl and has been used by Robert Leslie in *Jesus and Logotherapy* (1965) to illumine the psychodynamics of Gospel stories. Frankl's psychotherapeutic approach identifies the finding of a *logos* or center of meaning for one's life as the secret of mental health, and indeed of survival, as he illustrates most movingly in his 1959 classic, *From Death Camp to Existentialism*, later retitled, *Man's Search for Meaning*. Emphasizing the capacity of each person to exercise the power of choice, Frankl identifies the three types of meaning that can be realized in life: creative meaning (generated from what one produces or makes), experiential meaning (from what one undergoes), and attitudinal meaning (from the attitude one adopts toward one's situation). Leslie sees Frankl's model and therapeutic methods operating diagnostically and therapeutically in the Gospel accounts of the ministry of Jesus—for example, in the temptation narrative and in the stories of Zaccheus, the Samaritan woman, the rich young ruler, the paralyzed youth, Mary and Martha, the Bethesda invalid, and the Gerasene demoniac. Other applications of Frankl's *logotherapy* are found in Wuellner and Leslie (1984), Kühn (1988), Gladson (1989), and Tweedie (1961).

Object relations psychology grew out of the work of American scholar, Melanie Klein, and British psychologists, W. R. D. Fairbairn and D. W. Winnicott; it represents a modification of the Freudian emphasis on the oedipal complex in childhood. Ralph L. Underwood, in his "Primordial Texts: An Object Relations Approach to Biblical Hermeneutics" (1997), suggests the contribution it can make to "reflection on the interpretive process." In object relations theory the key relationship is between mother and infant.

> In psychoanalysis the term "object" refers to persons or to mental representa-tions of persons . . . . An assumption of all psychoanalytic theory is that . . . [for the infant] fragments of body parts, emotional impressions, and the like, are organized into wholes, objects within the psyche that represent other per-sons, in however distorted or realistic a fashion. . . . Such processes make out-side realities available internally to be the object of the investment of emo-tional energy.[60]

In relationship to the mother it is hoped that "an organized psyche with a stable sense of self and other in contact with external reality" will "eventuate . . . in the child's development."

In applying this to biblical studies, Underwood focuses on the object rela-tions "myth" as "a resource for understanding the *process* of biblical interpre-tation," especially on the "relational nature and imaginative character of inter-pretation" when the Bible functions as a psychologically freighted "object" for the reader. Underwood observed the states of "trust" and "distrust" among the various types of biblical readers and scholars. These led him to ask, "Can we learn to trust biblical texts and ourselves in the midst of reasonable distrust?" He found his answer in object relations psychology, which "suggests that bib-lical interpretation is an ongoing process that forms and transforms dynamic relations with biblical texts." This process is characterized by "a trust/distrust dynamic" that energizes the way persons and communities exercise imagina-tion to forestall doubts about the text and give birth to trust in the text.[61] Addi-tional applications of object relations theory to the Bible and related themes are found in Henderson (1975), McDargh (1983), and Hopkins (1989).

The **"Wir" (we) psychology** of Fritz Kunkel (1889–1956) was heavily influenced by Freud, Adler, and Jung. Kunkel focuses on the need for the individual to emerge from an ego-centered stage to a mature stage that acknowledges the larger self, or the "we," as the rightful object of one's atten-tion and energy. He applies his theory in a commentary on Matthew, *Cre-ation Continues: A Psychological Interpretation of the First Gospel* (1947). John A. Sanford has also applied Wir psychology to biblical interpretation. In *Fritz Kunkel: Selected Writings* (1984), Sanford's essay, "Kunkel's Psychology and the Bible," uses Kunkel's fivefold model of personality types to evaluate the mature (or immature) psychological development in the biblical portray-als of Herod, of Jesus during his temptation in the wilderness, of the woman with the ointment, of the wealthy ruler, of the man who did not know it was Jesus who cured him, and of the man in the parable who buried his talent.[62]

A number of other psychological approaches are being adopted by biblical scholars. The *post-Freudian psychoanalytic theory* of Jacques Lacan and feminists Luce Irigary and Julia Kristeva, mentioned earlier, is discussed in the essay on "Psychoanalytic Criticism" in *The Postmodern Bible* (1995)—with additional treatment of Lacan elsewhere by Hackett (1982) and Handelman (1983). The *self psychologies*, or *humanistic psychologies* of Carl Rogers and Erich Fromm, with their focus on "self-realization" and "self-actualization" as the primary goals of life, have been used widely in therapeutic and pastoral counseling, but also as models in biblical interpretation. For Rogers, see the work of Lucker (1980); for Fromm, see his own biblical works (1931, 1966). For Heinz Kohut's related work on narcissism and the self, see Castelein (1984), Greenlee (1986), and Chapman (1991).

The *individual psychology* of Alfred Adler, concerned with the "inferiority complex" and the struggle for significance and competence within the social field in which one finds oneself, is applied to biblical materials by W. C. Klein (1956), Haley (1969), Wohlgelernter (1988), Gladson and Lucas (1989), and Watts (1992). For work on the *social psychology of families and family systems* see the essay of M. L. Rogers (1979). Rollo May's *existential psychology* shifts focus from the problem of constructing a model of the self to the problem of understanding the self as it comes into existence in a world that requires the development of personal relations, social change, and pain and suffering as well as ecstasy and joy. May's approach provides the model for James Snell's analysis of the teachings of Jesus in Matthew (1978). Richard Batey (1976) and Rosemary Haughton (1974) have applied the models of Eric Berne's *transactional analysis* to the interpretation of the ministry of Jesus and the message of the Gospels.

Finally, individual instances of psychology used in biblical studies include: the *frame analysis* of E. Goffman applied as a social psychological approach to the parables of Jesus (King 1991); Boris Uspensky's literary-critical strategy of examining four "planes" of a document—ideological, phraseological, spatial/temporal, and the "plane of psychology"—applied to a reading of the Gospel of Mark (Petersen 1978);[63] Milton Erickson's *social learning and communication theory* applied to Luke's parable of the unjust steward (Blessing 1993); and Murray Bowens's *systems psychodynamics* applied to the parable of the prodigal son (Blessing 1995).

Representative Applications to the Bible and Its Interpretation

Having surveyed the variety of approaches to psychological biblical criticism developed since the late 1960s, we turn now to a summary of the kinds of biblical materials and interpretive issues to which they have been applied. What follows is a sketch of the effective agenda that psychological biblical criticism has adopted to date, divided into primary categories of biblical texts, figures, and issues. (The bulk of publication in the field has centered on the first two.)

• *Psychological interpretation of specific text genres.* This has focused on myth, legend, symbol, parable, and apocalypse, with the work of Eugen Drewermann dominating the field.[64]

• *Psychological analysis of biblical personalities.* This was popular for the first half of the twentieth century and became the leading cause of estrangement between psychology and biblical studies, as noted earlier in reference to Schweitzer's critique of psychiatric approaches to Jesus. The three figures most commonly "analyzed" were Moses, Jesus of Nazareth, and Paul of Tarsus.[65] (Just how seriously such research should be taken will be discussed in chapter 5, pp. 127–30.)

• *Analysis of psychodynamic factors in biblical narrative and personality portraits.* Though closely related to the previous area, this one focuses on the literary construct of the biblical figure rather than presuming to deal with the historical figures themselves. Research is generated by one of three motives: literary critical, psychohistorical, or didactic. The first seeks to understand the psychodynamics that make a story work the way it does; the second seeks to identify the genesis of certain defining myths in western culture (for example, identifying Adam and Eve with "original sin," the priority of the male, and the seductiveness of the female); the third seeks to find in the figure or story a positive or negative model for human behavior. The figures and their stories that have been studied this way include Adam and Eve, Abraham, Jacob, Joseph, Joshua, Samuel, Saul, David, Elijah, Isaiah, Jeremiah, Hosea, the author of the Song of Songs, the woman at the well, and "doubting Thomas."[66]

• *Religious phenomena in biblical culture and cultus.* This ranges from research on totemic meals, circumcision, eucharist, baptism, and women's religion, to prophetic inspiration and utterance and other psycho-spiritual experiential phenomena classified by some researchers as parapsychological.[67]

• *Dreams and dreaming.* Though a subdivision of the previous category, this stands in a class by itself because of the extensive attention it has received recently.[68]

• *Psychological hermeneutics.* As noted earlier, considerable groundwork has been done here by Paul Ricoeur on Freud and Peter Homans on Jung.

• *Exegetical commentary from a psychological perspective.* Beginning with John Sanford's 1993 commentary on the Fourth Gospel, this area is still in its formative state. Similar studies have been done on Genesis, especially the story of the Fall, and on the Psalms, Ecclesiastes, and the sayings of Jesus.[69]

• *Linguistics.* In his 1972 article, "Implications of Contemporary Linguistics for Biblical Scholarship," Eugene Nida states the importance of psychology's contribution of the notion of "patterns of the mind" that are evident in language systems and speaking everywhere:

> There was a time when modern linguistics reacted so strongly against improper psychologizing about language that linguistics tended to reject any and all efforts to relate language to thought processes. At the same time, doctrinaire behaviorist theories preferred to describe the mind as a kind of tabula rasa and to depict the learning of a language as merely the result of accumulated impressions. There is no generally recognized psychological theory which is adequate to explain all that is involved in language acquisition, competence, and performance, but it is quite clear that many universal features of language point to a number of what may be called "predispositions" of mental activity and structure. The recognition of these "patterns of the mind," if one may employ such a terminology, has important implications for the biblical exegete and translator.[70]

• *Archaeology.* This area uses psychological categories in its analysis of artifacts. In "Women's Popular Religion, Suppressed in the Bible, Now Revealed by Archaeology," William Dever makes a case for the systematic suppression in the Hebrew Bible of references or allusions to the popular women's cult of Asherah, the great Mother Goddess of Canaan, which, on the basis of archeological evidence (and the vigor of the polemic against it), was a flourishing reality in ancient Israel. In analyzing why a "male-dominated religious establishment" is bent on marginalizing an unofficial religion popular among women, Dever writes:

> There is more to all this than simply orthodoxy's instinct for self-preservation, particularly in the suppression of the cult of the Mother Goddess. I am convinced that the essential phenomenon we confront is a matter not so much of history as of psychology: the deep-seated ambivalence of men regarding women.[71]

Though Dever's specific psychological judgment invites further and more precise development, his citation of psychological factors as likely being at work in the social history of the Hebrew cultus suggests the unavoidability of such considerations in evaluating the material and textual remains of the culture.

• *Biblical psychology.* This area is amply demonstrated by works reaching from Delitzsch to Bultmann.

• *The use of the Bible in pastoral psychology and counseling.* Here the Bible is explored not only as a repository of therapeutic models but also a therapeutic text that can be employed in counseling

• *The Bible's contribution to contemporary psychological theory and models of humanity.* A number of writers, including Karl Menninger, Dominique Stein, and J. Harold Ellens, are exploring this area.[72]

In light of all that has been said in this chapter, it appears that psychological biblical criticism has begun to establish a credible presence within the ranks of biblical-critical scholarship. As Gerd Theissen has so aptly phrased it, while the latter's collective aim is "to make texts intelligible on the basis of their context in life," the former's is to focus on the "psychic factors and aspects" of that life context. Our task now is to cull out from the variety of approaches and applications some defining qualities that are common to psychological biblical criticism as a whole.[73]

Part Two
Prospect

4
What Is Psychological
Biblical Criticism?

Definition and Model

I am content to leave the Semitic philologist to grapple with
the origins and affinities of Hebrew, the psychologist to discourse on the relation of words and mind, and the philosopher to investigate the truth of propositions and the mystical
bond between words and the objects they denote.

G. B. Caird[1]

If every statement has psychological content, then every
statement may be scrutinized for its psychological significance, for what it means to soul. . . . Statements from any
field whatsoever thus become psychological, or revelations
of psyche, when their literalism is subverted to allow their
suppositions to appear.

James Hillman[2]

No matter how low anyone's opinion of the unconscious
may be, he must concede that it is worth investigating; the
unconscious is at least on a level with the louse, which, after
all, enjoys the honest interest of the entomologist.

Carl Gustav Jung[3]

You will never explore the furthest reaches of the soul, no
matter how many roads you travel.

Tertullian, citing Heraclitus[4]

When F. C. Grant announced in his 1968 article, "Psychological Study
of the Bible," that "Psychological Criticism opens up a wholly new and
vast, far-reaching scene," he offered no definition of the field nor a program of
study, but did suggest some topics for research. One was the psychology of

symbols. A second was the "psychological truth" of the Bible (as opposed to the historical or literary critical "truth"). A third was the effect of biblical texts on readers, for good and for ill.[5]

In chapters 4–6, we will pick up where Grant left off. In the present chapter we will propose a working definition and description of the field of psychological criticism, building on elements discussed in the preceding historical overview. In the next two chapters we will spell out an exegetical and hermeneutical agenda.

The present chapter consists of four sections. The first section identifies three fundamental elements for research in the field of psychological biblical criticism: its premise, its objective, and its criteria of interpretive adequacy. The second section provides historical definitions of *psyche*, *soul*, and *self*, proposing that within a psychological context the three are effectively synonymous terms for the complex psychic unity that constitutes the individual. Section three advances a working model of the psyche/soul/self that can serve as presuppositional for research in the field. Section four identifies the rudiments of a psychological critical perspective on the Bible and its interpretation.

Toward a Definition of the Field

Over the past thirty years, research in the field of psychological biblical criticism has led to identifying three defining elements: a fundamental premise that informs work in the field; a twofold objective that drives the work in the field; and the criteria of validity by which work in the field can be evaluated.

A Fundamental Premise

The premise that informs research in the field of psychological biblical criticism and that constitutes the insight that gave birth to the discipline can be stated as follows: *From a biblical-critical perspective, the Bible is to be seen as part and product, not only of a historical, literary, and socio-anthropological process, but also of a psychological process. In this process, conscious and unconscious factors are at work in the biblical authors and their communities, in the texts they have produced, in readers and interpreters of these texts and in their communities, and in the individual, communal, and cultural effects of those interpretations.*

The force of this premise is evident in the descriptions of psychological biblical criticism rehearsed in chapter 3 under the heading "Defining the Field" (pp. 75–78). Theissen, for example, suggested that the goal of psychological exegesis is to "make texts intelligible on the basis of their context in life," with "psychic factors and aspects" understood to be constitutive elements of that context. Ellens proposed that psychology is a "lens through which it is possible to see any text and understand dimensions of it and the way it reflects the living human documents behind it which could not be understood if one did not employ this lens." Its purpose, he says, is to understand "how humans function, what they tend to say, why they say what they say the way they say it, and what messages mean." Exum and Clines proposed that "a psychoanalytic criticism can take as its focus the authors of texts, the texts themselves, or the readers of the texts," suggesting that some of the phenomena that might be observed would include "unconscious drives embedded within texts" or "the psychology of characters and their relationships within the text."[6]

The common factor in these definitions is recognition that the Bible and its interpretation are, among other considerations, part and product of a "psychic context" constituted by the conscious and unconscious domains of author, text, and reader.

A Twofold Objective: Psychological Context and Psychological Content

From the preceding fundamental premise, there follows the twofold research objective of examining the *psychological context* and *psychological content* of the Bible and its interpretation. The first part of this objective can be formulated as follows: The first purpose of a psychological-critical approach is to examine texts and their interpretations (including their origination, authorship, and modes of expression, their construction, transmission, translation, reading, and interpretation, their transposition into kindred and alien art forms, and the history of their personal and cultural effect), as expressions of the nature, structure, processes, and habits of the human psyche/soul, both in individual and collective manifestations, past and present.

Getting at the psychological context requires developing a critical eye for what James Dittes has called the "habits of the soul."[7] These include the perennial ways the human psyche/soul finds itself touched by meaning, the forms in which it expresses that meaning, the purposes it chooses that meaning to serve, the words it finds congenial for translating that meaning into other languages and forms, the choice of media it makes to celebrate that meaning in word, sound, color, action, or silence, and above all, the function of that meaning within the life, ontogeny, and economy of the psyche/soul. The goal will be to discern these factors at work in the text, its reading, its interpretation, and its ongoing effect.

The second part of the objective can be formulated as follows: The second purpose of a psychological-critical approach is to study the implicit and explicit understanding of the psyche/soul in the Bible, which includes biblical concepts of illness and health of the soul, and biblical prescriptions for the care or cure of souls.[8]

To achieve this purpose, the psychological biblical critic will want to examine the complete biblical corpus, appreciating the variety of perceptions of the self to be found in its wide range of genres.

In summary: *The twofold objective of psychological biblical criticism is to enhance the repertory of critical perspectives on the Bible by adding to it a vision of the text as itself a psychic product, reality, symptom, and event, and as a source of commentary on the nature, life, habits, pathology, health, and purpose of the psyche/soul.*

Criteria of Interpretive Adequacy

Two efforts have been made to date to establish criteria of interpretive adequacy for psychological biblical-critical research, which in the end, prove to apply to all branches of biblical exegesis and hermeneutics.

In 1995, Martin Leiner proposed three criteria: coherence, correspondence, and consensus. *Coherence* requires that research in psychological exegesis be contradiction-free in terms of scholarly standards of procedure and proof. *Correspondence* requires a reasonable correlation between research results and current scholarly commentary on a given text. *Consensus* requires that psychological critical interpretation be at least as convincing as previous theories about the text and that they comport with historical conventions of research.[9]

In 1997, D. Andrew Kille explored the question of "interpretive adequacy" along the lines of a Ricoeurian model. Working with the mythic symbolism of Genesis 3 and the highly diverse history of its interpretation, Kille raises the question "If symbols are by nature polyvalent, and multiple interpretations are always possible, is there any basis for evaluating the relative adequacy of different interpretations?" With Ricoeur, Kille offers a positive answer, arguing that although we cannot positively *verify* any single interpretation, we can *validate* some interpretations as better than others. He proposes the following three "criteria for adequacy" in determining "a more valid interpretation" of a text:

- It will deal with the text "as a whole."
- It will deal with the text "as an individual," that is, respecting the uniqueness of the text in terms of authorship, genre, and literary and linguistic habits and structures.
- It will "account for the greatest number of factors found in the text, and will demonstrate greater convergence between the aspects considered."[10]

Though they did not focus on psychological biblical criticism, the criteria for "adequate interpretation" proposed by Schneiders in 1991 should also be mentioned. A valid interpretation, she states, is one that fulfills the following requirements:

• It "accounts for the text as it stands" (without "gratuitous rearrangement and emendation").

• It is "free from internal contradictions."

• It is "valid for the text as a whole and the whole of the text" (Schneiders comments that Mary Ann Tolbert defended the superiority of one psychoanalytic interpretation of the parable of the prodigal son over another because the former did "a better job of respecting both the integrity of the interpreter's model and the integrity of the text").

• It offers the best explanation of anomalies in the text.

• It is "compatible with what is known from other sources, both biblical and extrabiblical."

• It uses "responsibly all the methods that are appropriate within the framework of interpretation chosen."[11]

In the end Schneiders proposes a "global criterion" that may prove to be the most decisive, all else being equal. It is the criterion of the "fruitfulness" of the interpretation, one that allows the text to "mean all that it can mean." She explains:

> An interpretation, even if new or startling, that "makes the text speak," that, for example, exploits the potentiality of the text to illuminate the faith of the community without violating the canons of good exegetical and critical method, should be taken seriously. This is actually the global criterion to which some forms of sociological, psychological, and liberationist interpretation are appealing at the present time."[12]

Psychological critical research to date seems to have observed these canons of interpretive adequacy, especially since trained biblical scholars have entered the field. But the task remains for future scholars to refine these criteria, especially in light of recent discussions of postmodern critiques of classical biblical scholarship.

Toward a Definition of Terms

Given the basic premise that the Bible is to be seen as part and product of a psychic process, it behooves psychological criticism to define terms, especially the word *psyche*, and its common translation, *soul*. We have argued earlier that the terms *psyche* and *soul* have both been employed historically to refer to the human person as a center of conscious and unconscious awareness, functioning as an emoting, sensing, perceiving, desiring, imagining, knowing, thinking, willing, dreaming, and developing organism, susceptible to physical and psychological illness and healing, and oriented around a conscious integrating center we often call the ego. In this section we turn to a historical review of the terms *psyche* and *soul*, along with a term that is recently being readmitted in academic psychological circles to designate the whole person, namely the *self*. Following a thumbnail sketch of the meaning of these terms in the history of psychology, I will contend that all three are, with slight differences, historically the most appropriate and currently the most acceptable terms for referring to the total system of conscious and unconscious life in the human personality. I do this, recognizing that the terms are slightly different, and that each enjoys popularity in different settings: *psyche* in the psychoanalytic and intellectual communities; *soul* in religious contexts and more recently in the culture at large, and *self* both in the culture at large and more recently among professional psychologists.

Psyche *in Historical and Contemporary Usage*

As noted in chapter 1, Aristotle's *Peri Psyches* (*Concerning the Psyche*) defines *psyche* as the animating principle that catalyzes life in the body and is the source of all the animating functions we associate with being human. He developed a catalogue of these functions—reason, will, desire, memory, sensation, perception, learning, motivation, emotion, socialization, personality and imagination—and provided a "systematic psychology" that set the standard for two thousand years. His successors in Greco-Roman philosophy and in Patristic, medieval, and scholastic theology add little to Aristotle's observations, at best debating finer points on a number of perennial topics concerning the nature and constitution of the soul. Aside from recurring philosophical and religious questions about the preexistence, immortality, and transmigration of the psyche, the term has functioned much as it does today, connoting the totality of the vital, animated self. This same comprehensive understanding of psyche informed the first appearance of the term *psychology* in the thought of Marco Marulic and Philipp Melanchton in the early 1500s, coined, it would appear, to devise an anthropological term for the spiritual faculties of humans (as opposed to animals and angels).

It is this same term, *psyche*, that Wilhelm Wundt, the father of modern psychology, retained as the controlling concept of his "new psychology." Though he issues a disclaimer, warning us that he will use *psyche* in a strictly scientific sense, dismissing metaphysical connotations acquired in Western philosophical and religious tradition, he leaves no doubt that he uses it in its classic sense, namely, to refer to the totality of the psychic life. The difference between Wundt and his immediate predecessors is in his research protocol: "As soon as the psyche is viewed as a natural phenomenon, and psychology as a natural science, the experimental methods must also be capable of full application to this science."[13]

Freud and Jung also turned to *psyche* to express the idea of the unified psychic self, freely employing the German *Seele* (soul) as a fitting translation (though like Wundt, dismissing all metaphysical considerations). The precedent for using *Seele* as a synonym for *psyche* in academic psychological circles is demonstrated in the work of two German psychologists at the University of Göttingen, Johann Friedrich Herbart (1776–1841) and his successor in the chair of philosophy, Rudolf Hermann Lotze (1817–81). Lotze's work carries what would appear to many twentieth-century psychologists as an oxymoronic title, *Medicinische Psychologie, oder Physiologie der Seele* (1852) (*Medical Psychology, or Physiology of the Soul*), leaving no doubt that Lotze regarded *Seele* as the standard German philosophical and psychological equivalent of *psyche*, serving "the traditional function" of attributing "unity to the mind."[14] What Herbart and Lotze, Freud and Jung meant to denote by the terms *psyche* and *Seele*, then, was the objective nature of the spiritual, mental, emotional, soulful self, not reducible to somatic and physical factors—the same self that Aristotle and his successors had studied and described. In Freud and Jung's case, however, the concept of psyche is enlarged to include the newly highlighted realm of the unconscious.

In the early 1900s the terms *psyche* and *soul* become problematic; an increasingly empirically oriented environment made it difficult to talk about realities that defy precise, scientific measurement. The result is a certain terminological uncertainty among psychologists, evident as early as 1910 in psychologist Sir William Hamilton's gerrymandering definition of psychology as "the science conversant about the phenomena or modifications, or states of the mind, or [of] *conscious subject, soul or spirit, or self or ego.*"[15] The roots of this terminological uncertainty can be traced to the influence of the seventeenth-century mechanistic psychology of René Descartes and the rise of British empiricism which led to a "banishment of the intangible."[16] Already in the 1600s, Thomas Hobbes had repudiated the term and concept of soul (psyche) as "pernicious Aristotelian nonsense," preferring instead to think of psychological phenomena as derivatives of the nervous system and brain. This drive to reduce "psychic" qualities to reflexes activated in the somatic system by environmental stimuli comes to fullest expression with the advent of behaviorism in the 1920s with J. B. Watson (1878–1958) and his celebrated successor B. F. Skinner (1904–90). Watson and Skinner eliminate not only psyche and soul, but add *instinct, consciousness, mind,* and *thinking* itself to the list of casualties, leading to the quip (when Skinnerism began to fade as the premier voice in the field), "Pity poor psychology, first it lost its soul, then its mind, then consciousness, and now it is having trouble with behavior."[17]

The result of this perspective shift in academic psychology between the 1920s and the 1960s (marked by various schools of thought and driven to no small degree by professional anxiety among psychologists to achieve recognition for psychology as a bona fide scientific discipline), is the virtual disappearance of the concept of psyche from academic psychological discourse, a loss felt yet today.[18] This shift resulted, as Bettelheim noted, in distorted English translations of Freud, degenerating his humane language into mechanistic jargon: rendering soul (*Seele*) as "mental," "structure of the soul" as "mental apparatus," "organization of the soul" as "mental organization," and in many instances completely eliminating Freud's references to soul.[19]

A second effect is conspicuously ironic. On the one hand, academic "psychology" finds itself virtually discarding the term *psyche*, presumably because of the difficulty of constructing an empirically verifiable model of the psyche. As a result, one looks in vain for references to *psyche* in introductory academic psychology texts, histories of psychology, and even texts on the psychology of religion.[20] On the other hand, we find professional psychologists, academic psychologists, psychotherapists, and psychological popularizers manufacturing psyche-rooted neologisms to describe new activities in the field, e.g. psychometrics, psychodynamics, psychosomatic, psychiatrist, psychotherapy, psychoanalysis, psychedelic, psychosocial, psychopathology, psychosexual, and psychohistory—but with no effort to define what the "psych" element in these terms might mean.

This apparent quarantine on the term *psyche* among academic psychologists did not go unchallenged. A "correction" set in with two developments in the 1960s and 1970s. The first was "third force" or "humanistic psychology"; the second, a resurgent interest in Freud and Jung.

Abraham Maslow advanced "third force" or "humanistic psychology" to provide an alternative to the theories of human nature of the two dominant psychologies of the time, behaviorism and Freudian psychoanalysis.[21] Psychologists who shared his objectives include Gordon Allport, Erich Fromm, Karen Horney, Carl Rogers, Viktor Frankl, Carl Jung, and Ira Progoff. Humanistic psychology confronted the dominant psychologies on four fronts. First, it challenged the reduction of human nature to the "material" and "efficient" causes of neurophysiology or environment, evident especially in behaviorism. Second, it contended that humans are driven ultimately not just by the need for Freudian *homeostasis* or inner balance, but by "final causes" manifested in the "organism's inherent tendency toward . . . self-transcendence." These "causes" impel humans beyond survival needs and physical needs to higher values, such as self-esteem and competence, and at the highest level, self-actualization, aesthetic pleasure, and understanding, where innate "potentialities, capacities, and talents" are actualized.[22]

Third, humanistic psychology repudiated the "cellar view" of the unconscious proposed by Freud, preferring Jung's formulation that holds the unconscious to be not just a repository of the repressed but, more importantly, the source of an intuitive function that guides the organism toward self-actualization. Carl Rogers writes, "Our organisms as a whole have a wisdom and purpose which goes well beyond our conscious thought." Fourth, humanistic psychology treats the individual as subject as well as object. It takes seriously the "individual's subjective experience of the world" as important data for constructing a model of the self, reclaiming the method of William James who welcomed the "facts directly observable in ourselves."[23]

As effective as humanistic psychology was in reclaiming a sense of psyche or soul, it did not construct a comprehensive model of the psyche. For the rudiments of such a model we must turn to the thought of Carl Gustav Jung.

Jung states that the study of the psyche/soul is his main business: "The reality of the soul is the hypothesis with which I work and my main activity consists in collecting factual material and describing and explaining it. I have neither worked out a system nor a general theory but only postulated concepts which serve as tools, as is usual in any science." Jung makes this statement against the background of the repudiation of the term *psyche* by theologians and psychologists, and of generally deficient notions of soul in the culture at large. In an interview in 1955, Jung told of his enjoyment in pointing out to medical students the "old textbook for the Medical Corps in the Swiss army which gave a description of the brain" as a "dish of macaroni, and the steam from the macaroni was the psyche." Jung's disdain for such mechanistic views of the psyche is matched by his single-minded commitment to its study.[24]

Jung uses the term *psyche* in its classical, historical sense to refer to the "totality of all psychic processes, conscious as well as unconscious," generally reserving *Seele* or *soul* to refer to the unconscious realm of the psyche, though sometimes using *psyche* and *Seele* interchangeably. For Jung the psyche is the matrix of all human culture. He sees it as the force "primarily responsible for all the historical changes wrought by the hand of man on the face of this planet," holding that all human artifacts, compositions, creations, and achievements are the product of the human psyche, and as such it is "the womb of all the arts and sciences."[25]

For this reason, Jung would maintain, the psyche deserves our keenest interest, despite the fact that "neither the great religions nor the philosophies nor scientific rationalism have been willing to look at it twice." He observes:

> At a time when all available energy is spent in the investigation of nature, very little attention is paid to the essence of man, which is his psyche, although many researches are made into its conscious functions. . . . Man's greatest instrument, his psyche, is little thought of, if not actually mistrusted and despised. "It's only psychological" too often means: it is nothing.[26]

But he also acknowledges the impossibility of offering any final or complete description of the psyche:

> The phenomenology of the psyche is so colourful, so variegated in form and meaning, that we cannot possibly reflect all its riches in one mirror. Nor in our description of it can we ever embrace the whole, but must be content to shed light only on single parts of the total phenomenon. Since it is a characteristic of the psyche not only to be the source of all productivity but, more especially, to express itself in all the activities and achievements of the human mind, we can nowhere grasp the nature of the psyche per se but can meet it only in its various manifestations.[27]

Even though it is "quite impossible to define the extension and the ultimate character of psychic existence," and even though the psyche is "an ineffable totality which can only be formulated symbolically," it is nevertheless real. As an empirical reality it warrants close attention, not only because it is the progenitor of human culture, but also because of its ineluctable role in the destiny of world affairs. Jung writes, "It seems to me far more reasonable to accord the psyche the same validity as the empirical world, and to admit that the former has just as much 'reality' as the latter."[28]

Soul in Historical and Contemporary Usage

The term *soul* has a similar history. It was introduced as an English translation for psyche in its Greek context, anima in its Latin context, and *Seele* in its German psychoanalytic context. Its past is more complex and problematic than that of psyche because of the tendency, especially in English-speaking religious circles, to use it exclusively as a reference to the disembodied self before or after death—a concept objectionable not only to Aristotle, but to Freud, Lotze, and Herbart as well, as earlier noted. The result is that for the first two-thirds of the twentieth century, *soul* was either absent from discourse among psychologists and theologians, or dismissed by translating Freud's *Seele* as *mind* or *mental*. Writing in 1967, James Hillman lamented the loss of the term *soul*:

> As a term, . . . [the word *soul*] has all but vanished from contemporary psychology; it has an old-fashioned ring, bringing echoes of peasants on the Celtic fringes or reincarnating theosophists. Perhaps it is still kept alive as some vestigial organ by village vicars and by seminary discussion of patristic philosophy. But it barely enters popular songs—who longs with "heart and soul"? Who puts his whole soul into anything? What girl has "soulful" eyes, what man a "great soul," what woman is a "good old soul"? Soul is the last four-letter word left that is unmentionable among the "in."[29]

Though calls for the reclamation of soul appeared sporadically in the first two-thirds of the twentieth century, neither Hillman nor academic psychology nor theology could have anticipated the resurgence of the term in academic and popular circles in the 1980s and 1990s.[30] One example from academic discourse is William Barrett's *Death of the Soul: From Descartes to the Computer* (1986). Barrett derides the materialistic, mechanistic reductionism of the physical sciences that would "snuff out this little candle [of soul] as unnecessary and paradoxical." He recalls with Kant "that it is the power of mind that creates the systems of mechanics that here seek to extinguish it." He urges a return to Descartes's dream, which he describes as "the universe as a single machine [that has] there, inside it, at its center, . . . that miraculous thing, his own consciousness, in the light of which he sees and meditates." The book closes with an apt biblical metaphor: "What shall it profit a whole civilization, or culture, if it gains knowledge and power over the material world, but loses any adequate idea of the conscious mind, the human self, at the center of all that power?"[31]

In a similar vein, Richard Swinburne, in his 1983–84 Gifford Lectures later published as *The Evolution of the Soul* (1986), issues the charge that "scientists have tended to regard the life of conscious experience as peripheral, not central to understanding man." But, he argues, "we must not fall into the trap of believing that that which we cannot explain . . . does not exist. The conscious life evidently exists—that we have sensations and thoughts, feelings and hopes is the most evident thing that there is." For Swinburne, soul denotes the conscious, moral, conative, affective, experiencing, sensate self, dominated by "mental life." He "takes seriously the fact of human conscious experience, its continuity and it causal efficacy." He sees the leap from the primordial soup of inanimate life as bringing into being the consciousness of mental life with its "sensations, thoughts, purposes, desires and beliefs." What relationship has conscious life to body? "Though dependent on physical processes," Swinburne states, "the soul (or mind) is not the body," which is an ordinary material object like the brain. But the body "is connected to a soul which is the essential part of a man, and which is the part which enjoys the mental life."

This "mental life" is characterized by two qualities that differentiate humans from other animals: "complex and logically ordered thought" and "awareness of moral goodness and obligation." Two additional differences are "free will" ("in the sense that their choices are not totally predetermined by their brain-states") and "structure of character."[32]

One of the most compelling calls for the reclamation of soul is found in the ten essays edited by social scientists Richard K. Fenn and Donald Capps, *On Losing the Soul: Essays in the Social Psychology of Religion*. The editors state that their purpose is "to expand the discourse of the social sciences about the self by reintroducing the word 'soul,'" noting that it has fallen out of use among sociologists and anthropologists (as well as psychologists).[33] One of the contributors, Bernice Martin, offers an autobiographical response to the question *What is "soul"?*

> Soul, to my mother and the people with whom I grew up in that working class industrial town, was a word used unself-consciously to mean the ultimate core or essence of the individual's being. . . . People talked of the soul as if it were the irreducible, indestructible part of the person which, perhaps, continued to exist after death. . . . The word . . . suggests to me the possibility of recognizing—hinting at—a level of discourse which accords some ultimate significance to the person beyond what can be said by the expert social scientific disciplines. The metaphysical and theological connotations of "soul" suggest a dimension of the integrity of persons, which is not fully captured by the vocabulary of "self" and "selfhood." The death of the soul is of greater moment than the death of the self.[34]

Another contributor, David Martin, characterizes soul as the "essential or animating element of any human being, and the spiritual quiddity, characterized ideally by reason and integrity and wholeness considered together."[35] Richard Fenn adds that it is also constituted by the "mystery" within a person that provides the capacity to act with freedom in the face of those "longstanding social and cultural forces" that some anthropologists, like Victor Turner, see as absolutely determinative. How do we measure soul or gather data on it? Fenn contends that "its presence, like a black hole, can only be inferred from its effects, since it cannot be seen directly."[36] Or as Martin adds, "Few would have been able to define it; the meaning lay in the usage and the usage, as often as not, involved the telling of stories and the repetition of 'sayings.'"[37]

As striking as the reclamation of soul is in academic quarters, its phenomenal renascence in popular culture in the 1980s and 1990s is all the more remarkable. Just the number of books with the word *soul* in its title is impressive: Alan W. Jones, *Soul-Making: The Desert Way of Spirituality* (1985); Gary Zukav, *The Seat of the Soul* (1989); Robert J. Drinan, *Stories from the American Soul* (1990); Larry Dossey, M.D., *Recovering the Soul: A Scientific and Spiritual Search* (1990); Thomas Moore, *Care of the Soul* (1991) and *Soul Mates* (1994); Jack Canfield and Mark Victor Hanson, *Chicken Soup for the Soul* (1993), with a series of sequels; Marjorie Thompson, *Soul Feast* (1995); William J. Doherty, *Soul Searching: Why Psychotherapy Must Promote Moral Responsibility* (1995); Henry H. Mitchell and Nicholas Cooper-Lewis, *Soul Theology: The Heart of American Black Culture* (1996). One of the most comprehensive studies of "soul language" across world cultures is the anthology edited by Phil Cousineau, *Soul, An Archaeology: Readings from Socrates to*

Ray Charles (1994), with one hundred and thirty literary selections, including an Egyptian Gnostic myth of the soul's origin, a West African folktale, essays by psychologists, theologians, anthropologists, novelists, mystics, shamans, poets, and philosophers, and selections from sacred texts.[38]

How is one to account for the resurgence of soul at the end of the twentieth century? From the perspective of the history of ideas, the shift can be seen as a popular manifestation of postmodern consciousness with its negative suspicions of the positivistic and scientistic approach of behaviorism and radically empirical psychology. From a psychodynamic perspective, the answer may be found in the Freudian concept of the "return of the repressed," demonstrated in this instance in the return of a long repressed cultural need for a term to speak of the complex but unified self that most people understand themselves to be, and that cannot simply be reduced to the somatic and physical factors that for so long had been enlisted by behaviorism and empirical psychology as justification for the banishment of *psyche* and *soul* from the language. Philip Cousineau confirms the existence of a universal linguistic need for a word to express the idea of *soul* when he lists the many terms that are "sacred words used by primal peoples the world over for the surge of life itself, linguistic cousins of what was called *sawol* in Old English, *sawal* by the Anglo-Saxons, *sala* by the Icelandic folk, and eventually, . . . what we now call *soul*.[39]

Self in Historical and Contemporary Usage

The term *self*, surprisingly, has had a history in psychological circles comparable to that of *psyche* and soul. It was often rejected by psychologists because it defied empirical description, but was reinstated when the need arose for a word to express the concept of the whole person.

Plato, Augustine, Descartes, Kant, and Hume had conceived of the *self* as that conscious inner agent that observes oneself having experiences. H. D. Lewis summarizes their idea of *self* as an "abiding subject distinct from all the particular items apprehended."[40] Kant and Hume, however, were not disposed to attempt a description of the self because of its unavailability to empirical observation. *Self* was a matter for philosophic speculation, not psychological study. British Associationist psychologists had "sloughed it off as no more than the connected chain of passing effects."[41]

Over against this position, William James, in his 1890 *Principles*, revived interest in the concept of *self* with a theory of its four dimensions: the material self, which includes body, family, and possession; the social self, consisting of interpersonal sentiments; the spiritual self, comprised of the "inner" or subjective sense of being, and of psychic faculties and dispositions; and the pure ego, which functioned as an inner principle of personal unity. James's most important contribution, however, was the distinction he drew between self as subject or knower (which he termed the "I") and self as object or known (the "me"); thus he effectively reintroduced the "subjective self" into a conversation from which it had long been excluded.[42]

James's theory was crowded out by the materialist views of behaviorism and the rational objectivism of early experimental psychology appearing in the early 1900s. One of his former students, Edward Titchener (1867–1927) of Cornell, was persuaded in time that "the concept of self should be left out of psychology because it would bring in the realm of meaning, that which . . . lay beyond the purview of psychology as a descriptive science." This point of view effectively excluded the concept of *self* from most academic psychological discourse for half a century.[43]

By the second half of the twentieth century, however, the term began to reappear under the sponsorship of clinical and developmental psychology, the arts, and the humanities. Alfred Adler spoke of the "creative self" as a key ingredient of his "individual psychology." The personality theories of Gordon Allport, Erik Erikson, and Erich Fromm began to speak of "self-concept," "self-attitudes," and "self-esteem." Jung spoke of self as the supreme archetype to which the individual aspires. Rogers and Maslow introduced the notions of "self-actualization" and "self-realization," referring to a unified drive or tendency within the organism to grow and to realize its potentialities. Karen Horney wrote of "self-analysis" and Heinz Kohut developed "self psychology."

By the last decade of the twentieth century, *self* had made its return within the guild of academic psychologists. In a chapter on "The Self in Process" in his 1991 volume, *Human Change Processes: The Scientific Foundations of Psychotherapy*, Michael J. Mahoney writes,

> The cognitive, developmental, and emotional (r)evolution(s) have redirected mainstream experimental psychology back "inside" the organism; and the "modern synthesis" in psychology is, in part, an attempt to integrate and transcend inside/outside and mind/body dualisms. What cognitive and life scientists found when they looked inside the most "promising primates," however, was much more than they had anticipated. The recent and ongoing (re)discoveries of emotionality, unconscious processes, and personal meanings are cases in point. But perhaps the single most important (re)discovery of twentieth century psychology has been that of the self, which has (again) become a cardinal concept after a moratorium that lasted over half a century. As Louis A. Sass quipped, "The 'self,' once banished by mainstream psychology to the cloudland of unobservable and irrelevant abstractions, seems to have returned with a vengeance." . . . Whether it is a vengeful return or simply the persistence of a centuries-old mystery, however, self studies are now center stage in psychological laboratories and clinics around the planet.[44]

Academic psychology on the eve of the twenty-first century is beginning to sense the loss of the *psyche* in psychology and the need for a model of the *self* that will honor the reality of an entity that James had described at the turn of the century and that Aristotle and the biblical tradition had recognized long before.

On the basis of the foregoing we would like to suggest that there is sufficient justification for reinstating the triad of *psyche*, *soul*, and *self* as the historically most appropriate terms and culturally the most fitting terms to refer to the total system of conscious and unconscious life in the human personality. By way of a single definition that encompasses all three, I offer the following:

The common semantic content of the terms psyche, soul, *and* self *includes reference to the totality of the conscious and unconscious individual. This totality encompasses:*

• *The individual's powers and functions: emotional, conative, affective, intuitive, imaginative, perceptive, rational, sensate, moral, spiritual, and aesthetic*

• *The individual's development, behavior, character, and acts, as these are informed, shaped, and motivated by instincts, aspirations, innate physical and psychodynamic proclivities and drives, as well as positive and negative external reinforcements*

• *The individual's personal capacities: self awareness, free will, aesthetic appreciation, moral judgment, seeking and creating of meaning, creativity, and spiritual sensitivity—all of which can be bent to constructive or destructive ends and, depending on the circumstances, be the expression of healthy or pathological states.*

This definition of the psyche/soul/self triad is necessarily incomplete, given the unknown depths of the subject. It seeks to emphasize the reality and complexity of the phenomenon to which the history of psychology and Scripture have long attested. This phenomenon is what psychological biblical criticism attends to as it seeks to explore the conscious and unconscious psychic functions and habits at work in the biblical author, biblical text, and biblical reader, and in the history of the exchange among them.

Toward a Psychological Model of the Psyche/Soul/Self

We turn now to providing a picture of those major structures, processes, and habits that characterize the psyche/soul/self. Our focus is on those defining aspects of the "anatomy of the soul" that are presuppositional for psychological biblical criticism—as well as for biblical psychology and, in fact, for much of modern culture. This working model is based largely on those developed in depth psychology, predominantly by Jung and Freud, but with marked affinities for the biblical perspective.[45] It is, of course, provisional; Jung himself acknowledged: "We can nowhere grasp the nature of the *psyche per se* but can meet it only in its various manifestations."[46]

In developing this model, we will look first at the nature of the unconscious as an autonomous factor in the human personality. Second, we will examine four other prominent features of the self from a psychoanalytic and biblical perspective: the dynamic character of the psyche; the postulate of psychological types; the theory of stages of human psychological development; and the importance of the psychology of the individual vis à vis the psychology of the masses.

The Unconscious

The most telling contribution of depth psychology to an understanding of the psyche/soul/self is the postulate of *the reality of the unconscious as an autonomous factor in the human personality*. As noted earlier, Freud, Jung, Adler, and Rank acknowledged that they were not the first to speak of the unconscious. As early as 1678, Ralph Duckworth, an English cleric and philosopher, wrote: "There may be some vital energy without clear consciousness or express attention, . . . a more interior kind of plastic power in the soul . . . whereby it is formative of its own cogitations, which it itself is not always conscious of." Near the end of the nineteenth century, Nietzsche advocated research into the unconscious to correct "the absurd overvaluation of consciousness." He wrote:

> Consciousness only touches the surface. . . . The great basic activity is unconscious. . . . The real continuous process takes place below our consciousness, the series and sequence of feelings, thought . . . are symptoms of this underlying process. . . . All our conscious motives are superficial phenomena; behind them stands the conflict of our instincts and conditions.[47]

By 1900 four functions were identified with the unconscious: the conservative function, that recorded or "conserved" memories and perceptions that escaped conscious attention; the dissolutive function, evidenced in the abnormal conditions of hypnotic states or schizophrenia; the creative function, expressed in innovative, inspired thinking; and the mythopoetic function, realized in fantasies and dreams that allowed an "escape from reality."[48]

It was Freud, however, who conceived of the unconscious as a "mental place," an autonomous presence within the self, signaled most commonly by dreams, slips of the tongue, involuntary actions, unintentional misdeeds, demonstrations during hypnotic states, and pathological symptoms. He was also among the first to work on a systematic theory about the unconscious. For Freud the unconscious was the repository of personal repressed thoughts and experiences, factors that are unknown to the individual but that are actively at work in the individual's behavior. It was also a nesting place for the wishful thinking an individual projects onto reality to soften the harshness of life. In his later work Freud also saw the unconscious as the bearer of archaic factors and mythic patterns dating back to primeval civilization.[49]

Jung expanded the notion of the unconscious to include the "collective unconscious" as the purveyor of "motifs which typify human fantasy in general." These motifs, Jung contends, "are not *invented* so much as *discovered*; they are typical forms that appear spontaneously all over the world, independently of tradition, in myths, fairytales, fantasies, dreams, visions [as well as in] the delusional systems of the insane."[50] Except in the cases of the mentally ill, these archetypal images serve a "transcendent function" for the individual or for societies as a whole, producing a "third" option when a problem seems incapable of being solved. The solution comes as a new thought, inspiration, dream, or vision, and opens the door to a new course of meaningful action for the individual or the culture.

Jung speaks also of an inherent religious function of the unconscious. "I did not attribute religious functions to the soul," Jung writes, "I merely produced the facts which prove that the soul is *naturaliter religiosa*, i.e. it possesses a religious function."[51] This parallels a statement by William James in the early 1900s: "That the conscious person is continuous with a wider self through which saving experiences come . . . is literally and objectively true." James typifies what Robert C. Fuller, in his 1986 volume *Americans and the Unconscious*, describes as the "decidedly religious character" of American psychologies of the unconscious. Fuller traces this character to a tradition ranging from William James and G. Stanley Hall, to Abraham Maslow and Carl Rogers (with theological parallels in the thought of Jonathan Edwards, Ralph Waldo Emerson, Horace Bushnell). They all see the unconscious (or the soul) as an innate guide for the individual "toward life's intrinsic values and ultimate mysteries." Over against the Freudian emphasis on the "lower end" of the unconscious, with its "forgotten memories, silly jingles, inhibitive timidities, and . . . psychopathological hysteria," they emphasize the "upper end," with its "sense of continuity . . . with a wider spiritual environment."[52]

Jung defines the unconscious in terms of five functions that relate both to personal and collective aspects of the self. These include:

> everything of which I know, but of which I am not at the moment thinking; everything of which I was once conscious but have now forgotten; everything perceived by my senses, but not noted by my conscious mind; everything which involuntarily and without paying attention to it, I feel, think, remember, want, and do; all the future things that are taking shape in me and will sometime come to consciousness: all this is the content of the unconscious.[53]

Both Freud and Jung are impressed by the autonomy of the unconscious. Freud is said to have remarked that the most serious disease to which we are subject is "that one cannot come to terms with the realization that . . . he is not the master in his own house." In similar fashion Jung comments:

> The individual imagines that he has caught the psyche and holds her in the hollow of his hand. He is even making a science of her in the absurd supposition that the intellect, which is but a part and a function of the psyche, is sufficient to comprehend the much greater whole. In reality the psyche is the mother and the maker, the subject and even the possibility of consciousness itself. It reaches so far beyond the boundaries of consciousness that the latter could easily be compared to an island in the ocean. Whereas the island is small and narrow, the ocean is immensely wide and deep and contains a life infinitely surpassing, in kind and degree, anything known on the island. . . . [T]he known range of consciousness is confronted with the unknown extension of the unconscious.

On the basis of decades of clinical observation, dream analysis, and study of culture, Jung, and to some degree Freud, began to appreciate the vast depth and breadth of the psyche and the unconscious. More than just a feature of the individual, it is a reality shared collectively by the entire human species. In some respects, the unconscious transcends the species; it is that place where are born the archetypal images, dreams, and visions of the future that take humanity to places undreamed of. These inner promptings have such force and abiding effect on consciousness that Jung is moved to conclude, "Ideas spring from something greater than the personal human being. Man does not make his ideas; we could say that man's ideas make him"—a notion not distant from the experiential report of poetic inspiration, scientific insight, or biblical revelation.[54]

Other Aspects of the Psyche/Soul/Self in Psychological Perspective

In addition to the unconscious, four other aspects of the depth-psychological model have a bearing on biblical criticism: the dynamic as opposed to the static character of the psyche; the postulate of psychological types; the stages of human psychological development; and the psychology of the individual vis-à-vis that of the masses.

1. The dynamic as opposed to the static character of the psyche. This aspect has bearing especially on the analysis of biblical narratives, the depictions of biblical personalities, and biblical counsel for the soul. Freud sees the psychic life constituted by the tension between the pleasure principles of the libido with its capacity for power and aggression (id), and the conformity principle of the superego, with its laws, constraints, and proscriptions. The goal of the process is homeostasis or balance, refereed by the reality principle of the ego. In addition, Freud finds the self challenged—even threatened—by the "necessities" or inevitabilities (*ananke*) of persons, places, or things that confront us. We can meet this situation in a number of ways, either with defense mechanisms (denial, repression, suppression, neurosis, compulsive behavior) or by the sublimations dictated by reason (*logos*) or love (*eros*).

Jung portrays the scenario differently. For him, there are five players in a process aimed inherently toward wholeness and individuation, "coming to one's unique individual self." These players are: the *ego* (with its self-centered concerns); the *persona* (the image one constructs of oneself for presentation to the outside world); the *shadow* (with its concealed burdens of inferiority and its potential for violence, aggression, and evil); the *anima/animus* (the projected images we have about the opposite gender, whether idealized or distorted), and the *Self* (the built-in archetypal image we have of ourselves when ego no longer dominates the scene). As we will see, the patterns of inner conflict and personal development that psychoanalytic theory finds in the structure and processes of the self are not foreign to patterns intuitively rehearsed in biblical stories and narratives.

2. The postulate of psychological types. Developed largely in Jungian circles, this has bearing especially on the analysis of biblical authors and interpretations. Jung devised the theory to explain the puzzling differences between Freud's, Adler's, and his own theories of the psyche, when they had based their views on what seemed to be virtually the same set of data. Jung's theory of psychological types postulates first, that humans adapt themselves to life's challenges, either as extroverts or introverts; second, they orient their response to life around one of four adaptive functions available in the psychic repertory: thinking (using reason and logic), feeling (evaluating what is right or wrong, good or bad), sensing (responding to physical cues), and intuiting (reflecting on the "meaning"). For the psychological biblical critic, this fourfold model of psychological types provides a tool for exploring the idiosyncratic psychological orientation of individual biblical authors as well as the special angle of vision that different readers bring to their reading of the text.

3. The stages of human psychological development. This has bearing especially on the analysis of biblical writers and readers, of personality portraits of biblical figures, and of models of comparative maturity in biblical psychology. The work of Piaget, Erikson, Fowler, and Kohlberg on childhood development, on the epigenetic life stages, and on religious and moral development have been added to those of Jung in applying developmental psychological insight to biblical interpretation.

Freud did not provide a model of psychological development that extended beyond childhood; instead he focused on the period from infantile sexuality to the Oedipal crisis. He did show interest, however, in the horizontal or synchronic development that can occur in therapy from neurosis to homeostasis, reestablishing the individual squarely in the realities of life.

Jung's model of psychological development divided the life cycle into a two-stage process aimed at "individuation." In the first stage, extending from birth to mid-life (late 30s or early 40s), the psychic task is to consolidate the "ego complex," to fashion a *persona*, and to experiment with attitudes (extraversion/introversion) and functions (thinking, sensing, feeling, intuiting). These help in adapting to life through the process of choosing a vocation, creating "family," and finding a place. The second stage is spent in *enantiodromia* ("running to the other side") through a maturing process of "looking under the hood" to recognize previously unrecognized (and often undesired) aspects of the self, and of reclaiming functions, gifts, and activities that were left undeveloped in the first half of life. The second stage is also marked by a tolerating of ambiguities and collapsing of polarities that one's younger ego would have found little patience with. This "conjunction of the opposites" serves to dislodge the ego from the command center of one's personality, replacing it with the archetype of the broader image of Self that awakens one to the vast complex of relationships of which one is a part.[55]

For both Freud and Jung the maturation process, whether it leads to homeostasis or individuation, is a psychological given, the fulfillment (or frustration) of which was a function of the health or pathology of the individual. Jung comments:

> Whatever man's wholeness or the Self may mean *per se*, empirically it is an image of the goal of life spontaneously produced by the unconscious, irrespective of the wishes and fears of the conscious mind. It stands for the goal of the total man, for the realization of his wholeness and individuality with or without the consent of his will. The dynamic of this process is instinct, which ensures that everything which belongs to an individual's life shall enter it, whether he consents or not, or is conscious of what is happening to him or not.[56]

Achieving this wholeness requires development of the capacity for reason (*logos*), for love (*eros*), for more and more consciousness, and for that degree of "legitimate" suffering that is inevitable in a psychically mature life—again, a pattern discerned in biblical narrative and articulated in biblical psychology.

4. The psychology of the individual vis-à-vis the psychology of the masses. This has bearing especially on the study of biblical ethics and biblical understanding of individual and group responsibility. Perhaps the greatest contribution of the Judaeo-Christian tradition to Western civilization and democracy is the high valuation it placed on the individual.[57] This valuation is mirrored in depth psychology by both Freud and Jung. Jung reports how impressed he became with the uniqueness of each of his clients: "It was one of the greatest experiences of my life to discover how enormously different people's psyches are." Beyond this he was also interested in the relation of the individual to culture, especially when entire cultures are infected by a "psychic epidemic," as was the case with National Socialism in Germany in the 1930s and 1940s. For both Freud and Jung, however, all cultural changes, good or evil, originate with the individual. Jung writes, "The psychopathology of the masses is rooted in the psychology of the individual, and if the individual is not truly regenerated in spirit, society cannot be either, for society is the sum total of individuals in need of redemption." Freud viewed the individual as standing bravely against the current; Jung, as "that infinitesimal unit on whom a world depends." This same psychological judgment is reflected in the prophetic tradition permeating both testaments of the Judaeo-Christian scriptures.[58]

Toward an Agenda:
Fundamental Aspects of a Psychological Critical Approach to the Bible and Its Readers

Seeing the Bible from a "psychological-critical" perspective—and here I anticipate the next two chapters—entails a re-visioning of the text in five respects: biblical origins, the text itself, biblical interpretation, "biblical history," and the fundamental purpose of the Bible.

Re-visioning biblical origins from a psychological-critical perspective draws the conversation away from dates, places, and historical events, to the initial "psychic events" (to borrow a phrase from Jung) that lie at the base of religious movements and texts, and that in turn are refracted through the succession of readers. Two of Jung's comments are particularly relevant:

> The primordial experience is not concerned with the historical bases of Christianity but consists in an immediate experience of God (as was had by Moses, Job, Hosea, Ezekiel among others) which "con-vinces" because it is "overpowering." But this is something you can't easily talk about.[59]
> It has yet to be understood that the mysterium magnum is not only an actuality but is first and foremost rooted in the human psyche.[60]

The task of psychological biblical criticism is to search out the character of those original "events" that gave rise to the text and to note their permutations in the "souls" of succeeding generations. It will also survey the context from which the text has emerged and its broader cultural context of proto-Hebrew or Greco-Roman culture, looking for psychic factors in the form of mythic themes, symbols, and archetypal images that may have had a finger in the construction of Judaeo-Christian consciousness and expression. Finally, it will examine individual writings for cues of psychic factors that might be at work in the author's choice of material, themes, images, and modes of expression, testing the hypothesis of James Hillman, that "If every statement has psychological content, then every statement may be scrutinized for its psychological significance, for what it means to soul."[61]

A psychological critical perspective will also occasion a *re-visioning of the text*. It does this in four ways:

1. It will ask how texts occasion meaning in the human mind; why humans are drawn to creating and valuing texts like the Bible; how texts and words come to be accepted as autonomous bearers of meaning apart from their authors; how texts take on power as "Sacred Scripture" generating a sense of numinous depth in the text itself, in the world to which it points, and in the reader.[62]

2. It will focus on the genres of biblical language, taking note of the unconscious as well as conscious factors mediated through symbol, archetypal image, apocalypse, and myth.

3. It will bring fresh psychological insight into the psychodynamic of religious phenomena, from glossolalia, to dreams, to demon possession, and prophetic inspiration. It will also help bring to light psychodynamic factors in biblical narrative in which, for example, familiar patterns of adaptation and defense are operative in the "players" in the text (repression, denial, sublimation, projections, displacement, transference, reaction formation). It will provide psychological insight into the dynamics at work in many areas: in biblical personality portraits (from Abraham to Paul); in biblical ethics (the psychology of deontological ethics vs. an ethics of conscience); in biblical religion (ranging from an analysis of projective language to an analysis of the religious function); and in biblical psychology (both the psychology postulated by the biblical writers—and developed by Delitzsch—about the nature, origin, powers, and destiny of the self, as well as the psychology implicit in their writing).

4. It will be interested in applying canons of psychological health and illness to the Bible, to identify the Bible's potentially pathogenic and therapeutic features.

A psychological-critical perspective will also foster a *re-visioning of biblical interpretation*, seeing the reader and the various modes and forms of biblical interpretation as demonstrations of the structures, processes, and habits of the human psyche. Turning to the reader, it will see the act of reading as a psychic event and will inquire along the lines of reader-response, ideological, deconstructionist, rhetorical, and contextual criticism into what the reader brings to the text (considering psychological type as well as personal history) and what the text brings to the reader. With respect to biblical interpretation, it will explore the modalities of interpreting the text, with attention, for example, to the Jungian modes of amplification and active imagination as strategies native to the human psyche for elaborating the meanings found in the text. These elaborative strategies include dance, sculpture, song, pageant, liturgical celebration, and acts of mercy.

A psychological-critical perspective will invite a *re-visioning of biblical history*, taking note of the Bible's post-history as well as pre-history, examining biblical effects as well as causes, and pondering not only what produced the Bible but what the Bible has created and produced. A psycho-critical hermeneutic will focus on the catalytic effect the biblical text has exercised on readers and whole communities, activating conscience, will, and imagination for new courses of creative, moral action, or triggering prejudice, animosity, belligerence, and inquisitional paranoia that in turn triggered pogroms, witch-burnings, racial suppression, and family violence and abuse. By thus chronicling both the therapeutic and the pathogenic effects occasioned by the text, it will provide insight into the psychodynamics of the processes that produce them.

Finally, a psychological-critical perspective will invite *re-visioning the fundamental purpose or* telos *of the Bible.* We know from form criticism that the text functions with multiple purposes through its range of genres, such as law, history, myth, legend, psalm, proverb, prophecy, gospel, epistle, parable, and apocalypse. But it also serves a collective function as canon. Psychological biblical criticism sees the intrinsic purpose of a canonical text as fundamentally therapeutic, that is, as preoccupied with the nature and destiny of the soul and with strategies for its "cure." As such, it invites the reader to listen for truths that the Bible, especially through its psalms and stories, awakens from deep within the soul. It invites the reader to be open to archetypal images of future possibility that the text inspires through parable and prophetic imagery, to search for insight into the meaning of human existence that the Bible celebrates through poetry and myth, to seek the gift of heightened consciousness and revelation that the text occasions through its "word," and to notice the models of human possibility and individuation it proposes in its laws and epic tales. From a psychological-biblical-critical perspective, the purpose of the text in all its genres is tutelage of the soul.

In summary, from a psychological-critical perspective the Bible is an artifact of the human soul, bearing witness to the habits, dispositions, and aspirations of the soul. And although it is part of a historical process, it is also part of a psychic process in which conscious and unconscious factors are at work. These factors in the end may prove to be the decisive determinants of what is said in the text, why it was remembered and recorded, how it is said, to whom and for what purpose it was said, as well as how it is read, how it is interpreted, and how that interpretation is received.

Keeping this perspective on the Bible in mind as presuppositional for a psychological-biblical-critical approach, we turn next to delineating a research agenda for the field. In chapter 5, we will consider the exegetical agenda; in chapter 6, the hermeneutical agenda.

5
The Exegetical Agenda

The World of the Text

Religious experience. . . in the end resists analysis and rational explanation. . . . We are obliged to ask whether or not in
addition to the supernatural factors which alone impressed
the early Christians, there were other factors involved in this
enthusiasm, factors which may be much more readily
understood by us. We must ask about the human and historical antecedents of this inspiration, and its psychological
conditionings.

Johannes Weiss (1913)[1]

The student of the New Testament must also understand
religious psychology, especially the various types of religious
experience to be met within the Jewish and the Hellenistic
world of the first two centuries.

F. C. Grant (1950)[2]

Numerous examples could be cited showing the necessity of
a collaborative effort on the part of exegetes and psychologists: to ascertain the meaning of cultic ritual, of sacrifice, of
bans, to explain the use of imagery in biblical language, the
metaphorical significance of miracle stories, the wellsprings
of apocalyptic visual and auditory experiences.

Pontifical Biblical Commission (1993)[3]

In focusing on the exegetical agenda for psychological biblical criticism, we
will use *exegesis* to refer to that branch of textual interpretation that focuses
on the world of the text, that is, on what the text says in its own words within
the framework of the world in which it is speaking.[4]

The present chapter identifies seven exegetical topics ripe for psychological-critical inquiry, reporting on research done to date and suggesting lines of

inquiry for future research. The topics are: the psychology of symbols and archetypal images; unconscious factors at work in the history of biblical motifs and cultic practices; psychodynamic factors in biblical narrative; the psychology of biblical personalities; the varieties of biblical religious experience or the phenomenology of biblical religion in psychological perspective; the psychology of biblical ethics; and biblical psychology.

The Psychology of Symbols and Archetypal Images

Symbols, myths, apocalypses, stories, and legends have been of interest to psychological critics for two reasons: their rich unconscious content, and their role in the life of individuals and cultures universally. Both dimensions came to light in the psychoanalytic work of Freud and Jung on dream symbolism, on the artwork of patients, and eventually on the role of symbol in the arts, culture, and religion. Freud and Jung made a case for the "symbolizing process" as a "natural and spontaneous function of the psyche,"[5] holding that symbols function as the native language of the psyche, emerging unbidden from the retorts of the psyche in the form of dreams, visions, poetry, myth, drawings, painting, sculpture, stories, or even hallucinatory states, with meanings that prove novel, surprising, startling, or inspiring to consciousness.

Four aspects or qualities of symbolic language that Freud and Jung highlighted have special relevance for the psychological biblical critic. First, *symbols, by virtue of the depth they intrinsically convey, are not to be confused with signs*. A sign (for example, "Exit") is invented and devised by the rational mind to point univocally and unambiguously to something that is usually quite unlike itself. But a symbol (for example, the American flag, the cross, the menorah, the upright clenched fist) is produced by a process that includes unconscious factors. It is an image "thrown together with" (*sym-ballein*) a reality in whose nature it is somehow felt to participate and whose essence it seeks to illumine, always with the implicit understanding there is more than meets the eye. Jung comments:

> A sign is always less than the things it points to, and a symbol is always more than we can understand at first. Therefore, we never stop at the sign but go on to the goal it indicates; but we remain with the symbol because it promises more than it reveals.
>
> Because there are innumerable things beyond the range of human understanding, we constantly use symbolic terms to represent concepts that we can't define or fully comprehend. This is one reason why all religions employ symbolic language or images.[6]

The goal of psychological criticism is to attend to the question of the unarticulated meanings in biblical images, both for the text and for the reader.

Second, *symbols are polyvalent* rather than univocal, reverberating with unconscious as well as conscious associations. The plenitude of meaning to be found in symbols stems not only from the complex mystery of the thing-in-itself that is symbolized, but from the spectrum of values the image can evoke in the consciousness of the symbol-maker or the symbol-reader. This occurs not only at the personal level, but at the socio-cultural level as well. For example, by comparing what the symbol of the "cross" might connote to various individuals—a first-century Roman, a second-century Christian, a medieval saint, a twelfth-century crusader, an exorcist, a member of the Ku Klux Klan—we highlight the exegetical necessity of considering the polyvalence a symbol can exercise in the conscious and unconscious perceptions of different authors and readers.

Third, *symbols are polyfunctional*, that is, they play on a range of psychological functions that include not only the rational, but also, as delineated by C. G. Jung, the feeling (or evaluating), intuitive, and sensing functions. Jung observes that the symbol

> certainly has one side that accords with reason, but it has also another side that is inaccessible to reason. . . . The prospective meaning and pregnant significance of the symbol appeals just as strongly to thinking as to feeling, while its peculiar plastic imagery when shaped into sensuous form stimulates sensation as much as intuition.[7]

The thinking function provides access to some dimensions of the text—for example, the biblical riddle, or the rabbinic logic of Paul—but the other functions also play a role. The sense function is necessary to "understand" the erotic elements in the Song of Solomon or to "comprehend" the horror of the war scene in 2 Kings 25:7. The feeling function is necessary to perceive Job's indignation or Nathan's confrontation of David. The intuitive function is necessary to fathom the "Holy, Holy, Holy" of Isaiah in the year King Uzziah died.

Fourth, *symbols provide a compensatory function* in the economy of the psyche. For both Freud and Jung the purpose of dream analysis was to generate conscious awareness of realities at work in oneself of which one is literally "unconscious." Jung, however, saw not only the dream but the whole apparatus of symbolization as a function of a self-regulating system that calls on the "wisdom" of the unconscious to compensate for the one-sidedness of conscious life and accordingly, to provide direction, integration, and health for the whole conscious/unconscious self. This compensation occurs as both an individual and cultural phenomenon. Just as the dream provides the individual with clues from the personal unconscious to compensate for one-sidedness, so also the literature, music, or art of a culture are "constantly at work educating the spirit of the age, conjuring up the forms in which the age is most lacking." One would be hard pressed to find any biblical symbol or passage that has not at sometime been pressed into service to compensate for the one-sided consciousness of an individual, a community, or a culture.[8]

A class of symbol that deserves special mention with respect to the function of redirecting consciousness is the *archetype* or *archetypal image* that Jung found as part of "a sphere of unconscious mythology whose primordial images are the common heritage of mankind," originating in what he called the "collective" or "objective unconscious." By studying his patients' dream images, myths, religious art, and drawings, Jung concluded that the unconscious consists not only of originally conscious contents that have become lost (à la Freud), but also of

> a deeper layer of the same universal character as the mythological motifs which typify human fantasy in general. These motifs are not invented so much as discovered. They are typical forms that appear spontaneously all over the world, independently of tradition, in myths, fairytales, fantasies, dreams, visions, and the delusional systems of the insane. On closer investigation they prove to be typical attitudes, modes of action, thought processes and impulses which must be regarded as constituting the instinctive behaviour typical of the human species. The term I chose for this, namely "archetype," therefore coincides with the biological concept of the "pattern of behaviour." In no sense is it a question of inherited ideas, but of inherited, instinctive impulses and forms that can be observed in all living creatures.[9]

Joseph Campbell characterized these archetypal images as "a cast of inevitable stock characters that have played through all time, through the dreams and myths of all mankind, in ever-changing situations, confrontations, and costumes" up to the present, when "the latest incarnation of Oedipus, the continued romance of Beauty and the Beast, stand this afternoon on the corner of Forty-Second Street and Fifth Avenue, waiting for the traffic light to change."[10]

Freud did not use the term *archetype*, but he did speak of an analogous phenomenon, namely, the presence of "archaic factors which were once dominant generally in the primeval days of human civilization," active in the "mental life of children today," and recurring in the history of the race. In *Moses and Monotheism* Freud adds: "There probably exists in the life of the individual, not only what he has experienced himself, but also what he brought with him at birth, fragments of phylogenetic origin, an archaic heritage."[11]

A prime example of an archetypal figure is the image of the hero elaborated by Joseph Campbell in *The Hero with a Thousand Faces*, which Campbell traces in various guises from Assyria, Babylon, Greece, and Rome, to Cambodia, Indonesia, Honduras, and Argentina, as well as to the Bible. Other archetypal images to be found in the Bible include the primordial garden, the divine child, the wise old man or woman, the satanic trickster, the sacred mountain, the tree of life, the coming golden age, the divine king, the wicked queen, the image of the cosmos, the archetypal themes of good vs. evil, of slavery and freedom, and of death and resurrection. Walter Wink, in his essay on Jacob's wrestling with God, observes that such classical images appear

> so frequently in widely scattered mythic traditions that we are justified in regarding [them] . . . as a standard component in spiritual development. The very pervasiveness of such stories . . . is evidence that we are dealing with something fundamental to the spiritual journey itself, and not merely with etiological legends invented to "explain" the origin of things.[12]

What does the foregoing imply for the future work of psychological biblical criticism? It suggests three types of projects. First, there is a need for an expanded biblical lexicography to include comparative psychological and anthropological research on symbols in other cultures and religious systems. Concretely, this means amplifying the already rich collection of archaeological, historical, and linguistic data gathered by biblical scholars, with the comparative mythological and symbolic analysis done by historians, anthropologists, phenomenologists, and psychologists of religion. The goal is to perceive as thoroughly as possible the range of values a given biblical symbol or motif can register in the human psyche.

As John Dominic Crossan suggested some years ago, "The full study of a biblical text . . . will demand in the future as much use, for example of James Pritchard's magisterial *Ancient Near Eastern Texts and Pictures* as of Stith Thompson's equally magisterial *Motif-Index of Folk-Literature.*" Work done to date in this area includes E. R. Goodenough's *Jewish Symbols in the Greco-Roman Period* (1953–68), and Eugen Drewermann's two-volume work on depth psychology and exegesis, examining dream, myth, story, saga, legend, visions, apocalypse, wisdom sayings, and miracle story. The objective will be to determine the extent, if any, to which such meanings might be at work in the biblical text.[13]

The second project needed is a renewed exegetical appreciation of the archetypal, polyvalent, and polyfunctional character of biblical symbols. This will add psychological insight to the work of contextual, feminist, reader response, ideological, rhetorical, and autocritographical critics who have already advanced theories on the multiple meanings of biblical texts and images. In his 1960 presidential address to the Society for Old Testament Study, "An Inquiry into the Biblical Theology of History," C. A. Simpson cited the contribution of depth psychology to the understanding of the chaos symbol and water imagery in biblical stories and traditions, maintaining that "water is the commonest archetypal image of the unconscious." Accordingly, biblical typology is "not merely an ingenious game" but "reflects the psychological constant which in part determined the pattern of men's response to what was apprehended as the activity of God in history." Similarly, D. Andrew Kille's analysis of the multiple psychological readings of the symbols of the serpent and the tree adds to the psychological judgment that "ineluctably cerebral" readings of the text run the risk of eclipsing the archetypal dimension and the meta-rational meanings inherent in the experiencing of a text. A psychological-biblical-critical approach would agree that "the goal of interpretation is to restore those levels of meaning lost to a rationalistic and literal-minded culture."[14] Mention should also be made of Walter Wink's epic trilogy on the imagery of "powers" in the Bible. He provides an incisive and panoramic "second reading" of the mythic, symbolic, archetypal, and unconscious depths of the biblical language of power as expressions "of the real but invisible spiritual dimension of personal and corporate earthly existence." Using analytical psychological tools, largely informed by the work of C. G. Jung, Wink unconceals what had previously been regarded to be the products of irrational, primitive mentality, as vivid expressions of lived experience in the communities of the biblical authors, with imposing analogies to experiences of "demons" and "angels" in personal lives and institutional structures in our own time.[15]

A third area of research, rooted in the theory that symbols are compensatory to consciousness, is a study of the catalytic effect of biblical symbols on individuals and cultures within the history both of the text and its interpretation. In his research on psychological aspects of Paul's theology, Gerd Theissen states that "the basic question of exegesis from the perspective of the psychology of religion is the question of the extent to which the religious symbolism contained in the Pauline texts could have effects in transforming experience and behavior." In his article on Johannine symbolism, Michael Willett Newheart focuses on such an effect within the text itself, contending that in the Fourth Gospel the transforming symbols of water, bread, and light, and the symbol of Christ as an exemplification of the archetype of the self, are transferred from their earlier identification with the Law to identification with Jesus. This compensates for the psychic loss of expulsion from the synagogue experienced by Johannine Christians, and providing a source of "psychic equilibrium" and "psychic grounding" in the trauma of their dislocation.[16] Outside the text, the testimonies of the catalytic effect of biblical texts on individuals and cultures are legion in the history of Judeo-Christian piety.

Finally, research on the archetypal effect of biblical imagery would suggest two additional lines of inquiry. The first has to do with the puzzling fact of the archetypal attraction of sacred texts themselves, a question Wilfred Cantwell Smith has raised in his trans-cultural study, *What Is Scripture?* Why is it that human cultures everywhere seem ineluctably drawn to the veneration and cultic celebration of sacred texts, written and "oral"? A second question has to do with the baffling phenomenon of the sudden and rapid spread of certain religious movements at particular times in history (for example, early Christianity, Islam, and the Sabbatai S'vi movement).[17] With respect to the spread of early Christianity, historical critics tend to attribute it to historical, economic, political, and social causes. A psychological approach such as that of Jung, however, would also consider a psychological cause, seeing the spread of Christianity as quintessentially an expression of events that transpired within the psyches of individuals and communities. Jung wrote in this regard:

> Christ would never have made the impression he did on his followers if he had not expressed something that was alive and at work in their unconscious. Christianity itself would never have spread through the pagan world with such astonishing rapidity had its ideas not found an analogous psychic readiness to receive them.[18]

Unconscious Factors at Work in the History of Biblical Motifs and Cultic Practices

A second exegetical topic of special psychological interest—and related to the preceding discussion of archetypal images and themes—is the possibility of unconscious factors at work in the cultural inheritance, transmission, and adaptation of religious motifs and cultural practices in the Bible. In a discussion of the extent to which the present Western psyche is shaped by that of the Christian Middle Ages, Jung notes that "we are also stamped by what existed before Christianity." Suggesting the possibility that remnants of the pre-Christian might reside unconsciously in Christian sacred texts (and by analogy, that pre-Israelite consciousness might be at work in Hebrew texts), he writes:

> Everything has its history, everything has "grown," and Christianity, which is supposed to have appeared suddenly as a unique revelation from heaven, undoubtedly also has its history. . . . I need not speak of the rites of the Mass and certain peculiarities of the priests' clothing which are borrowed from pagan times, for the fundamental ideas of the Christian Church also have their predecessors. But . . . we are all overcome by the impression of the uniqueness of Christianity. It is exactly as if we had built a cathedral over a pagan temple and no longer knew that it is still there underneath.[19]

Jung's observation suggests a line of inquiry for psychological biblical criticism that would see a text being shaped not only by the personal conscious and unconscious depths of individual authors, but also by collective motifs and mythemes at work, often unconsciously, in the culture at large to which the individual and the culture fall heir. Such mythemes can have their origin in specific past cultural events or experiences, or they can be seen as archetypal themes integral to the human species and recurring in changed garb in successive civilizations and cultures.

As an example of a cultic symbol operative in a series of cultures, Erwin R. Goodenough comments on the recurrence of the image of the cup in Mesopotamian, Jewish, Greco-Roman, Hellenistic, and Christian cultures. He notes that the psychological values attached to a symbol in one culture are frequently preserved in succeeding cultures, even when the culture from which it was derived may be publicly repudiated and denounced. Thus, "the cup containing the divine fluid" is a symbol that "can be traced not only to early Christianity, but to the followers of Dionysus, and even to early Mesopotamia. In the form of a vase it was one of the most important symbols for the ancient Egyptians."[20]

Freud makes comparable observations. In his essay, "Great is Diana of the Ephesians," a title drawn from Acts 19:28, he links the cult of Diana to that of Mary in Ephesus, suggesting that "important people are apt to be 'revenants' of still earlier figures." To this we might add Freud's speculative works on *Totem and Taboo* and *Moses and Monotheism*, in which he postulates that certain biblical cultic practices and laws are the unconscious replay of a primordial tribal patricide and its cultural re-enactment. Though Freud's theory of patricide of the tribal leader by the "primal horde" has been repudiated by cultural anthropologists and has been an embarrassment even to Freud's admirers (who object to Freud's analyzing a culture as he would an individual by unearthing traumas of the past), a recent work by Robert Paul, *Moses and Civilization*, suggests the possibility of its psychological value. Paul points out that in terms of contemporary psychoanalytic theory, Freud's primal horde theory may cast light on "what persistent unconscious fantasy, or, . . . what persistent myth inherited from the past, continues to determine aspects of our thought and action in ways of which we might not be fully aware." Though Paul rejected Freud's primal horde myth as a story rooted in history, Paul argues for it as "a useful interpretive construct":

> What Freud reconstructed as ancient history . . . is an almost perfectly accurate model of the myth that we already know to be the central organizing master narrative of the Judeo-Christian tradition, namely the Bible. The mythic paradigm of the primal horde is . . . the most widely known, read, and performed sacred story we have, whose influence on the West . . . has been

incalculable. This consideration opens up . . . horizons for new understand-
ings of the Bible, of Freud, of Western civilization, and of the primal-horde
paradigm.

Though Robert Paul rejects the primal horde motif as originating in the
"unconscious collective memory of the West," he does concede it is a myth
whose values and meanings exceed consciousness, and have unconscious
effect on thought and action.[21]

From the perspective of psychological biblical criticism, these observations suggest the need to expand the horizons of exegetical expectations of the
text by engaging in what Paul Ricoeur calls a literary and cultural "archaeology of the subject."[22] The study of unconscious as well as conscious values
mediated in the preservation, adaptation, and transformation of ancient Near
Eastern stories, themes, and practices in the Hebrew Scriptures, and possibly
echoed in the New Testament, will provide grist for this research mill. It could
encompass examining pre-biblical tales of creation and the flood, metaphors
for the deity, ritual and civil laws and taboos, sacrificial motifs and holy days,
symbolic uses of the images of water, bread, and wine, paradigms of male and
female, images of the realms of heaven, the cultic use of altars and sacred
books and the cultic stories that accompany and account for them—all as part
of the pre-history, history, and even post-history of biblical texts, possibly providing a link between contemporary and pre-biblical experience.

Psychodynamic Factors in Biblical Narratives

The psychological exegesis undertaken in the last quarter of the twentieth
century, either by seasoned psychologists with a knowledge of biblical scholarship or by seasoned biblical scholars with psychological background, has
tended to transcend the "psychologizing" of an earlier era. This new work has
begun to demonstrate that when an experienced psychological eye is trained
on the text, observations emerge which the traditional exegete might have
missed.

One of the primary objectives of such exegesis is a psychodynamic analysis of the text. The goal of psychodynamic analysis is to observe how the habit-
ual strategies and thought patterns of the human psyche might be manifest in
a text. These strategies, drawn from psychoanalytic theory, would include at
least the five strategies Freud identified that the "inner censor" devises to con-
ceal the true meaning of a dream: substitution, displacement, condensation,
conversion, and inversion.[23] They would also include the defensive strategies
of repression, sublimation, denial, intellectualization, projection, introjection,
reaction formation, and rationalization, along with the patterns of transference, dissociation, cognitive dissonance, and obsessive compulsion. On a

larger scale they would include patterns of extraversion, introversion, neurosis, psychosis, regression, individuation, homeostasis, and other dynamics related to psychological development.

To date, four types of research on the psychodynamic factors in biblical texts and interpretations have emerged. The first is a variety of specialized studies on psychodynamic patterns in biblical discourse. Earlier examples include the work of Freud and Jung. Freud drew attention to the compulsive-obsession factors in ritual law, the projection implicit in the construction of God images, and the repression implicit in taboos. Jung's *Answer to Job* focused on the odd psychological dynamics between Job and the Yahweh-Satan coalition, the psychology of the evolution of the God-concept from Job to early Christian concepts of a God-man, and the spontaneous emergence of unconscious elements in the violent imagery of the Apocalypse. Between 1910 and 1925 Ludwig Levy and Eduard König wrote on the dynamics of sexual symbolism in the stories of the Tower of Babel, the Samson Saga, the Paradise story, and the Song of Songs.[24]

More recent contributions have broadened this field. In 1975, John Gager introduced the analytic concept of cognitive dissonance to explain how early Christians dealt with the delay of the parousia, namely by reinforcing those elements of experience that were consonant with eschatological expectation, and repressing those that were not. Myron Gubitz (1977) examined the Biblical "myth" of Israelite hostility to the Amalekites as an illustration of the dynamic process of dissociation. Françoise Dolto and Gérard Sévérin (1979) produced a brief, conversational volume of Freudian analytical insights into the dynamics operative in the Gospels, from the birth stories, to the young Jesus in the temple, the wedding at Cana, the parable of the good Samaritan, the death of Lazarus, and the passion and resurrection accounts.

In the 1980s, Heinz Westman published his two volumes on archetypal motifs in Genesis and Job: *The Structure of Biblical Myths* and *The Springs of Creativity: The Bible and the Creative Process of the Psyche*. Walter Ong probed the psychodynamics of oral memory and narrative in the Bible. In 1984 Gerd Theissen explored the dynamics of the conversation between Jesus and the Syrophoenician woman in light of social-psychological analysis of relations between Jews and Gentiles in Tyre and Galilee (Mark 7:24–30). That same year Wilhelm Wuellner and Robert Leslie produced an exploratory volume on "psychological insights from the New Testament," providing commentary on the substance or effect of the psychodynamic aspects of fourteen New Testament passages. Theissen's previously mentioned major study, *Psychological Aspects of Pauline Theology* (1987) refracted five sets of Pauline passages through the lenses of learning theory, cognitive psychology, and the psychodynamic theories of Freud and Jung, shedding light on the psychological dynamics at work in these passages. Brooke Hopkins (1989) offered a psycho-dynamic reading of the resurrection narratives from the perspective of object relations theorist D. W. Winnicott.

One of the first examples of a "psychological commentary" appeared in 1993 with John Sanford's *Mystical Christianity: A Psychological Commentary on the Gospel of John*. Combining his training in analytical psychology and scripture, he explored the psychological dynamics operative in the Johannine dialogues of Jesus with Nicodemus, Nathaniel, the woman at the well, the paralytic at Bethesda, Judas, the woman taken in adultery, the man born blind, and Pilate. In 1995, Naomi H. Rosenblatt, psychotherapist and lecturer on the Bible, cowrote *Wrestling with Angels*, a compelling analysis at a popular level of the family dynamics of the Genesis saga, observing that Genesis offers "a comprehensive framework for exploring human nature and for embracing adult life with all its rewards and responsibilities." In 1995, Lyn Bechtel used developmental psychological theory to interpret Genesis 2–3; in 1997, psychotherapist Richard Q. Ford, applied psychoanalytic insight to eight of the synoptic parables by reporting what he finds when he listens to the psychodynamic exchange between the characters in the story. In 1997, Andrew Kille added a masterful historical summary and analysis of the history of the psychological interpretations of this passage. Also in 1995, Kille produced a compelling biblical psychological exegetical analysis of the narrative structure of the Jacob saga as a "journey toward wholeness" from the standpoint of the Jungian theory of individuation. In that article Kille offered the following observation concerning the search for psychodynamic factors at work within texts:

> Even when a story shows no concern for "psychological" issues [as biblical stories do not], the . . . [psychological] processes are still operating. In fact, as Jung remarked about modern literature, "in general, it is the non-psychological novel [in contrast to the psychological novel] that offers the richest opportunities. . . . [S]uch a tale is constructed against a background of unspoken psychological assumptions, and the more unconscious the author is of them, the more this background reveals itself.[25]

The second type of research on the psychodynamics of biblical texts focuses on the dynamic elements in the "deep structures" of the mind that produces narratives. This approach was suggested by the turn-of-the-century structuralist critic Ferdinand de Saussure, succeeded by A. J. Greimas, Rolande Barthes, Vladimir Propp, Claude Lévi-Strauss, and in the United States, Daniel Patte. Its line of inquiry turns from observing patterns of psychological behavior acted out in the relationships within biblical scenarios, to patterns of relationship among the structural components with which the mind constructs narratives—what Saussure called its "deep structures."

The Bible and Culture Collective, which co-authored *The Postmodern Bible*, defines Structuralism as "a general theory of the intelligibility of the products of mind based on the view that what makes things intelligible is their perceived relatedness, rather than their qualities as separate items." This suggests that the mind "thinks" in terms of "perceived relatedness" and that it has a proclivity for speaking, writing, and narrating in binary opposites. Elijah pits fire against water; the Fourth Gospel pairs life and death, truth and falsehood, light and darkness, the upper and the lower. Lévi-Strauss suggests that dealing with the world in this way is an innate human tendency. He proposes that sets of opposites (for example, mortal/immortal, male/female, parent/child) are the building blocks of myth in its attempt to make the world comprehensible, if not tolerable and controllable. It was Lévi-Strauss's conviction that the rules governing myths—and language itself—merge from such identical unconscious structures.[26] Why the mind behaves this way is a matter of psychological inquiry, and research on the question would seem to offer insight into why the biblical authors construct stories the way they do and why these stories seem so expert at capturing the human imagination.

A third type of research follows the lines of narrative criticism, inquiring into the psychodynamic relationship between the "implied" writer, narrator, narratee, and reader. Bracketing questions of historical background, authorial intent, or sources, the narrative critic looks at "the closed universe of the story-world" of the text, with special interest in the "implied author" (the authorial presence projected by the text), the "narrator" (the speaking voice in the narrative), the "narratee" (the person or group directly addressed in the narrative), and the "implied reader" (the person projected by the text as its ideal reader). Among the few who have included psychological considerations in their analysis of these narrative "personalities" is Norman Petersen, who analyzes the narrator's role in Mark's Gospel. Much work remains to be done in examining the psychodynamic relationship between these fictive "personalities" as elements in a standard pattern of composition to which the human psyche resorts in constructing a narrative.[27]

The fourth research area—even more daunting than the previous one—involves a consideration of what the biblical text tells us about the unconscious as well as conscious factors at work in its authors. We shall see in the next section that such factors are rarely visible to us at this distance from the ancient text, though evidence of their presence occasionally surfaces. In any event, we can hardly deny that such factors exist, as is now recognized by the virtually universal application of Ricoeur's "hermeneutics of suspicion" by ideological, rhetorical, and feminist critics, who readily concede the presence of a complex of ulterior editorial motives, conscious and unconscious, informing the content and design of the text. Michael Willett Newheart is not far off the mark in observing that as "a reader attempts to solve his or her own complexes through reading," so "an author attempts to resolve complexes through writing a piece of literature."[28] Psychological biblical criticism can begin to ferret out these and other factors, adding psychological considerations to the earlier work of redaction criticism.

The Psychology of Biblical Personalities

Recent psychological-critical studies of biblical personalities have developed along two lines: analysis of literary depictions of biblical personalities (for example, the narrative descriptions of Adam, Eve, Abraham, Jacob, Job, and Judas), and analysis, based on hints in the text, of biblical personalities themselves (for example, Ezekiel and Paul).

The first of these, the psychological study of literary depictions of biblical personalities, offers a character analysis of the literary construct of a biblical figure, analyzing the psychic habits, strategies, and defenses implicit in the textual portrait, commenting on the conscious as well as unconscious factors and intentions built into the narrative. Examples are found in John Sanford's analyses of Jacob, Joseph, Moses, Adam and Eve, and Saul, "the tragic hero"; in Edward Edinger's studies of Abraham, Jacob, Moses, Joshua, Gideon, Samson, Ruth, Saul, David, Solomon, and other Old Testament prophets and kings; in André and Pierre-Emmanuel LaCocque's study of Jonah; in Andrew Kille's study of Jacob as a model of individuation; in Schuyler Brown's analysis of the beloved disciple; in the stream of literature on the figure of Jesus, as surveyed (and amplified) by John W. Miller in *Jesus at Thirty: A Psychological and Historical Portrait* (1997).[29] Other studies of biblical figures include Cain,[30] Samuel,[31] Isaiah,[32] Hosea,[33] Amos,[34] Judas,[35] and Pilate.[36]

The contribution of this literature is twofold: it adds a psychological dimension to the work of the new literary and narrative criticism by drawing attention to psychodynamic factors; and it provides psychological insight into the appeal of some of these figures as models and exemplars for Bible-reading communities. For example, both Freud and Jung found themselves drawn to Paul. For Freud, Paul was "a man with a gift for religion, in the truest sense. . . . Dark traces of the past lay in his soul ready to break through into the regions of consciousness." For Jung, Paul was a model of individuation, of special relevance to a fundamental concept in Jung's psychological theory:

> Always Paul's experience on the road to Damascus hovered before me, and I asked myself how his fate would have fallen out but for his vision. Yet this experience came upon him while he was blindly pursuing his own way. As a young man I drew the conclusion that you must obviously fulfill your destiny in order to get to the point where a *donum gratiae* might happen along. . . .

> From this you can easily see the origin of my psychology: only by going my
> own way, integrating my capacities headlong (like Paul), and thus creating a
> foundation for myself, could something be vouchsafed to me or built upon
> it.[37]

The second approach is psychoanalytic and focuses on the biblical personalities themselves, drawing on autobiographical traces found in their writing. Of course, a psychoanalysis of biblical figures in the strictest sense is the-
oretically ruled out, given the absence of the analysand. And though the
defects of "bad psychoanalysis" have been enumerated by Albert Schweitzer
(as noted in chapter 3), a number of recent studies have suggested that psychoanalytic observations in the hands of seasoned analysts can provide persuasively meaningful and compelling insight into the psychodynamic factors
at work in author and text. Among these are David Halperin's work on Ezekiel,
and the psychological commentary of Richard Rubenstein and Robin Scroggs
on the apostle Paul.[38]

In his classic *Understanding the Old Testament*, Bernhard Anderson comments that "Ezekiel *himself* was an unusual person whose psychic peculiarities
make a fascinating psychological study." Halperin fleshed out Anderson's intuition with his *Seeking Ezekiel, Text and Psychology* (1993). Taking as his point
of departure a reexamination of a 1946 article on "Ezekiel's Abnormal Personality" by Edwin C. Broome, Halperin offered an imposing psychological
analysis of Ezekiel, based on four passages, 8:7–12; 16; 23; 24:15–27. Armed
with data from the text, Halperin takes the daring psychoanalytic step of tracing the source of Ezekiel's violent and sexually abusive imagery to the
prophet's childhood experience.

Critics have faulted Halperin for attempting such an analysis, arguing
that "it is never completely safe to guess at the 'psychic significance' of a
piece of literature to the author of the work, even that of a candid living
author." Others have felt that although Halperin may have overdrawn his
conclusions, he is correct in seeing that the text of Ezekiel, especially in
chapter 16, "cries out most loudly for an analysis along psychological
lines."[39] Halperin is certainly correct in concluding that Ezekiel's skewed
perspective on the feminine and his willingness to advance an imaginative
depiction of God as one who violates his surrogate daughter, "Jerusalem,"
tell us something about his inner life and most likely about the personal
biography that gave rise to it. Though Halperin may not be able to prove his
theory concerning Ezekiel's personal history, he has succeeded in illuminat-
ing a troubling and probably unconscious drama in the mind that stands
behind the document.

Among New Testament authors, Paul has been the most frequent subject
of psychological analysis, and one of the most explicitly psychoanalytic stud-

ies of the Pauline "autobiography" is Richard Rubenstein's *My Brother Paul* (1972), written from a Freudian perspective.[40] Rubenstein tells us that, beginning in his youth as a student preparing for the rabbinate, he was attracted to the writings of Paul, particularly the Epistle to the Romans, and specifically chapter 7 in which Paul describes the conflict he experienced between the demands of the Law and the "other" laws operative within him. In Paul, Rubenstein found an enlightening parallel to his own experience, dominated by scrupulous observance of the Law, driven by fear of death at the hands of a judging God, and marked with an unconscious quest for omnipotence. For Paul, the resolution of the conflict came through Christ; for Rubenstein it came through "psychoanalytic experience." But the outcomes, from Rubenstein's perspective, were the same, namely the discovery that one must dare to trust one's own experience over against the monolithic and repressive authority of tradition. What Rubenstein contributes to contemporary biblical scholarship is the thesis (notwithstanding Krister Stendahl) that at the heart of Paul's life and letters was an experience of personal despair and transformation in which conscious and unconscious factors played a role, and that to understand Paul it is necessary to get a bead on the psychodynamics of that experience.

Rubenstein's second contribution is the suggestion that Paul was a master symbolist who intuitively selected images such as baptism, the eucharist, and the Last Adam, to take us beyond the normal and ordinary to "hints of the deeper and true meaning of the human world." With these symbols Paul succeeded, consciously or unconsciously, in tapping primordial desires and needs typical of the human condition: the longing for rebirth (baptism), the desire to devour and ingest the holy (eucharist), and the aspiration to identify with a transcendent, primordial humanity (the Last Adam). Declining to go as far as assigning psychoanalytic skills to Paul, Rubenstein instead prefers Gershom Scholem's description of Paul as a "revolutionary Jewish mystic" whose work anticipates the world of twentieth-century psychoanalysis:

> Almost two thousand years before the depth psychology that his religious imagination helped to make possible, Paul of Tarsus gave expression to mankind's yearning for a new and flawless beginning that could finally end the cycle of anxiety, repression, desire and craving—the inevitable concomitants of the human pilgrimage.[41]

Another psychoanalytic study of Paul, also in the Freudian tradition, is Robin Scroggs's *Paul for a New Day* (1977), and its interpretive sequel, "The Heuristic Value of a Psychoanalytic Model in the Interpretation of Pauline Theology" (1978). Whereas Rubenstein interpreted Paul from the standpoint of personal experience, Scroggs used the "later Freud as interpreted by Norman

O. Brown and Herbert Marcuse" as a heuristic model to "plumb the depth of the apostle's thinking" and to unveil the living realities to which "Paul's mythological world" points. Scroggs writes out of the conviction that Paul's vision of civilization and the vision of psychoanalysis share "the same deep insights into human reality and dynamic" and the same "sense of the dynamic of salvation . . . despite the apparent enormity separating the language systems." The society and civilization in which Brown and Marcuse find modern humanity caught is coterminous with the world Paul describes. Both worlds are characterized by a cultural system governed by the performance principle, preoccupied with personal status (the importance principle), marked by a repressive super-ego of law that demands unflinching obedience, and consequently troubled by hostility and aggression. The way out involves a "new spirit" and a cultural transformation. Achieving this involves abolishing the "performance principle" and "importance principle," advocating a "life of unrepression that mirrors a person's original possibility . . . in God's creation intent," acting out of eros (love, joy, peace, patience, kindness, goodness, and so forth) rather than possession and domination, maintaining relationships marked by forgiveness rather than guilt, emphasizing grace rather than "law-demand"—in general, establishing a society driven by a new spirit in which law, repression, death, and sin are not the bottom line.[42]

The contribution of approaching Paul through this psychoanalytic model is threefold. First, it not only provides psychoanalytic insight into Paul's perception of the world, it also hints of what he experienced to get there, enabling us to enrich Pauline biography. Second, it has hermeneutical significance because it gives us "a little better grasp of how . . . embedded in the Christian symbol structure is a depth dynamic of human transformation out of a performance-principle world into the new community of grace," and this dynamic is applicable to human societies extending far beyond Paul's world. Third, it proposes consideration of the thesis that "divine transformative acts can be described in psychoanalytic terms as well as theological ones."[43]

The Psychology of Biblical Religious Experience

As early as 1950, F. C. Grant saw the need for "the student of the New Testament . . . [to] understand religious psychology, especially the various types of religious experience to be met within the Jewish and Hellenistic world of the first two centuries."[44] In mentioning "religious experience" Grant may have had in mind William James's classic, *The Varieties of Religious Experience*, which provided a model of psychological insight (and empathy) into the phenomenology of religious experience, ranging from sickness of soul to saintliness. One of the tasks of psychological biblical criticism is to follow James's lead in documenting, describing, and providing psychological insight into religious experience, ritual, and cultic practice in the Bible.

The psychological study of the phenomenology of biblical religion involves research in three major areas.[45] The first is *conventional (as opposed to paranormal) religious experience*. This includes prophetic inspiration, "enthusiasm," and ecstasy; prophetic and apocalyptic visions, photisms and auditions;[46] the phenomenon of glossolalia; biblical dreams and biblical dream interpretation; conversion and the religious life. The latter encompasses the processes and experiences of repentance,[47] sin and forgiveness,[48] grace and sanctification,[49] faith,[50] temptation,[51] anger,[52] guilt,[53] grief,[54] religious psychopathology, the experience of evil,[55] messianic and millennial thinking,[56] and the use of theological language.[57]

The second is the psychology of *religious practice*. This includes cultic rituals (circumcision, baptism, eucharist,[58] foot washing, and sacrificial rites and atonement[59]), religious objects and holidays (the menorah,[60] passover,[61] sabbath), prayer, and cultic law. A third area is *paranormal experience*. This includes demon possession and exorcism, the experience of angels,[62] miracle stories and faith healing,[63] and parapsychological experiences (telepathy, clairvoyance, telekinesis, and out-of-body experience).[64]

For our present discussion we will focus on six of these topics, sampling current research on each: Hebrew prophecy, glossolalia, dreams and dream interpretation, conversion, initiatory rituals (circumcision and baptism), and demon possession and exorcism.

Hebrew prophecy — with its subthemes of revelation, inspiration, spiritual possession, and religious ecstasy — has sustained more psychological-biblical-critical research in the twentieth century than any other biblical topic. Three approaches stand out. The first, undertaken by H. Wheeler Robinson between 1911 and 1946, aimed at clarifying prophecy within the framework of Hebrew psychology. Though Robinson admits that "their psychology no more satisfies us to-day than does their mythological account of creation or their moralistic way of writing history," he makes a significant contribution to the study of biblical psychology with his careful differentiation between the biblical and modern view of "the constitution of human personality."[65] The second approach was taken by Martin J. Buss in his 1980 article, "The Social Psychology of Prophecy," where he focuses on the social psychological issues of "role" and "selfhood," and invites further research on such topics as the psychology of "communication," the cognitive structure of groups and individuals, and "the origin and dynamics of a sense of justice."[66] The third approach analyzed prophetic phenomena through a variety of contemporary psychological models. Examples are J. W. Povah's study of Hebrew prophecy from the perspective of the "new psychology"(1925); Boyce Bennett's analysis of prophetic "vision and audition" in light of recent brain research and EEG studies of altered states of consciousness (1978); Dan Merkur's Freudian analysis of prophetic initiation and the practices of apocalyptic visionaries (1985, 1988, 1989); and R. P. Carroll's work on prophecy and dissonance theory (1977, 1980).

Glossolalia has been another subject of extensive psycho-critical research. In the 1980s two major studies appeared: H. Newton Malony and A. A. Lovekin's *Glossolalia: Behavioral Science Perspectives on Speaking in Tongues* (1985) and Gerd Theissen's *Psychological Aspects of Pauline Theology* (1987). The former is the most comprehensive psychological study of the phenomenon to date. Though focused on tongues-speaking today, it also provides rich case studies and a spectrum of psychological analyses (from William James to ego psychology) that cast light on the phenomenon as we meet it in the Bible and classical antiquity. Theissen's work integrates contemporary psychological analysis with biblical exegesis. Opening with the caveat of Hermann Gunkel that glossolalia "is a matter of real psychological events, not of phrases or of superstitions,"[67] Theissen proceeds with a masterful survey of analogous phenomena in the Greco-Roman world (Bacchanalian frenzy, Platonic inspiration, and the heavenly language of Apocalyptic). He then undertakes a psychological analysis from three perspectives: contemporary learning theory, psychodynamic theory (Freud, Jung), and cognitive psychology. From the standpoint of *learning theory*, glossolalia can be seen socio-dynamically as learned behavior, with the community serving as reinforcer and model. Its goal is to promote emotional cohesion among diverse social classes, and a clear marker of exclusion for outsiders. From the standpoint of *psychodynamic theory*, glossolalia can be seen as the eruption of unconscious repressed contents, manifested in a behavioral pattern that regresses to the childhood experience of learning speech. Paul's comment, "When I was a child, I spoke as a child" (1 Cor. 13:11), alludes to this. From the standpoint of *cognitive psychology*, glossolalia can be seen as a form of speech without specific semantic content, but which nevertheless succeeds in communicating through cryptosemantic elements (for example, "Abba," "maranatha"), its secondary linguistic forms—what Paul calls "various kinds of tongues" (1 Cor. 12:11)—as well as non-verbal cues such as posture and emotional output, and "situative factors" (*where* a person speaks). The effect of such speech, Theissen said, is a "cognitive restructuring of social perception," the kind of incorporation and exclusiveness that Paul seeks explicitly to expose.[68]

Dreams, dreaming, and dream interpretation are religious experiences that psychological biblical critics are finding increasingly interesting. As noted earlier, dream research in the modern era was initiated by Freud, but Jung provided a theoretical view of dreams that was most compatible with biblical perspective. He saw the dream not simply as a covert expression of repressed personal contents, but, above all, as an expression of a depth dimension (collective unconscious), echoing the biblical view of dreams as having a transcendent function, "sent by God" (Job 33: 14–18). Though contemporary dream theory categorically rules out dream analysis without the dreamer present, it nevertheless believes that what is being learned about dreams today can contribute to the study of dreams in antiquity in three ways. First it can supply historical background on the understanding of dreams in history, as Morton Kelsey demonstrated in his book, *Dreams: The Dark Speech of the Spirit* (1968),[69] with its survey of dream theory in the Hebrew Bible, the Apocrypha, Philo, Greco-Roman literature,[70] and the early church. Second, it can apply its typology of dreams (recurrent dreams, "big dreams," initial dreams) to the classification of biblical dreams. Third, contemporary dream theory can offer comparative analysis and assessment of biblical scenarios of dream interpretation—for example, the well-known dream interpretation scenes in the Joseph saga (Gen. 37; 40; 41) and the narrative of Peter's dream (Acts 10:9–16)—in light of dream interpretation protocol today. During the second half of the twentieth century, dream research has enabled biblical criticism to reclaim the substantial lode of dream material in the Bible as legitimate subject matter for critical research and as a contribution to the history of dream research.

Conversion has been a major focus in psychological research on biblical religious experience for more than a century. In 1861, Franz Delitzsch included a major section on "The Conscious and Unconscious Side of the Work of Grace" in the second edition of *A System of Biblical Psychology*. In 1912, M. Scott Fletcher included two sections on conversion in *The Psychology of the New Testament*. One was on "The Conversion of Paul," taking up Pfleiderer's suggestion that psychological factors relating to Paul's earlier life as a persecutor of Christians played a role. The second was on "Spiritual Conditions of Entrance to the New Life." More recent studies on the conversion experience of Paul appear in Alan F. Segal's, "Paul's Conversion: Psychological Study" and John Gager's "Some Notes on Paul's Conversion." Gager discusses "post-conversion dissonance" and other instinctual, mechanical psychological patterns associated with conversion. The premier study on the theme is Cedric Johnson and H. Newton Malony's 1982 volume *Christian Conversion: Biblical and Psychological Perspectives*.

Robin Scroggs captured the consensus of psychological-critical opinion regarding conversion when he observed that "salvation means changes, changes in how we think, in how we feel, in how we act. And that means, or so it seems to me, that psychological intuitions and, perhaps, even explicitly psychological models and terminology can give us insight into what these changes are."[71] Even so, the range of terminology for the conversion event is broad, including the concepts (experiences) of reconciliation, sanctification, liberation, transformation, justification, new being, rebirth, and repentance. The task of psychological biblical criticism is to attempt clarifying the differences conceptually in terms of human experience.

Biblical *initiatory rituals of circumcision and baptism* have also commanded the interest of psychological biblical critics. For Theodor Reik, circumcision resembles archaic puberty rites of initiation, still practiced today. In the biblical context he suggests circumcision is a substitute or mitigated form of the sacrifice of the first born, symbolizing and enacting the father's renunciation of infanticidal impulses and adverting instead to a rite that reconciles fathers and sons in perpetuity. Ilona Rashkow, in *The Phallacy of Genesis: A Feminist-Psychoanalytic Approach* (1993), adds other considerations, asking why the penis is chosen as the "token" to seal the covenant. Why not a "more obvious part of the body, . . . e.g. piercing the ear or nose"? The obvious answer for Rashkow is that "the male organ is linked with power," so that sexual symbolism is at work, underlining the primacy of male procreativity in relation to the deity. The act of circumcision, however, is threat as well as promise, a symbolic reminder that those who do not "cut" the covenant will be "cut off" (Gen. 17:14). Thus, circumcision exalts maleness but also establishes "the vulnerability of Abraham's organ and Abraham's dependence upon God and fertility."[72]

Patrick Henry discussed baptism in a chapter on the psychology of "water, bread, and wine symbolism" in his 1979 volume, *New Directions in New Testament Study*. Drawing on the insights of Richard Rubenstein and Mircea Eliade, Henry highlights the initiatory function of baptism as native to religious experience, "coexistent with any new revelation of spiritual life." Central to the ritual is water symbolism. He cites Rubenstein's observation of Paul's ingenious ability "to bring to the surface of powerful symbolic expression [in this case, water] the hidden dynamics of the human unconscious," and the reason for this ability: "he [Paul] was able to give objectified expression to his own unconscious mental processes." From Eliade, Henry derives the symbolic value of immersion as "a return to the pre-formal, a total regeneration, a new birth, for immersion means a dissolution of forms, a reintegration into the formlessness of pre-existence; and emerging from the water is a repetition of the act of creation in which form was first expressed."[73]

The dual phenomenon of *demon possession and exorcism* is another aspect of religious experience that has been the subject of substantial psychological-critical research. In 1912, M. Scott Fletcher pointed to the line of analysis that most psychological studies would take:

Of special importance psychologically are the cases of demonic possession. . . . Victims of demonic possession were most probably sufferers from some physical or psychical disorders who yet were amenable to treatment which seemed to cast out some sub-personal agency that subjugated the personality of the patient. Now, modern psychology recognizes the existence of abnormal mutations of self, such as alterations of the memory, split personality, and even mediumship. . . . The personality may be so disintegrated that the self seems to be replaced by one or more other selves. These abnormal psychic states have been called Diseases of Personality.[74]

Subsequent works bear out Fletcher's insight. They include Carroll Wise's 1956 classic, *Psychiatry and the Bible*, Vernon McCasland's 1951 book, *By the Finger of God: Demon Possessions and Exorcism in Early Christianity in Light of Modern Views of Mental Illness*, and Paul Bach's 1979 article, "Demon Possession and Psychopathology: A Theological Relationship." All agree that the so-called demon-possessed are suffering from multiple personality disorder or, as Wise put it, are "persons in whom destructive energies have overcome creative energies, whose life and energies are not organized and directed toward satisfying goals."[75]

Stevan Davies in his 1995 *Jesus the Healer*, agrees that demon possession and multiple personality disorder "represent parallel dissociative disorders with similar etiologies." But he advances a portrait of Jesus as not just a therapist, but a "spirit-possessed leader" whose "treatment" of the possessed corresponds more closely to the phenomenology of the gospel description than is sometimes supposed. Thus he corroborates Freud's comment that medieval interpretations of hysterical phenomena as possession by a demon seemed closer to the truth than medical theories of his time.[76]

From the six topics just discussed, it seems likely that research opportunities in the psychology of religious experience in the Bible are unlimited. The goal of such research, to repeat the words of Oskar Pfister, is to "make redemption, rebirth, and sanctification understandable to a modern person," that is, to trace theological, cultic, and religious forms to their roots in experienced reality. G. Stanley Hall, founder of the American Psychological Association, anticipated the contributions of psychology to religious understanding. His 1904 editorial in the first issue of the new *American Journal of Religious Psychology and Education* offers a litany of topics:

We cannot here characterize or perhaps even name all the old problems that are beginning to glow with a new light. . . . Sacrifice, poverty, obedience, chastity, asceticism, renunciation and its motives and forms, creeds, dogma and doctrine, worship including sacraments, rites, ritual and ceremonies, priests and saints, the psycho-pedagogic aspect of miracles, especially those of

healing, as related to mental states, the nature, value and limitations of personality, the feminine aspects and functions of religion and Mariolatry, the
Sabbath as a philosophical institution and the uses of rest from fatigue of
body and soul, the relation of religion to art and aesthetics, the place and
form of symbols, vows and oaths, the psychology of sects, the relations of religious feeling and belief to morals and conduct: —all these and many more
topics have anthropological sides which theology has too often failed adequately to recognize which are quite distinct from, and to some extent, independent of, historical criticism or textual exegesis.[77]

The Psychology of Biblical Ethics

Biblical ethics is a virtually untapped field for psychological research. In his
foreword to Erich Neumann's *Depth Psychology and a New Ethic* (1948), Jung
cited the need "to formulate the ethical problem anew" from a psychological
perspective, in view of the "tremendous revolution of values that has been
brought about by the discovery of the unconscious" and by the recognition of
the "psychological foundation" out of which all ethical systems come. But neither in his time nor since has extensive psychological commentary developed,
either on ethics in general, or on biblical ethics.[78]

In the early part of the nineteenth century, Freud made forays into the
field of biblical ethics with his observations on the unconscious origins and
repressive function of tribal laws and taboos, and his theories concerning the
repressive super-ego function of cultural and religious norms that emerge with
the development of civilization. In 1983, Gerd Theissen addressed the psychological ethical issues in Romans 7—one of the few passages on which psychological commentary has regularly been made—citing the evaluations of
Pfister (1920) and Fischer (1974), to the effect that the pre-Christian Paul's
"attachment to the law" and "his compulsive ritual" constituted a defense
against the psychic tensions within him between law and libido. They also
constituted a defense against the Christians, who both attracted him by their
daring freedom from the law, and repulsed him by their repudiation of the very
law that was the foundation of his personality. In effect, the Christian freedom
from the law activated "mechanisms of suppression." As Fischer put it:

> Paul must not admit to himself that in the depths of his being he envies the
> Christian for the freedom from the law; he therefore needs to respond to the
> secret sympathy for Christians with an even stronger hatred for them.

Theissen adds an original and compelling proposal to this psychodynamic
analysis of Romans 7 and Phil. 3:4–6, namely, that "Phil. 3:4–6 reflects the consciousness of the pre-Christian Paul [confident with his righteous observance of

the law], while Romans 7 depicts a conflict [also of the pre-Christian Paul] that was unconscious at the time, one of which Paul became conscious only later."[79]

Additional examples of psychological commentary on biblical ethics involve the analysis of three biblical ethical systems: a deontological or nomistic ethic, an aretaic ethic, and an ethic of consciousness.

A *deonotological or nomistic ethic*—that is, an ethic of principle and law, often perceived as "laid down" from above—can be perceived from two psychological perspectives. From a Freudian perspective, it is seen as compulsive obsessive behavior, driven by fear of what will happen if the code is violated. Paul Ricoeur labels this type of ethic "theistic" because it is perceived as sanctioned by an omnipotent and morally absolutistic God, an image Ricoeur regards as a projection inspired by the disappointed realization of human weakness. Jung describes it as the "old ethic [that] unconsciously imitates, or actually prefers, the procedure of an absolute monarchy or a tyrannical one-party system."[80]

Another perspective on a deontological ethic is offered by archetypal psychology, which sees the Law as transcendentally desirable: "more to be desired than . . . much fine gold; sweeter also than honey" (Ps. 19:10). From this perspective "the Law" is an archetypal image, rooted in the collective unconscious of humanity, surfacing to consciousness for the health and benefit of the species. Thus, to be enthralled by the Law, is to share in a beneficent and universal, psychologically necessary human (and divine) longing.

An *aretaic ethic* is based on excellence or character. It invites incorporating into oneself the qualities of "excellent" persons (for example, Abraham's faith, Ezekiel's prophetic courage, Jesus' love, Dorcas's magnanimity) or values (the omni-competence of the "good wife" of Proverbs 31, the enjoinder in Philippians 4:8–9 to ponder and carry out "whatever is true, . . . honorable, . . . just" and so forth). From the standpoint of archetypal psychology, aretaic ethics encourages openness to "transcendent" models of behavior or being that fortuitously address consciousness along life's way, providing guideposts for the journey. From the standpoint of an "individuational psychology," however, aretaic ethics can foster an "ethic of imitation," born of a sense of lack of self and even of a fear of becoming oneself. Jung comments on the shadow side of an imitation ethic in a letter to a friend:

> [Christ] took himself with exemplary seriousness and lived his life . . . regardless of human convention and in opposition to his own lawful tradition, as the worst heretic. . . . But we? We imitate Christ and hope he will deliver us from our own fate. . . . Christ and his cross deliver us from our conflict, which we simply leave alone, . . . mindful only of the imitatio Christi but not of our own reality which is laid upon us. . . . Instead of bearing ourselves, i.e. our own cross, ourselves, we load Christ with our unresolved conflict. . . . Whoever imitates

Christ and has the cheek to want to take Christ's cross on himself when he
can't even carry his own has in my view not yet learnt the ABC of the Christian
message.[81]

A third ethical system—recommended but never developed by Jung
though he found it sanctioned in the New Testament tradition—is *an ethic of
consciousness*. He liked to cite its centerpiece, a variant reading of Luke 6:4
from the fifth-century Codex Bezae: "Man, if indeed thou knowest what thou
doest, thou art blessed; but if thou knowest not, thou art cursed, and a transgressor of the law." Jung notes: "Here the moral criterion is *consciousness*, and
not law or convention."[82]

An ethic of consciousness appreciates the moral objectives and ideals of
the deontological ethic. But it also takes note of the unconscious and even
neurotic factors that can be at work in its conception, promulgation, and
enforcement. Jung, drawing from his clinical experience, hints at a number of
truths presuppositional for an ethic of consciousness: that most ethical situations are fraught with moral ambiguity; that absolute "oughts" and "musts" are
frequently inapplicable and often unhelpful; that in many ethical dilemmas
one can do evil at the same time one does good (for example, a physician con-
cealing the truth from a patient about the patient's condition); that "one can
hardly think of a single rule that would not have to be reversed under certain
conditions"; "that ethical problems are always intensely individual"; that "the
collective rules of conduct offer at most provisional solutions, but never lead
to those crucial decisions which are the turning-points" in a person's life; and
finally, that lurking in every decision and every precept is the possibility of the
unconscious presence and interests of the shadow side of the self.[83]

The goal of an ethic of consciousness is to increase conscious appreciation not only of the precepts of a deontological ethic but also of the ambiguities in life and of the dark motives that can arise from the unconscious,
then, having done that, to—in Luther's words—"sin bravely" (*pecca for-
titer*). In such a decision the ego, with its pretensions, self-interest, and self-
deception, is displaced by the larger Self: a broader sense of moral enmesh-
ment in the totality of things, as ambiguous and problematic as they and the
ego are.

Jung finds an example of an ethic of consciousness particularly in Paul. For
Jung, Paul is aware of his own intellectual and moral limitations (1 Cor. 13:
8–12), has given up the pretension of perfection (Phil. 3:12), has experienced
another face of the law in its ability to inspire perversity and its inability to work
internal transformation and a desire for the good (Romans 7). In Paul, Jung further finds someone who is willing to live with the ambiguity that although "all
things are lawful" they are not always helpful (1 Cor. 10:23), whose writings do
not contain a single law code, who tenders conflicting bits of moral advice to

different constituencies (1 Cor. 7:1–3; 8:7–10), who relies for moral guidance on the exemplary teaching of Christ (1 Cor. 7:12) but also demonstrates willingness to risk his own moral judgment (1 Cor. 7:4). Above all, Jung sees Paul as attesting to having had his "ego" displaced by a new "self" of the spirit and mind of Christ (Gal. 2:20; 1 Cor. 2:16; 2 Cor. 5:17). Jung comments:

> Mankind is . . . still in a state of childhood—a stage that cannot be skipped. The vast majority needs authority, guidance, law. This fact cannot be overlooked. The Pauline overcoming of the law falls only to the man who knows how to put his soul in the place of conscience. Very few are capable of this. . . . And these few tread this path only from inner necessity, not to say suffering, for it is sharp as the edge of a razor."[84]

The aim of this and other psychological-critical approaches to biblical ethics is to help disclose how each of the conscious and unconscious habits, nature, and processes of the psyche that may be operative in biblical ethical systems and precepts can contribute to, or detract from, psychic wholeness.

Biblical Psychology

A footnote to "Anthropological Concepts of Paul" in Rudolf Bultmann's 1951 *Theology of the New Testament* lists four works on biblical psychology: *A System of Biblical Psychology* by Franz Delitzsch (1867), "Hebrew Psychology in Relation to Pauline Anthropology" by H. Wheeler Robinson (1926), *The Psychology of the New Testament* by M. Scott Fletcher (1912), and "The Psychology of Paul" by A. B. D. Alexander (1910). In this unexpected move by a scholar known for his antipathy to psychology, Bultmann seemed willing to acknowledge that biblical psychology constitutes a legitimate subcategory of biblical anthropology and represents a tradition tracing back to Tertullian, Augustine, Aquinas, and Melanchton, flowering by the end of the twentieth century in the work of Delitzsch. This is also true of works Bultmann does not mention: *The Soul: An Enquiry into Scripture Psychology* by George Bush (1845), "Olshausen's New Testament Psychology" by Hermann Olshausen (1859), *Biblical Psychology* by Jonathan Langstaff Forster (1873), *The Bible Doctrine of Man, or, The Anthropology and Psychology of Scripture* by John Laidlaw (1879), "Psychology of the Bible" by John Fletcher Hurst (1896), and *Biblical Psychology: A Series of Preliminary Studies* by Oswald Chambers (1900).

With few exceptions, the work done in biblical psychology since Bultmann did not appear until the 1970s. A partial list would include two works on the biblical concept of anger by Pedersen (1974) and Cerling (1974); John Carter's "Maturity, Psychological and Biblical" (1974); a dissertation by P. H.

Benson on "New Testament Concepts for a Sociopsychological Model of Personality Development" (1979); Joel Weinberg's "Der Mensch im Weltbild des Chronisten: seine Psyche" (1983); Allen Groff's "Biblical Psychology of Christian Experience"(1983); David Powlinson's "Which Presuppositions: Secular Psychology and the Categories of Biblical Thought" (1984); David Clark's "Interpreting the Biblical Words for the Self" (1990); and Michael J. Boivin's "The Hebraic Model of the Person: Toward a Unified Psychological Science among Christian Helping Professionals" (1991). As noted earlier, research in the field is aided by the appearance of two American journals, *The Journal of Psychology and Theology* (1973) and *Journal of Psychology and Christianity* (1982), with articles representing diverse psychological approaches on a broad spectrum of issues in the interdisciplinary field of psychology and biblical studies.

What is biblical psychology and what role does it play within the field of psychological-biblical-critical research? Traditionally the phrase refers to the study of the Bible's perspective on the nature, origin, powers, health, and destiny of the human psyche in its individual and corporate manifestations. But it can also be used in a secondary sense to refer to any theological or psychological system rooted in the Bible and adopting the Bible's psychological perspective.[85] The present work uses the phrase in its traditional sense, but allows for the possibility of theological or psychological stances that believe the "psychology" of the Bible has a depth and breadth of insight which can contribute meaningfully to contemporary psychological perspective.

Though the phrase *biblical psychology* is singular, it clearly refers to multiple biblical psychologies. This was demonstrated, for example, in specialized studies of the psychology of Paul, or the Chronicler. One of the tasks for the future is to refine those differences even further by developing an expanding collection of studies that focus on the discrete psychological perspectives of the various biblical authors.

The goal of research in biblical psychology can be defined in terms of an agenda that is descriptive, prescriptive, and comparative. The *descriptive agenda* for biblical psychology is virtually spelled out in the chapter headings of the "biblical psychologies" written to date—for example, those of Delitzsch, Fletcher, and Robinson. But these need refinement in terms of new psychological theories that have emerged since the early twentieth century and the new questions and perceptions of the self that they introduce. This requires identification, description, and analysis of the Bible's perspective on a wide range of aspects of the psyche in its individual and social manifestations. These include, for example, the constituent elements of the self (soul, heart, mind, body, flesh, spirit, "bowels"), psychic functions (intelligence, reason, free will, desire, conscience, imagination, dreaming), the substance of the "inner" and "outer" self of which the Bible speaks, biblical language that suggests recognition of an unconscious dimension of the self,[86] the biblical understanding of human drives and emotions in the life of the psyche (affect, appetite, libido, love, hate, anger, ecstasy, fear, anxiety, terror, grief, joy, sorrow), and biblical perceptions on the psychology of behavior (work, play, sexuality, socialization, war, crime, and punishment). In summary, the descriptive agenda of biblical psychology is to identify, catalogue, and analyze the complex of entities, functions, faculties, and behavioral patterns—along with the typical predicaments, problems, and possibilities—that the Bible understands as constitutive of the life of the human psyche, both individually and collectively.

The *prescriptive agenda* for biblical psychological research turns to another fundamental feature of the Bible's interest in the human psyche: its concern with what a human psyche/soul is, and perhaps more fundamentally, with what a human psyche/soul can be. Accordingly, this research will focus on what the Bible teaches about the care, nourishment, proper development, and goal of the human psyche. It will elaborate on the Bible's views of health and sickness, physically, morally, and spiritually (sin, suffering, death, demonic possession, fallenness, salvation, grace, rebirth, transformation, reconciliation); on its perceptions and models of human development (concepts of maturity and immaturity, the *psychikos* vs. the *pneumatikos*, the laws governing successful human behavior); and the role of spirituality in the life of the soul (prayer, piety, God-consciousness, obedience to the law, faith, hope, love, vice and virtue, and images of the holy framed by the psyche).

The data for constructing such a biblical psychology are in two sources. The most obvious is the catalogue of biblical passages that speak explicitly of the nature, habits, and destiny of the human soul. A second source, however, would be biblical passages in which the perspective on the nature and habits of the soul is implicit, but not consciously explicated. A negative example would be the "texts of terror" noted by Phyllis Trible, stories of awesome violence that seem to leave the biblical mind and the textual authors unfazed. Such stories bear witness to enigmatic, even neurotic, obsessively destructive, or psychotic qualities that are so operant in the biblical conception of "normalcy," they are not explicitly commented on or acknowledged.[87] A positive example would be the apocalyptic visions of the survivors of the "great tribulation" in Revelation, the Gospel parable images of the good Samaritan, the prodigal, and the publican, the portrait of the "poor in spirit" in the Beatitudes, the legends of the patriarchs as "example stories," and the soliloquies of Jeremiah. All these bear witness implicitly to a vision of the nature, mettle, and developmental potential of the human soul.

The *comparative agenda* for biblical psychological research turns attention to a critical comparison of the biblical perspective on the self and that of contemporary psychology. The task can be framed as two questions: "What has the Bible to learn from psychology?" and "What has psychology to learn from the Bible?" Though the apparent incongruity between biblical and psychological scholarship has always seemed sufficient to preclude meaningful exchange, there are signs, as noted in chapter 3, of a thaw in the relationship and of the possibility of mutual learning taking place.[88] With respect to the question, "What has the Bible to learn from psychology?" it is evident from the growing corpus of work in the field of psychological biblical criticism that, despite the pronouncement of psychoanalyst-theologian Dominique Stein that "exegesis has nothing to expect from psychoanalysis," exegesis has had something to learn from psychology. We have outlined much of this "learning" above. William Meissner's observation on the contribution of psychological insight to the study of religion characterizes its parallel contribution to biblical studies. He notes that psychology helps us see "the religious belief system and its tradition" in "increasingly realistic terms," affirming "their inherent tensions and ambiguities," and accepting "the relativity, partiality, and particularity of the beliefs, symbols, rituals and ceremonials of the religious community."[89]

What does psychology stand to learn from the Bible? In his essay on "Biblical Psychology," theologian Emil Brunner comments on the relationship between two approaches to the soul—one scientific psychological; the other, biblical psychological. Concerning the first, he writes:

> Empirical psychology, which takes as its model the freedom from prejudice of the natural sciences, has without doubt brought to light a great store of important knowledge which we should be loath to do without. But we must from the beginning draw attention to the fact that this psychology, like every psychology, is based on a definite world-view as its axiomatic presupposition.

He identifies the worldview of scientific psychology as "naturalistic positivism," which "conceives of the soul and psychological realities as objects among objects," rather than as subjects that constitute the observer-self. He goes on to suggest that the biblical forms—story, legend, myth, parable, saga, psalm, proverb, letter, apocalypse—capture dimensions of the self not susceptible to scientific observation but quintessential to a full portrait of the human psyche/soul.[90]

A number of researchers in the field of biblical psychology have suggested specific dimensions of the soul that do not submit to rigorous scientific description, but that are identified and addressed in biblical literature as fundamental features of the self. Psychology would do well to reflect upon these qualities. In speaking of the contribution of biblical psychology to counseling, for example, J. Harold Ellens identifies eight insights from the Bible that are important for fully understanding "the living human document." He calls these: "the biblical theology of (a) human personhood, of (b) alienation, of (c) sin, of (d) discipline, of (e) grace, of the (f) wounded healer, of (g) mortality, and of (h) celebration."[91] Similar views have been expressed by Karl Menninger and D. Andrew Kille. Menninger has recommended re-appreciation of the concept of "sin" from a psychological perspective.[92] Kille has recommended probing the psychological value of the biblical notions of the fall, repentance, redemption and grace, and eschatological consciousness. He states that "each of these themes highlights an issue that might be used to critique aspects of modern psychology." The biblical notion of creation, for example, avoids both the apotheosization and the degradation of humans; the notion of the fall crystallizes the reality of the brokenness and incompleteness of life; repentance critiques psychological determinism and attests to the possibility of transformation; the notion of redemption and grace contravenes the theory of a directionless and purposeless universe.[93]

Contemporary psychological biblical critics have joined M. Scott Fletcher who, in 1912, identified the biblical concept of the "spirit"—with its attendant experiential categories of new creation, transformation, and rebirth—as a psycho-anthropological element meriting consideration in understanding the life and experience of the psyche.[94] In 1946, Brunner referred to the Spirit as the "theologian's stepchild," implying that the empirical positivism of the mid-nineteenth century had even affected theology.[95] Perhaps the most eloquent apologia for reclaiming a sense of "spirit" is voiced by Carl Jung:

> We moderns are faced with the necessity of rediscovering the life of the spirit; we must experience it anew for ourselves. It is the only way in which to break the spell that binds us to the cycle of biological events. . . . The wheel of history must not be turned back, and man's advance toward a spiritual life, which began with the primitive rites of initiation, must not be denied. . . . Scientific thought, being only one of the psyche's functions, can never exhaust all of its potentialities. The psychotherapist must not allow his vision to be colored by pathology; he must never allow himself to forget that the ailing mind is a human mind and that, for all its ailments, it unconsciously shares the whole psychic life of man. He must even be able to admit that the ego is sick for the very reason that it is cut off from the whole, and has lost its connection not only with mankind but with the spirit. . . . For thousands of years, rites of initiation have been teaching rebirth from the spirit; yet, strangely enough, man forgets again and again the meaning of divine procreation. Though this may be poor testimony to the strength of the spirit, the penalty for misunderstanding is neurotic decay, embitterment, atrophy, and sterility. It is easy enough to drive the spirit out of the door, but when we have done so the meal has lost its savor—the salt of the earth.[96]

Biblical psychology needs to be reclaimed as a legitimate and significant rubric within biblical scholarship. For readers of the Bible, it can shed new light on human self-understanding. For professional psychologists, it can engender a deeper and broader understanding of the nature, origin, habits, powers, possibilities, and purpose of the human psyche.

The above threefold agenda—descriptive, prescriptive, and comparative—represents the beginnings of what psychological criticism might contribute to biblical exegesis. The ultimate goal of such criticism, indeed of the entire apparatus of critical biblical scholarship, is, in the words of Carl Jung, "to create more and more consciousness." Psychological criticism can contribute to that goal by heightening awareness of the text as an expression of a psychic as well as historic process. In doing so, it will build on the promethean achievements of historical and literary criticism, and join the host of other critical disciplines that have emerged during the past two decades. As Gerd Theissen has observed with respect to New Testament scholarship:

> We do not yet grasp what historical forces brought forth and determined early Christianity. But beside and within this external history there is an inner history. . . . Anyone who thinks that this religion can be illumined historically and factually without psychological reflection is just as much in error as one who pretends that everything about this religion can be said in this fashion.[97]

6
The Hermeneutical Agenda

Between Text and Reader

The inspection of one's personal presuppositions involves both social and psychological elements. Such an inspection is necessary because interpreters should know and be conscious of the baggage that they bring to the task of biblical interpretation.

Daniel Harrington, S. J.[1]

But this teacher, Mr. Martin, was the first to give me a feeling for what words are. . . . Through him I started to sense that words not only convey something, but are something; that words have color, depth, texture of their own, and the power to evoke vastly more than they mean; that words can be used not merely to make things clear, . . . but to make things happen inside the one who reads them or hears them.

Frederick Buechner[2]

But divine inspiration necessarily comes through a human heart and a mortal mind, through personal prejudice and communal interpretation, through fear, dislike, and hate as well as through faith, hope, and charity.

John Dominic Crossan[3]

We turn now to "the world in front of the text," the world of interaction between text and reader, traditionally the area of hermeneutics. But we do so with the recognition that interpretation is not a one-way street: texts "interpret" readers as much as readers interpret texts. The effect of both text and reader on one another, far greater than earlier recognized, is the subject of this chapter.[4] Our discussion, accordingly, will focus on three aspects of the interpretive process from a psychological-critical perspective: the text and its effect on the reader; the effect of the reader and reading on the text; and the psychology of biblical effects (*Wirkungsgeschichte*). In all three discussions our goal is to review research done to date and to identify issues for future consideration.

Of course, critical reflection on the transaction between text and reader is not new. Our purpose is to build on the work already undertaken by Paul Ricoeur and Hans-Georg Gadamer, by the post-structuralist analyses of deconstructionist, ideological, rhetorical, and reader-response criticism, and by the new specialized fields of (among others) African-American, feminist, liberationist, womanist, Hispanic, and Asian critics, adding observations and questions from a psychological critical perspective.

The Text and Its Effect on the Reader in Psychological Perspective

The question of "how the text 'works,' . . . how it engages the reader in the production of meaning" has been explored in recent biblical scholarship by literary critics, structural analysts, narrative critics, and poetic analysts.[5] Approaching this question from a psychological perspective draws attention to two new aspects of the text: its psychic constitution, and its psychic function.

The Constitution of Texts in Psychological Perspective

It is a fundamental psychological assumption that any text is in part constituted, shaped, and informed by factors of which the author and the author's community are not consciously aware. The presence of such unconscious factors has long been noted by literary critics who maintained that a text often "means" more than either author or reader suspects. This insight is echoed in the 1993 report of the Pontifical Biblical Commission, "The Interpretation of the Bible in the Church," which notes that there are spiritual truths in the biblical text, "the fullest depths of which the authors themselves do not perceive." Ricoeur's ascription of the "surplus of meaning" in texts suggests a similar perception, as does deconstructionist theory in its contention that a text is a "place of intersection in a network of signification" so vast that both reader and writer have only an inkling of the full import of what they read or write.[6]

A recognition of unconscious factors at work in texts is implicit in Ricoeur's concept of a "hermeneutic of suspicion," grounded in the psychological insight that "the human mind can deceive itself in varieties of ways, often in the interest of individual or of social power." Ricoeur's hermeneutic aims at unconcealing the text's ulterior motives. It is modeled on three prototypes: Marx's suspicion that texts secretly ideologize the class status of the author, Nietzsche's suspicion that texts advance the interests of class power, and Freud's suspicion that texts manifest Oedipal conflicts in persons whose desires are repressed by cultural prohibitions.[7]

Identification of unconscious factors in the text is not new. Numerous schools of contemporary biblical criticism—ideological criticism, deconstructionism, the post-structuralist criticism of Michel Foucault, structuralist criticism, Jungian psychology, and theorists on the role of imagination in textual creation—all have uncovered such factors. Their work points to seven types of unconscious factors. The first three reflect a "hermeneutic of suspicion," aimed at disclosing unconscious specialized interests in the text; the last four refer to constructive unconscious structures that produce meaning in texts.

1. Ideologies operant in texts. Identified by ideological criticism, these ideologies can be racial, ethnic, sexist, social, or nationalistic. The goal of ideological criticism is to expose "the various ways the text's system of representation operates to instanciate [*sic*] and empower particular notions of truth—whether individual, corporate, or transcendental truth—and particular values and actions." For the ideological critic, the ideology "pre-exists" the text; it is to be found in "both what a text says and what it does not say"; no text is ideology-free and any part of a text, "plot, author, characters, narrator as well as reader," can be the carrier of that ideology. Of special interest to the psychological critic is the contention that "the ideology of the text defines, operates and constitutes that ideology in ways unpremeditated, so to speak by ideology itself." This suggests that ideology functions in a form not always recognized by the conscious mind. Accordingly, the goal of ideological criticism in psychological perspective is to ask not only on whose behalf a text is written, but in the service of what motives.[8]

2. Systems of exclusion and inclusion operant in texts. The deconstructionist literary approach of Jacques Derrida has been described as an interpretive method that "seeks out those points within a system where it disguises the fact of its incompleteness," that is, it leaves out what it regards as marginal or secondary, or at the unconscious level, what is denied or repressed.[9] What does it leave out or repress? For feminists it is women or the feminine; for Derrida it is apartheid or "deviant modes of thought"; for Foucault it is "the sick, the insane, criminals and sexual 'deviations.'" Deconstructionist theory offers a catalogue of the "exclusions" it finds typical of the value system inherent in the collective psyche of the Caucasian West, noting that in each pair, the first element is almost always "privileged," and the second marginalized:

transcendent-immanent, intelligible-sensible, spirit (mind, soul)-body, neces-sary-contingent, primary-secondary, simple-complex, nature-culture, male-female, white-black (brown, red, yellow), inside-outside, object-representation, history-fiction, conscious-unconscious, literal-metaphorical, content-form, text-interpretation, speech-writing, presence-absence, and so on.[10]

The result is a value system of "hierarchical violence rather than equal partnership" in which the second element is either excluded or radically devalued. Though this list of binary opposite values may be more a feature of the modern world than the biblical world, it suggests a topic for psychological critical exploration, testing for the presence of an analogous set of binary oppo-sites unconsciously at work in the text.[11]

3. The quest for power operant in texts. Post-structuralist Michel Foucault contends that "the will to truth and the will to power always work hand in glove. Power circulates everywhere within the social body," either as a con-scious goal or an unconscious ulterior motive. One of the goals of psychologi-cal criticism would be to join forces with ideological and Foucauldian analysis to lay bare "the complex nature of power relations that produce texts, construct the institutional contexts of texts and their reception, and affect readers of those texts in their particular social locations."[12] Examples of how psychologi-cal analysis might expose the ways power is sought and exercised in the bibli-cal text and its interpretation include the following: in social formation and social order (*parenesis*); in establishing boundaries of acceptance or rejection of certain members (Acts 15); in maintaining order (Pastoral Epistles); in defining acceptable behavior (biblical legal codes); in setting interpretive lim-its (Rev. 22:18); in assigning authority (2 Corinthians 10); and in advocating competing soteriologies (various evangelists and letter writers).[13]

4. The text as a place of intersection in a network of signification. This implies that a text is a vortex of meaning in which both author and reader are caught up, and of which they are only partially conscious. From such a per-spective, every "signified" subject of discourse in the text is, in turn, a signifier of another "signified" or deeper discourse beyond the literal text. Or as Fou-cault observes, "There is nothing absolutely primary to be interpreted, since fundamentally everything is already interpretation. . . . Every sign is . . . but the interpretation of other signs."[14]

The goal of biblical scholarship from this perspective can no longer be conceived as biblical historians once saw it, namely as the "gradual refinement of methods [that] enabled a progressive and inexorable matching of scholarly description to historical fact."[15] The goal is not just to master the text, or the historical facts behind it, but to become engaged in a larger, overarching world of meaning of which both text and reader are part. The text, therefore, is to be seen not only as the product but also as the creator of the author, whose identity *qua* author is generated by what he or she addresses in the writing.

The implication for psychological criticism is that large tracts of the text-reader-meaning event consist of unconscious psychic content (associations, memories, intuitions, complexes) wafting in the virtually endless network of signification in which the text participates, out of which the text was generated, and in behalf of which the text speaks. Such a view of the text is hinted at in the "experience/interpretation" model of textual interpretation proposed by Luke Timothy Johnson, which "takes seriously the deeply human character of the writings, the experiences and convictions that generated them, and the cultural and historical symbols they appropriate." Accordingly, Johnson proposes, "the writings of the New Testament [and one can assume, of all Scripture] can respond to questions about the experiences and convictions that generated their composition, about the symbolic worlds used to interpret those experiences, and about the ways in which the interaction of experience and symbol created new worlds of meaning within the first-century world"—and, we might add, within succeeding worlds as well.[16]

5. Unconscious structures operant in the production of stories and texts. This unconscious dimension of the text is hinted at, but not developed, by structuralist theoreticians Ferdinand de Saussure, A. J. Greimas, Claude Lévi-Strauss, and Daniel and Aline Patte. Structuralism is defined as a "general theory of the intelligibility of the products of mind based on the view that what makes things intelligible is their perceived relatedness, rather than their qualities as separate items." Reference to "a theory of the intelligibility of the products of mind" and to "what makes things intelligible" suggests a model of the human psyche that has a built-in, meaning-producing mechanism. For example: Saussure speaks of a linguistic model, focusing on *langue* as "the system of relationships that constitute language" (as opposed to *parole*, a sentence or word within that system); Greimas speaks of an actantial model (of sender, object, receiver, and so forth) operant in the meaning-producing mechanism of language; and Lévi-Strauss's mythical model draws attention to the "deep structures" in language and the innate human tendency to mythicize the world in terms of the binary opposites of life/death, male/female, nature/culture.[17]

Though none of the structuralists has developed a psychological model of the mind, Daniel and Aline Patte acknowledge that their objective as structuralist critics has been to explore the "subconscious framework" of the "semantic universe" within which "the user of these systems of signs lives and thinks." Making "no pretense" of offering "an objective description of the manner in which aspects of the meaning of a narrative are produced and apprehended by the human mind," they simply attempt to describe and represent these phenomena.[18] Accordingly, although structuralism does not construct a psychology of the mental mechanism that produces narratives and texts, it presupposes the existence of such a mechanism as a function of the largely unconscious structure that makes meaningful texts possible. Psychological biblical criticism, in mapping the nature and habits of the psyche at work in the biblical texts and its interpretation, would want to explore such a mechanism.

6. Personal and collective unconscious elements operant in texts. As noted in chapter 2, Jung proposes that an author's personal and collective unconscious are at work in a text. The personal unconscious is the theoretical host to all the ulterior motives, power drives, and rhetorical objectives cited above. The collective unconscious (or the objective unconscious), however, is the hypothetical postulate that Jung described as "a sphere of unconscious mythology whose primordial images are the common heritage of mankind." Though the collective unconscious "will forever elude our attempts at understanding," Jung would maintain that its traces can be detected in many genres of scriptural expression: for example, in its symbols, archetypal images, dream narratives, stories, myths, epic narratives, apocalypses, and stories of heroic figures. The concept of the collective unconscious is of special interest vis-à-vis a "hermeneutic of suspicion," insofar as it proposes that texts are not only the perpetrators of unconscious exclusions, ideological agendas, and power plays, but are also the mediators of archetypal images that provide models of inclusiveness, service, and empowerment. Having been dredged from the unconscious and awakened in the biblical writer's consciousness, these models now wait in the text as psychic images, ready to catalyze the consciousness of the reader.[19]

7. The role of imagination in the production of texts. In her landmark study, *The Revelatory Text*, Sandra Schneiders discusses the role of imagination in the Bible. She does not develop a psychology or psychoanalytic theory of imagination—nor, in fact, does she identify it specifically as a psychic function or explore it as a part of the unconscious resources of the human psyche. But she does point to the imagination's importance as a conceptual tool for historical-critical biblical scholarship:

> For understandable historical reasons, some people will be more than a little uneasy with the suggestion that the gospels are works of the imagination appealing to the imagination, for just as they tend to equate historical facts with reality (which I have just tried to show is fallacious), so they tend to equate imagination with fantasy or unreality (which is equally fallacious).[20]

Schneiders advances the concept of "constructive imagination" or, as she generally refers to it, "Paschal Imagination," alluding specifically to the drive of the Gospel writers to integrate, focus, and promulgate images of the "Christ event." The function of "constructive imagination" is to "construct a world," to create wholes, to synthesize and integrate impressions, and to articulate their essence with an array of dynamic, heuristic, tensive images. These images, when they "correspond to reality," can conspire to "organize, enrich, and deepen" experience (or when they do not, to "deform and impoverish" it). They do this by drawing together a constellation of "disparate facts and experiences, . . . historical, transhistorical, and interpretive" elements, that coalesce into a meaningful whole.

Speaking specifically of the gospel *kerygma*, Schneiders contends:

> The Gospel is not primarily an historical text in the usual sense of the word. The subject matter of the text is not exclusively or exhaustively the historical Jesus. Rather, the historical Jesus is the symbolic medium for the presentation of the proclaimed Jesus. The proclaimed Jesus is not coextensive with the historical Jesus but is a construction of the Christian theological/spiritual imagination.

Looking at the four Gospels (as opposed to just one), Schneiders states that each is "the product of the paschal imagination, a function of the Jesus-image, which is not a mental drawing or an ossified memory of the earthly Jesus but a tensive and creative principle of ever-new presentations of Jesus that, true and relatively adequate, are never exhaustive of him." She adds that the goal of the imaginative process is "to elicit the faith response of the hearer/reader."[21]

Though Schneiders makes no attempt to analyze the psychodynamics of imagination nor spell out its possible links with the unconscious, she acknowledges that we require more than the tools of conventional historical criticism to understand the origin and nature of the biblical text:

> Because the purpose of the text is to proclaim Jesus as the Christ and thereby to foster the faith of disciples, it is not only legitimate but of primary importance that research not be limited to historical investigation. Biblical research into the theological, religious, and spirituality dimensions of the text is even more important, ultimately, than historical research, even though such substantive interpretation depends in a very real sense on historical research. In the last few decades scholars have come to realize that it also depends upon literary criticism, and can be enriched by psychological, sociological, and ideological criticism.

It remains for psychological criticism specifically to take up the challenge to elaborate a fuller portrait of the human psyche that honors the imaginative function with the same enthusiasm with which it honors the critical mind, and to employ a range of psychological and psychoanalytic tools to understanding more fully the imagination's prodigious virtuosity and its constructive (and sometimes destructive) role in the creation of the biblical text, of the traditions that the text mediates, and of the meanings that the text catalyzes in the souls of readers.[22]

The Function of Texts in Psychological Perspective

We turn now to what can be said psychologically about how a text "moves" readers—or, more precisely, how a text, as a complex of conscious and unconscious factors, functions and exercises power in the life of the psyche. Models that show promise in this regard have been advanced from eight quarters: rhetorical criticism, reader-response criticism, learning theory, cognitive psychology, structuralist criticism, the philosophical psychology of Hans Georg Gadamer, speech-act theory, and Jungian psychology.[23]

1. The model from rhetorical criticism. Here the focus is on "the means by which a text establishes and manages its relationship to its audience in order to achieve a particular effect."[24] From a rhetorical critical perspective, the noncognitive and affective elements of a text are the defining factors in the power it exercises in the lives of readers. "Exegetes fail, for the most part, to take adequate account of the affective semantics of biblical literature, of the power of the Bible to *move*."[25] For the rhetorical critic, the Bible stands as an "archetypal example of how power is constituted by discourse." To be more specific:

> Rationality and the conscious are never fully in charge in any human interaction, and the meaning that happens in any rhetorical situation is generated largely by processes unconscious to speaker or hearer. The power released by effective speech not only affects the hearers in ways the speaker could not anticipate; it also makes the speaker say things he never anticipated saying (the phenomenon of "getting carried away by one's own rhetoric"). "Deep calls to deep" (Psalm 42:7)—any rhetorical event is a transaction between unconsciousnesses as well as rationalities. . . . This suggests an increased attention to myths and to the persuasive use of the arts in religion, which have "a rhetoric of their own to move the mind or the emotion" and raises again acutely the issue of the unconscious in rhetoric.[26]

Taking the lead from rhetorical criticism, psychological critical analysis needs to construct a model that explores the non-rational, often unconscious, affective power of discourse in the determination of understanding.[27]

2. The model from rhetorical and reader-response criticism. This helps in examining the psychic function of biblical texts. Wayne Booth's *The Rhetoric of Fiction* explores the "rhetorical strategy" by which authors engage, persuade, and shape the perception of their readers by projecting an image of themselves (the "implied author") and an image of their reader (the "implied reader"). A fundamental objective of every author is "consciously or *unconsciously*, to impose his fictional world upon the reader." This world includes "points of view, norms, and standards of judgment." Or as others have put it, through the "use of plot, character, dialogue, irony, etc.," the author projects the "appropriate subjectivity to participate in the dynamics of the text," creating "a world within which, and according to whose dynamics, the reader operates for the duration of the aesthetic experience." A matter of interest to psychological biblical criticism would be how this happens and why it is that the human psyche is susceptible to the "persuasion" of the biblical texts.[28]

3. The model from learning theory. Gerd Theissen used this in *Psychological Aspects of Pauline Theology*. Rooted in behavioral psychology, learning theory focuses on the behavioral change that takes place in response to the urging or inspiration of external stimuli. The goal of learning theory is thus to understand the specific psychological factors that generate change in the life of the reader. Of interest to psychological biblical criticism would be the stimuli ("associative learning"), new reinforcers ("operant learning") and new models ("imitative learning") that are at work in the stories, laws, injunctions, and exemplary acts and persons of Scripture, and that work consciously and unconsciously in the reader to reinforce present modes of behavior or to generate new ones.[29]

4. The model from cognitive psychology. Also appropriated in Theissen's work, this model draws attention to the cognitive restructuring or revisioning of the world that occurs in response to an event or a text. This restructuring takes places through the cognitive processes of new causal attribution, new anticipations, new self-assessment, and new role-options that a text can generate or facilitate. These enable readers to transcend and re-vision "cognitively dissonant" elements in life—such as sin, lostness, meaninglessness, suffering and despair—through a newly constructed vision (cognition) of their world. For psychological biblical criticism, cognitive psychology offers special promise in the analysis of "conversion" stories, both within the biblical text and in the history of response to the text.[30]

5. The model from structuralist and narratological criticism. This involves the "defamiliarization," "disorientation," or "de-habitualization" that can be experienced in reading a text. It suggests that one of the functions of a text is to generate a sufficient sense of psychic disequilibrium to activate conscious change and reconceptualization on the part of the reader.[31] Hans Robert Jauss, one of the leading proponents of Reception Theory, proposes that every reader brings to the text a "horizon of expectation," a mindset, system of references, and viewpoint. Of interest to psychological biblical criticism is the fact that the text can unsettle or "subvert" this horizon of expectation, even reverse it. Such a reversal is anticipated, for example, in the parable of the laborers in the vineyard (Matt. 20:1–15), where a horizon of expectation, "shaped and determined by the demands of justice," is transmuted by a judgment of grace.[32]

6. The model from philosophical psychology. Derived from the work of Hans-Georg Gadamer, this is remarkably similar to the structuralist analysis of Jauss. Gadamer speaks of a text challenging readers to expand the "horizon" of their own perception to incorporate or "fuse" with the perceptual "horizon" offered by the text. In *New Horizons in Hermeneutics* (the title reflects Gadamer's influence), Anthony C. Thiselton describes Gadamer's fundamental premise and theory:

> We approach questions of knowledge . . . from within horizons already bounded by our finite situatedness within the flow of history. But it is possible for these finite and historically conditioned horizons to be enlarged, and to expand. In actualization of understanding or encounter between readers and texts, the boundaries of horizons may be extended and moved, and thus come to constitute new horizons.[33]

According to this model, a text creates a new world into which the reader is invited. But this world is not, as Sandra Schneiders reminds us, the

> imaginative, fictional world of the work, for example, the land of Oz or the inn to which the Good Samaritan took the victim of the robbers. . . . This different world is the world before the text, the world that the text generates and projects and invites the reader to enter. . . . This world is variously named in the text itself: Paul speaks of living "in the Spirit" rather than in the flesh; John talks of . . . being "born from above" and living by the Spirit rather than being "of this world"; . . . the synoptic gospels present Jesus as inviting his hearers to discern in their midst an alternative sphere called the "reign of God."[34]

The ultimate function of the text from Gadamer's position, therefore, is a "fusion of horizons." The reader's horizon fuses with that of the text. The result is that the reader, like someone watching a play or absorbed by a painting, comes out of the experience as a different person. The psychological question of why the self is susceptible to the persuasions of another horizon of meaning, and toward what end within the economy of the psyche, will be a subject for psychological-critical analysis.[35]

7. The model from speech-act theory. This relates specifically to the covenantal, declarative, and promissory character of much of biblical language and its documentable effect on readers. The controlling insight of speech-act theory lies in the discovery of the capacity of certain types of language to *perform acts.* The theory originated with the observation that some transactions take place in "inter-personal situations of oral speech" where words have real, and sometimes irreversible, effects on their recipients. The statements, " I forgive you," or " I authorize you. . .," or "I do" (in the marriage ceremony), have performative force, affecting the conscious (and unconscious) status of the person addressed. Performative speech commonly includes the verbs to bless, ordain, pardon, rebuke, confer, give, love, pledge, promise, trust, pardon, proclaim, confess, comfort, encourage, exhort, urge, thank, and praise. Such language leaves "neither the speaker nor the hearer uninvolved and unchanged." In fact it is often so absolute that it leaves no way to revoke or annul the force of the statement or its effect. We have no procedure, for example, for saying "I unbaptize this infant" or "I uncommit her ashes to the ground."

Thiselton proposes that although speech-act theory has been applied primarily to inter-personal exchange, it can be applied to the transactions that occur between text and reader as well:

> The biblical writings . . . embody an institutional framework of covenant in which commitments and effects become operative in acts of promise, acts of blessing, acts of forgiveness, acts of pronouncing judgment, acts of repentance, acts of worship, acts of authorization, acts of communion, and acts of love.

Thus one of the possible effects or functions of the biblical text can be performative, imparting to the reader a conviction of change in status or being. In working with the effect of performative biblical language, speech-act theorists acknowledge that the speech-act event is more than a linguistic phenomenon and that one must "look 'behind the scenes' at the extra-linguistic content." This extralinguistic content will include consideration of psychic factors, making it especially interesting to psychological-biblical criticism. These factors include the wishes and desires of speakers and hearers and their degree of commitment and resolve (insofar as these are retrievable in the text), as well as shifts in perception, cognition, will, expectation, and affect that transpire in the speech-act event.[36]

8. The model from archetypal psychology. This explicitly psychological model emerges from Jung's theory of archetypes. Jung held that great literature and art are often the bearers of recurrent images that constitute the common heritage of humanity and have the power to catalyze the human will, imagination, conscience, and thought. They are stock figures that play through the dreams and myths of all time in ever-changing forms. Walter Wink comments that they appear

> so frequently in widely scattered mythic traditions that we are justified in regarding [them] . . . as a standard component in spiritual development. The very pervasiveness of such stories [and images] . . . is evidence that we are dealing with something fundamental to the spiritual journey itself.[37]

According to Jung, the production of these images is an "inherited mode of psychological functioning." But the structural tendency within the human species that produces such images also responds to such images, as Jung observed in his analysis of the response to the historical Jesus in the first century C.E.:

> Christ would never have made the impression he did on his followers if he had not expressed something that was alive and at work in their unconscious. Christianity itself would never have spread through the pagan world with such astonishing rapidity had its ideas not found an analogous psychic readiness to receive them.[38]

When archetypal images appear in art or literature, for example, they introduce images of human possibility that prove compensatory to the one-sidedness of human consciousness. When individuals or cultures have lost their way, archetypal images offer a correction to consciousness, advancing new possibilities and options. As such they release "the hidden forces of instinct, to which the ordinary conscious will alone can never gain access" and catalyze the reader to get on with life and the task at hand, enlivened by a new image of present possibility. Thus from Jung's standpoint the unconscious is not just adversarial to consciousness as Freud postulated—sneaking inferior motives and drives past the censorship of consciousness—but is also compensatory to consciousness, expanding conscious awareness through human imagination, visions, and dreams of possibilities for psychic growth and even human advancement.[39]

In summary, a psychological critical approach to the content and function of the biblical text operates out of a vision of the text as a psychic event, an expression and product of an occurrence within the psyche/soul of the author and the author's community, creating another event in the psychic life of the reader and the reader's community. Unlike the historical-critical approach which sees the text as a historical artifact, the psychological-critical approach sees the text as a product of, and participant in, a complex psychic event, riddled with conscious and unconscious factors. As such, the text appears as an autonomous literary, historical, and psychic entity, whose meaning can no longer be reduced simply to what the author intended. Rather, it participates in the galaxy of meaning that gave birth to the author as author (of which the author as person is only partially conscious), and can change the lives of readers, extending as far as conscious and unconscious reckoning can reach.

The Reader and Reading in Psychological Perspective

We turn now from a study of the effects of texts on readers, to an examination of the effects of readers on texts, and the psychodynamic factors at work in the reading experience. Though biblical scholarship has long recognized that readers impose their presuppositions on texts, it has, toward the end of the twentieth century, tended to formulate this judgment increasingly in psychological terms. As Schneiders notes:

> It is not only the presuppositions that we inherit in language and culture, not only the accepted understanding of physical reality or cosmology, not only the officially sanctioned religious beliefs and norms of the community, but also the ideological distortions of our sense of reality as a whole that shape unconsciously both the writing and the reading of the text.[40]

Cedric Johnson was one of the first to identify and analyze the psychological factors at work in biblical readers from the perspective of contemporary psychological and psychoanalytic theory. His 1983 volume, *The Psychology of Biblical Interpretation*, designed for the popular rather than technical reader, was the product of cross-disciplinary research at the Fuller Graduate School of Psychology and the Rosemead Graduate School. Johnson recounts that "Over the past few years I have had a growing suspicion that my ideas about biblical truth do not come entirely from the study of the Bible. . . . Each one forms his or her theological system with some reference to personal psychohistory." Referring to theological factions within his own evangelical background, Johnson contends that "the dispensationalists, covenant theologians, neo-orthodox people, and others cannot disguise psychohistory." He reinforces this claim with a quotation from the evangelical biblical scholar, G. C. Berkouwer:

> Do not all people read Scripture from their own current perspectives and presuppositions? Do they not cast it in the form of their own organizing systems, with all kinds of conscious or subconscious preferences, ways of selection which force the understanding of Scripture into one particular direction?[41]

Johnson's first chapter discusses "The Mind in Search of Meaning." Taking Gestalt psychology and the Piagetian notions of assimilation and accommodation as his point of departure, he explores the psychological processes in constructing and changing one's perspectives. Chapter 2, "Personality and Interpretation," describes the unconscious motivational processes (transference, reaction formation, selective attention), the cognitive styles (analytic and global, right and left brain), and the perceptual distortions ("mind sets") at work in individual psychologies. Chapter 3, "The Influence of Society and Culture on Interpretation," scans the cultural and socio-political conditioning of authors and texts. Chapter 4, "A Psychological Hermeneutic—Insight and Responsibility," closes with a call to critical self-consciousness and awareness of the personal and cultural psychological conditioning that shapes one's interpretation of the Bible, dramatizing the point with a story of arctic explorer Robert E. Peary:

> Peary relates that on his polar trip he traveled one whole day toward the north, making his sleigh dogs run briskly. At night he checked his bearings to determine his latitude and noticed with great surprise that he was much further south than in the morning. He had been toiling all day toward the north on an immense iceberg drawn southwards by an ocean current.

Johnson concludes: "The iceberg of unconscious motivation and other psychological factors need to be heeded, surveyed, and mastered in the hermeneutical task."[42]

Johnson's work and that of postmodern biblical criticism point to at least four types of psychological factors affecting biblical interpretation: the personal and socio-cultural location of the reader; the psychological type and personality of the reader; psycho-dynamic factors in the reading process; and the psychology of textual performance (using media of expression such as painting, music, dance, pageant, and so forth to convey aspects of the text's meanings that seem "beyond words").

Personal and Socio-Cultural Location of the Reader in Psychological Perspective

In the last quarter of the twentieth century an increasing number of biblical scholars included autobiographical notes in their writing, identifying the significance of their gender or of their personal, religious, intellectual, educational, ethnic, cultural, or vocational history as factors that qualify the way they approach, read, and interpret Scripture. Daniel Harrington includes such an autobiographical note in his 1979 survey, *Interpreting the New Testament*:

The inspection of one's personal presuppositions involves both social and psychological elements. Such an inspection is necessary because interpreters should know and be conscious of the baggage that they bring to the task of biblical interpretation. I am a white American male living in the middle to late twentieth century, born of immigrant parents (from Ireland), raised in the Boston area, the product of parochial schools, a Jesuit now for twenty years, a Roman Catholic priest, a teacher of Scripture in a seminary in Cambridge, Massachusetts, holding a doctoral degree in biblical languages from Harvard, and so on. Each and every one of these elements has some impact upon the way I approach a biblical text. Remove one or two of them from my biography and substitute something else, and surely my reading of the text would change. I will spare the reader an inventory of my psychological strengths and weakness, but this omission should not be taken as suggesting that the interpreter's psychological predispositions are not important. Good interpreters must know themselves in order to distinguish between the message of the text and the social and psychic interference that they bring to it."[43]

Two features of Harrington's literary *confessio* are of special interest to the psychological biblical critic: his personal location, and his social-cultural location. The psychological factors he attributes to his personal location include his vocational orientation as priest and professor, his personal identity, growth, and development as a male, and his "psychological strengths and weaknesses." To this list, a postmodern biblical critical approach would want to add the six psycho-dynamic features noted earlier as unconscious factors operative in "the constitution of texts," but which, as we will now see, can also be operative in readers. They are:

• the ideologies of the reader that instanciate and empower particular notions of truth, whether personal, racial, ethnic, religious, sexual, social, or political.

• the strategies of exclusion (Derrida) that maintain an illusion of completeness but at the same time repress, eclipse, or deny those ideas, persons, or realities that our minds, consciously or unconsciously, hold to be marginal or secondary.

• the power-seeking interests of the reader, however subtle (Foucault), that can control the interpretation of texts, define social status, interpret right belief, determine acceptable behavior, and legitimate authority.

• that complex network of signification (Derrida) in which reader and text alike are unconsciously caught up, far exceeding human comprehension, in which everything that is "signified" is in turn a "signifier" of something further. Or as Julia Kristeva's work suggests with its theory of "intertextuality": "each text is situated for each reader in an ever-changing web composed of innumerable texts."

• the subconscious meaning-producing "deep structure" mechanism (structuralism) operative in every human being that creates language, defines coherent thought, and leads to the production and interpretation of meaningful texts.

• the repository of archetypal images that consciously and unconsciously populate and frequently motivate what a reader thinks, writes, dreams, and hopes.

• the power of the constructive imagination to synthesize, integrate, and utilize the word it hears in Scripture as *prima materia* for the construction of the reader's world.

All of these call for recognition as factors in one's personal location, affecting the way one reads and interprets.[44]

A second factor Harrington finds psychologically affecting one's reading is *social-cultural location*, which in his case consists of rootedness in a mid-twentieth-century American, Irish, Roman Catholic, Bostonian, parochial-school culture. In the last quarter of the twentieth century, social-cultural location has been noted as a significant hermeneutic factor especially by liberation biblical interpreters, Hispanic, "Latin American, Asian (Minjung in South Korea), Mujerista, African American, South African, feminist, and gay and lesbian theologians." Such factors affect not only *how we read texts* (most often touching on matters of class, gender, race, and ethnicity), but also, *who is regarded as a legitimate reader.*[45]

That social-cultural location can affect how we read texts is discussed by Cedric Johnson in his previously noted chapter on the influence of society and culture in *The Psychology of Biblical Interpretation*. Johnson points to the light that social psychology can cast on how biblical interpretation is influenced by "the actual, imagined or implied presence" of "others" within a specific socio-cultural circle. Dominant customs, habits, and traditions of social location can affect perceptions, expectations, and valuations, unconsciously and consciously. Johnson observes that these "culture bound" constraints can extend even to the interpretation of individual words:

> Even as apparently universal a category as father (of obvious importance to theology for its metaphoric use in reference to God) turns out to have quite diverse meanings depending on a number of factors: is the society bilineal like ours, patrilineal like those of Bible times, or matrilineal like a number of contemporary societies? Is the father regarded as a remote, forbidding authority figure or is he close and indulgent? Is the adult male authority figure for a child his biological father, or his mother's brother? And so on.[46]

Social-cultural location can also be an unconscious or conscious determinant of who is regarded as a legitimate interpreter of the text. The new liberationist "readings from below," for example, demonstrate how the Bible is read differently outside the confines of white, male, logocentric, Eurocentric culture. This leads us to consider unconscious socio-cultural presuppositions that can legislate whether an interpretation is correct or incorrect, whether an exegetical or hermeneutical approach is legitimate or illegitimate, or in Derrida's terms, whether a specific reading or type of reading is to be included or excluded. The types of readings regularly excluded from most of twentieth-century biblical scholarship are those of non-specialists, of dissenting scholars within the guild, and of readers who come from a theological or a non-objectivist faith perspective — resulting in the irony that issues of theology and faith have often been banned from critical biblical studies, even those conducted in theological schools.[47]

Reader-response critic Stanley Fish notes the *de facto* power of the interpretive community or the scholarly guild in establishing socially defined conventions for reading, by placing constraints over the production of readings, and in training, licensing, and in the end, legitimating certain kinds of readers and disenfranchising others. Fish accordingly challenges the concept of a "privileged reading," holding that every reading, including that of the scholarly guild, is to be seen as a "contextualized reading" that devises and employs "camouflaging jargons" that it "has decided is true for itself," noting that "different readers of biblical texts (whether they be male or female, white, black, Latino, Asian, and so on) stand in asymmetrical relationships concerning power and in their ability to speak about the text even within the same general interpretive community."[48]

In sum, consideration of the reader's personal and socio-cultural location suggests two tasks for psychological biblical criticism. The first is to add to the contribution of rhetorical, ideological, and reader-response critics by probing the psychological components, conscious and unconscious, at work in the social, political, and ideological constraints that affect the reader before, during, and after reading. Such an enterprise is important not only for increased psychological consciousness and intellectual honesty, but also for ethical integrity, in view of the profound social, cultural, and political effects such readings and constraints can exercise in the culture at large, such as racism, anti-Semitism, child abuse, slavery, religious persecution, radical nationalism. (These will be explored below in our discussion of pathogenic effects of texts and interpretations.)[49]

A second task is to develop a history of the text's reception, following the school of Hans Robert Jauss, that has begun to write histories of the reception of specific texts in specific sociohistorical settings. Biblical studies still does not take seriously the reception-history of biblical texts. It needs to catalogue not just the range of responses a given text evokes in readers over the centuries, but also the range of ways in which readers in different personal and socio-cultural locations have received, refracted, and transmitted a given text. As *The Postmodern Bible* states: "If the cherished history of exegesis in biblical studies were ever to become self-conscious, self-reflexive, and self-critical praxis, it could be transformed into a rich and exciting history of reception."[50]

Psychological Type and Personality of the Reader

One of the first modern psychological theories of personality types was proposed by Carl Gustav Jung in his 1921 volume, *Psychological Types*. (It has since become the basis for the Myers-Briggs Type Indicator, perhaps the most widely applied personality theory in the last half of the twentieth century.[51]) Opposing the Freudian notion that personalities are fundamentally the same, namely, driven by the psychodynamic interaction of ego, instinct, super-ego, and the eros and thanatos drives, Jung maintained that individual human personalities differ in fundamental ways. Though they are armed with the same sets of instincts and psychic structure, they differ in the "function" and "attitude" they adopt (or adapt) toward life.

Jung identified four functions available to human consciousness: the *thinking* function, concerned with objectivity and rationality; the *feeling* (or evaluating) function, sensitive to the value or agreeableness of things; the *sensing* function, attentive to the feel, taste, sound, smell, and appearance of things; and the *intuitive* function that ponders the "whence," "whither," and "why" of things. To this typology he appends two additional markers of psychological type: the attitudes of *extroversion* and *introversion*. In the case of the former, one's libido or psychic energy tends to move outward from the self; in the latter, the energy flows inward.

According to Jung's theory, each of us begins life cultivating one of these attitudes and one of these functions as a dominant adaptive mode, leaving two of the functions only partially utilized and one of them in a state of almost total neglect. In the second half of life, however, a compensatory shift in psychological type occurs: the neglected functions and attitude begin to be reclaimed as part of a natural psychic process bent on psychological wholeness.

Jung's theory was forged from a desire to find a psychological explanation for the disparate theories of the self developed by Freud, Adler, and himself when the three of them had worked from shared data. In coming to the theory that human beings are born either as extroverts or introverts, and that they develop a discrete mode of functioning at a very early age, Jung provided a key for solving the riddle. He also, as Laurens van der Post reports, provided a basis for understanding the differences between the "classical and romantic urges in art, the Apollonian and Dionysian in the mind, the Greek and Trojan in legend and history, . . . and so on up to the vitalists and mechanists in the sciences of our own day."[52]

Jung's theory is only one of many personality theories advanced in Western thought since Galen's second century C.E. humoral theory of the four temperaments (phlegmatic, choleric, melancholic, and sanguine) or the remarkably modern-sounding theory of Christian Thomasius (1655–1728), founder of the University of Halle, who "worked out a scheme for measuring personality by assigning numerical scores to various traits of character."[53] Other twentieth century theoreticians include:

• Gordon Allport, who established and identified personality "traits" as standard units of personality measurement

• E. Spranger (on whom Allport built his theories), who predicated six basic personality types, corresponding to the six value orientations that may dominate life: theoretic, economic, aesthetic, social, political, and religious

• Hermann Rorschach, who developed projective tests to identify psychological type

• Jean Piaget and Erik Erikson, who related personality or psychological type to an individual's growth stage along a developmental scale, echoing in the work of Lawrence Kohlberg on stages in moral development and James Fowler on stages in faith development

Other psychologists have differentiated personalities on the basis of cognitive styles. Notable among them are H. A. Witkin and Nobel Prize winner Roger W. Sperry. Witkin distinguishes between a "field independent" (analytic) and a "field dependent" (global) style. From these he derives two cognitive types: the "objective, analytic and rational," and the "subjective, synthesizing and intuitive." This theory has been applied to discerning different cognitive styles within church communities: the "word-oriented" analytic person, and the "spirit-oriented" intuitive person. Sperry's discovery of the difference between right hemisphere and left hemisphere functioning provided the basis for a personality theory based on hemispheric dominance: the "right-brained" tending toward the linear, logical, and analytic; the "left-brained" toward the intuitive and global.[54]

Though there is no unifying model among these theories of personality types, there is clear consensus that psychological disposition, orientation, function, and attitudes influence the ways we perceive, conceptualize, and interpret things. It will be the work of psychological biblical criticism to probe the effect of personality type on interpretation. Doing so will encourage a certain hermeneutic of suspicion regarding the ways one's psychological type can skew one's reading of the text. As Daniel Harrington expressed it, "Good interpreters must know themselves in order to distinguish between the message of the text and the social and psychic interference that they bring to it."[55]

But a second, equally important contribution that psychological biblical criticism can make is to appreciate the special angle of vision innate in each psychological type, and the special insight each offers. One of the primary benefits of psychological type theory is to increase appreciation for the diverse ranges of meanings in a text, for the diverse aptitudes for sensing those meanings, and for the possible legitimacy of all of them for a holistic approach. The privileging of a rational approach to the text by classical biblical scholarship has had the effect of disregarding the other types of meaning (sensate, feeling, and intuitive) that readers have found.

Psychological biblical criticism will also want to revisit two ancient models. The first is the fourfold rabbinic model of biblical interpretations: *peshat*, focusing on the literal meaning; *remez*, seeking out the allegorical or typological meaning; *derash*, probing or searching; and *sod*, seeking out the "secret mysteries" of the text. The second is the fourfold medieval model of Augustine of Denmark: literal, allegorical, moral, and anagogical. Both of these are conscious institutionalizations of the psychological fact that readers differ in function and attitude, and that different hermeneutical approaches from the perspective of different psychological types are not only legitimate but necessary to catch the full meaning of a text.

The Psychodynamics of the Reading Process

In the preceding sections, we examined two reader characteristics that affect reading: personal and socio-cultural location, and personality type. We turn now to the psychodynamics of the reading process itself. We will examine six psychological theories on the ways the reader catalyzes the production of meaning in the reading process and the kinds of meaning that are produced: interactive reader-response theory, psychological reader-response theory, object-relations theory, theories of imagination and "illusion processing," philosophically oriented hermeneutical theory, and psychoanalytically oriented hermeneutical theory.

1. Interactive Reader-Response Theory. Early reader-response theory (that of Stanley Fish, Wolfgang Iser, and Wayne Booth) held that meaning in reading is to be found, not in the "past" of the text, but in the "present experience" of the reading process. A text is unrealized until it is read; reading "reorganizes" thought-systems invoked by the text:

> Through its literary conventions and strategies, the text presents a puzzle, which the reader must solve to gain understanding. The reader is drawn into the adventure not only by what the text spells out but also by what it withholds. To understand literature, the reader must begin to fill in the gaps, to infer what is not given.[56]

At the root of reader-response criticism is a premise fundamental to Gestalt psychology, that the process of reading involves looking for patterns of meaning that address one's needs at the moment. What one "sees" or "finds" is shaped significantly by the largely unconscious "wisdom of the organism," which programs the self to search for elements of meaning that will engender balance and homeostasis.[57]

The psychological dimensions of Iser's theory are evident in his description of the phenomenology of reading as the movement of a "recreative" reader who "travels along inside" the text with a "wandering viewpoint" that engages with the text in a dialogue of "anticipation and retrospection." The reader is driven by a psychological need to generate or find a Gestalt that will make consistent sense of the "blanks," "gaps," and "spots of indeterminacy." Isher describes the process: "We look forward, we look back, we decide, we change our decisions, we form expectations, we are shocked by their nonfulfillment, we question, we muse, we accept, we reject. . . . This is the dynamic process of recreation."[58]

2. Psychological Reader-Response Theory. A second theory of reader-response criticism, oriented explicitly along psychoanalytic lines, has been developed by Norman Holland and David Bleich. Holland's hermeneutic, based on his "ego psychology," draws on the tradition of Freud. It sees texts as evoking defensive strategies in the reader's conscious self. The reader uses these strategies to render the text's meaning in ways that will reinforce his or her identity. Holland defines identity as the sense of that "unchanging essence" or "central-unifying pattern" that defines the reader's personality or character.

Holland has supported his theories with experimental psychological research, as described in his 1975 work, *Five Readers Reading,* in which he compares the responses of five readers to the same texts, concluding that the differences correlate with differences in each reader's sense of identity, personality type, and narrative experience. The constructive implication of Holland's theory for psychological biblical criticism, is that readers can enhance their self-understanding in conversation with a text. The negative implication is that they can simply "replicate" themselves, rather than hear the text and be changed by its otherness.[59]

3. Object-Relations Theory. The object-relations research of Ralph L. Underwood stresses the dynamic relation-building exchange between text and reader. As noted earlier, Underwood advances the thesis in his 1997 article, "Primordial Texts: An Object Relations Approach to Biblical Hermeneutics," that the relation between reader and text is analogous to the imaginative relationship between infant and mother. Based on Freud's psychoanalytic theory, object-relations theory predicates that "relations with primary others are introjected inside the person, in the psyche, where in due course they take up residence as stable mental images." An "object," accordingly, "refers to persons or to mental representations of persons [that become an] object of investment of emotional energy."[60] Healthy growth and mental stability develop out of relation and dialogue with such "objects."

The model Underwood advances to illustrate the point is a game that British psychologist D. W. Winnicott played in research sessions with children. Underwood describes Winnicott as presenting a "line or drawing that had no particular meaning [a "squiggle"], and the child was to draw and make something from this squiggle. Then the child could draw a squiggle, and Winnicott would make something of it." Out of this process two realizations grew: a sense of relationship, intimacy, and trust between the two; and a clearer sense of self. Underwood writes:

> The squiggle game is like the process of developing a relationship with a text and of being in a position to interpret the relationship in a meaningful way. Similarly, hermeneutics emerges out of a process of relationship building such that our interpretations of texts are hunches or declarations about our relationship with these texts. An object relations approach frames hermeneutics as a dynamic relationship between text and readers. Hermeneutics is not simply a task of making a meaning from the text that suits the needs of the readers, nor simply a task of unlocking some a priori meaning ensconced in the text. Rather, hermeneutics is a process in which a unique relationship between text and readers evolves, . . . where there is no complete dominance of either objectivity or subjectivity.[61]

The process involves a history of changing dynamics built on imaginative and illusional interplay in which the relationship is always in a state of evolution and growth. The illusional dimension for Underwood consists of that necessary creativity, theorizing, religious imagination, and inner fantasy that is essential to the creation of new meaning. For Underwood, "an object relations approach suggests that biblical interpretation is an ongoing process that forms and transforms dynamic relations with biblical texts . . . [with the ultimate] potential to form and reform persons, communities and cultures."[62] This is not unlike the relationship between text and reader in rabbinic tradition or the piety of an individual who spends a lifetime with the Bible.

4. Theories of Imagination and "Illusion Processing." These two models were developed independently; the first by Wilfred Cantwell Smith, a comparative historian of religion, and the second by Paul Pruyser, a clinical psychologist and psychologist of religion. They both speak of a creative function innate and indispensable to the human psyche for formulating the transcendent meanings generated in the encounter with texts and with life.

Smith proposed a model of "imagination" in his monumental study, *What Is Scripture? A Comparative Approach.* Though he is not wont to use psychological language in discussing the relationship between "scripture" and its "reader/hearer," Smith does endorse Northrup Frye's proposal that the faculty of imagination is primarily responsible for the phenomenon of the "massive role" the Bible has come to play in the course of Western civilization. The closest that Smith comes to a psychological analysis of the phenomenon is in his description of imagination (following Samuel Taylor Coleridge) as a "distinctive and central capacity of human living," and in his citation of the sentiment of C. C. Everett, a nineteenth-century American philosophic theologian, that imagination is "the eye of the soul." Smith sees imagination as the capacity of humans to deploy concepts and tools, including the tool of reason, in their search for transcendence. Left unanswered, however, is the question of the nature and function of imagination within the economy of the psyche. This task has been taken up in the work of John Dourley, Alan Jacobs, Ann Ulanov, and as we shall see, Paul Pruyser and D. W. Winnicott.[63]

The concept of "illusion processing," an alternate designation for the imaginative faculty, is advanced by post-Freudian clinical psychologist Paul Pruyser. It is influenced by the thought of object-relations theorist, D. W. Winnicott, and of sociologists Peter L. Berger and Thomas Luckman, proposing that "illusions are the cultural fabric from which science, as well as religion, is formed" and that the primary component of any culture is its "shared subjective experience." All visual arts, music, literature, the physical sciences, and religion "entail in some essential way the skillful processing of illusion."[64]

Pruyser notes that the root meaning of "illusion" is the Latin *ludere* (to play). Thus illusion comes from the "play of human imagination." As David Wulff describes Pruyser's thought in *Psychology of Religion*, the world of illusion is a world of "tutored fantasy, adventurous thinking, orderly imagination, inspired connections, verbalizable images, . . . the world of play, of the creative imagination in which feelings are not antagonistic to thinking, in which skills and talents are used to the utmost, and where pleasure is found without categorical abrogation of the reality principle." With Freud, Pruyser differentiates between "illusion" and "delusion," the former referring to a creative, imaginative, constructive function of the psyche; the latter to a conviction held at the expense of both reason and contrary evidence. But whereas Freud holds religious "illusion" to be nothing more than an expression of wish-fulfillment, Pruyser sees it, along with art and music, as "a valid and inevitable part of life."[65]

Pruyser finds that "illusion" constitutes a third world of knowing that stands in contrast to two other worlds, "the private, inner world of autistic fantasy" and "the public outer world of realistic and verifiable sensory perception"—the two of which were, at one time, "the only well-defined alternatives in the psychoanalytic literature." The world of illusion "falls neither into the world of private images nor in the world of ordinary sense perception" but generates a new genre of images, for example, "deities, ideal human virtues, and ultimate spiritual states," including the repertory of transcendent images to be found in the Bible.[66] It is in this illusionistic mid-world that religion finds itself, because

> the transcendent, the holy, and mystery are not recognizable in the external world by plain realistic viewing and hearing, nor do they arise directly in the minds as pleasurable fictions. They arise from an intermediate zone of reality that is also an intermediate human activity—neither purely subjective nor purely objective.[67]

How do "illusion" and its characteristic field of images function in the life of the human psyche? To answer this, Pruyser turns to the object-relations theory of David Winnicott, who holds that a prime function of science as well as of religion is to provide "transitional objects," that is, coherent images of the non-self world that accompany us in the transition from childish autism to the imaginative creation of culture. The process begins with "the child's play with transitional objects and culminates in 'playful' participation in the adult world of human culture." The function of illusion-processing both for science and religion is to find a name, read a purpose, and identify a reality that can represent the meaning of the whole. Religion, accordingly, generates a constellation of meaningful, "playful" constructs or symbol systems in an "open-ended *search* in a universe pervaded by mystery."[68]

Pruyser warns that these playful constructs and illusionary images are "delicate and vulnerable" and that their creators and preservers must never give in to the temptation to confuse such images with either the autistic or the "realist" side. He laments for example, the foolishness of pitting "the illusionistic perspective and language of the Bible against the realistic outlook and expressions of Darwin, rather than recognizing that each may be true within its own sphere," just as he would proscribe pitting the "illusionistic" process of biblical interpretation and theological construction against the realistic constructs of physics and chemistry.[69]

He does suggest, however, that illusion-processing is constantly taking place, whether one is dealing with the multiple-armed images of tantric Hindu tradition, the vast world of biblical myth, poetry, legend, song, parable, and apocalyptic vision, or the vast and varied world of exegetical and hermeneutical constructs, ranging from higher criticism to postmodern biblical criticism. In all such instances, illusion-processing is providing transitional objects for the road, constructs for the soul, as it were, as one moves from infancy to maturity—a process on which cognitive psychology and constructivistic psychology promise to cast additional light.

5. Philosophically Oriented Hermeneutical Theory. This model comes from the hermeneutical theory of Sandra Schneiders in *The Revelatory Text*, rooted in the thought of Paul Ricoeur and Hans-Georg Gadamer. Though none of the three presents a developed theory of the psychodynamics of reading and understanding, they lead us to the threshold of psychological reflection by frequently hinting at psychological dimensions in their discussion of three stages in the interpretive process: preunderstanding, exegesis, and meaning.

The first stage, "preunderstanding," raises a number of psychological questions. It is predicated on the recognition that any interpretive act begins with an "initiating guess that sets the process of interpretation into motion; . . . not a wild guess but an educated guess or hypothesis [that provides the] basis for planning . . . a methodical process of investigation." And while "the quality and content of *consciousness* that enables this originating hypothesis . . . is both complex and subject to scrutiny, . . . without it no entrance into the meaning of the text is possible." Schneiders does not describe the process and phenomenology of "preunderstanding" in psychological terms, but the concept is ripe for psychological inquiry into its etiology and role as a function emerging spontaneously within the conscious and unconscious operation of the psyche.[70]

The second stage in the interpretive process, exegesis, ordinarily does not occasion psychological comment by virtue of its apparently straightforward, research-oriented battery of historical, literary, and "Sach"-critical strategies and methods. As Schneiders observes, however, Gadamer, along with postmodern criticism, raises questions about the conventional perception of exegesis as a "methodologically antiseptic grasp by an objective mind of a free-standing knowable resulting in 'objective knowledge.'" With his theory of an "effective history" of the text and an "effective historical consciousness" of the interpreter, Gadamer is predicating an "ever-changing involvement of the consciousness of the knower" along with an ever-changing re-contextualization and re-conception of the text in successive generations of readers. All this prevents the knower from assuming a "transcendent, stationary, detached point of view," and the text from assuming a constant identity in the perception of readers over time. From Gadamer's perspective, neither the text nor the interpreter is a stationary object. In identifying this phenomenon as characteristically human, Gadamer invites an in-depth consideration, from the perspective of a psychology of the individual and society, of the history, disposition, and function of exegesis and its time-bound agenda in post-Enlightenment consciousness.[71]

The third stage in the interpretive process, meaning, especially invites psychological commentary. It is called "application" (Gadamer), "appropriation" (Ricoeur), or "aesthetic surrender" (Schneiders)—all of which express the moment when meaning is found and owned by the reader in the text-reader encounter.

Gadamer's theory of "application" of meaning focuses on the subjectivity of the reader in the production of meaning. For him, "one can only truly understand something as 'applied,' when it is integrated into one's own world of meaning (one's understanding in the ontological sense), . . . [one's] effective historical consciousness."[72] Gadamer advances the thesis, not unlike that of Norman Holland above, that the understanding of a text occurs only when its "application" or relevance to some aspect of the reader's existence is consciously or unconsciously recognized. Understanding a text always means applying it to ourselves. In effect, the meaningful subject matter of any text for any reader is defined by its capacity to evoke an applicable association within that reader's effective historical consciousness.

Ricoeur's theory of "appropriation," on the other hand, focuses more on the text, its "surplus of meaning," and the "strangeness" and "otherness" that provides the text with its capacity to question the reader's perspective and to invite a broadening of the horizons of the reader's world. Such a psychodynamic process of transformation warrants further psychological analysis.[73]

Schneiders's treatment of the process goes a step further toward "psychological analysis" with her discussion of "aesthetic surrender," which is a consciously adopted attitude that renders the reader susceptible to the meaning offered by the text. For Schneiders, "aesthetic surrender" is part of a three-phase movement. The first phase (as Ricoeur suggests) is an initial act of conscious distancing ("distanciation") from the text, using the tools of classical biblical criticism and a Ricoeurian "hermeneutic of suspicion" that "sifts the text for error and deceit" and seeks to overcome the limitations of a primally "naive" reading.[74]

But this critical distanciation from the text must be overcome if one is to appropriate its meaning:

> If the reader remains the critic, she or he is like the person who goes to a play but can never forget that the actors are acting, that the action is a play, and that the play's world is a stage. Unless the reader can, in a postcritical moment, be caught up in the text, the text cannot function for that person as transformative mediation of meaning.

The overcoming of the distance between text and reader is the second phase, and it requires a "deliberately fostered" attitude of "aesthetic surrender." Schneiders describes this as

> not necessarily surrender to the subject matter but a certain way of entering into the text, not in order to extract information, but in order to live in the world projected by the text. To enter in this way into the text the reader must suspend disbelief, suppress the distance that makes one say, "this isn't real; it's just a story." Like the spectator who, having finished reading the reviews, settles back as the lights dim and the curtain goes up. . . . The reader . . . puts aside specific reflection on historical details and scholarly arguments about authorship and begins to participate in the play of the text. . . . The text is experienced in its immediacy and transparency. The parable is my story, redescribing my world as challenged and transformed by the values of the reign of God.[75]

Having surrendered to the possibility of meaning in terms of the world projected by the text, the reader reaches the third phase of the process, a "critical existential interpretation" of that meaning, or, in Gadamer's terms, "radical personal engagement with . . . the truth claims of the text" toward the end of "life-integration through self-transcendence toward the horizon of ultimate value." This engagement consists of "genuine dialogue with the text, that like all dialogue, not only permits but demands development of both the interpreter and the text." On the one hand this dialogue affirms the reader's freedom to repudiate "morally unacceptable" subject matter of the text (patriarchal ideology, sexist language, trivialization and marginalization of women), but on the other hand it acknowledges the reader's right (and the right of the text) to celebrate its truth claims. This transformative, dialectical interpretation, Schneiders says,

> is not blind submission to the text as answer but an in-depth engagement of the text's subject matter, of its truth claims, in terms of the developed Christian consciousness of the contemporary believer within the contemporary community of faith. . . . Appropriation of the meaning of the text, the transformative achievement of interpretation, is neither a mastery of the text by the reader (an extraction of its meaning by the application of method) nor a mastery of the reader by the text (a blind submission to what the text says) but an ongoing dialogue with the text about its subject matter.[76]

Ricoeur, Gadamer, and Schneiders do allude from time to time to the psychological dimensions of the processes of preunderstanding, the fusion of horizons, and the acts of appropriation, application, and aesthetic surrender. Ricoeur in fact employs explicitly Freudian psychoanalytic categories to characterize the interpretive event as "an emptying of the narcissistic ego in favor of a selfhood which develops itself with the help of the text."[77] But what that selfhood consists of, consciously and unconsciously, what devices and strategies it habitually enlists in seeking its ends, and what those ends are (for example, homeostasis, individuation, self-realization) as functions native to the human psyche—all these remain significant questions for psychology, psychoanalysis, and scriptural scholarship.

6. Psychoanalytically Oriented Hermeneutical Theory. Two models for using a psychoanalytic approach as tools for understanding to the psychodynamics of reading are proposed by biblical scholars Ilona Rashkow and Stephen Moore, who find the act of biblical interpretation illumined by comparing it to the analysand-analyst transaction in the psychoanalytic process.

Rashhkow draws our attention to two parallels between the processes of biblical reading and psychoanalysis. The first is the two-stage experience of "identification" and "catharsis." The identification can transpire in the exchange either with biblical figures or with the analyst, and to either positive or negative effect. The "catharsis," involving purgation and pleasurable relief, leads to a transformation of "seeing," both at the conscious and unconscious levels, and to a breakdown of "old schemata" we use for viewing the world. The second parallel between the processes of biblical reading and psychoanalysis is seen in the motive that seems to be operative in both, namely the drive to gratify wishes and defeat fears (reminiscent of Holland's contention that reading is driven by the desire to reinforce one's identity). Rashkow, in effect, identifies the psychodynamics of hermeneutics with the psychodynamics of psychoanalysis, advancing a psychological interpretation of the motive, process, and outcome common to both.[78]

Stephen Moore takes another tack. He focuses not on the psychology of hermeneutics, but on the psychodynamics of the struggle of the biblical authors with such perennial issues as God, guilt, prescription and subversion of gender roles, and "reconfiguring the past," which he proposes are similar to the issues with which psychoanalysis is engaged. On the basis of these "striking similarities between biblical and psychoanalytic thought," Moore suggests there can be "a cross-fertilization that could enrich biblical studies and psychoanalytic theory," and that this connection has implications for a psychological interpretation of hermeneutics. However he does not spell out the details. At most, he offers the observation that psychoanalysis is a "para-religious discourse," but he leaves the implications for biblical interpretation and hermeneutics to future reflection.[79]

Both Rashkow and Moore, in highlighting the parallels between psychoanalysis and hermeneutics (Rashkow) and between psychoanalysis and biblical theology (Moore), are advocating the need to recognize the psychodynamic factors in all of these processes. Thus they are acknowledging not only that dimensions of biblical studies can be enlightened by psychoanalysis, but as Moore hints, possibly also the reverse.

Textual Performance as Hermeneutics in Psychological Perspective

Another set of issues raised by a psychological and psychoanalytic approach to the Bible concerns the various kinds of meaning we find in texts, the various forms we enlist to "perform" those meanings, and the various human faculties we exercise and appeal to in the process.

James Wiggins has observed that "we have tended in historical studies to focus on the rationalistic theologizing [of Origen, Clement, Jerome, and Augustine] through which the intelligentsia were wooed to Christianity . . . [but] have been less sensitive to the quantitatively far greater tradition through which the masses encountered Christian communication—sermons, commentaries, romances, legends, lives of the saints and history."[80] Post-Enlightenment hermeneutics, as Wiggins suggests, has tended to be logocentric and ratiocentric, employing words and reason as the primary mode of communication.

From a psychoanalytic or psychological perspective, however, hermeneutics is to be conceived in broader anthropological terms, namely as the act of a self that is equipped with a variety of sensitivities and a range of faculties of expression. It envisions the psyche as endowed with a capacity and propensity to perceive and mediate meaning in many forms, to attune itself to many modes of perception, and to enlist the meanings it finds in the service of many different dimensions of the self—the conative, affective, moral, and intuitive—as well as the rational and the cognitive. Frances Young observes that the "actualization of textual meaning" can be seen as analogous to the "performance of music and art," and in fact has, throughout the history of Judaeo-Christianity, been mediated through both.[81]

The psychological justification for a hermeneutic that is not limited to the strictly rational and verbal rests on two presuppositions. The first is that the text contains unconscious as well as conscious factors that can trigger comparable responses in the reader which, in turn, require forms of expression beyond reasoned discourse to communicate their full meaning. The second is that different psychological types (as discussed above) are oriented toward different kinds of meanings in the text and inclined toward different modes of conveying those meanings. The hermeneutical task, accordingly, is to find ways to "read" and "interpret/perform" the text that will honor the unconscious content of the text and the various modes of perception and performance intrinsic to the various types of readers.

A method of honoring these unconscious factors and the possibility of different interpretive modes is suggested by the psychoanalytic strategies of free association (Freud) and the techniques of "amplification" and "active imagination" (Jung).[82] The more developed of these is Jung's, which invites the reader to "translate" the meaning perceived in the text into a new form—whether clay, painting, liturgy, pageant, dance, or song. Jung's comment, as noted earlier, applies here as well: "Often the hands know how to solve a riddle with which the intellect has wrestled in vain."[83]

A survey of Judaeo-Christian tradition provides ample evidence that active imagination has in fact been employed for centuries. Biblical texts have been recast in the form of sermons, midrashic commentary, the fourfold forms of medieval biblical interpretation (literal, moral, allegorical, and anagogical), Bible study group discussions, teaching, miracle plays, liturgies, cantatas, soup kitchens, hospitals, schools, stained glass windows, paintings, statuary—whatever way the psyche may have seized upon to amplify and reimage the story of the text.[84] Until the post-Enlightenment period, the Judaeo-Christian tradition held the literal and verbal interpretation of the text to be only one mode among others for translating or "performancing" the text, regularly resorting to the imaginative, artistic, eleemosynary, and liturgical modes to fill in the picture. In the process, new dimensions of the text were unconcealed and new depths of the text were realized in concrete form. In many instances—for example, with religious art, literature, liturgy, music, or drama—the new form became the primary mediator of the meaning of the text, even more than the text itself, "speaking" persuasively to the will, conscience, imagination, and intuition, as well as to the rational mind, and affecting the audience at levels that exceed rational consciousness.

It is noteworthy that this same hermeneutic process has, in fact, been operative within the history of the biblical text itself, visible in the prodigious production of biblical myth, legend, psalm, religious tale, parable, hymn, and apocalypse. These were penned, not simply *de novo*, but in answer to the texts, oral or written, to which the biblical authors themselves were responding. In effect, three millennia of biblical interpretation, beginning with the text itself as an interpretive document, provide a vast panorama for observing the resourcefulness of the psyche in amplifying the proleptic power of biblical and pre-biblical images and symbols, personally and collectively, performing and harvesting their meaning in a spectrum of artistic, moral, liturgical, doctrinal, social, spiritual, and cultural expression designed to speak to and for the full aptitude of the soul.

The History of Biblical Effects in Psychological Perspective: Pathogenic and Therapeutic Effects

In 1971, historian of religion Wilfred Cantwell Smith called for a new generation of biblical scholars who would approach the history of the biblical text in a new way, examining not only its background but its foreground, chronicling not only its past history but its forward history, researching not only the powers that have produced the Bible but also those the Bible has itself produced—for better and for worse. For Smith, the story of the *Nachleben* ("after-life" or "continuing history" or "forward history") of the text is as much a part of biblical history as the story of its past, and merits just as much observation.[85]

Smith's proposal has been echoed in other quarters. Gadamer announced in the early 1970s the need for a new "effective-historical consciousness" (*wirkungsgeschichtliches Bewusstsein*) that would note the impact the Bible has had on those who interpret it and how this, in turn, affects the way they perceive and read the text.[86] In 1967, Jauss introduced the concept of "reception history" (*Rezeptionsgeschichte*), pointing to the various ways the text has been "received" in various sociohistorical settings and, by implication, the different "effects" texts can generate in readers.[87] In 1977, biblical scholar John Dominic Crossan, in his article "Perspectives and Methods in Contemporary Biblical Criticism," called for study of the "post-history" as well as "pre-history" of the biblical text. Finally, in 1994, Martin Hengel, in his presidential address to the Society of New Testament Scholars, issued a call for research on "the history of effects" (*Auslegungs- und Wirkungsgeschichte*) as well as on "the history of interpretation."[88]

One of the objectives of psychological biblical criticism will be to provide insight into the causes and histories of these "effects," as well as into the roles they have played and continue to play in the psychic economy of individuals and groups, focusing on two genres of effect, the pathogenic and the therapeutic.

Pathogenic Effects

It is no longer a secret in scholarly and even ecclesiastical literature that the Bible and its interpretation can have pathogenic effects on individuals and cultures—an acknowledgment that has been both liberating and dismaying for those who treasure the text. Smith, for example, would have us recognize as part of biblical history "the appalling harm that from time to time scriptures have wrought, the suffering that on occasion they have not only condoned but instigated." He adds:

Historical instances abound. Scripture served as the chief moral justification for slavery among those who resisted proposals to abolish that institution; and indeed as sanctifying many an oppressive status quo against movements for justice. . . . Again, it has served the degradation of women. . . . Another: the mighty force of a scripture's binding a community together has worked to make sharp, and often relentless, divergence between communities. Especially in the case of the Western triad—Jewish, Christian, Islamic—the scripture-based disparagement of those deemed outsiders has been, and continues to be, disastrous.[89]

Ideological critics draw attention to a striking irony, namely that a biblical text may be liberating for one person or group but oppressive to another. A case in point is the story of the Exodus. When refracted through the experience of liberationist theologians and civil rights leaders, the Exodus functions as a symbol of freedom. But refracted through the experience of the Native American, whose identity is not with the conquering Israelites but with the invaded Canaanites, it becomes a symbol of oppression. Robert Allen Warrior, an Osage Indian, contends that the Exodus saga provided "Puritans and other European settlers in North American with a biblical text whose particular ideological reading justified the destruction of indigenous peoples."[90]

Biblical scholars Phyllis Trible, Renita Weems, and Sandra Schneiders, along with feminists Rita Brock, Joanne Brown, and Rebecca Parker, have documented the oppressive posture toward women both within Scripture and in the cultural institutions that have used Scripture as justification for their stance.[91] Robert Carroll has traced the "ferocities, contradictions, and opacities" of Christian persecutions to scriptural roots. Philip Greven's *Spare the Child*, as the title suggests, traces the roots of some child abuse to Scripture. René Girard and Robert Hamerton-Kelly have raised awareness of the ways biblical texts have provided sanctions for violence. Gerd Lüdemann has probed the potential of violence seeded in the biblical notions of election and holy war in the Hebrew Scriptures and in the anti-Judaism to be found in the New Testament. John Dominic Crossan speaks of the lethal effect that the passion narrative came to have with the changing political fortunes of the early Christian community:

In its origins and first moments, . . . Christian propaganda was fairly innocent. Those first Christians were relatively powerless Jews, and compared with them the Jewish authorities represented serious and threatening power. As long as Christians were the marginalized and disenfranchised ones, such passion fiction about Jewish responsibility and Roman innocence did nobody much harm. But, once the Roman Empire became Christian, that fiction turned lethal.[92]

Pastoral counselors and psychologists of religion have added their voice on potentially pathogenic elements in the biblical texts and possible pathological effects of biblical interpretation. Donald Capps comments on the seeds of permission for child abuse some have found in the text, and Jungian analyst John Dourley in *The Illness That We Are* cites the pathology that has resulted from the systematic exclusion of materiality, the feminine, and the sexual-instinctual from the God-concept, as well as from the projection of a "militant monotheistic faith that kills" in Western Christian and biblical tradition.[93]

It will be the task of psychological biblical criticism to amplify the work already undertaken by feminist, ideological, and history-of-religions critics. This means earmarking the dark biases that enjoy advocacy in certain biblical texts and continue to cause harm in human affairs both within and outside communities of faith as they are refracted through the psyches of readers. It means attending to interpretations of the Bible, as well as to the original texts themselves, for the pathologies they can propagate from time to time. It means publicizing the fact that texts invite projections, and even the most sublime of texts can be bent, consciously or unconsciously, to the service of the darkest and most harmful motives.[94] Finally, it means raising the consciousness of readers to the labyrinth of powers latent in the text and themselves, heeding the caveat of Cedric Johnson that, "Being on our own, each of us must take personal responsibility of coming to know the wolf within or we risk becoming the lamb that slaughters the rest of the flock."[95]

Therapeutic Effects

Scholarly interest in the pathogenic aspects of the Bible has been matched at the end of the twentieth century with renewed interest in its therapeutic dimension. As much as the Bible provides evidence of pathogenic potential, even more does it provide evidence that it can transform consciousness, change behavior patterns, and open up a new cognition of reality in ways that have affected individuals and shaped entire cultures for generations.

Evidence for this is implicit in the philosophic and psychological hermeneutical models discussed above. Gadamer speaks of the fusion of horizons between text and reader that leads to expanded consciousness. A Jungian perspective sees the text as a galaxy of archetypal stories, models, and images that are compensatory to consciousness and nourish the development of the self in the process of individuation. An object-relations approach finds in the ongoing process of Bible-reading a potentially transformative experience for the reader on the move between infantile narcissism and maturity. A cognitive psychological perspective sees the text leading to a revisioning and restructuring of one's world. From a learning theory perspective the Bible reinforces and generates new models of behavior. Speech-act theory takes note of the power of biblical language to change the reader with its words of promise, command, blessing, or forgiveness. Norman Holland's psychological reader-response theory understands reading as a psychodynamic process aimed at reinforcing one's identity.

Professional biblical scholarship—though somewhat tardily—has also begun to turn its hand to the task of exploring the therapeutic nature, function, and effect of the Bible and its interpretation. As a result of the major research shift in biblical scholarship in the 1970s from the exclusive use of diachronic historical models to the inclusion of synchronic models (see chapter 3), we hear new voices. Canonical criticism speaks of the text within the context of a believing community, expressing interest in the Bible's saving power. Contextual criticism, with its focus on the ability of the Bible to address different types of communities, underlines the character of the text as a mediator of a personal and socially redemptive and liberating Word. Feminist criticism attests to the transformative, liberational, and egalitarian promise and power of the Bible despite its pockets of misogynist repression and violence.

To these efforts, psychological criticism promises to add its voice, focusing on two aspects of the text's therapeutic function: as a text that is innately therapeutic, dedicated to the healing task of the cure and care of souls; and as a text that generates therapeutic effects.

1. The Innately Therapeutic Purpose of Religious Texts. In his essay on "The State of Psychotherapy Today," Carl Jung writes that "religions are psychotherapeutic systems in the truest sense of the word. . . . They express the whole range of the psychic problem in mighty images; they are the avowal and recognition of the soul, and at the same time the revelation of the soul's nature." For him, their principal function is to recognize the reality of the psyche (soul), to plumb its nature, to divine its maladies and prescribe its cures. "Not only is religion not the enemy of the sick," Jung writes, "it is actually a system of psychic healing, as the use of the Christian term 'cure of souls' makes clear, and as is also evident from the [Bible]."[96]

Jung's point of view on the therapeutic function of religion and of the Bible is echoed elsewhere. Calvert Stein's 1976 article on "Psychotherapy in the Bible" in the *Journal of the American Academy of Psychiatry and Neurology*, identifies analogues to psychotherapeutic strategies at work in the biblical text, including psychosomatics, psychodrama, and group therapies. Robert Leslie and Wilhelm Wuellner, in *The Surprising Gospel: Intriguing Psychological Insights from the New Testament* (1984), find the therapeutic function quintessential to the purpose of the biblical text, adducing comparisons between therapeutic models in the text and psychological models from contemporary culture (Carl Jung, Viktor Frankl, Henry Stack Sullivan, Rollo May, Virginia Satir).[97]

To these voices can be added the testimony of the Bible itself, which frequently identifies its *raison d'être* as that of healing the mind, the soul, the self, and the community. In the Hebrew Scriptures the psalmist envisions the law as an agent for reviving the soul, making wise the simple, rejoicing the heart, and being sweeter to the soul than the drippings of the honeycomb (Ps. 19: 7–10). The wisdom literature self-consciously aims at providing patterns of fruitful living with words of insight and instruction in wise dealing, righteousness, justice, prudence, knowledge, and discretion (Prov. 1:1–5).

The New Testament is no different. John tells us the *telos* of the Gospel is that the reader "may have life" (John 20:31). Paul announces that the purpose of "whatever was written in former days" is to serve "for our instruction, that by steadfastness and by the encouragement of the scriptures we might have hope" (Rom. 15:4). We read in Hebrews 4:12, "The word of God is living and active, sharper than any two-edged sword, piercing to the division of soul and spirit, of the joints and marrow, and discerning the thoughts and intentions of the heart."

Finally, the vocabulary of the Bible regularly plays on a glossary of terms that speak of the healing of self or society: sanctification, reconciliation, redemption, transformation, liberation, and justification. From the standpoint of talmudic tradition, the writings of the early church, the reformers, scholastics, and contemporary biblical theology, the text reveals and mediates wholeness to its readers and to the community that treasures and studies its words. Origen voices this perspective in his fourth-century essay, "First Principles":

> One must register the thoughts of the holy Scriptures in one's soul in a triple manner. The simple man will be edified by what we may call the flesh of Scripture, by which we mean its obvious interpretation; he who has made some progress will be edified by its soul; whilst the perfect man . . . will be edified by "the spiritual law." . . . For just as man consists of body, soul and spirit, so too does the Scripture which God has provided for the salvation of men.[98]

A major undertaking for psychological biblical criticism will be to develop a critical method for identifying, measuring, and assessing the degree to which the text presents itself as the mediator of a therapeutic agenda, to come to an understanding of the strategies it recommends for achieving this agenda, to compare it with contemporary therapeutic models, and to consider what insight it can add to collective scholarship and thought on the *cura animarum* in our own time.

2. Therapeutic Effects of the Bible. That the Bible has exercised therapeutic effects on its readers for centuries is undeniable in light of a sea of testimony. It ranges from the classic statement in Deuteronomy 30:11–14 on the power of the "word" within the self, to John Wesley's experience of his heart being "strangely warmed," to contemporary psychological research on the effects of the biblical text on readers. Ernest Wall's 1973 article, "The Kerygma's Psychology and Human Distress," discerns the "instruments of therapy" in the Gospels that can restore equilibrium by overcoming doubt, guilt, and fear, mobilizing inner forces, and inspiring self-maximalization. More recently, psychiatrist Robert Coles documents the effects of biblical stories, personalities, and images on the spiritual life of children:

> Biblical stories have a way of being used by children to look inward as well as upward. It should come as no surprise that the stories of Adam and Eve, Abraham and Isaac, Noah and the Ark, Abel and Cain, Samson and Delilah, David and Goliath, get linked in the minds of millions of children to their own personal stories as they explore the nature of sexuality and regard with awe, envy, or anger the power of their parents, as they struggle with brothers and sisters, as they imagine themselves as actual or potential lovers, or as actual or potential antagonists. The stories are not mere symbolism, giving expression to what people go through emotionally. Rather, I heard children embracing religious stories because they are quite literally inspiring—exciting their minds to further thought of fantasy and helping them become more grown, more contemplative and sure of themselves."[99]

One of the richest sources of clinical information on the effects of the Bible on its readers is the information gathered by pastoral counselors, and one of the most useful offerings of that information to date is Donald Capps's *Biblical Approaches to Pastoral Counseling*.[100] His work is particularly helpful in providing psychological insight into the constructive and therapeutic effect of certain types of biblical passages in characteristic counseling situations. Capps begins by acknowledging the pathogenic potential of the text, especially in the counseling setting, issuing a caveat against the use of Scripture to moralize, to coerce, to work a magic cure, or to encourage obsessive ritualistic behavior. Beyond that, Capps sets forth a heuristic typology of therapeutic uses of Scriptural texts in counseling settings. These uses include:

• the application of scriptural texts (Proverbs) as an aid to moral realism and as a form of reality therapy.

• the use of the Bible as an aid to emotional catharsis and renewed hope (with examples from the Psalms of prayer models for clarifying experiences of loss and renewal).

• the employment of Scripture as an aid to perceptual reorganization (citing the recent parables research on the cognitive reorientation implied in this biblical genre).

• the utilization of Scripture as a diagnostic tool, deploying the biblical stories and characters as associative devices for identifying the reader's conscious and unconscious complexes, fears, ideals, and needs.

• the serious study of Scripture for historical-critical insight that can liberate one from oppressive biblical literalism (for example, the enjoinder for wives to obey their husbands, which, when taken to extreme, can be read as a divine mandate for passive submission to spousal abuse).

• the mining of Scripture for archetypal paradigms, providing the reader with liberating and inspiring models for future action, perception, and behavior.

Capps concludes with the added observation that the therapeutic biblical effect is a function not only of a single "inspiring" idea or text, but also of an encounter with a person or counselor who has internalized and exemplifies a "biblical perspective" (for example, a sense of providence, repentance, forgiveness, grace, of vocation, justice, faith, hope, love, and awareness of "the holy"). Such a person demonstrates the viability of living out of the constellation of realities that Scripture advances as necessary for the healing of the soul, and mediates those to the hearer as a possibility for his or her own being—all as an expression of biblical "effect."

A primary goal of psychological biblical criticism will be to come to understand in greater psychological and psychoanalytic detail the secret of the therapeutic and catalytic effect of the biblical text and the role it plays in the habits, strategies, and agendas of the human psyche. Perhaps this is what Carl Jung had in mind when he spoke about the therapeutic power of words:

> Whoever speaks in primordial images speaks with a thousand voices; he enthralls and overpowers, while at the same time he lifts the idea he is seeking to express out of the occasional and transitory into the realm of the everenduring. He transmutes our personal destiny into the destiny of mankind, and evokes in us all those beneficent forces that ever and anon have enabled humanity to find a refuge from every peril and to outlive the longest night.[101]

Notes

Preface

1. Carl Gustav Jung, *The Collected Works of C. G. Jung*, vol. 20, Bollingen Series, eds. Gerhard Adler et al. (Princeton: Princeton University, 1953–78), 11:172 (reference is to volume 11, paragraph 72 in the *Collected Works* [henceforth, *CW*], following the general index, which employs paragraph numbers rather than page numbers).

2. Gerd Theissen, *Psychological Aspects of Pauline Theology*, trans. John P. Galvin (Philadelphia: Fortress Press, 1987), 398.

3. Joseph A. Fitzmyer, S.J. *Scripture, the Soul of Theology* (New York: Paulist, 1994), 51–52.

4. The phrase was used by F. C. Grant, "Psychological Study of the Bible," in Jacob Neusner, ed., *Religions in Antiquity: Essays in Memory of Erwin Ramsdell Goodenough*, *Numen*, Spl. XIV (Leiden: Brill, 1968), 112. Gerd Theissen has employed optional phrases, "psychological exegesis" or "a hermeneutically oriented psychology of religion" (*Psychological Aspects*, 1–4). D. Andrew Kille proposed the adoption of the phrase used in this volume. See the discussion on "naming the field" in chap. 3, p. 75.

5. Fitzmyer, *Scripture*, 51–52.

6. James E. Dittes, "Analytical (Jungian) Psychology and Pastoral Care," in *Dictionary of Pastoral Care and Counseling*, ed. R. Hunter (Nashville: Abingdon, 1990), 30.

7. Jung, *Collected Works*.

Chapter 1: Biblical Psychology

1. Franz Delitzsch, *A System of Biblical Psychology*, 2d ed., trans. R. E. Wallis (1869; reprint, Grand Rapids: Baker Book House, 1966), 3.

2. *De Anima* 14.5.

3. "Psychology," in *The New Encyclopedia Britannica: Macropedia* (Chicago: Encyclopedia Brittanica, Inc., 1989), 322.

4. Delitzsch, *System*.

5. Morton Hunt, *The Story of Psychology* (New York: Doubleday, 1993), 128.

6. Delitzsch, *System*, 3, 5.

7. The English word *soul* (and the German *Seele*), which usually translates the Biblical term *psyche* (or the Hebrew *nephesh* or *nishamah*), is at root a psychological term in that it serves as a semantic vehicle for talking about the phenomenon for which the Greek word *psyche* was devised (and which it regularly translates). Thus the three terms, Greek *psyche*, along with the Latin *anima* and the Anglo-Saxon *soul* as translations of Biblical *psyche*, are to be seen as semantically contiguous terms referring to a common semantic field, symbolizing a common phenomenon, namely the emoting, sensing, perceiving, desiring, imagining, knowing, thinking, willing, dreaming, developing self. At the same time, depending on their use, they may denote quite different and even opposing aspects or features of that phenomenon: for example, preexistence, corporeality, and/or immortality. Eighteenth century psychology (especially empirical psychology) began to disuse the English term *soul* when its connotation became limited to dogmatic and metaphysical considerations, though in many psychological and psychoanalytic circles, *soul* or *Seele* remained viable as a synonym for *psyche*. In recent times, both in popular culture and in some psychological and psychoanalytic research, *soul* is being reinstated as a psychological term, adverting to the self as a center of conscious and/or unconscious awareness and functioning. In the present work we will use the words *psyche*, *soul*, and *anima* as largely interchangeable translation terms when referring to their usage during most of the history of psychology in the West. See W. Barrett, *Death of the Soul: From Descartes to the Computer* (New York: Doubleday, 1986); D. Capps and R. K. Fenn, eds., *On Losing the Soul: Essays in the Social Psychology of Religion* (Albany, N.Y.: SUNY Press, 1995); P. Cousineau, ed., *Soul: An Archaeology: Readings from Socrates to Ray Charles* (San Francisco: HarperSanFrancisco, 1994); R. Swinburne, *The Evolution of the Soul* (Oxford: Clarendon, 1986). For a fuller discussion of *psyche*, *soul*, and *self*, see chap. 4, pp. 95–111.

8. The term *psychology* appears two centuries earlier than the names for its two sister disciplines, "biology" (1802, Jean-Baptiste Lamarck) and "sociology" (1840, Auguste Comte); see F. H. Lapointe, "Origin and Evolution of the Term 'Psychology,'" *American Psychologist* 25 (1970): 640; H. Van de Kemp, "Origin and Evolution of the Term 'Psychology': Addenda," *American Psychologist* 35 (1980): 774; Morton Hunt, *The Story of Psychology* (New York: Doubleday Anchor, 1993), 59. Melanchton, like many theologians between the second century and the Reformation, borrowed the title from Aristotle's classic study of the psyche, *Peri Psyches*, known more commonly in Latin translation, *De Anima*. Delitzsch, *System*, 6–7, reports that Melanchton read Aristotle in the Greek unlike his scholastic predecessors who used the Latin.

9. D. Hothersall, *History of Psychology*, 3d ed. (New York: McGraw Hill, 1995), 36; Lapointe, "Origin," 640; D. J. Murray, *A History of Western Psychology* (Englewood Cliffs, N.J.: Prentice-Hall, 1983), 64. Goeckel is often referred to by his Latin *nom de plume*, Goclenius.

10. Denis Diderot in the 1750s reinforced the distinction, speaking of a "science en psychologie experimentale et psychologie raisonnée"; see Lapointe, "Origin," 641. Thomas Hardy Leahey, *A History of Psychology: Main Currents in Psychological Thought*, 2d ed. (Englewood Cliffs, N.J.: Prentice-Hall, 1987), 55, 144.

11. Van de Kemp, "Origin," 774.

12. *Leviathan*, chap. 46; see Hunt, *Story of Psychology*, 73.

13. In Lapointe, "Origin," 644.

14. The universities include Clark, Harvard, Columbia, Pennsylvania, Toronto, Yale, Brown, Catholic University of America, Cornell, Iowa, McGill, Michigan, Nebraska, Princeton, Stanford, and Wisconsin.

15. From Hall's presidential address on "History and Prospects of Experimental Psychology in America," delivered at the first annual meeting of the American Psychological Association at the University of Pennsylvania, December 17, 1892; cited in Hothersall, *History*, 357. A full bibliographic picture of eighteenth-century psychology appears in the third volume of James M. Baldwin, ed. *Dictionary of Philosophy and Psychology* (New York: Macmillan, 1901–05); see also, Van de Kemp "Origin," p. 774; Lapointe, "Origin," 644.

16. Lapointe, "Origin," 645.

17. Lapointe, "Origin," 645. The subject index of David Hothersall's 3d edition *History of Psychology* (1995) contains no entry either for *psyche* or for *soul*.

18. *Encyclopedia Britannica*, s.v. "Psychology," 322.

19. M. D. Lemonick et al., "In Search of the Mind: Glimpses of the Brain," *Time* 146 (3/1955): 49. See also examples of the broad cultural use of the word *soul* in Cousineau, *Soul*.

20. Hunt, *Story of Psychology*, 310.

21. *System*, 3.

22. Lapointe, Origin," 640. The tables of contents of current histories of psychology uniformly begin the story of psychology in classical antiquity. Hunt (*Story of Psychology*) begins the story in classical Greece, classifying all psychology prior to Wundt (1879) as "pre-scientific." David Hothersall (*History of Psychology*) follows suit, classifying pre-Wundt psychology under the rubric, "Psychology and the Ancients" and "Philosophical and Scientific Antecedents of Psychology." Thomas Hardy Leahey (*A History of Psychology: Main Currents in Psychological Thought*) devotes six chapters to the rubric, "Background to

Psychology," covering the classical world, the medieval and renaissance thinkers, and the philosophic-psychologic tradition of the seventeenth to nineteenth centuries. David J. Murray (*A History of Western Psychology*) similarly covers the pre-Wundt tradition with six chapters, beginning with "The Beginnings of Psychology" (Hellenistic and Roman), "Early Christian and Medieval Psychology" (Augustine, Aquinas et al.), and with separate chapters on the sixteenth and seventeenth centuries (Descartes), focusing on German, British, and French traditions prior to 1879. R. S. Peters, ed. *Brett's History of Psychology, Revised and Abridged* (Cambridge, Mass.: M.I.T. University Press, 1962) is an abridgement of the masterful three-volume work by G. S. Brett first published in 1912. The abridgement announces on its cover that it retains "the astonishing erudition of Brett's classic work" which "unfolds the full sweep of the history of psychology beginning with the speculations of the ancient Greeks through to the present." Eleven of its fifteen chapters are devoted to the history of psychology prior to Wundt.

23. R. S. Peters and C. A. Mace, "Psychology" in *The Encyclopedia of Philosophy*, ed. Paul Edwards, vol. 7 (New York: Macmillan, 1967). Peters and Mace define psychology as "the study of the mental life and activities of animals and men," admitting that the value of the term has been drastically reduced from its base meaning as the "study of the soul"; 1–27.

24. Peters and Mace, "Psychology," 1.

25. Robert I. Watson, *The Great Psychologists*, 4th ed. (Philadelphia: J. B. Lippincott, 1978), 146.

26. *Discourse on Method*, IV; see Hothersall, *History*, 46.

27. *Discourse on Method*, IV; see Hunt, *Story of Psychology*, 64 n.5.

28. Richard Lowry, *The Evolution of Psychological Theory: A Critical History of Concepts and Presuppositions*, 2d ed. (New York: Aldine, 1982), 61–62.

29. Hunt, *Story of Psychology*, 139.

30. Hunt, *Story of Psychology*, 559, 644.

31. Peters and Mace, "Psychology," 1, 4. See the discussion of Aristotle's "psychology" in Hunt, *Story of Psychology*, 27, and Leahey, *History*, 47–52. The latter notes that Aristotle's tri-partite model of the psyche originates with Plato.

32. Hunt, *Story of Psychology*, 6–7. For elaboration on Greco-Roman "psychology" as developed below, see Hothersall, *History*, 1–33, especially 28–29; Leahey, *History*, 34–57, especially, 45, 52, 55; Murray, *History*, 8–38, especially 25, 27, 28–29, 37; Peters and Mace, "Psychology," 1–6.

33. *On the Sacred Disease*, attributed to Hippocrates. See Hunt, *Story of Psychology*, 18.

34. Galen, *On the Passions and Errors of the Soul*, cited in Hothersall, *History*, 21.

35. Murray, *History*, 61, cites the publication of 46 new commentaries (along with the reprinting of earlier commentaries) on Aristotle's *De Anima* in the sixteenth and seventeenth centuries.

36. G. De Vries, *Bijdrage tot de psychologie van Tertullianus* (Utrecht: Kemink en Zoon, 1929); Johannes Quasten, *Patrology*, vol. 2. The Ante-Nicene Literature After Irenaeus. (Westminster, MD: Newman Press, 1953), 289–90.

37. Bro. Daniel F. Stramara, OSB, "The Use of Psychology According to Vatican II," *The Pecos Benedictine* (March 1990): 2–3; H. Misiak and V. S. Sexton, *History of Psychology* (New York: Grune & Stratton, 1966), 8; see Hothersall, *History*, 35, who adds, "the label seems premature, but Augustine's *Confessions* is still of great interest for its analysis and description of one man's psyche."

38. His work, *Concerning the Psyche and the Body*, is cited by Eusebius and Jerome; Delitzsch, *System*, 1–2.

39. Gregory Thaumaturgus wrote an essay entitled, "On the Subject of the Soul."

40. Murray, *History*, 43.

41. Lactantius discusses the creation and immortality of the soul in *De Opificio Dei* and *Divinae Institutiones*; see Quasten, *Patrology*, 2:392–410.

42. Delitzsch, *System*, 4, reports that Gregory's copious works contain "abundant psychological elements," especially his *Peri Psyches kai Anasteos Pros Ten Adelphen Makrinan* (*Dialogus de anima et resurrectione qui inscribitur Macrinia*). Gregory relates how she "examined human nature in a scientific way," discussing the "philosophy of the soul." See Quasten, *Patrology*, 3:261.

43. His treatise, *Peri Physeos Anthropou*, attempts to construct a Platonically based portrait of the psyche that will be consonant with Christian teaching. In the process he provides a directory of Hellenistic philosophical anthropology, citing Plato, Aristotle, Epicurus, Galen, Aetius, Ammonius, Plotinus, Porphyry, Jamblichus, and others; see Quasten, *Patrology*, 3:353; F. L. Cross and E. A. Livingstone, eds. *The Oxford Dictionary of the Christian Church*, 2d rev. ed. (Oxford: Oxford University Press, 1990) [henceforth, ODCC], 959.

44. He defends a Neoplatonist theory against the substantialist view of Faustus of Riez who "held that the soul as a created substance was of a corporeal and extended character'; see Delitzsch, *System*, 4; ODCC, 299.

45. His *De Anima* systematically delineates the nature of the soul in twelve chapters, beginning with a definition of terms. He founded two monasteries as academies in which secular and religious learning were integrated,

reinforcing the monastic tradition of preserving the classical culture of Europe during the Dark Ages; Delitzsch, *System*, 4; ODCC, 246–47.

46. His writings are largely commentaries on Aristotle, including one on the *De Anima*. See Delitzsch, *System*, 4–5; *Encyclopedia Britannica* 14th ed., s.v. Joannes Philiponus.

47. Though an avid Neoplatonist, Aeneas rejected the Platonic notion of the pre-existence of the soul on Biblical grounds; see Delitzsch, *System*, 4–5; ODCC, 21.

48. Delitzsch, *System*, 5; ODCC, 594–95.

49. Quasten, *Patrology*, 2:287–90, questions De Vries's phrase, "first Christian psychology," on the grounds that the document is written to correct "contemporary errors," not to construct a "psychology." Though Quasten correctly identifies Tertullian's motive, he underestimates Tertullian's achievement. See Delitzsch, *System*, 3.

50. De Praescr. 7; see Quasten, *Patrology*, 2:320–21.

51. The severest critics of classical philosophy include Irenaeus, Peter of Alexandria, Cassiodorus, and Jerome. Irenaeus regarded cultural and philosophical influences a threat to faith. Those who embraced classical thought as a helpmate of theology include Clement of Alexandria, Lacantius, Ambrose, Augustine, and Aquinas; see Leahey, *History*, 54; Quasten, *Patrology*, 2:20, 264, 289, 321.

52. He cites Wis. of Sol. 6:1, "God searches hearts"; see Prov. 24:12; Matt. 5:28; 9:4; Rom. 10:10; *De Anima* 15, 3–5.

53. Tertullian makes an empirical observation compatible with experimental dream psychology today, that even infants dream, observing "how they toss in their sleep, wag their heads, and sometimes smile" (49. 1–2).

54. CW 4:739; 6:19, 28; 11:771; 15:195; 17:310. Jung alternates the term "Christianus and religiosus," predicating that the God archetype functions in humans from early childhood.

55. For Augustine, Greek *psyche* is usually rendered with Latin *anima*, though on occasion Augustine can also render *psyche* as *spiritus* or *mens*; *Civ.* 11.26. *Sol.* 1.7. See Gerard O'Daly, *Augustine's Philosophy of Mind* (Berkeley: University of California Press, 1987), 1, 7–8. See Leahey, *History*, 61.

56. Ernest L. Fortin, "Augustine's *De Quantitate Animae* or the Spiritual Dimensions of Human Existence," in Agostino D'Ippona, ed., *De Moribus Ecclesiae Catholicae et de Moribus Manichaeorum; De Quantitate Animae* (Palermo: Edizioni "Augustinus," 1991), 136–38.

57. *Quantitas* does not refer to corporeal size of the soul, since Augustine denies its corporeality. It refers to the dimensions and parts of the soul. Augustine tells his interlocutor, Evodius, "Now let me . . . assist you to an appreciation of how great the soul is, not in regard to extension in space and time, but

in regard to its power (*vis*) and capacity (*potentia*) (*quant. an.* 32,69). See Ernest Fortin, *De Quantitate*, 136, 155.

58. Other essays of Augustine's on the soul are *Soliloquia* ("The Soliloquies"); *De Ordine* ("Concerning Order"); *Contra Priscillianistas et Origenistas* ("Against the Priscillians and the Origenists). See Langdon Gilkey, "Ordering the Soul: Augustine's Manifold Legacy," *Christian Century*, 105 (April 27, 1988): 427.

59. *De v. rel.* 39, 72. Augustine is indebted to the neo-Platonist, Plotinus, for this introspective method; K. J. Weintraub, "St. Augustine's Confessions: The Search for the Christian Self," in Donald Capps and James E. Dittes, ed., *The Hunger of the Heart: Reflections on the Confessions of Augustine*, Society for the Scientific Study of Religion Monograph Series, Number 8 (West Lafayette, Ind.: Society for the Scientific Study of Religion, 1990), 11–12. See Quasten, *Patrology*, 4:406–7; Peters and Mace, "Psychology," 5.

60. Gilkey, "Ordering the Soul," 427.

61. *De Quant.* 79. Augustine makes no absolute claim either for his "psychology" or "theology." He acknowledges that these same five phenomena can be differentiated in countless other ways. See O'Daly, *Augustine's Philosophy*, 7, 14–15.

62. *Gn. litt.* 7.18.24; 12.23.49; 12.30.58;12.15.31; see O'Daly, *Augustine's Philosophy*, 81, 115–17, 179.

63. See O'Daly, *Augustine's Philosophy*, 43–47, 111.

64. Leahey, *History*, 64.

65. *Conf.* 10.21; 10.26; *Trin.* 12.23; see O'Daly, *Augustine's Philosophy*, 133, 136; Murray, *History*, 46.

66. *C. Acad.* 1.7; *Mag., par.* 40; see O'Daly, *Augustine's Philosophy*,164, 175; Murray, *History*, 47; Wayne G. Rollins, *Jung and the Bible* (Atlanta: John Knox, 1983), 388–89.

67. *En Ps.* 31, 2,6; see Quasten, *Patrology*, 4:413–14; Murray, *History*, 47; R. W. Crapps, "Augustine of Hippo," in *Dictionary of Pastoral Care and Counseling* [henceforth, *DPCC*], ed. Rodney L. Hunter (Nashville: Abingdon, 1990), 58.

68. "Recurrent Questions in Psychology" in Hothersall, *History*, 1–2.

69. Quasten, *Patrology*, 3:352–53.

70. Peters and Mace, "Psychology," 4; Murray, *History*, 44, 47.

71. *Letter* 9; see F. J. Braceland and M. Stock, *Modern Psychiatry* (Garden City, N.Y.: Doubleday, 1963), 42.

72. *Adv. Haer.* 5, 9, 1; Quasten, *Patrology*, I:310.

73. Quasten, *Patrology* 2:388; see Plato, *Phaedo*, 72–73.

74. Murray, *History*, 43, 55.

75. Albertus Magnus wrote commentaries on the psychological works of Aristotle, with dependence on Avicenna, Boethius, and St. John of Damascus.

Duns Scotus wrote *The Spirituality and Immortality of the Human Soul* and *Concerning Human Knowledge*, commenting on mental illusions and studies of intelligence. See Murray, *History*, 54–55.

76. Murray, *History*, 48–51; Leahey, *History*, 64–67.

77. Leahey, *History*, 66–67.

78. Leahey, *History*, 73, suggests that Aquinas's separation of reason and revelation as independent modes of knowing lays the ground for the separation of science and religion four centuries later. See Hunt, *Story of Psychology*, 55.

79. Leahey, *History*, 72; Hunt, *Story of Psychology*, 55–57.

80. Hothersall, *History*, 36.

81. Murray, *History*, 61.

82. Murray, *History*, 62–64.

83. Hothersall, *History*, 35.

84. Delitzsch comments that although many "psychological 'writings of the scholastics surpassed Melanchton's in fullness and depth of thought, Melanchton's work nonetheless was' elegant in learning, sound, liberal . . . more serene"; Delitzsch, *System*, 6.

85. Delitzsch, *System*, 26–28.

86. Delitzsch, *System*, 9–12.

87. Delitzsch, *System*, 9–12. For a fuller bibliography of psychological works of the period and of "biblical psychologies" in particular, see J. M. Baldwin, ed. *Dictionary of Philosophy and Psychology* (New York: Macmillan, 1901–05); and H. Van de Kemp, *Psychology and Theology in Western Thought, 1672–1965: A Historical and Annotated Bibliography* (Millwood, N.Y.: Kraus International, 1984).

88. *Die Religion in Geschichte und Gegenwart*, 1958 ed., s.v. Franz Julius Delitzsch; see also Samuel Ives Curtiss, *Franz Delitzsch: A Memorial Tribute* (Edinburgh: T. & T. Clark, 1891), especially Delitzsch's "autobiography," 82–85, and bibliography, 85–96.

89. Originally located in Leipzig, it was refounded in Münster by K. H. Rengstorf in 1948.

90. Delitzsch, *System*, 267, 432. Delitzsch's pietism is evident especially in his inclusion of a sermon on Romans 8:18–23 in an appendix, in which he develops the notion of inner transformation of humanity into the image of the "God-man."

91. M. Scott Fletcher, *The Psychology of the New Testament*, 2d ed. (New York: Hodder & Stoughton, 1912), v, vii.

92. Fletcher, *Psychology*, 4–6, 14–16, 18–19.

93. Fletcher, *Psychology*, vii.

94. Fletcher, *Psychology*, 175, 179–81.

95. Fletcher, *Psychology*, 107.

96. Fletcher, *Psychology*, 145.

97. Fletcher, *Psychology*, 9–10, 164, 205–6, 302.

98. *Psychological Aspects of Pauline Theology* (Philadelphia: Fortress Press, 1987), 10, 28, 394. The volume was originally published as *Psychologische Aspekte paulinischer Theologie* (Göttingen: Vandenhoeck & Ruprecht, 1983).

Chapter 2: Freud and Jung

1. Sigmund Freud, "An Autobiographical Study," *The Standard Edition of the Complete Psychological Works of Sigmund Freud*, ed. James Strachey (London: Hogarth Press and the Institute of Psychoanalysis, 1953–74) 20: 8 (volume 20, page 8) [henceforth *SE*].

2. C. G. Jung, *The Visions Seminars*, vol. 1 (Zurich: Spring Publications, 1976), 156; see Edward Edinger, *The Bible and the Psyche: Individuation Symbolism in the Old Testament* (Toronto: Inner City Books, 1986), 11.

3. Peters and Mace, *Philosophy*, 23–24, 26. In the context of late nineteenth and early twentieth century psychology, Freud and Jung stand in the tradition of "philosophical psychology" or "philosophy of mind," in continuity with the earlier *psychologia rationalis* of Kant, Leibniz, and Hegel. Contemporary psychology acknowledges more readily than earlier positivists that although some psychology has to be done "on a laboratory stool, in a bird watcher's blind, or behind a one-way screen," other legitimate psychological work "can properly be done in an armchair." Even the behaviorist, it is admitted, has to sit in the armchair to come up with the notions of stimulus and response before proceeding to log the behavior of pigeons.

4. W. H. Auden, "In Memory of Sigmund Freud" (1940), in John Frederick Nims, ed., *The Harper Anthology of Poetry* (New York: Harper & Row, 1981), 630.

5. Carl Gustav Jung, *Memories, Dreams, Reflections*, trans. R. Winston and C. Winston (New York: Pantheon, 1963), 150.

6. Sigmund Freud, *Letters*, trans. Tania and James Stern; ed. Ernest Freud (New York: Basic Books, 1960), 427; see Stanley A. Leavy, *In the Image of God: A Psychoanalytic View* (New Haven: Yale University Press, 1988), 101.

7. *CW* 10:367.

8. *SE* 20: 8.

9. Joachim Scharfenberg, *Sigmund Freud and His Critique of Religion*, trans. O. C. Dean, Jr. (Philadelphia: Fortress Press, 1988), 27.

10. Paul C. Vitz, *Sigmund Freud's Christian Unconscious* (New York: Guilford, 1988), 34, 127; see Théo Pfrimmer, *Sigmund Freud, Lecteur de la*

Bible (Thesis, Protestant Faculty, University of Strasbourg, 1981), 284–308; 371–80.

11. Pfrimmer, *Lecteur*, 372–73; Vitz, *Unconscious*, 40–41, 127.

12. G. Papini, "A Visit to Freud," in H. Ruitenbeek, ed., *Freud as We Knew Him* (Detroit: Wayne State University Press), 99; see Vitz, *Unconscious*, 107.

13. Vitz, *Unconscious*, 107.

14. Vitz, *Unconscious*, 115.

15. Scharfenberg, *Critique*, 28.

16. Vitz, *Unconscious*, 104.

17. Vitz reports that "In all things religious, ambivalence was Freud's dominant attitude." *Unconscious*, 47.

18. *SE* 4: 197; see Vitz, *Unconscious*, 36.

19. Jewishness was a barrier to social, academic, and political advancement in late nineteenth and early twentieth century Austria. Freud knew of the "dramatic and immediate advancement" Gustav Mahler had experienced in the music world of Vienna when he converted from Judaism. Vitz, *Unconscious*, 81.

20. Ernest Jones, *The Life and Work of Sigmund Freud*, vols. 1–3 (New York: Basic Books, 1957), 194; see Vitz, *Unconscious*, 199.

21. Vitz, *Unconscious*, 3, 8–12.

22. Peter A. Gay, *A Godless Jew: Freud, Atheism, and the Making of Psychoanalysis* (New Haven: Yale University Press, 1987), 74–75, 83.

23. Sigmund Freud and O. Pfister, *Psychoanalysis and Faith: The Letters of Sigmund Freud and Oskar Pfister*, ed. E. L. Freud and H. Meng, trans. E. Mosbacher (New York: Basic Books, 1963), 76; see Vitz, *Unconscious*, 175. An additional note bearing on the occasional "religious" side of Freud is that his correspondence with Pfister reflects remarkable ease with traditional Christian terminology, regularly sprinkled with biblical phrases, with references to "Easter" and "Pentecost," and with casual asides, such as "God only knows"; see Vitz, *Unconscious*, 174–78.

24. Vitz, *Unconscious*, 63, 69, 77–78; Sigmund Freud, *Letters of Sigmund Freud*, ed. E. L. Freud, trans. T. Stern and J. Stern (New York: Basic Books, 1960), 302; *SE* 5: 469.

25. In a letter to his friend, Eduard Silberstein; see Dan Merkur, "Freud and Hasidism," in *The Psychoanalytic Study of Society*, eds. L. Bryce Boyer, Ruth M. Boyer, and Howard F. Stein (Hillsdale, N.J.: Analytic Press, 1994), 341.

26. Scharfenberg, *Critique*, 44.

27. Vitz, 200; Freud, *Letters*, 366–67.

28. Thomas Hardy Leahey, *A History of Psychology: Main Currents in Psychological Thought*, 2d ed. (Englewood Cliffs, N.J.: Prentice-Hall, 1987), 214.

29. Dan Merkur, in personal correspondence, citing David Bakan, *Sigmund Freud and the Jewish Mystical Tradition* (Boston: Beacon Press, 1958), 245.

30. H. L. Philp, *Freud and Religious Belief* (New York: Pitman Publishing Corp., 1956), 92; Vitz, *Unconscious*, 105; Scharfenberg, *Critique*, 45; 150 n. 26.

31. Philp, *Freud*, 400–40.

32. Robert A. Paul, *Moses and Civilization: Freud and the Judeo-Christian Master Narrative* (New Haven: Yale University Press, 1996), 219–21.

33. During this period he revises and systematizes his earlier work, at the same time turning to cultural analysis with two critiques of religion and culture, *The Future of an Illusion* (1927) and *Civilization and Its Discontents* (1930).

34. Freud adopted the motto of the enlightenment, *sapere aude* ("dare to take a taste") and enjoyed repeating the saying, *pour épater le bourgeois* ("to shock the conventional middle class"). Erich Fromm, *Sigmund Freud's Mission: An Analysis of His Personality and Mission* (New York: Harper & Row, 1959), 2, 9.

35. Vitz, *Unconscious*, 122, 177.

36. Scharfenberg, *Critique*, 119.

37. Scharfenberg, *Critique*, 47.

38. Scharfenberg, *Critique*, 150 n. 26. He characterizes the anonymous article he published on "The Moses of Michelangelo" (1914) as a "love child."

39. Scharfenberg, *Critique*, 46–47.

40. Philp, *Freud*, 92–93; Scharfenberg, *Critique*, 47.

41. Vitz, *Unconscious*, 202; Ernest Jones, *The Life and Work of Sigmund Freud*, vol. 1–3 (New York: Basic Books, 1957), 370; Philp, *Freud*, 94; R. W. Clark, *Freud: The Man and the Cause* (New York: Random House, 1980), 523–24.

42. Scharfenberg, *Critique*, 2.

43. Scharfenberg, *Critique*, 88; J. Samuel Preus, "Psychogenic Theory: Sigmund Freud," in *Explaining Religion: Criticism and Theory From Bodin to Freud* (New Haven: Yale University Press, 1987), 179.

44. See H. F. Ellenberger, *The Discovery of the Unconscious: The History and Evolution of Dynamic Psychiatry* (New York: Basic Books, 1970); L. L. Whyte, *The Unconscious Before Freud* (New York: Julian Friedmann Publishers and St. Martin's Press, 1978).

45. Leahey, *History*, 208.

46. See the imaginative, though occasionally extravagant work of Roman Catholic Freudian analysts, F. Dolto and G. Séverin, *The Jesus of Psychoanalysis: A Freudian Interpretation of the Gospel*, trans. Helen R. Lane (New York: Doubleday, 1979).

47. On transference see Scharfenberg, *Critique*, 97–99. Stanley Leavy introduces the term *unconcealing* to refer to the analytic task of bringing repressed elements to consciousness; see *In the Image of God: A Psychoanalytic View* (New Haven: Yale University Press, 1988), 105.

48. Freud speculated that theories of demon possession in the Middle Ages seemed closer to the truth than contemporary scientific theories on hysteria; Scharfenberg, *Critique*, 39.

49. Vitz, *Unconscious*, 191–92.

50. Though Freud never promulgates a doctrine of sin, his description of the human condition approximates the biblical notion of "fallen humanity" in almost Augustinian terms. Freud speaks of the "innate inclination of people toward evil, aggression, destruction and thus also toward cruelty, "even if the "dear little children did not want to hear it." Freud also focuses on "suffering" as an unavoidable reality. With his insistence on the primacy of the reality principle over the pleasure principle, Freud replicates the biblical conviction that on occasion suffering may be the only route to achieving the good. As Freud cryptically comments, "As long as a person suffers, he can still accomplish something"; Scharfenberg, *Critique*, 118, 145.

51. Philp, *Freud*, 127.

52. Freud borrowed these mottos from a book by E. D. Dekker, entitled *Multatuli*. Freud ranked *Multatuli* first in a list of "ten best books" he was asked to make for a Viennese bookstore in 1907; see Scharfenberg, *Critique*, 34–35.

53. Freud wrote to Pfister, "I have, as you grant, done a lot for love." Scharfenberg, *Critique*, 133–34.

54. Augustine proposed such a principle (similar to Freud's in its emphasis on love) in stating that "Whoever seems to himself to have understood the divine scriptures in such a way that he does not build up that double love of God and neighbor, has not yet understood." Freud would want to add "reason" to Augustine's formula, but the two would agree that some sovereign standard is necessary as critique of culture, religion, and text.

55. *Zygon* 13 (1978): 142–43.

56. See chapter 3 for a fuller description of the various approaches and applications of psychological and psychoanalytic theory.

57. "Freud and Jung: Contrasts"; CW 4: 773–74, 777, 781.

58. Carl Gustav Jung, *C. G. Jung Letters, 2: 1951–1961*, eds. Gerhard Adler and Aniela Jaffé, trans. R. F. C. Hull; Bollingen Series 95:2 (Princeton: Princeton University Press, 1975), 346.

59. *MDR*, 43; Carl Gustav Jung, "Approaching the Unconscious," in *Man and His Symbols* (New York: Doubleday, 1964), 94, 102.

60. CW 8:528; CW 11:34, 461–63; Jung, *Letters* 2:207.

61. Jung, *Letters* 2:88, 89, 91, 115–16.

62. Carl Gustav Jung, *Memories, Dreams, Reflections* (New York: Pantheon, 1963), 43, 73, 91.

63. Jung, *Memories*, 233.

64. *Letters* 2:257–58.

65. Jung, *Visions*, 1:156.

66. C. G. Jung, *The Zofingia Lectures*, ed. W. McGuire (Princeton: Princeton University Press, 1983), xiii; Gerhard Wehr, *Jung: A biography*, translated by David M. Weeks (Boston: Shambala, 1988), 58–60. Wehr tells of "Jung's ability to fascinate his colleagues in lectures of all sorts . . . on the most controversial topics possible," for example, "On the Limits of Exact Science" or "The Value of Speculative Research."

67. Jung, *Memories*, 97.

68. For example, Matthew 13:35, "I will open my mouth in parables; I will utter things which have been kept secret from the foundation of the world"; or Luke 12:49, "I am come to send fire on the earth."

69. N. Schwartz-Salant, "Patriarchy in Transformation: Judaic, Christian, and Clinical Perspectives," in ed. M. Stein and R. L. Moore, *Jung's Challenge to Contemporary Religion* (Wilmette, Ill.: Chiron, 1987), 64.

70. Jung, *Letters*, 2:17–18, 20, 116.

71. CW 11:555–56.

72. Two topics that enjoy more columns of entries than "Bible" are "Animals" (36 columns) and "Alchemical Writers and Texts" (27 columns).

73. P. Homans, "Psychology and Hermeneutics: Jung's Contribution," *Zygon* 4 (1969): 349.

74. See CW 11, 13, 15.

75. CW 15: "Introduction" and 133; 11:1.

76. CW 11:749 n. 2; 15:101, 156, 162.

77. Carl Gustav Jung, *Psychological Reflections: A New Anthology of His Writings, 1905–61*, vol. 31, eds. Jolande Jacobi and R. F. C. Hull, Bollingen Series (Princeton: Princeton University Press, 1953), 342.

78. CW 15:125, 135.

79. CW 15:130.

80. CW 15:131.

81. CW 9.2:79; Jung, *Memories*, 38.

82. For example, the book of David Halperin, *Seeking Ezekiel, Text and Psychology* (University Park, Pa.: Pennsylvania State University Press, 1993), echoing an observation of Bernhard W. Anderson in his classic *Understanding the Old Testament*, 4th ed. (Englewood Cliffs, N.J.: Prentice-Hall, 1986), 429, that "Ezekiel *himself* was an unusual person whose psychic peculiarities make a fascinating psychological study."

83. See "The Psychology of Biblical Religious Experience" in chapter 5, p. 130 ; also, John J. Pilch, "Psychological and Psychoanalytical Approaches to Interpreting the Bible in Social-Scientific Context," *Biblical Theology Bulletin* 27 (1997): 112–16.

84. CW 10:367.

85. See Donald Capps, *Biblical Approaches to Pastoral Counseling* (Philadelphia: Westminster, 1981); "The Bible's Role in Pastoral Care and Counseling: Four Basic Principles," *Journal of Psychology and Christianity* 3 (4, 1984): 5–15; Wayne Oates, "The Diagnostic Use of the Bible: What a Man Sees in the Bible Is a Projection of His Inner Self," *Pastoral Psychology* 1 (1950): 43–46; *The Bible in Pastoral Care* (Philadelphia: Westminster, 1953); and Carroll A. Wise, *Psychiatry and the Bible* (New York: Harper & Row, 1956).

86. CW 11:696.

87. CW 9.2:276.

88. See chapter 6 for a fuller discussion; Cedric Johnson's, *The Psychology of Biblical Interpretation* (Grand Rapids: Zondervan, 1983), is one of the first examples of psychological research in this area.

89. For a fuller picture of the influence of the Bible in Jung's life and work, see Wayne G. Rollins, "Psychology, Hermeneutics, and the Bible," in *Jung and the Interpretation of the Bible*, ed. David L. Miller (New York: Continuum, 1995), 9–39.

90. *Bible and the Psyche*, 13.

91. CW 11:148; 13:74.

92. CW 15:113–14.

93. Dr. Elizabeth Boyden Howes and Dr. Sheila Moon, founders of the San Francisco based Guild for Psychological Studies, were among the first to develop this method to interpret the life and teachings of Jesus. Walter Wink elaborates on the basics of this approach in his *Transforming Bible Study* (Nashville: Abingdon, 1980), integrating a Jungian hermeneutic method with classical Biblical scholarship.

94. Janet Dallett, "Active Imagination in Practice," in *Jungian Analysis*, ed. Murray Stein (Boston: Shambala, 1984), 174.

95. CW 8:180.

96. MDR, 326.

97. Laurens van der Post, *Jung and the Story of Our Time* (New York: Vintage, 1975), 189.

98. Eugen Drewermann, *Tiefenpsychologie und Exegese: Die Wahrheit der Formen: Traum, Mythos, Märchen, Sage, und Legende*, vol. 1 (Olten/Freiburg: Walter, 1984a); Ulrich Luz, *Matthew in History: Interpretation, Influence, and Effects* (Minneapolis: Fortress Press, 1994), 9; David Cox, *Jung and St. Paul: A Study of the Doctrine of Justification by Faith and Its Relation to the Concept of Individuation* (New York: Association, 1959); Edward Edinger, *Bible and Psyche.*

Chapter 3: Psychological Biblical Criticism in the Twentieth Century

1. F. C. Grant, "Psychological Study of the Bible," in J. Neusner (ed.), *Religions in Antiquity: Essays in Memory of Erwin Ramsdell Goodenough* (Leiden: Brill, 1968), 112–13.

2. Gerd Theissen, *Psychological Aspects of Pauline Theology*, trans. John P. Galvin (Philadelphia: Fortress Press, 1987), 28.

3. Scharfenberg, *Critique*, 2.

4. Jung, *Letters*, vol. 1 (Bollingen Series; ed. G. Adler and A. Jaffé; Princeton: Princeton University Press, 1973), 29–30; Robin Scroggs, "Psychology as a Tool to Interpret the Text: Emerging Trends in Biblical Thought," *Christian Century* (March 24, 1982): 335; Theissen, *Psychological Aspects*, 1. See also Gerd Theissen, *A Critical Faith: A Case for Religion* (Philadelphia: Fortress Press, 1979), viii, citing the suspicion he aroused by becoming involved "in such 'godless' matters as sociology and psychoanalysis." Patrick Henry, *New Directions in New Testament Study* (1979), 203, similarly observes, "If, as [John] Gager says [in *Kingdom and Community*], New Testament study has remained until now a special 'enclave' in its resistance to sociological analysis, it has been even more resistant to the viewpoint of psychology."

5. J. M. Baldwin, ed., *Dictionary of Philosophy and Psychology* (New York: Macmillan, 1901–05), x.

6. Others from the period include Theodor Simon, *Die Psychologie des Apostels Paulus* (Göttingen: Vandenhoeck & Ruprecht, 1897); G. Waller, *The Biblical View of the Soul* (London & New York: Longmans, Green & Co., 1904); J. Stalker, *Christian Psychology* (New York and London: Hodder & Stoughton , 1914); L. S. Keyser, *A Handbook of Christian Psychology* (Burlington, Iowa: The Lutheran Literary Board, 1928); for a review of literature prior to 1896 see J. F. Hurst, "Psychology of the Bible," in *Literature of Theology: A Classified Bibliography of Theological and General Religious Literature* (New York: Hunt and Eaton, 1896), 173–74.

7. (London: SCM Press, 1936), 136–78.

8. Rudolf Bultmann, *Theology of the New Testament* (New York: Charles Scribner's Sons, 1951), 393. Bultmann includes Delitzsch (1867; Eng.); Laidlaw (1895); Dickson (1883); Lüdemann (1872); Gutbrod (1934); Burton (1918); Fletcher (1912); Käsemann (1933); Torge (1909); and Kümmel (1948). He refers, for example, to Archibald B. D. Alexander's chapter on "The Psychology of Paul" in his study of *Ethics of Saint Paul* (Glasgow: Maclehose and Sons, 1910). Alexander offers a standard definition of "psychology" in the biblical psychology sense, as "the attempt to exhibit in their order and connection the Pauline presuppositions with regard to the nature of the unregenerate man" as well as to discern the "substratum of powers, physical, mental, and moral" constituting the "raw material of the new creature in Christ," 60. Bultmann also mentions H. Wheeler Robinson's, *The Christian Doctrine of Man* (Edinburgh: T. & T. Clark, 1911), the most comprehensive example of biblical psychology from the period. "Virtually unchanged" over the course of three editions up to 1926, and reprinted in the 1950s, the book features major sectional headings on topics such as "the characteristics of primitive psychology," "the evolution of the psychological terms" in the Hebrew Bible, and Pauline psychology, with detailed analysis of the vocabulary of "Hebrew psychology" (e.g. *neshâmah, nephesh, ruach, lêb, bâsâr*) and of Paul (*psyche, pneuma, kardia, syneidesis, nous*); 6–7, 11–27, 104–12. Don Browning in his essay "The Influence of Psychology on Theology" in *The New Shape of Pastoral Theology: Essays in Honor of Seward Hiltner*, ed. William B. Oglesby, Jr. (Nashville: Abingdon, 1969), 121–35, contends that theologians like "Bultmann and Tillich are already using a psychology of sorts in their interpretation of Jesus, existentialism, although it is one that lacks a 'phenomenology of genesis' and is therefore incapable of recognizing the fact that some of the structures of consciousness may have a developmental history. See John W. Miller, *Jesus at Thirty* (Minneapolis: Fortress Press, 1997), 138.

9. Martin Leiner, *Psychologie und Exegese: Grundfragen einer textpsychologischen Exegese des Neuen Testaments* (Gütersloh: Chr. Kaiser, 1995), 41–45, 238–39.

10. Delitzsch, *System*, 422–23; Fletcher, *Psychology*, 179–81, 302.

11. See Werner Georg Kümmel, *The New Testament: The History of the Investigation of Its Problems*, trans. S. McLean Gilmour and Howard C. Kee (Nashville: Abingdon, 1972), 93–95, 149, 152, 237, 284–85; Albert Schweitzer, *The Psychiatric Study of Jesus: Exposition and Criticism*, trans. Charles R. Joy (1913; Boston: Beacon Press, 1948), 7, 74. The four psychiatric studies were *Jesus Christus vom Standpunkte des Psychiaters* (Bamberg: Handels-Druckerei, 1905) by George Lomer (writing under the pseudonym George de Loosten); *Eine vergleichende psychopathologische Studie* (Leipzig:

Julius Zeitler, 1905) by Emil Rasmussen, a Dane; *Religion and Civilization: The Conclusions of a Psychiatrist* (New York: The Truth Seeker, 1912) by William Hirsch, an American; and *La Folie de Jesus* (4 vols.; Paris: Maloine, 1910–15) by Charles Binet-Sanglé, a Frenchman.

12. Schweitzer states that he was not making a blanket condemnation of psychology or of psychopathological analysis: "The psychopathological method, which conceives its task to be the investigation of the mental aberrations of significant personalities in relation to their works, has recently fallen into disrepute. This is not because of the method, which with proper limitations and in hands of professional investigators can produce and has produced valuable results, but because it has been faultily pursued by amateurs"; *Psychiatric*, 33. On the exclusion of "religion" in psychological journals, see Benjamin Beit-Hallahmi, "Psychology of Religion 1880–1930: The Rise and Fall of a Psychological Movement," in *Current Perspectives in the Psychology of Religion*, ed. H. Newton Malony (Grand Rapids: Eerdmans, 1977), 17–26.

13. Kümmel, *History*, 149, 152, 223, 237, 239, 285, 288. Kümmel customarily dismisses psychological studies as "spiritualizing" or "liberal." Only once (280) does he allow a positive cast on psychology, namely in citing Johannes Weiss's call for new research into the "psychological conditionings" and "human" antecedents of biblical inspiration.

14. William James, *The Varieties of Religious Experience* (New York: Longmans, Green & Co., 1902), 233.

15. William Sanday, *Christology and Personality* (New York: Oxford University Press, 1911), 137–38, 231. James was not correct in his dates on the discovery of the unconscious. Discussion begins with Carl Gustav Carus and his follower Eduard von Hartmann, though it was with Freud that the unconscious became a "practical medical concept." See Carl Gustav Jung, *C. G. Jung Speaking: Interviews and Encounters*, Bollingen Series 47, eds. William McGuire and R. F. C. Hull (Princeton: Princeton University Press, 1977), 252–53; also L. L.Whyte, *The Unconscious Before Freud* (London & New York: Julian Friedmann Publishers and St. Martin's Press, 1978), who contends that "the general conception of unconscious mental processes was *conceivable* . . . around 1700, *topical* around 1800, and *fashionable* around 1870–80"; see the unpublished paper by Daniel Merkur, "Mythology into Metapsychology: Freud's Misappropriation of Romanticism" (1990), 8–10. See chapter 4 of the present volume for a more thorough discussion of the unconscious.

16. Vincent Taylor, "Christology and Psychology," in *The Person of Christ in New Testament Teaching* (London: Macmillan, 1959), 277–78. Taylor also urges consideration of the "researches of Freud and of Jung into the nature of the unconscious," 282.

17. See the work of Jacob Hyman Kaplan (1906); G. C. Joyce (1910); D. E. Thomas (1914); W. Jacobi (1920); John Walter Povah (1925); H. Wheeler Robinson (1946); George Widengren (1948); Walter C. Klein, (1956). More recently see Martin J. Buss (1969, 1980).

18. Gunkel, *Die Wirkungen des Heiligen Geistes* (Göttingen: Vandenhoeck & Ruprecht, 1888), iv-v (Eng. trans.: *The Influence of the Holy Spirit*, trans. R. A. Harrisville and P. A. Quanbeck II [Philadelphia: Fortress Press 1979]); see, Theissen, *Psychological Aspects*, 268.

19. J. Weiss, *Earliest Christianity: A History of the Period A.D. 30–150*, tr. F. C. Grant (New York: Harper Torchbooks, 1959), 650; see Kümmel, *History*, 280, 444–45 n. 346.

20. Bousset, *Kyrios Christos* (Göttingen: Vandenhoeck & Ruprecht, 1913), 99; see Theissen, *Psychological Aspects*, 16; Deissmann, *Paul: A Study in Social and Religious History*, 2d rev. ed., tr. William E. Wilson (New York: Doran, 1926); see Wayne A. Meeks, ed. *The Writings of St. Paul* (New York: Norton, 1972), 385–86; Streeter (London: Macmillan), 391–92; Hoskyns (London: Faber & Faber, 1947), 319.

21. Henry J. Cadbury, "Current Issues in New Testament Studies: An Address Delivered at the Harvard Divinity School, November 26, 1953," *Harvard Divinity School Bulletin* (1953–54), 54. I am indebted to Paul N. Anderson for notice of Cadbury's investment in "motive criticism," to be discussed in a forthcoming book *"The Eclipse of the Historical Jesus" and Other New Testament Essays by Henry J. Cadbury* (Harrisburg, Pa.: Trinity Press International).

22. C. A. Simpson, "An Inquiry Into the Biblical Theology of History," *Journal of Theological Studies* 12 (1961): 1–2.

23. Grant, "Psychological Study," 112–13. As early as 1950, Grant had urged that "the student of the New Testament must also understand religious psychology, especially the various types of religious experience to be met with in the Jewish and the Hellenistic world of the first two centuries"; *Introduction to New Testament Thought* (New York: Abingdon), 26.

24. Walter Wink, *The Bible in Human Transformation: Toward a New Paradigm for Biblical Study* (Philadelphia: Fortress Press, 1973) 1. See the discussion of Wink's statement in section III below. Harsch and Voss (Stuttgart: KBW Verlag); the essays focus on John 2:1–11, illustrating what each discipline contributes to its interpretation. Grelot, *Nouvelle Revue Theologique* 98 (1976): 481–511; Lewis S. Mudge, "Paul Ricoeur on Biblical Interpretation," in *Essays on Biblical Interpretation*, ed. Lewis S. Mudge (Philadelphia: Fortress Press, 1980), 12.

25. John Dominic Crossan, "Perspectives and Methods in Contemporary Biblical Criticism," *Biblical Research* 22 (1977), 41. Cheryl Exum and David J. A. Clines writing in 1995 predicted that "by the end of this decade

approaches that may now present some degree of novelty or even shock value to traditional biblical critics will be incorporated into the daily practice of mainstream scholars (just as the language and interests of the formalist rhetorical critics and narratologists of the 60s and 70s have become part of the common professional stock in trade)"; *The New Literary Criticism and the Hebrew Bible* (Sheffield: Sheffield Academic Press, 1995), 12. It should be added that the mark of these new disciplines is their common synchronic view of the text as a vital entity that can be observed at work in different settings (social, cultural, political, anthropological, psychological) both as product and agent, as opposed to the earlier diachronic view of the text primarily as an artifact and as a window to the past.

26. Tillich writes that "the problem of the relation between the theological and the psychotherapeutic understanding of men has come more and more into the foreground of my interest, partly through a university seminar on religion and health at Columbia University, partly through the great practical and theoretical interest that depth psychology has aroused in Union Seminary, and partly through personal friendship with older and younger analysts and counselors. I do not think that it is possible today to elaborate a Christian doctrine of man [sic] . . . without using the immense material brought forth by depth psychology"; Paul Tillich, "Autobiographical Reflections of Paul Tillich," in *The Theology of Paul Tillich* (New York: Macmillan, 1952), 18–19; see also comments of Tillich scholars on 40, 63, 157.

27. John Gager, *Kingdom and Community: The Social World of Early Christianity* (Englewood Cliffs, N.J.: Prentice-Hall, 1975), 43. David Aune, *The New Testament and Its Literary Environment* (Philadelphia: Westminster, 1987), 59. Anderson, *Old Testament*, 429. For a detailed assessment of the "psychologization" of Western culture, see Leiner, *Psychologie*, 17–41, 77–118.

28. David K. Miell, "Psychological Interpretation," in *A Dictionary of Biblical Interpretation* (London: SCM, 1990), 571.

29. The 1902 classic of William James on the *Varieties of Religious Experience* that was reprinted thirty-eight times in the thirty-three years following its publication is still standard fare in college courses, and has done more to make psychology "user-friendly" to theologians, clergy, pastoral counselors, and biblical scholars than any other single factor.

30. Jung's thought was promoted by two of his premier spokespersons in the United States, Morton Kelsey and John Sanford, both episcopal priests, by Roman catholic theologians Victor White and Josef Goldbrunner, and by mythologist Joseph Campbell.

31. For example, in an article by Stanton L. Jones in the APA publication, *American Psychologist*, on "A Constructive Relationship for Religion with the

Science and Profession of Psychology" (March 1994):184–99, and a paper read at a 1997 sectional meeting of the APA in Denver, Colorado, by clinical psychologist Dennis Shulman, "A Psychoanalytic Perspective on Abraham's Binding of Isaac: Implications for Who We Are and How We Change."

32. Bruce Narramore, "Perspectives on the Integration of Psychology and and Theology," *Journal of Psychology and Theology* 1 (1993): 3, 4, 17; the *Journal of Psychology and Christianity* is the official organ of the Christian Association for Psychological Studies founded in 1957, preceded by the *Proceedings* (1957–74) and *The Bulletin* (1974–82).

33. J. Harold Ellens, "The Bible and Psychology, an Interdisciplinary Pilgrimage," *Pastoral Psychology* 45 (1997): 195.

34. J. Cheryl Exum and Mark G. Brett, "Editorial Statement," *Biblical Interpretation: A Journal of Contemporary Approaches* 1 (1993): i. Their interdisciplinary posture ironically complements a recommendation Carl Jung made to the newly inaugurated *Psychoanalytic Review* (1913) eighty years earlier, when he congratulated the editors for their plans "to "unite in their journal the contributions of . . . specialists in various fields, "adding, "we need not only the work of medical psychologists, but also that of philologists, historians, archaeologists, mythologists, folklore students . . . biologists" and "theologians"; Jung, *Letters*, 2: 85.

35. Participants in the "Bible and culture collective" are George Aichele, Fred W. Burnett, Elizabeth A. Castelli (editor), Robert M. Fowler, David Jobling, Stephen D. Moore (editor, and primary author of the essay on "Psychoanalytic Criticism"), Gary A. Phillips (editor), Tina Pippin, Regina M. Schwartz (editor), and Wilhelm Wuellner. The volume will be cited henceforth as *Postmodern Bible*.

36. The present writer submitted the program proposal in 1990. An adjunct feature of the group was an online psychology/biblical studies seminar, dubbed PsyBibs by its author, Charles T. Davis, III, with an e-mail address of <listserv@listserv.appstate.edu> for information exchange on new research in the field, comments on papers, and shared bibliographic notes.

37. Miell, "Psychological Interpretation," 571–72.

38. Sandra M. Schneiders, *The Revelatory Text: Interpreting the New Testament as Sacred Scripture* (San Francisco: HarperSanFrancisco, 1991), 117–18, 120.

39. Russell Pregeant, *Engaging the New Testament* (Minneapolis: Fortress Press, 1995), 25–26, 401–2.

40. "The Interpretation of the Bible in the Church" was published by *Catholic International* (March 1994): 109–47, and by *Origins* (January 6, 1994). It is also available as a pamphlet from the Society of St. Paul in Boston;

Joseph A. Fitzmyer, S. J., *Scripture, the Soul of Theology* (New York: Paulist, 1994), 51–52.

41. Martin Leiner, *Psychologie*, follows Theissen's lead in using the phrase, "psychological exegesis." The first instance of the phrase, "psychological criticism," is probably G. Stanley Hall's use of it in his essay, "The Jesus of History and of the Passion versus the Jesus of the Resurrection," *The American Journal of Religious Psychology and Education* 1 (1, 1904): 64. In all probability F. C. Grant was not familiar with the essay. The use of the fuller phrase "psychological biblical criticism" was suggested by D. Andrew Kille in personal communication.

42. Theissen, *Psychological Aspects*, 28, 394, 398.

43. Drewerman's two principal works *Tiefenpsychologie und Exegese: Die Wahrheit der Formen: Traum, Mythos, Märchen, Sage, und Legende*, vol. 1, and *Tiefenpsychologie und Exegese: Die Wahrheit der Werke und der Worte: Wunder, Vision, Weissagung, Apokalypse, Geschichte, Gleichnis*, vol. 2 (Olten/Freiburg: Walter, 1984). See also Bernhard Lang, *Eugen Drewermann, interprète de la Bible* (Paris: Cerf, 1994).

44. J. Cheryl Exum and David J. A. Clines, eds. *The New Literary Criticism and the Hebrew Bible* (Sheffield: Sheffield Academic Press, 1993), 18.

45. Ilona N. Rashkow, *The Phallacy of Genesis: A Feminist-Psychoanalytic Approach*, Literary Currents in Biblical Interpretation (Louisville: Westminster/John Knox Press, 1993), 22–25, 110.

46. *Postmodern Bible*, 222.

47. Wayne G. Rollins, "Rationale and Agenda for a Psychological-Critical Approach to the Bible and Its Interpretation," in *Biblical and Humane*, eds. David Barr, Linda Bennett Elder, and Elizabeth Struthers Malbon (Atlanta: Scholars Press, 1996), 160.

48. Ellens, "Bible and Psychology," 207.

49. "De connaître l'univers mental des traditions bibliques." A. Vergote, "Psychanalyse et interprétation biblique," in *Supplément au Dictionnaire de la Bible*, eds. H. Cazelles and A. Feuillet, vol. 9 (Paris: Letouzey & Ané, 1973–75), col. 259.

50. Hall, "Jesus of History," 64; Wink, *Human Transformation*, 1–2.

51. Miell, "Psychological Interpretation," 571–72. See also Walter Wink, "On Psychologizing," in *Transforming Bible Study: A Leader's Guide*, 2d rev. ed. (Nashville: Abingdon, 1989), 163–65.

52. Jung, CW 15: 98–100.

53. Miell, "Psychological Interpretation," 572.

54. Pregeant, *Engaging*, 26. See also Miell, "Psychological Interpretation," 571; Krister Stendahl, "The Apostle Paul and the Introspective Con-

science of the West," *Harvard Theological Review* 56 (1963): 199–215; Pilch, "Psychological Approaches," 112–16.

55. See the section on "Historische Psychologie oder Übertragung gegenwärtiger psychologischer Theorien auf die Vergangenheit?" in Leiner, *Psychologie*, 243–47, for a telling critique of Berger. Leiner's main point is that the "historical psychologist" is no less burdened with presuppositions than the contemporary psychologist in describing the psychological experience and state of persons in antiquity, comparable to a deep sea diver and a fisherman, both after the same "prey" but using different methods, but both confined to work in a medium (the Sea) that is foreign to both. See also the comment of Sandra Schneiders, *The Revelatory Text*, 118, that "although the ancient writers probably did not share our interests in personal psychological dynamics and certainly did not have our scientific categories for describing or analyzing them, they did frequently present their readers with rounded pictures of complex personalities. . . . Thus, the fact that the human and personality sciences are modern developments that were unknown to the biblical authors does not invalidate their use in interpretation provided that the interpreter does not attribute to the author or the biblical characters conscious concerns that neither could have had."

56. Pregeant, *Engaging*, 26.

57. Pregeant, *Engaging*, 26. Works in social psychology and the Bible include Jesse Hickman Bond, *Industrial Influence on the Psychology of Jesus. A Study of the Origin, Processes and Results of Psychological Conflict in His Ethical Struggle* (Boston: R. G. Gorman, 1925); Martin J. Buss, "The Social Psychology of Prophecy," in *Prophecy: Essays Presented to Georg Fohrer on His Sixty-fifth Birthday*, ed. J. A. Emerton (Berlin: Walter de Gruyter, 1980), 1–11; Charles Thomas Holman, *The Cure of Souls: A Sociopsychological Approach* (Chicago: University of Chicago Press, 1932); J. R. King, "The Parables of Jesus: A Social Psychological Approach," *Journal of Psychology and Theology* 19 (1991): 257–67.

58. Theissen, *Psychological Aspects*, 5–10.

59. Theissen, *Psychological Aspects*, 29–39.

60. Ralph L. Underwood, "Primordial Texts: An Object Relations Approach to Biblical Hermeneutics," *Pastoral Psychology* 45/3 (January 1997): 182.

61. Underwood, "Primordial Texts," 191.

62. Fritz Kunkel, *Creation Continues: A Psychological Interpretation of the First Gospel*. 2d ed.; eds. Elizabeth Kunkel and Ruth Spafford Morris (Waco, Tex.: Word Books, 1973), 11; John Sanford, ed. *Fritz Kunkel: Selected Writings* (Mahwah, N.J.: Paulist, 1984), 333–52.

63. Norman R. Petersen, "Point of View' in Mark's Narrative," *Semeia* 12 (1978), 116–18. Uspensky differentiates the descriptions of human behavior in literary narratives as either external (from the standpoint of an observer) or internal ("from the point of view of the person himself or . . . an omniscient observer who is permitted to penetrate the consciousness of that person"); in the second type, internal processes are described ("thoughts, feelings, sensory perceptions, emotions").

64. See the psychodynamic analysis of character relationships in the parables of Jesus by psychotherapist, Richard Q. Ford, *The Parables of Jesus: Recovering the Art of Listening* (Minneapolis: Fortress Press, 1997) and the psychoanalytic approach to apocalypse by Dereck Daschke (1999).

65. In addition to Freud's *Moses and Monotheism*, studies of *Moses* include Theodor Reik, *Mystery on the Mountain: The Drama of the Sinai Revelation* (New York: Harper 1959) and John A. Sanford's study in *The Man Who Wrestled with God: Light from the Old Testament on the Psychology of Individuation* (King of Prussia, Pa.: Religious Publishing, 1974). On *Jesus* see, for example, Granville Stanley Hall, *Jesus, the Christ, in the Light of Psychology* (Garden City, N.Y.: Doubleday, 1917); A.W. Hitchcock, *The Psychology of Jesus: a Study of the Development of His Self-Consciousness* (Boston: Pilgrim, 1907); Hanna Wolff, *Jesus der Mann. Die Gestalt Jesu in tiefenpsychologischer Sicht*, 10 ed. (1977; Stuttgart: Radius-Verlag, 1990). Additional studies on Paul include A. B. D. Alexander, "The Psychology of Paul," in *Ethics of Saint Paul* (Glasgow: Maclehose and Sons, 1910); J. G. Bishop, "Psychological Insights in St. Paul's Mysticism," *Theology* 78 (1975): 318–24; David Cox, *Jung and St. Paul: A Study of the Doctrine of Justification by Faith and Its Relation to the Concept of Individuation* (New York: Association Press, 1959); Robert G. Hamerton-Kelly, "A Girardian Interpretation of Paul: Rivalry, Mimesis and Victimage in the Corinthian Correspondence," *Semeia* 33 (1985): 65–81; Robert L. Moore, "Pauline Theology and the Return of the Repressed: Depth Psychology and Early Christian Thought," *Zygon* 13 (1978): 158–68; Richard Rubenstein, *My Brother Paul* (New York: Harper & Row, 1972); John A. Sanford, "Jesus, Paul, and Depth Psychology," *Religious Education* 68 (1973): 673–89; Robin Scroggs, *Paul for a New Day* (Philadelphia: Fortress Press, 1977); Theodor Simon, *Die Psychologie des Apostels Paulus* (Göttingen: Vandenhoeck & Ruprecht, 1897); Walter Rebell in his *Gehorsam und Unabhängigkeit. Eine sozialpsychologische Studie zu Paulus* (Munich: Kaiser, 1986) rejects attempts at a psychological analysis of Paul's personality, advocating instead a social psychological and more "methodologically sound" approach.

66. Dorothy Zelig, *Psychoanalysis and the Bible: A Study in Depth of Seven Leaders* (New York: Bloch, 1974) devotes a chapter apiece to Abraham, Jacob, Joseph, Samuel, Saul, David, Solomon; John A. Sanford, *Wrestle*, does the same with Jacob, Joseph, Moses, Adam and Eve. Additional studies on individual personality portraits include D. Andrew Kille, "Jacob—A Study in Individuation," in *Jung and the Interpretation of the Bible*, ed. David L. Miller (New York: Continuum, 1995), 40–54; Michael Shiryon, "Joshua—The Underestimated Leader: The Use of Psychology in the Book of Joshua," *Journal of Psychology and Judaism* 19 (Fall 1995): 205–25; on Elijah, Charles Binet-Sanglé, "Le Prophète Elisée. Arch. di Anthropologia criminale." *Psichiatria e med. legale* 20 (1905): 136–41; Dan Merkur, "The Prophecies of Jeremiah," *American Imago* 42.1 (1985): 1–37; Adolf Allwohn, *Die Ehe des Propheten Hosea in Psychoanalytischer Bedeutung* (Giessen: 1926); Eduard König, "Die Sexualität im Hohenlied und ihre Grenze," *Zeitschrift für Sexualwissenschaft* 9 (1922): 1–4; Adrian van Kaam, *The Woman at the Well* (Denville, N.J.: Dimension, 1976); Dennis L. Gibson, "Doubting Thomas, the Obsessive," *Journal of Psychology and Christianity* 4.2 (1985): 34–36.

67. See the discussion of "the psychology of biblical religious experience" in chapter 5. The only major study of parapsychology in the Bible is Laurence Tunstall Heron's *ESP in the Bible* (1974). The Biblical material Heron identifies as "psychic phenomena" are instances of "telepathy, clairvoyance, clairaudience, clairsenience, photism, apparitions, mediumship, glossolalia, detachment and trance, precognition, and dreams"; 187.

68. See chapter 5, V, on "The Psychology of Biblical Religious Experience," and chapter 2, I and II on dream theory in Freud and Jung.

69. John A. Sanford, *Mystical Christianity: A Psychological Commentary on the Gospel of John* (New York: Crossroad, 1993). See the sections on the exegetical and hermeneutical agendas for psychological biblical criticism in chapter 6. Studies of individual subjects include L. F. Greenlee, Jr., "Kohut's self psychology and theory of narcissism: Some implications regarding the fall and restoration of humanity," *Journal of Psychology and Theology* 14 (1986): 110–16; J. E. Gelberman and D. Kobak. "The Psalms as Psychological and Allegorical Poems," in *Poetry Therapy*, ed. Jack Leedy (Philadelphia: Lippincott, 1969); Lorenz Wachinger, "Spiegelung und dunkles Wort: Tiefenpsychologische Schriftauslegung—am Beispiel des Ps 91 (90)," in *Liturgie und Dichtung, II*, eds. H. Becker and R. Kaczynski (St. Ottilien: Eos, 1983), 335–57; Frank Zimmermann, "The Book of Ecclesiastes in the Light of Some Psychoanalytic Observations," *American Imago* (1948): 301–5; John A. Sanford, *The Kingdom Within* (Philadelphia: Lippincott, 1970).

70. Eugene A. Nida, "Implications of Contemporary Linguistics for Biblical Scholarship," *Journal of Biblical Literature* 91 (1972): 77.

71. William Dever, "Women's Popular Religion, Suppressed in the Bible, Now Revealed by Archaeology," *Biblical Archaeology Review* 17.2 (March-April 1991): 65.

72. Karl Menninger, *Whatever Became of Sin?* (New York: Hawthorn Books, 1973); Dominique Stein, "Une lecture psychanalytique de la Bible," *Revue des Sciences Philosophiques et Théologiques* 72 (1988): 95–108; J. Harold Ellens, "The Bible and Psychology, an Interdisciplinary Pilgrimage," *Pastoral Psychology* 45.3 (1997): 193–208. See the section on Biblical Psychology in chapter 5; for the use of the Bible in pastoral counseling see the section on "therapeutic effects" in chapter 6, III.

73. Theissen, *Psychological Aspects*, 28.

Chapter 4: What Is Psychological Biblical Criticism?

1. G. B. Caird, *The Language and Imagery of the Bible* (London: Duckworth, 1980), vii.

2. James Hillman, *Archetypal Psychology: A Brief Account* (Dallas: Spring, 1983), 18.

3. Carl Gustav Jung, "Approaching the Unconscious," *Man and His Symbols* (New York: Doubleday, 1964), 32.

4. *De Anima* 2.6.

5. Taking the lead from Erwin R. Goodenough, in whose *Festschrift* Grant's article appeared, Grant recommended we begin reading biblical symbols for their psychological depth as bearers of unconscious as well as conscious meaning. He also suggested that the "truth" of Job, for example, is "not that a man by that name once lived somewhere in the East and suffered vicissitudes," nor is it found in discussions of the text's literary unity. The "real truth is . . . its psychology," as expressed in the words 'Though he slay me, yet will I trust in him'" (13:15), a confession "*lived* by ancient Israel and by ancient individual Israelites, and by multitudes of Jews ever since." On "biblical effects" he cited as an example of "good" effect the new "psychological orientation" the Gospels generated among Christians in the "new world . . . of the early Caesars." An example of "ill" effect would be the unconscious license for cruelty that the Bible seems to generate from time to time with its descriptions of violence against enemies of the faith. Grant, "Psychological Study," 117, 119, 121–23.

6. Chapter 3, III; Theissen, *Psychological Aspects*, 28; Ellens, "Bible and Psychology," 206–7; Exum and Clines, *New Literary Criticism*, 18.

7. James E. Dittes, "Analytical (Jungian) Psychology and Pastoral Care," in *Dictionary of Pastoral Care and Counseling*, ed. R. Hunter (Nashville: Abingdon, 1990), 30.

8. For an earlier version of this definition see the author's article, "Rationale and Agenda for a Psychological-Critical Approach to the Bible and Its Interpretation," in *Biblical and Humane*, eds. David Barr, Linda Bennett Elder, and Elizabeth Struthers Malbon (Atlanta: Scholars Press, 1996), 160.

9. Leiner, *Psychologie*, 314–15.

10. D. Andrew Kille, "Psychological Biblical Criticism: Genesis 3 as a Test Case" (Ph.D. Diss., Graduate Theological Union, 1997), 70–74.

11. Schneiders, *Revelatory Text*, 164–66.

12. Schneiders, *Revelatory Text*, 165.

13. Hunt, *Story of Psychology*, 129, citing Wundt, *Contributions to the Theory of Sense Perception* (1862).

14. C. G. Carus adopted a similar title in 1846, *Psyche: Zur Entwicklungsgeschichte der Seele* (Pforzheim: Flammer u. Hoffmann). Freud used Herbart in developing his concept of the unconscious. See Peters and Mace, "Psychology," 18.

15. Sanday, *Christology*, 137; italics added.

16. Robert C. Fuller, *Americans and the Unconscious* (New York: Oxford, 1986), 76.

17. "Psychology," in *The New Encyclopedia Britannica: Macropedia*, 15 ed., vol. 26 (Chicago: Encyclopedia Britannica, Inc., 1989), 322.

18. The period is also marked by an increasing disaffection with psychology of religion and with the concepts of consciousness and unconsciousness. See Benjamin Beit-Hallahmi, "Psychology of Religion 1880–1930: The Rise and Fall of a Psychological Movement," in *Current Perspectives in the Psychology of Religion*, ed. H. Newton Malony (Grand Rapids: Eerdmans, 1977), 17–25, especially 21; Fuller, *Americans*, 75–76, 123; "An unsigned editorial in a 1924 issue of the *Journal of Abnormal Psychology* bemoaned the endless writings on the unconscious as possessing no more worth than the German mark."

19. Bruno Bettelheim, "Reflections: Freud and the Soul," *New Yorker* (March 1, 1982): 52–93, republished in book form as *Freud and Man's Soul* (New York: Knopf, 1982). See Donald Capps, "Enrapt Spirits and the Melancholy Soul: The Locus of Division in the Christian Self and American Society," in *On Losing the Soul: Essays in the Social Psychology of Religion*, eds. Richard K. Fenn and Donald Capps (Albany, N.Y.: SUNY Press, 1995), 138–40.

20. For example, David M. Wulff's widely used *Psychology of Religion: Classic and Contemporary Views* (New York: John Wiley and Sons, 1991) lists no occurrences of the term *psyche*, though includes ten references to *soul*.

21. Abraham Maslow. *Toward a Psychology of Being* (Princeton, N.J.: D. Van Nostrand Co., 1962).

22. Fuller, *Americans*, 155, 158–59. As Walter Weisskopf, one of the founding editors of the *Journal of Humanistic Psychology*, expresses it, "The *causae efficientes* have eclipsed the *causae finales*."

23. Fuller, *Americans*, 88; see William James, *A Pluralistic Universe* (New York: E. P. Dutton, 1971), 196.

24. C. G. Jung, *Speaking*, 262; Gerhard Wehr, *Portrait of Jung: An Illustrated Biography*, trans. W. A. Hargreaves (New York: Herder & Herder, 1971), 153–54 n. 189.

25. Jolande Jacobi, *The Psychology of C. G. Jung*, 7th ed. (New Haven: Yale University Press, 1968), 5; see R. A. Muller, "Soul," in *Dictionary of Pastoral Care and Counseling* [henceforth, *DPCC*], 1202. Hans Schaer reports that Jung hoped *Seele* would be translated soul "when the context carries with it any moral, metaphysical or theological implications, leaving 'psyche' as a purely psychological term," though Schaer comments that in practice it is difficult to determine whether a given context is psychological or religious; *Religion and the Cure of Souls in Jung's Psychology* (Zurich: Rascher Verlag, 1946), trans. R. F. C. Hull; Bollingen Series 21 (New York: Pantheon, 1950), 1; originally *Religion und Seele in der Psychologie C. G. Jungs* (Zurich: Rascher Verlag, 1946); C. G. Jung, *CW* 15:133; 10:526.

26. C. G. Jung, *Man and His Symbols*, 93.

27. *CW* 15: Introduction: "Psychology and Literature."

28. *CW* 11:140; 13:75.

29. James Hillman, *Insearch: Psychology and Religion* (New York: Scribner's), 41.

30. Hubert Gruender, *Psychology without a Soul: A Criticism* (St. Louis: B. Herder, 1912); Otto Rank, *Psychology and the Soul*, trans. William D. Turner (Philadelphia: University of Pennsylvania Press, 1950); William H. Crawshaw, *The Indispensable Soul* (New York: Macmillan, 1931); John W. Drakeford, *Psychology in Search of a Soul* (Nashville: Broadman Press, 1964); Carl Jung, *The Spiritual Problem of Modern Man* (also titled *Modern Man in Search of a Soul*), *CW* 10.

31. William Barrett, *Death of the Soul: From Descartes to the Computer* (New York: Doubleday, 1986), 164, 166.

32. R. Swinburne, *The Evolution of the Soul* (Oxford: Clarendon, 1986), 2–4.

33. Richard K. Fenn, "Introduction: Why the Soul?" in *On Losing the Soul: Essays in the Social Psychology of Religion*, eds. Donald Capps and Richard K. Fenn (Albany, N.Y.: SUNY Press, 1995), 1.

34. Bernice Martin, "Whose Soul Is It Anyway?" in *On Losing the Soul: Essays in the Social Psychology of Religion*, eds. Donald Capps and Richard K. Fenn (Albany, N.Y.: SUNY Press, 1995), 69–70.

35. David Martin, "Bedeviled," in *On Losing the Soul: Essays in the Social Psychology of Religion*, eds. Donald Capps and Richard K. Fenn (Albany, N.Y.: SUNY Press, 1995), 39.

36. Richard K. Fenn, "Introduction: Why the Soul?", 15, 4.

37. Bernice Martin, "Whose Soul Is It Anyway?", 70.

38. Phil Cousineau, ed. *Soul: An Archaeology: Readings from Socrates to Ray Charles* (San Francisco: HarperSanFrancisco, 1994).

39. Cousineau, *Soul*, xx. Cousineau lists the following sacred words for soul found in various cultures: "psyche, anima, atman, savira, semangat, nephesh, otachuk, loákal, tunzi, prana, duk, and geist."

40. H. D. Lewis, "Philosophy of Self," in *Dictionary of Pastoral Care and Counseling*, ed. R. Hunter (Nashville: Abingdon, 1990), 1125.

41. Hunt, *Story of Psychology*, 157.

42. Michael J. Mahoney, *Human Change Processes: The Scientific Foundations of Psychotherapy* (New York: BasicBooks, Harper Collins, 1991), 215–16; Hunt, *Story of Psychology*, 157.

43. Mahoney, *Human Change*, 216.

44. Mahoney, *Human Change*, 211.

45. On the rootedness of Freud and Jung in the biblical tradition, and on the affinities between Jung's psychology and a "biblical psychological" perspective, see chapter 2.

46. CW 15: Introduction: "Psychology and Literature."

47. Lancelot Law Whyte, "Unconscious," in *The Encyclopedia of Philosophy*, ed. Paul Edwards (New York: Macmillan, 1967), 186.

48. Fuller, *Americans*, 4.

49. "The Question of Lay Analysis," in Freud, *SE* 20: 211–12. See Cyriac Kottayarikil, *Sigmund Freud on Religion and Morality: A Challenge to Christianity*, vol. 3 (Innsbruck: Resch, 1977), 262–63. See the discussion of Freud in chapter 2.

50. CW 3:565–66.

51. CW 12:14.

52. Fuller, *Americans*, 5–6, 86, 241.

53. Carl Gustav Jung, *Memories, Dreams, Reflections* (New York: Pantheon, 1963), 401; see CW 8:185.

54. Jung, C. G. CW 11:141; 4:769. For a discussion of the recognition of the unconscious in antiquity, including the Bible, see Theissen, *Psychological Aspects*, 95: "The analysis of the history of the tradition has shown that the

'unconscious' is not a modern discovery. The idea of an unconscious region with the human is already approximately expressed in ancient texts."

55. For example, Jung postulated that the Christ figure served as an exemplification of the archetype of the "Self" for Christians; see his essay on "Christ, A Symbol of the Self"; CW 9:2.

56. CW 11:745.

57. Erwin R. Goodenough, *Toward a Mature Faith* (Lanham, Md.: University Press of America, 1955), 124.

58. CW 10:285, "The Meaning of Psychology for Modern Man"; CW 10:445, "The Fight with the Shadow"; CW 10:588, "The Undiscovered Self."

59. Jung, *Letters* 2: 424.

60. *Psychological Reflections*, 351 = CW 12:13.

61. Hillman, *Archetypal*, 18.

62. See the magisterial discussion of this question by Wilfred C. Smith, *What Is Scripture? A Comparative Approach* (Minneapolis: Fortress Press, 1993). See also the discussion of Smith in chapter 6 of the present work, on the role of imagination in the Psychodynamics of the Reading Process, 166–69.

Chapter 5: The Exegetical Agenda

1. Werner Georg Kümmel, *The New Testament: The History of the Investigation of Its Problems*, trans. S. McLean Gilmour and Howard C. Kee (Nashville: Abingdon, 1972), 280.

2. *Introduction to New Testament Thought* (New York: Abingdon), 26.

3. Pontifical Biblical Commission, "The Interpretation of the Bible in the Church," *Catholic International* 5 (3, 1994): 122.

4. Chapter 6, on hermeneutics, will focus on the "world in front of the text" or "between text and reader."

5. Lucy Bregman, "Symbolism/symbolizing," in *DPCC*, 1249.

6. CW 18:482; *Man and His Symbols*, 21. See Michael Willett Newheart, "Johannine Symbolism" in *Jung and the Interpretation of the Bible*, ed. David L. Miller (New York: Continuum, 1995): 79. Jung charges Freud with treating symbols as signs, especially in his dream analysis: "For Freud . . . symbols . . . are not truly symbols but *signs* or *symptoms* of the subliminal [repressive] processes. The true symbol differs essentially from this, and should be understood as an expression of an intuitive idea that cannot yet be formulated in any other or better way. When Plato, for instance, puts the whole problem of the theory of knowledge in his parable of the cave, or when Christ expresses the idea of the Kingdom of Heaven in parables, these are genuine and true symbols, that is, attempts to express something for which no verbal concept yet exists"; CW 15:105.

7. See M. Philipson, *Outline of a Jungian Aesthetics* (Evanston, Ill.: Northwestern University Press, 1963), 71.

8. CW 15:130.

9. CW 3:565.

10. Joseph Campbell, ed. *The Portable Jung* (New York: Viking, 1971), xxx-xxxi; *The Hero with a Thousand Faces* (New York: Pantheon, 1949): 4.

11. See J. Samuel Preus, "Psychogenic Theory: Sigmund Freud," in *Explaining Religion: Criticism and Theory From Bodin to Freud* (New Haven: Yale University Press, 1987), 181; *SE* 20:211–12.

12. Walter Wink, "On Wrestling with God: Using Psychological Insights in Biblical Study," *Religion in Life* 47 (1978): 142.

13. John Dominic Crossan, "Perspectives and Methods in Contemporary Biblical Criticism," *Biblical Research* 22 (1977): 45; Erwin R. Goodenough, *Jewish Symbols in the Greco-Roman Period*; Bollingen Series 37 (New York: Pantheon, 1953–68); volume 4 provides Goodenough's psychological presuppositions on the nature of symbols and their interpretation. Eugen Drewermann, *Tiefenpsychologie und Exegese: Die Wahrheit der Formen: Traum, Mythos, Märchen, Sage, und Legende*, vol. 1 (Olten/Freiburg: Walter, 1984a) and *Tiefenpsychologie und Exegese: Die Wahrheit der Werke und der Worte: Wunder, Vision, Weissagung, Apokalypse, Geschicte, Gleichnis*, vol. 2. (Olten/Freiburg: Walter, 1984b). Eugen Drewermann proposes that the "dream like" symbols, myths, and legends of the Bible have an "*unhistorische*" (dis-historical) meaning that far transcends the "historical" meaning on which the historical-critical method has focused and that has tended to obscure the timeless and yet forever timely archetypal truths of these images. See also Bernhard Lang, *Eugen Drewermann, interprète de la Bible* (Paris: Les éditions du Cerfs, 1994): 9.

14. C. A. Simpson, "An Inquiry into the Biblical Theology of History." *Journal of Theological Studies* 12 (1961): 1–13. Simpson acknowledges his debt to F. W. Dillistone, *Christianity and Symbolism* (London, 1955): 183, 188. See also D. Andrew Kille, "Psychological Biblical Criticism: Genesis 3 as a Test Case." (Ph.D., Graduate Theological Union, 1997): 162–64. Michael Willett Newheart, in his article on "Johannine Symbolism" in *Jung and the Interpretation of the Bible*, ed. David L. Miller (New York: Continuum, 1995): 75, raises the question whether "'ineluctably cerebral' readings" might not be a "defense against the unconscious issues which the symbols raise"; Lucy Bregman, "Symbolism/symbolizing," in *Dictionary of Pastoral Care and Counseling*, ed. R. Hunter (Nashville: Abingdon, 1990): 1246.

15. Walter Wink, *Naming the Powers: The Language of Power in the New Testament* (Philadelphia: Fortress Press, 1984), xi, 142; *Unmasking the Powers:*

The Invisible Forces that Determine Human Existence (Philadelphia: Fortress Press, 1986), 2.

16. Gerd Theissen, *Psychological Aspects*, 394. Luke Timothy Johnson comments on the effects of symbol as a subject for biblical research: "The writings of the New Testament can respond to questions about the experiences and convictions that generated their composition, about the symbolic worlds used to interpret those experiences, and about the ways in which the interaction of experience and symbol created new worlds of meaning within the first-century world"; *The Real Jesus: The Misguided Quest for the Historical Jesus and the Truth of the Traditional Gospels* (San Francisco: HarperSanFrancisco, 1997), 104; Michael Willett Newheart, "Johannine Symbolism," 71–91.

17. Sabbatai S'vi (or Sebi) was a seventeenth-century Jewish mystic who claimed to be the Messiah. He inaugurated a messianic movement that spread from Jerusalem to Venice, Amsterdam, Hamburg, and London just prior to 1666, the year in which he expected the millennium.

18. CW 11:713.

19. *Psychological Reflections*, 342 = "Basel Seminar" (1934), 84.

20. Erwin R. Goodenough, *Toward a Mature Faith* (Lanham, Md.: University Press of America, 1955), 70.

21. Vitz, *Unconscious*, 91–92. Theodor Reik theorizes along the same lines in *Pagan Rites in Judaism* (New York: Farrar, Straus, 1964). Robert A. Paul, *Moses and Civilization: Freud and the Judeo-Christian Master Narrative* (New Haven: Yale University Press, 1996), 220–21. James J. DiCenso, "*Totem and Taboo* and the Constitutive Function of Symbolic Forms," *Journal of the American Academy of Religion* LXIV (3, 1996): 573, makes a similar point. Though he dismisses Freud's "causal mechanistic" theory of the origins of religion in *Totem and Taboo*, he affirms the work as a "figurative presentation of qualitative transformations of personality" that occur "within symbolic structures," such as religious systems, that display the cultural dynamics of "displacements, supplementarity, and symbolism."

22. Anthony C. Thiselton, *New Horizons in Hermeneutics: The Theory and Practice of Transforming Bible Reading* (Grand Rapids: Zondervan, 1992), 371.

23. Kille, *Genesis* 3, 117; Robert C. Fuller, *Americans and the Unconscious* (New York: Oxford, 1986), 111.

24. Ludwig Levy, "Die Sexualsymbolik der Bibel und des Talmud," *Zeitschrift für Sexualwissenschaft* 1 (1914): 273–79; 318–26; "Die Sexualsymbolik des Ackerbaus in Bibel und Talmud." ZS (1915): 437–44; "Sexualsymbolik in der Simsonsage," ZS 3 (1916): 256–71; "Sexual symbolik in der biblischen Paradiesgeschichte," *Imago* 5 (1917–19): 16–30; Eduard

König, "Die Sexualität im Hohenlied und ihre Grenze," ZS 9 (1922): 1–4.

25. John Gager, *Kingdom*, 43; see Theissen, *Psychological Aspects*, 32; Myron B. Gubitz, "Amalek: The eternal adversary Amalek: The eternal adversary," *Psychological Perspectives* 8 (1, 1977): 34–58; Françoise Dolto and Gérard Séverin, *The Jesus of Psychoanalysis: A Freudian Interpretation of the Gospel*, trans. Helen R. Lane (New York: Doubleday, 1979); Heinz Westman, *The Structure of Biblical Myths: The Ontogenesis of the Psyche* (Dallas: Spring Publications, Inc., 1983); *The Springs of Creativity: The Bible and the Creative Process of the Psyche* (Peru, Ill.: Chiron Publications, 1986/1961); see also Stephen Carter Scott, "A Biblical Analysis of Reality Therapy: A Comparison of the Nature of Mankind in Genesis 1–11 and in Reality Therapy," (MA thesis: Pacific Lutheran University, 1982); W. Ong, "The Psychodynamics of Oral Memory and Narrative: Some Implications for Biblical Studies," in *The Pedagogy of God's Image: Essays on Symbol and the Religious Imagination*, ed. R. Masson. (Chico, Calif.: Scholars Press, 1982); Gerd Theissen, "Local—und Sozialkolorit in der Geschichte von der syrophönikischen Frau (Mk 7:24–30)," *ZNTW* 75 (3–4, 1984): 202–25; Wilhelm H. Wuellner and Robert C. Leslie, *The Surprising Gospel: Intriguing Psychological Insights from the New Testament* (Nashville: Abingdon, 1984); Brooke Hopkins, "Jesus and Object-Use: A Winnicottian Account of the Resurrection Myth," *International Review of Psycho-Analysis* 16 (1989): 93–100; John A. Sanford, *Mystical Christianity: A Psychological Commentary on the Gospel of John* (New York: Crossroad, 1993), 77, 30, 107–19, 131–32, 230–40, 313–16, 170, 203; Naomi H. Rosenblatt and Joshua Horwitz, *Wrestling with Angels* (New York: Delacorte Press, 1995), xiv; Lyn M. Bechtel, "Genesis 2.4b-3.24: A Myth about Human Maturation," *Journal for the Study of the Old Testament* 67 (1995): 3–26; Richard Q. Ford, *The Parables of Jesus: Recovering the Art of Listening* (Minneapolis: Fortress Press, 1997), see 1–2, 9–10; D. Andrew Kille, "Psychological Biblical Criticism: Genesis 3 as a Test Case" (Ph.D., Graduate Theological Union, 1997); D. Andrew Kille, "Jacob—A Study in Individuation," in *Jung and the Interpretation of the Bible*, ed. David L. Miller (New York: Continuum, 1995), 41.

26. *Postmodern Bible*, 70–71. Structuralist Vladimir Propp in 1928 proposed a "deep structure or grammar of possibile relationships which all fairy tales obey." One of the most celebrated structural analyses of biblical narratives is Roland Barthes's, "The Struggle with the Angel" (1974), maintaining that "all narratives obey a fundamental narrative grammar." See *A Dictionary of Biblical Interpretation*, s.v. "Structuralism," 651, 652, 655.

27. Norman R. Petersen, "'Point of View' in Mark's Narrative," *Semeia* 12 (1978):97–121; *Postmodern Bible*, 85–88.

28. Newheart, "Johannine Symbolism," 89.

29. John A. Sanford, *The Man Who Wrestled with God: Light from the Old Testament on the Psychology of Individuation* (King of Prussia, Pa.: Religious Publishing Co., 1974); *King Saul, The Tragic Hero: A Study in Individuation* (New York: Paulist, 1985); Edward Edinger, *The Bible and the Psyche: Individuation Symbolism in the Old Testament* (Toronto: Inner City Books, 1986). Bernhard Anderson comments that "Today, Saul would be regarded as a fit subject for a study in abrnomal psychology . . . haunted by dark moods and inflamed by insane jealousy and rage . . . "; *Old Testament*, 174–75; Schuyler Brown, "The Beloved Disciple: A Jungian View," in *The Conversation Continues: Studies in Paul and John in Honor of J. Louis Martyn*, eds. R. T. Fortna and B. R. Gaventa (Nashville: Abingdon Press, 1990), 388–99.

30. Reik (1917); Chorisy (1953); Felber (1956); Westman (1961); Monchy (1962); Cole (1978); Gregory (1980).

31. Binet-Sanglé (1903); Zeligs (1974).

32. Micklem (1926); Seierstad (1946); Carroll (1977).

33. Povah (1924); Micklem (1926); Allwohn (1926).

34. Micklem (1926); Seierstad (1934) (1946); Kille (1993).

35. Nicole (1924); Schendler (1954); Tarachow (1960); Reider (1960).

36. Foxe (1943).

37. *Moses and Monotheism*, trans. Katherine Jones (New York: Alfred A. Knopf, 1939), 110. Jung, *Letters* 2:257. Jung emphasizes the need to "examine carefully the psychological aspects of the individuation process in the light of Christian tradition, which can describe it for us with an exactness and impressiveness far surpassing our feeble attempts"; *CW* 9.2:45.

38. An analogy might be the psychological judgments that seasoned biographers make on deceased public figures.

39. B. W. Anderson, *Old Testament*, 429; David J. Halperin, *Seeking Ezekiel* (University Park: Pennsylvania State University Press, 1993); Edwin C. Broome, "Ezekiel's Abnormal Personality," *Journal of Biblical Literature* 65 (1946): 277–92; N. H. Cassem, "Ezekiel's Psychotic Personality: Reservations on the Use of the Couch for Biblical Personalities," in *Word in the World*, ed. R. Clifford (Cambridge, Mass.: Weston College Press, 1973), 59–68; John J. Schmitt, "Yahweh's Foundling: Psychological Reflections on Ezekiel 16" (paper delivered at the Society of Biblical Literature meeting, Chicago, 1994), 10; Ilona N. Rashkow, "Review of David Halperin, *Seeking Ezekiel: Text and Psychology*," *Journal of the American Academy of Religion* (Fall 1996): 680.

40. A. B. D. Alexander, "The Psychology of Paul" in *Ethics of Saint Paul* (Glasgow: Maclehose and Sons, 1910); J. G. Bishop, "Psychological Insights in St. Paul's Mysticism," *Theology* 78 (1975): 318–24; R. A. Cowley, "The Concept of Guilt in the Writings of St. Paul in the Light of Contemporanean

Psychotherapists" (University of Bristol), 1973; David Cox, *Jung and St. Paul: A Study of the Doctrine of Justification by Faith and Its Relation to the Concept of Individuation* (New York: Association Press, 1959); J. Faur, "De-authorization of the Law: Paul and the Oedipal Model," in *Psychoanalysis and Religion*, eds. J. H. Smith and S. A. Handelman (Baltimore: Johns Hopkins, 1990), 222–43; R. A. Hughes, "The Cain Complex and the Apostle Paul," *Soundings* 65 (1982): 5–22; John A. Sanford, "Jesus, Paul, and Depth Psychology," *Religious Education* 68 (1973): 673–89; Alan F. Segal, "Paul's Conversion: Psychological Study," in *Paul the Convert: The Apostolate and Apostasy of Paul the Pharisee* (New Haven: Yale University Press, 1990), 285–300; Sidney Tarachow, "St. Paul and Early Christianity: A Psychoanalytic Study," in *Psychoanalysis and the Social Sciences*, ed. G. Roheim et al. (New York: International Universities Press, 1947–58), 1–5; Theissen, *Psychological Aspects* (1987); Krister Stendahl, "The Apostle Paul and the Introspective Conscience of the West," *Harvard Theological Review* 56 (1963): 199–215. See also the early study of C. Moxon,"Epileptic Traits in Paulus of Tarsus," *Psychoanalytic Review* 9 (1922): 60–66; also, M. Scott Fletcher's *The Psychology of the New Testament*, 2d ed. (New York: Hodder & Stoughton, 1912), 175–81, emphasizes the importance of considering the psychodynamic factors in Paul's conversion and career. Fletcher states that "historical criticism fails to reveal the deepest spring of Paul's convictions," ignoring the "emotional factor" and failing to recognize that "Paul's inward state was really one of great complexity psychologically." Speaking of the pre-Christian Paul he writes that "Saul of Tarsus carried in the depths of his mind an idea and an image. . . . Ideas and images may be suppressed, but they live and work in the sub-conscious realm of personality until some crisis or experience brings them into the light of full consciousness." Rubenstein, *Brother Paul*, 6, 11.

41. Rubenstein, *Brother Paul*, 19, 22, 173. Rubenstein's judgment is partially echoed in psychiatrist Stanley Leavy's observation that "Paul, no mean psychologist, is . . . helpful in reminding us of our inability to carry out the law as he understood it"; *In the Image of God: A Psychoanalytic View* (New Haven: Yale University Press, 1988), 8.

42. *Paul for a New Day* (Philadelphia: Fortress Press, 1977); Robin Scroggs, "The Heuristic Value of a Psychoanalytic Model in the Interpretation of Pauline Theology" in *The Text and the Times* (Minneapolis: Fortress Press, 1993), 125–50. Originally published in *Zygon* 13 (1978): 136–57. See *The Text and the Times*, 125, 127, 134, 138–39, 150.

43. Robin Scroggs, "Heuristic," 150; "Psychology as a Tool to Interpret the Text: Emerging Trends in Biblical Thought," *Christian Century* (March 24, 1982): 338.

44. Frederick C. Grant, *An Introduction to New Testament Thought* (New York: Abingdon, 1950), 26.

45. Topics that are unannotated will be the subjects of fuller discussion below.

46. See Boyce M. Bennett, "Vision and Audition in Biblical Prophecy," *Parapsychology Review* 9 (1, 1978): 1–12. Jung frequently cites contemporary examples of photism and auditions. See his Carl Gustav Jung, *Psychology and Religion: The Terry Lectures* (New Haven: Yale University Press, 1938), 42, 45; also, "Approaching the Unconscious" in *Man and His Symbols*, 31.

47. P. Sladeck, "Kehret um! (Mark 1:15): Die Umkehrforderung des Evangeliums im Lichte einer christlichen Tiefenpsychogie," *Ordens-Korrespondenz* 15 (1974): 173–84.

48. See J. L. Henderson and M. Oakes, *The Wisdom of the Serpent: The Myths of Death, Rebirth and Resurrection* (New York: Collier, 1963) on an object relations approach to the idea of original sin, and Thomas Auchter, "Zum Schuldverständnis in der Psychoanalyse im Alten und Neuen Testament," *Wege zum Menschen* 30 (1978): 208–25, on the Biblical understanding of sin.

49. Delitzsch, *System*, 398–99, insists on seeing the experience of grace as a psychological issue. See Fletcher *Psychology*, 203.

50. Fletcher, *Psychology*, 211–27; Hjalmar Sunden, "Der psychologische Aspekt in der Rechfertigung durch den Glauben," *Kerygma und Dogma* 32 (2, 1986): 120–31.

51. Wayne E. Oates, *Temptation. A Biblical and Psychological Approach* (Louisville: Westminster/John Knox, 1991).

52. John E. Pedersen, "Some Thoughts on a Biblical View of Anger," *Journal of Psychology and Theology* 2 (3, 1974): 210–15; Barbara Horton Johnes, "Anger: Psychological and Biblical Perspectives" (Colorado State University, 1990).

53. T. Reik, *Myth and Guilt* (New York: George Braziller, 1957); R. A. Cowley, "The Concept of Guilt in the Writings of St. Paul in the Light of Contemporanean Psychotherapists" (University of Bristol, 1973); Rashkow, *Phallacy*, reminds us that the concepts of guilt and shame are more at home in the psychoanalytic lexicon than in the conventional moral vocabulary such as "ethical," "righteous," and so forth.

54. R. S. Sullender, "Grief and Growth: Perspectives from Life-Span Psychology and Pauline Theology" (Claremont School of Theology, 1978); Jeannette G. Rodenbough, "The Healing Journey: The Use of Biblical Narrative in the Grief Process" (Columbia Theological Seminary, 1993).

55. On psychological insight into the biblical concept of "principalities and powers," see the three-volume work by Wink, *Naming the Powers* (1984);

Unmasking the Powers (1986); and *Engaging the Powers* (1992). Also, Rivkah Schärf Kluger, *Satan in the Old Testament*, trans. H. Nagel, Studies in Jungian Thought (Evanston: Northwestern University Press, 1967).

56. William W. Meissner, *Thy Kingdom Come: Psychoanalytic Perspectives on the Messiah and the Millennium* (New York: Sheed & Ward, 1996).

57. Lindsay Dewar, *The Holy Spirit and Modern Thought: An Inquiry into the Historical, Theological, and Psychological Aspects of the Christian Doctrine of the Holy Spirit* (London: Mowbray, 1959).

58. Patrick Henry, "Water, Bread, Wine: Patterns in Religion," in *New Directions in New Testament Study* (Philadelphia: Westminster, 1979), 212–15.

59. See Bakan (1968) on Job; Wellisch (1954) on Isaac; Van der Wolk (1921) on incense offerings; and Girard (*multi*) and Hamerton-Kelly (1985) on sacrifice and violence; David Bakan. "Sacrifice and the Book of Job," in *Disease, Pain, and Sacrifice: Toward a Psychology of Suffering* (Chicago: University of Chicago, 1968), 95–128; E. Wellisch, *Isaac and Oedipus. A Study in Biblical Psychology of the Sacrifice of Isaac, the Akedah* (London: Routledge and Kegan Paul, 1954); P. C. Van der Wolk, "Zur Psychologie des Rauchopfers," *Imago* 7 (1921): 131–41; Robert G. Hamerton-Kelly. "A Girardian Interpretation of Paul: Rivalry, Mimesis and Victimage in the Corinthian Correspondence," *Semeia* 33 (1985): 65–81.

60. Renato J. Almanasi, "A Psychoanalytic Interpretation of the Menorah," *Journal of the Hillside Hospital* 2 (1953): 80–92; "A Further Contribution to the Psychoanalytic Interpretation of the Menorah," *Journal of the Hillside Hospital* 3 (1954): 3–18.

61. L. Grinberg, "Psychoanalytic Considerations on the Jewish Passover Totem Sacrifice and Meal," *American Imago* 19 (1962): 391–424.

62. M. J. Field, *Angels and Ministers of Grace: An Ethno-psychiatrist's Contribution to Biblical Criticism* (New York: Hill and Wang, 1972).

63. Edward Romilly Micklem, *Miracles and the New Psychology: A Study of the Healing Miracles of the New Testament* (New York: Oxford University Press, 1922); J. Tenzler, "Tiefenpsychologie und Wunderfrage," *Münchener Theologische Zeitschrift* 25 (1974): 118–37; Morton Kelsey, *Healing and Christianity in Ancient Thought and Modern Times* (New York: Harper & Row, 1976); John A. Sanford, *Healing and Wholeness* (New York: Paulist Press, 1977).

64. Little of substance is found in this area to date. Heron, *ESP in the Bible* (Garden City, N.Y.: Doubleday, 1974) is the work of a popular journalist. Michael Perry, "Psi in the Bible," *Parapsychology Review* 10 (3 1979): 9–14, explores Saul and the "medium" of Endor. Bennett, "Vision and Audition,"

recommends caution in the study of biblical parapsychological phenomena because of distance from the actual events.

65. *The Christian Doctrine of Man* (Edinburgh: T. & T. Clark, 1911); *Inspiration and Revelation in the Old Testament* (Oxford: Clarendon Press, 1946), 69–74, 191.

66. In *Prophecy: Essays Presented to Georg Fohrer on His Sixty-fifth Birthday*, ed. J. A. Emerton (Berlin: Walter de Gruyter, 1980), 1–11.

67. Hermann Gunkel, *Die Wirkungen des Heiligen Geistes*, 2d ed. (Göttingen: Vandenhoeck & Ruprecht, 1888), iv–v.

68. Malony and Lovekin, *Glossolalia: Behavioral Science Perspectives on Speaking in Tonogues* (New York: Oxford University Press, 1985); Theissen, *Psychological Aspects*, 267–342.

69. (New York: Doubleday). See also John A. Sanford, *Dreams: God's Forgotten Language* (Philadelphia: Lippincott, 1968); Isaac Lewin, "The Psychological Theory of Dreams in the Bible," *Journal of Psychology and Judaism* 7 (2, 1983): 73–88.

70. Greco-Roman commentators on dreams range from Homer, Plato, Aristotle and the Greek playwrights, to Hippocrates, Galen, Vergil, Cicero, and Plutarch.

71. Delitzsch, *System*, 401–6; Fletcher, *Psychology*, 164–88, 189–209. Alan Segal in *Paul the Convert: The Apostolate and Apostasy of Paul the Pharisee* (New Haven: Yale University Press, 1990), 285–300; John Gager, in *New Testament Studies* 27 (1981): 697–703; Johnson and Malony in the Rosemead Psychology Series (Grand Rapids, Mich.: Zondervan, 1982); Scroggs, "Psychology as a Tool," 336.

72. See J. W. Miller, "Psychoanalytic Approaches to Biblical Religion," *Journal of Religion and Health* 22 (1983): 23–24; Rashkow, *Phallacy*, 91–93.

73. Henry, "Water, Bread, Wine," 207–12, with citations from Mircea Eliade, *Patterns in Comparative Religions* (Sheed & Ward, 1958), 188, and Rubenstein, *My Brother Paul*, 29.

74. Fletcher, *Psychology*, 159.

75. Wise, *Psychiatry and the Bible* (New York: Harper & Row, 1956), 25; Vernon McCasland, *By the Finger of God* (New York: Macmillan, 1951); Paul Bach, "Demon Possession," *Journal of Psychology and Theology* 7 (1, 1979): 22–26.

76. Stevan L. Davies, *Jesus the Healer: Possession, Trance, and the Origins of Christianity* (New York: Continuum, 1995), 87; Scharfenberg, *Critique*, 86.

77. See Scharfenberg, *Critique*, 3; Hall, *The American Journal of Religious Psychology and Education* 1,1 (May 1904):3.

78. Carl G. Jung, "Foreword," in Erich Neumann, *Depth Psychology and a New Ethic* (New York: Harper Torchbooks, 1973 [1948]), 12. Examples of

work in the field include Eugen Drewermann, *Psychoanalyse und Moraltheologie* (Mainz: Grünewald, 1982–84); T. O'Connor, "Psychological Health According to Karen Horney Compared with the Moral Theme in the Pauline Writings" (Pontificiae Univ. S. Thomae de Urbe; Dallas, Texas, 1976); Richard G. Shepard, "Biblical Progression as Moral Development: The Analogy and Its Implications," *Journal of Psychology and Theology* 22 (Fall 1994): 182–86; John R. Tisdale, "Transpersonal Psychology and Jesus's Kingdom of God," *Journal of Humanistic Psychology* 34 (3, 1994): 31–47; Ernest Wallwork, "Thou Shalt Love Thy Neighbor as Thyself: The Freudian Critique," *Journal of Religious Ethics* 7 (2, 1982): 264–319.

79. Theissen, *Psychological Aspects*, 235–36, citing H. Fischer, *Gespaltener christliche Glaube: Eine psychoanalytische orientierte Religionskritik* (Hamburg: Reich, 1974), 56–57; Oskar Pfister, "Die Entwicklung des Apostels Paulus. Eine religionsgeschichtliche und psychologische Skizze," *Imago* 6 (1920): 243–90.

80. See David Wulff, *Psychology of Religion: Classic and Contemporary Views* (New York: John Wiley and Sons, 1991): 358; Jung, "Foreword," *Depth Psychology*, Neumann, 18. It should be mentioned that one of the attendant theological and psychological deficiencies of a deontological ethic from Jung's perspective is its inability to deal satisfactorily with the problem of evil. It tends to project evil either on the "evil one" or the "enemy," rarely if ever tracing evil to its own doorstep.

81. On "aretaic ethics," see Don Browning, *Religious Thought and the Modern Psychologies* (Philadelphia: Fortress Press, 1987), 11; Jung, *Letters* 2:76.

82. CW 11:696.

83. Jung, "Foreword," *Depth Psychology*, 11–16.

84. CW 7:401.

85. See Emil Brunner, "Biblical Psychology," in *God and Man: Four Essays on the Nature of Personality* (London: SCM Press, 1946), 137; "Biblical psychology . . . must mean . . . doctrine about the soul on the basis of Christian or Biblical faith."

86. Theissen, *Psychological Aspects*, makes a convincing case for biblical acknowledgment of the unconscious in his section on "The Secrets of the Heart: The Disclosure of Unconscious Motives Through Pauline Theology," especially pages 81–114. See also the section on "The Unconscious," in chapter 4 of the present volume, section III, 106–8.

87. Phyllis Trible, *Texts of Terror: Literary-Feminist Readings of Biblical Narratives* (Philadelphia: Fortress Press, 1984).

88. J. Harold Ellens, founding editor of the *Journal of Psychology and Christianity*, has been a consistent advocate of "mutual illumination" between

psychology and religion, and most recently between psychology and biblical studies. See Ellens, "Biblical Themes in Psychological Theory and Practice," in *Christian Counseling and Psychotherapy*, ed. D. G. Benner (Grand Rapids: Baker, 1987), 23–33; *God's Grace and Human Health* (Nashville: Abingdon, 1982); "The Bible and Psychology, an Interdisciplinary Pilgrimage," *Pastoral Psychology* 45 (3, 1997): 193–208.

89. Dominique Stein, "Is a Psycho-Analytic Reading of the Bible Possible?" in *Conflicting Ways of Interpreting the Bible*, eds. Hans Küng and J. Moltmann (New York, Edinburgh: Seabury, T. & T. Clark, 1980), 24–32; William Meissner, in *Psychoanalysis and Religious Experience* (New Haven: Yale University Press, 1984), 157. See Dan Merkur,"Freud's Atheism: Object Relations and the Theory of Religion," *Religious Studies Review* 16/1 (January 1990): 14.

90. Brunner, "Biblical Psychology," 138.

91. "The Bible and Psychology, an Interdisciplinary Pilgrimage" *Pastoral Psychology* 45 (3 1997):200.

92. *Whatever Became of Sin?* (New York: Hawthorn Books, 1973).

93. Kille in personal communication in the course of his doctoral work in psychology and biblical studies at the Graduate Theological Union, Berkeley, California.

94. Fletcher contends that the Bible contains "psychological material of the highest value" providing a "new view of human personality." A chief feature of of this new view is its doctrine of the spirit as a distinctive feature of regenerate humans; *Psychology*, 10, 146, 287.

95. Brunner, "Biblical Psychology," 113.

96. Jung, CW 4:780–83.

97. Jung, *Memories*, 326; Theissen, *Psychological Aspects*, 398.

Chapter 6: The Hermeneutical Agenda

1. Daniel Harrington, *Interpreting the New Testament* (Wilmington, Del.: Michael Glazier, 1979), 132.

2 Frederick Buechner, *The Sacred Journey* (New York: Harper & Row, 1982), 68.

3. "Who Killed Jesus? Crossan Responds to Brown," *Explorations* 10 (1, 1996): 2–4.

4. Sandra Schneiders, *The Revelatory Text*, 169–72, notes that biblical criticism in the last quarter of the twentieth century has come to appreciate the need for critical distanciation between readers and texts, recognizing both that *texts need protection from readers* (given the proclivity of readers to project themselves and their values upon texts in a way that renders the text "unable

to say anything the reader does not already think" and that accordingly fails to recognize the "strangeness" and "otherness" of the text), and that *readers need protection from texts* (that is, from the possible errors, "deceits," ideologies, and domination strategies that the text can kindle in the conscious or unconscious haunts of the reader).

5. Schneiders, *Revelatory Text*, 125.

6. Pontifical Biblical Commission, "Bible," 133; on deconstruction theory see, *Postmodern Bible*, 130, and the extended discussion, 119–25, 128–35. Sandra Schneiders proposes, in light of Ricoeur, that "in virtue of the text's relative semantic autonomy and freedom from the coordinates of its composition, the textual meaning entails both a surplus of meaning and susceptibility to recontextualization. Therefore, the text always actually means something other than, and in the case of a classic, more than, its author could have intended or its original audience could have understood"; *The Revelatory Text*, 163.

7. Lewis S. Mudge, "Paul Ricoeur on Biblical Interpretation," in *Essays on Biblical Interpretation*, ed. Lewis S. Mudge (Philadelphia: Fortress Press, 1980), 5; *Postmodern Bible*, 281.

8. *Postmodern Bible*, 273–74, 295, 299, 302.

9. *Postmodern Bible*, 120.

10. *Postmodern Bible*, 122.

11. *Postmodern Bible*, 121–22, 143–44.

12. *Postmodern Bible*, 273.

13. *Postmodern Bible*, 140–43; see Elizabeth A. Castelli, *Imitating Paul: A Discourse of Power*, Literary Currents in Biblical Literature (Louisville: Westminster/John Knox, 1991), 48–49; Sandra Schneiders also notes the religious institutional power-wielding that "regards women as derivative and defective, that maginalizes, trivializes, and even demonizes women, that excludes women from full religious participation and legitimates male domination" (at the same time prescribing a hermeneutic that can repudiate "the morally unacceptable subject matter of the text without repudiating the text itself and its truth claims"); *Revelatory Text*, 175.

14. *Postmodern Bible*, 139–40; see Michel Foucault, "Nietzsche, Freud, Marx" in *Cahiers de Royaumont philosophie 6, Nietzsche* (Paris: Minuit, 1967): 188. This perspective rejects the "epistemological conviction that the text has a determinate meaning, that the text is a transparent window to an extra-textual reference, and that the referent can be discussed with some degree of accuracy"; Fred Burnett, "Postmodern Biblical Exegesis: The Eve of Historical Criticism," *Semeia* 55 (1990): 53.

15. *Postmodern Bible*, 139.

16. *Postmodern Bible*, 130–31; Luke Timothy Johnson, *The Real Jesus: The Misguided Quest for the Historical Jesus and the Truth of the Traditional Gospels* (San Francisco: HarperSanFrancisco, 1997): 174, 104.

17. *Postmodern Bible*, 70–71, 76–80. The phrase, "actantial model," was adopted by Greimas to refer to the acts, actors, and things acted upon in a narrative. He identified these elements as sender, receiver, helper, opponent, subject, and object, all of them standard elements in narratives. Greimas used this model "to map units of story action down to the most elementary so that the story can be analyzuzed as an interlocking set of actantial models"; see David Jobling, "Structuralism and Deconstruction," in *Dictionary of Biblical Interpretation*, ed. John H. Hayes, vol. 2 (Nashville: Abingdon, 1999), 511.

18. Daniel and Aline Patte, *Structural Exegesis: From Theory to Practice* (Minneapolis: Fortress Press, 1978), 7, 12.

19. CW 15:125, 135.

20. Schneiders, *Revelatory Text*, 102.

21. Schneiders, *Revelatory Text*, 101, 102, 103, 106, 109.

22. Schneiders, *Revelatory Text*, 114. A selection of psychological studies of imagination include the following: Janet Dallett, "Active Imagination in Practice" in *Jungian Analysis*, ed. M. Stein (Boston: Shambala, 1984), 173–91; John P. Dourley, "Jung's Critique of Biblical Imagination: An Appreciative Undermining," in *The Goddess, Mother of the Trinity: A Jungian Implication* (Lewiston, N.Y.: Edwin Mellen, 1990); Alan Jacobs, "Psychological Criticism: From the Imagination to Freud and Beyond," in *Leland Ryken*, ed. Clarence Walhout (Grand Rapids: Eerdmans, 1992); P. Pruyser, "The Tutored Imagination in Religion," in *Religion in Psychodynamic Perspective: the Contributions of Paul M. Pruyser*, eds. H. N. Maloney and B. Spilka (New York: Oxford University Press, 1991), 101–15; Pruyser, *The Play of the Imagination: Toward a Psychoanalysis of Culture* (New York: International Universities Press, 1983); Ann Belford Ulanov, *The Healing Imagination: A Meeting of Psyche and Soul* (Mahwah, N.J.: Paulist, 1991); D. W. Winnicott, *Playing and Reality* (London: Tavistock, 1971).

23. Thiselton, *New Horizons*, 17, 33, notes that after 1970, hermeneutical theory began to pay attention to "the capacity of biblical texts *to produce certain transforming effects*, rather than only to transmit certain disclosures." The lack has been increasingly compensated for in the theories cited below. Thiselton classifies theories about the effect of texts on readers under one of three models: the speech-act model; the narrative-world model, and the model of inter-personal understanding.

24. Dale Patrick and Allen Scult, *Rhetoric and Biblical Interpretation*, Bible and Literature Series 26 (Sheffield: Almond, 1990), 12.

25. *Postmodern Bible*, 172.

26. *Postmodern Bible*, 167; 170, citing George A. Kennedy, *New Testament Interpretation Through Rhetorical Criticism* (Chapel Hill: University of North Carolina Press, 1984), 158.

27. Cheryl Exum makes the same point in her definition of an agenda for psychological biblical criticism: "We can turn our focus upon empirical readers, and examine the non-cognitive effects that reading our texts have upon them"; Exum and Clines, *The New Literary Criticism and the Hebrew Bible*, 18.

28. Italics added; Wayne C. Booth, *The Rhetoric of Fiction*, 2d ed. (Chicago: University of Chicago Press, 1983), xiii, 138; *Postmodern Bible*, 32–33; Schneiders, *Revelatory Text*, 173.

29. Theissen, *Psychological Aspects*, 5–10, chapter 1, "Learning Theory: Religion as Socially Learned Experience and Behavior."

30. Theissen, *Psychological Aspects*, 29–39, chapter 3, "The Cognitive Approach: Religion as Construction of an Interpreted World." With both models, that of learning theory and cognitive psychology, Theissen's objective is to clarify the "psychic factors and aspects" that resulted in "new patterns of experience and behavior that appeared with ancient Christianity" as evidenced in the New Testament text. Analogously the contemporary psychological critic will focus on the "new patterns of experience and behavior" that have appeared in response to the biblical text. Examples of the application of cognitive behavioral theory to the analysis of biblical passages include Thomas Anthony Reed, "An Analysis of Christ's Behavior toward Simon Peter in Matthew's Gospel following the Contemporary Cognitive-Behavioral Model of Reality Therapy" (University of San Francisco, 1985); Siang-Yang Tan, "Cognitive-behavior Therapy: a Biblical Approach and Critique," *Journal of Psychology and Theology* 15 (1987): 103–12; Uri Wernik, "Frustrated Beliefs and Early Christianity: A Psychological Enquiry into the Gospels of the New Testament," *Numen: International Review for the History of Religions* 22 (August 1975): 96–130.

31. *Postmodern Bible*, 93. See Hugh White's use of "defamiliarization" in *Narration and Discourse in the Book of Genesis* (Cambridge: Cambridge University Press, 1991), 18; see Roland Barthes's use of "disorientation" in "The Struggle with the Angel: Textual Analysis of Genesis 32:23–33," in *Structural Analysis and Biblical Exegesis: Interpretational Essays*, ed. Roland Barthes et al. (Pittsburgh: Pickwick, 1974), 21–31.

32. Thiselton, *New Horizons*, 33–34.

33. Thiselton, *New Horizons*, 6.

34. Schneiders, *Revelatory Text*, 167–68.

35. Schneiders, *Revelatory Text*, 172.

36. Thiselton, *New Horizons*, 16, 18, 19, 32, 293, 298–300.

37. Wink, "Wrestling," 142.

38. Jung, *CW* 11:713.

39. Rollins, *Jung and the Bible*, 75, 77.

40. Schneiders, *Revelatory Text*, 160, 171; italics added. Schneiders comments that for Gadamer, "the knower . . . is always implicated in the knowing and therefore in the known."

41. A licensed clinical psychologist in private practice, Johnson taught at Western Conservative Baptist Seminary in Portland, Oregon, and holds degrees from the University of South Africa, Fuller Theological Seminary, and Fuller Graduate School of Psychology; Cedric B.Johnson, *The Psychology of Biblical Interpretation* (Grand Rapids: Zondervan, 1983), 7, 10; G. C. Berkouwer, *Studies in Dogmatics: Holy Scripture* (Grand Rapids: Eerdmans, 1979), 106; italics added.

42. Johnson, *Psychology*, 13.

43. Harrington, *Interpreting*, 132.

44. *Postmodern Bible*, 130. See the discussion above on "The Constitution of Texts in Psychological Perspective," discussing the psychological significance of the critical theories of ideological critics, Derrida, Foucault, structuralists, and Jungian psychology. Psychotherapist/biblical scholar Hal Childs offers an impressive ideological and personal critical analysis of John Dominic Crossan's quest(s) for the historical Jesus, arguing that "objective structures of deep-subjectivity determine the narrative structure of history" for Crossan and for every other historian. Childs proposes a "new paradigm for the quest of the historical Jesus that combines a phenomenological and hermeneutic analytical psychology with a historical criticism that is aware of history as myth"; Hal Childs. "The Myth of the Historical Jesus and the Evolution of Consciousness: A Critique and Proposed Transformation of the Epistemology of John Dominic Crossan's Quest for the Historical Jesus from the Perspective of a Phenomenological Reading of C. G. Jung's Analytical Psychology"; Ph.D., Graduate Theological Union, 1997; ii, 370–73. On autobiographical criticism, which emphasizes the need for authors to identify their personal location, see Janice Capel Anderson and Jeffrey L. Staley, eds., "Taking It Personally: Introduction," in *Taking It Personally: Autobiographical Biblical Criticism* (Atlanta: Scholars Press, 1995), 15–16. Examples of pioneering autobiographical criticism can be found in Richard Rubenstein, *My Brother Paul* (New York: Harper & Row, 1972) and Marcus Borg, *Meeting Jesus Again For the First Time: The Historical Jesus and the Heart of Contemporary Faith* (San Francisco: HarperSanFrancisco, 1994), both of whom provide personal life stories as presuppositional for understanding their approaches.

45. *Postmodern Bible*, 281. See Fernando F. Segovia, "Towards a New Direction in Johannine Scholarship: The Fourth Gospel from a Literary Perspective," *Semeia* 53 (1991): 16–17.

46. Johnson, *Psychology*, 81; 61–89; see Charles Taber, "Is There More than One Way to Do Theology?" *Gospel in Context* (January 1978): 8.

47. See *Postmodern Bible*, 49, 177.

48. *Postmodern Bible*, 57–59, 176–77. The "Bible and Culture Collective" also offers the psychological observation of the need "to expose the ideology or psychology that has led generations of biblical scholars to suppress their responses to their own reading experience"; 24. See Stanley E. Fish, *Is There a Text in This Class? The Authority of Interpretive Communities* (Cambridge, Mass.: Harvard University Press, 1980).

49. *Postmodern Bible*, 65, 166, mentions the need for "all biblical critics to take ethical and political responsibility for the contextualization of their readings." On the ethics of interpretation, see Daniel Patte, *Ethics of Biblical Interpretation: A Reevaluation* (Louisville: Westminster John Knox Press, 1995); Elisabeth Schüssler Fiorenza, "The Ethics of Interpretation: De-Centering Biblical Scholarship," *Journal of Biblical Literature* 107 (1988): 3–17; Mary Ann Tolbert, "When Resistance Becomes Repression: Mark 13:9–27 and the Poetics of Location," in *Readings from this Place: Social Location and Biblical Interpretation in Global Perspective*, eds. Fernando F. Segovia and Mary Ann Tolbert, vol. 2 (Minneapolis: Fortress Press, 1995), 331–46.

50. *Postmodern Bible*, 36 n.16. The notes cites Robert M. Fowler's, *Let the Reader Understand: Reader-Response Criticism and the Gospel of Mark* (Minneapolis: Fortress Press, 1991) as one of few studies that have applied reception theory to the history of biblical interpretation. See also Schuyler Brown's volume on "biblical empirics" as a form of reception theory that focuses on "what *actually occurs* when a real reader reads the sacred text"; *Text and Psyche: Experiencing Scripture Today* (New York: Continuum, 1998), 44.

51. The Myers-Briggs Type Indicator developed by Isabel Myers and her mother Katheryn Briggs, adopted Jung's work on psychological types to develop a tool for identifying sixteen different personality types. It has been used widely as an instrument for hiring, for employee mediation, for crisis counseling, and for psychological type differentiation in business, social, and church settings, classifying temperament and type on a scale measuring extraversion [E], introversion [I], sensation [S], intuition [N], thinking [T], feeling [F], perceiving [P], and judging [J]. See I. Myers, *Manual: The Myers-Briggs Type Indicator* (Palo Alto, Calif.: Consulting Psychologists Press, 1962).

52. Laurens van der Post, *Jung and the Story of Our Time* (New York: Vintage Books, 1977), 191.

53. Hunt, *Story of Psychology*, 313.

54. Out of the series of tests that were developed along the lines of Allport's research to identify individual personalities with respect to a scale of traits, such as the Minnesota Multiphasic Personality Inventory and the California Psychological Inventory, five traits have emerged at the end of the twentieth century as basic dimensions of personality: 1) extraversion: sociability, activity, interpersonal involvement; 2) neuroticism: emotionality, emotional stability, and adjustment; 3) openness to experience: intellect, intelligence, "intellectance"; 4) agreeableness: likeability, altruism, trust, sociability; 5) conscientiousness: superego strength, dependability, restrained self-discipline. See Hunt, *Story of Psychology*, 348; Wulff, *Psychology of Religion*, 547–50; Johnson, *Psychology*, 51, 52, 62.

55. Harrington, *Interpreting*, 132.

56. Margaret Davies, "Reader-Response Criticism," in A *Dictionary of Biblical Interpretation* (London: SCM Press, 1990), 578–80.

57. Thiselton, *New Horizons*, 517.

58. *Postmodern Bible*, 31–32; see Wolfgang Iser, *The Act of Reading: A Theory of Aesthetic Response* (Baltimore: Johns Hopkins University Press, 1978), 108–9.

59. Thiselton, *New Horizons*, 529–31; *Postmodern Bible*, 28–29; Norman H. Holland, *Five Readers Reading* (New Haven, Conn.: Yale University Press, 1975); "Transactive Criticism: Re-Creation Through Identity," *Criticism* 18 (1976): 334–52; A *Reader's Guide to Psychoanalytic Psychology and Literature-and-Psychology* (New York: Oxford University Press, 1990).

60. Ralph L. Underwood, "Primordial Texts: An Object Relations Approach to Biblical Hermeneutics," *Pastoral Psychology* 45 (3, 1997): 182–83.

61. Underwood, "Primordial Texts," 186–87.

62. Underwood, "Primordial Texts," 191.

63. Wilfred C. Smith, *What Is Scripture? A Comparative Approach* (Minneapolis: Fortress Press, 1993), 225, 361 n. 29. See the discussion of Sandra Schneider's concept of the *constructive imagination* at work in *textual production* in section I above. See also, for example, Ray Hart, *Unfinished Man and the Imagination* (Atlanta: Scholars Press: 1968); Gordon D. Kaufman, *The Theological Imagination: Constructing the Concept of God* (Philadelphia: Westminster, 1981).

64. H. Newton Malony and Bernard Spilka, eds. *Religion in Psychodynamic Perspective: The Contributions of Paul W. Pruyser* (New York: Oxford University Press, 1991), 212; Wulff, *Psychology of Religion*, 339.

65. Pruyser retains the Freudian term, *illusion,* preferring it to *imagination* or *symbolization,* despite its adverse connotations in English, but also in Latin, where it denotes "mocking and irony " (*illusio*) and "to make sport of, mock, ridicule" and to "destroy" or "ruin" (*illudo*). See Paul Pruyser, "The Seamy Side of Current Religious Beliefs," in *Religion in Psychodynamic Perspective: the Contributions of Paul M. Pruyser,* eds. H. N. Maloney and B. Spilka (New York: Oxford University Press, 1991), 47–65, 210–12. Alfred Adler finds the words "illusion" less satisfactory than the phrase "useful fiction" to refer to the God language that creative humans have produced "to organize their individual *and* communal perceptions of reality around strivings toward perfection in ways that sanctify human life, the relationship between human beings, and the human community itself"; see Robert L. Powers, "Religion: Adler's View," in *International Encyclopedia of Psychiatry, Psychology, Psychoanalysis, and Neurology,* ed. Benjamin B. Wolman (New York: Van Nostrand Reinhold Company, 1976), 427–29.

66. Wulff, *Psychology of Religion,* 339.

67. Paul W. Pruyser, *Between Belief and Unbelief* (New York: Harper & Row, 1974), 111–13; Wulff, *Psychology of Religion,* 340.

68. Wulff, *Psychology of Religion,* 341.

69. Wulff, *Psychology of Religion,* 340–41, alluding to Pruyser, *The Play of the Imagination: Toward a Psychoanalysis of Culture* (New York: International Universities Press, 1983), 166–67.

70. Schneiders, *Revelatory Text,* 158.

71. Schneiders, *Revelatory Text,* 158–60. As noted earlier, psychotherapist Hal Childs has argued that "objective structures of deep-subjectivity determine the narrative structure of history" that objectivist historians construct; he accordingly urges the development of a historical-criticical approach that is aware of history as myth; "The Myth of the Historical Jesus and the Evolution of Consciousness: A Critique and Proposed Transformation of the Epistemology of John Dominic Crossan's Quest for the Historical Jesus from the Perspective of a Phenomenological Reading of C. G. Jung's Analytical Psychology."

72. Schneiders, *Revelatory Text,* 161; Werner G. Jeanrond, *Text and Interpretation as Categories of Theological Thinking,* trans. Thomas J. Wilson (New York: Crossroad, 1988), 12.

73. Schneiders, *Revelatory Text,* 171.

74. Schneiders, *Revelatory Text,* 169.

75. Schneiders, *Revelatory Text,* 172–73.

76. Schneiders, *Revelatory Text,* 174–75, 177.

77. Jeanrond, *Text and Interpretation,* 52.

78. Rashkow, *Phallacy of Genesis*, 22–25. Rashkow states that her "theoretical approach is literary, not psychoanalytic, although it is clearly informed by psychoanalytic theory." Her strategy is to read the Bible "*while reading* Freud," not "in *light* of Freud [and in this sense, to] . . . appropriate Freud's psychoanalytic approach as another tool for biblical interpretation"; 111.

79. *Postmodern Bible*, 222–23. Although the authorship of the *Postmodern Bible* is attributed to "the Bible and Culture Collective," the authorship for each chapter was undertaken by individual members of the group. In correspondence with one of the editors, I was informed that Stephen Moore is the primary author of the chapter on "Psychoanalytic Criticism, " 187–224. Schuyler Brown and Richard Q. Ford make similar comparisons between the psychoanalytic process and reading. Schuyler Brown, *Text and Psyche*, 96, draws an analogy between the psychoanalytic process and transformative biblical reading; Richard Q. Ford, between the therapist-client relationship and the parable-listener relationship, *The Parables of Jesus: Recovering the Art of Listening*, 9.

80. James Wiggins, *Religion as Story* (New York: Harper & Row, 1976), 9.

81. F. Young, *The Art of Performance: Towards a Theology of Holy Scripture* (London: Darton, Longman, and Todd, 1990); see Thiselton, *New Horizons*, 3.

82. A fuller discussion of these strategies is found in chapter 2, sections I and II.

83. CW 8:180.

84. Walter Wink, *Transforming Bible Study: A Leader's Guide.* 2d rev. ed. (Nashville: Abingdon, 1989), proposes exercises in "active imagination" as applied to biblical interpretation.

85. Wilfred Cantwell Smith, "The Study of Religion and the Study of the Bible," *Journal of the American Academy of Religion* 39 (1971): 131–40.

86. Hans-Georg Gadamer, *Truth and Method* (New York: Seabury, 1975) Part II; Schneiders, *Revelatory Text*, 67–68, 159–60; Ulrich Luz, *Matthew in History: Interpretation, Influence, and Effects* (Minneapolis: Fortress Press, 1994), 3.

87. *Postmodern Bible*, 35.

88. *Biblical Research* 22 (1977): 44. Crossan notes Robert Polzin's succinct summary of the Carleton University (Ottawa) symposium in Fall 1977: "that we who for so long have looked at the Bible and worked *backwards* to its origins might profitably study it by working *forwards* towards ourselves, through its successive traditional interpretations"; Hengel, "Aufgaben der Neutestamentlichen Wissenschaft," *New Testament Studies* 40 (1994): 355.

89. Wilfred C. Smith, *What Is Scripture? A Comparative Approach* (Minneapolis: Fortress Press, 1993), 213–14.

90. Robert Warrior, "Canaanites, Cowboys, and Indians: Deliverance, Conquest, and Liberation Theology Today," *Christianity and Crisis* 29 (1989): 262, 265; see also the work of "conservative Jewish theologian" Marc Ellis who relates the Exodus motif to the situation of the Palestinians in late twentieth-century Israel, suggesting that the the Israeli government (not the Jewish people) paradoxically has become the modern counterpart to Egypt, a case of the oppressed becoming oppressor; Marc H. Ellis, "Critical Thought and Messianic Trust: Reflections on a Jewish Theology of Liberation," in *The Future of Liberation Theology: Essays in Honor of Gustavo Gutierrez*, eds. Marc H. Ellis and Otto Maduro (Maryknoll, N.Y.: Orbis, 1989), 375–89; *Postmodern Bible*, 282, 285, 293. See also William R. Hutchison and Hartmut Lehmann, eds. *Many Are Chosen: Divine Election and Western Nationalisms* (Minneapolis: Fortress Press, 1994), on the biblical rhetoric of "chosenness" and its potentially dangerous effects in the nationalist ideologies of South Africa, Switzerland, Republic of France, Germany, Israel, America, Great Britain, and Sweden.

91. Phyllis Trible, *Texts of Terror: Literary-Feminist Readings of Biblical Narratives* (Philadelphia: Fortress Press, 1984), citing the violence toward women in four episodes in the Hebrew Bible; Renita Weems, *Battered Love: Marriage, Sex, and Violence in the Hebrew Prophets* (Minneapolis: Fortress Press, 1995), citing battery, infidelity, rape, and mutilation of women; Schneiders, *Revelatory Text*, 174, identifies the moral-hermeneutical issue in observing that "the biblical text contains not only historical inaccuracies, scientific errors, mythological assumptions that are unassimilable by the modern mind, but also morally objectional positions. Feminist criticism in particular, by exposing the patriarchal ideology, androcentric presuppositions, and sexist languge and teaching of the New Testament, has raised the problem of how a sacred text that is rife with morally unacceptable material can continue to function normatively for a faith community. . . . The hermeneutical question is how we can understand the interpretive process by which the reader identifies and repudiates the morally unacceptable subject matter of the text without repudiating the text itself and its truth claims." Feminist Rita Brock has pointed to the fact that the theological framing of the story of the crucifixion and death of Jesus as imposed by God the Father has resulted in a "glorification of suffering, which has served as the theological-christological basis for abuse of women"; *Journeys by Heart: A Christology of Erotic Power* (New York: Crossroad, 1988), 52–53. More radically Joanne Brown and Rebecca Parker have commented, "Is it any wonder that there is so much abuse in modern society when the pre-dominant image or theology of culture is of 'divine child abuse'—God the Father demeaning and carrying out the suffering and death of his own son?"; "For God

So Loved the World?" in Joanne Carlson Brown and Carol R. Bohn, eds., *Christianity, Patriarchy, and Abuse: A Feminist Critique* (New York: Pilgrim, 1989), 26–27; *Postmodern Bible*, 300–301.

92. Robert P. Carroll, *The Bible as a Problem for Christianity* (Valley Forge, Pa.: Trinity International Press, 1991); Philip Greven, *Spare the Child: The Religious Roots of Punishment and the Psychological Impact of Physical Abuse* (First Vintage Books Edition, New York: Vintage Books, Random House, 1992); René Girard, *The Bible, Violence, and the Sacred: Liberation from the Myths of Sanctioned Violence* (San Francisco: Torch, 1991); Robert G. Hamerton-Kelly, *Sacred Violence: Paul's Hermeneutic of the Cross* (Minneapolis: Fortress Press, 1992); Gerd Lüdemann, *The Unholy in Holy Scripture: The Dark Side of the Bible* (Louisville: Westminster/John Knox, 1997); John Dominic Crossan, "Who Killed Jesus? Crossan Responds to Brown," *Explorations* 10 (1, 1996): 3.

93. Donald Capps, *The Child's Song: The Religious Abuse of Children* (Westminster/John Knox, 1995); John P. Dourley, *The Illness That We Are: A Jungian Critique of Christianity* (Toronto: Inner City Books, 1984).

94. A striking example is the Fourth Gospel, perhaps the most "Jewish" and certainly the most sublime of the Gospels, which became a primary de facto progenitor of anti-Semitism because of its numerous references, especially in the crucifixion narratives in chapter 18, to the *Ioudaioi* (inappropriately translated "Jews"), providing fertile soil for the projections of anti-Semitic neurosis. See also Bernard McGinn, *Antichrist: Two Thousand Years of the Human Fascination with Evil* (Dunmore, Pa.: Torch, 1994), on how the figure of the Antichrist is projected on target individuals and groups to demonize them in the public eye.

95. Johnson, *Psychology*, 118.

96. CW 10:367; 16:249; in the second passage Jung speaks specifically of the therapeutic power of the "Old Testament," citing two passages of perennial meaning for him, Ps. 147:3, "He heals the brokenhearted and binds up their wound," and Job 5:18, "For he wounds, but he binds up; he smites, but his hands heal." On the comprehensive role of the Bible in Jung's life and work, see Rollins, "Psychology, Hermeneutics, and the Bible," in David L. Miller, ed., *Jung and the Interpretation of the Bible* (New York: Continuum, 1995), 9–39.

97. Calvert Stein, "Psychotherapy in the Bible," *Journal of the American Academy of Psychiatry and Neurology* 1 (2–3, 1976): 67–70. Another example of a study that perceives patterns of therapy in the Bible is Michele Matto's, *The Twelve Steps in the Bible* (Mahwah, N.J.: Paulist, 1991).

98. "On First Principles," IV, 2, 4. *Die griechischen christlichen Schriftsteller der ersten drei Jahrhunderte* (Leipzig and Berlin, 1897–) vol. 22, 305–23;

see Maurice Wiles and Mark Santer, eds., *Documents in Early Christian Thought* (New York: Cambridge University Press, 1975), 140–41.

99. E. Wall, "The Kerygma's Psychology and Human Distress," *Journal of Psychology and Theology* 1(4, 1973): 48–56. I am grateful to Thomas Faucher for the reference to Robert Coles, *The Spiritual Life of Children* (Boston: Houghton Mifflin, 1990), 121.

100. Donald Capps, *Biblical Approaches to Pastoral Counseling* (Philadelphia: Westminster, 1981); see also D. Capps, "The Bible's Role in Pastoral Care and Counseling: Four Basic Principles," *Journal of Psychology and Christianity* 3 (4, 1984): 5–15; Wayne Oates, *The Bible in Pastoral Care* (Philadelphia: Westminster, 1953); Carroll A. Wise, *Psychiatry and the Bible* (New York: Harper & Row, 1956).

101. CW 15:129

Bibliography

Abraham, Karl. "Der Versöhnungstag." In *Psychoanalytische Interpretationen Biblischer Texte*, ed. Yorick Spiegel. 117–27. Munich: C. Kaiser, 1972 [1920].

Aichelle, George, and Tina Pippin, eds. *Fantasy and the Bible. Semeia* 60. Atlanta: Scholars Press, 1992.

Alcorn, D. E. "New Testament Psychology." *British Journal of Medical Psychology* 16 (1937): 270–80.

Alexander, A. B. D. "The Psychology of Paul." In *Ethics of Saint Paul*. Glasgow: Maclehose and Sons, 1910.

Allen, Charles Livingstone. *God's Psychiatry: the Twenty-Third Psalm, the Ten Commandments, the Lord's Prayer, the Beatitudes*. Westwood, N.J.: Fleming H. Revell Co., 1953.

Allport, Gordon. *The Individual and His Religion*. New York: Macmillan, 1950.

_____. "William James and the Behavioral Sciences." *Journal of the History of Behavioral Sciences* 2 (1966): 145–47.

Allwohn, Adolf. *Die Ehe des Propheten Hosea in Psychoanalytischer Bedeutung*. Giessen: A. Töpelmann, 1926.

Almanasi, Renato J. "A Psychoanalytic Interpretation of the Menorah." *Journal of the Hillside Hospital* 2 (1953): 80–92.

_____. "A Further Contribution to the Psychoanalytic Interpretation of the Menorah." *Journal of the Hillside Hospital* 3 (1954): 3–18.

Alter, Margaret G. *Resurrection Psychology: An Understanding of Human Personality Based on the Life and Teachings of Jesus*. Chicago: Loyola University Press, 1994.

_____. "Prophet as a Psychological Construct in Mark 5:24–34: A Clinician's Perspective." Unpublished SBL paper, Philadelphia, 1995.

Altschule, Mark D. "The Two Kinds of Depression According to St. Paul." *British Journal of Psychiatry* 113 (1967): 779–80.

Anderson, Bernhard W. *Understanding the Old Testament*. 4th ed. Englewood Cliffs, N.J.: Prentice-Hall, 1986.

Anderson, F. A. "Psychopathological Glimpses of Some Biblical Characters." *Psychoanalytic Review* 14 (1927): 56–70.

Anderson, Janice Capel, and Stephen D. Moore, eds. *Mark and Method: New Approaches in Biblical Studies*. Minneapolis: Fortress Press, 1992.

Anderson, Janice Capel, and Jeffrey L. Staley. "Taking It Personally: Introduction." In *Taking It Personally: Autobiographical Biblical Criticism*, eds. Janice Capel Anderson and Jeffrey L. Staley. 7–18. Atlanta: Scholars Press, 1995.

Anderson, Paul N. *The Christology of the Fourth Gospel: Its Unity and Disunity in the Light of John 6*. Valley Forge, Pa.: Trinity Press International, 1996.

Andreson, J. J. "Biblical Job: Changing the Helper's Minds." *Contemporary Psychoanalysis* 27 (1991): 454–81.

Arnold, Patrick M. "Masculine Identity and Biblical Literature." *Listening* 23 (1988): 106–14.

Atkinson, Harley T. "Reinforcement in Learning: Integrating Skinner and Scripture." *Christian Education Journal* 14 (Autumn 1993): 58–72.

Auchter, Thomas. "Zum Schuldverständnis in der Psychoanalyse im Alten und Neuen Testament." *Wege zum Menschen* 30 (1978): 208–25.

Bach, Paul J. "Demon Possession and Psychopathology: A Theological Relationship." *Journal of Psychology and Theology* 7 (1 1979): 22–26.

Baentsch, B. "Pathologische Züge in Israels Prophetentum." *Zeitschrift für wissenschaftliche Theologie* (1907): 52–81.

Bakan, David. "Sacrifice and the Book of Job." In *Disease, Pain, and Sacrifice: Toward a Psychology of Suffering*, 95–128. Chicago: University of Chicago Press, 1968.

_____. *Slaughter of the Innocents: A Study of the Battered Child Phenomenon.* San Francisco: Jossey-Bass, 1971.

Baker, Oren H. "Paul: A Study in Conflict." *Pastoral Psychology* 2 (June 1951): 29–40.

Bal, Mieke. *Murder and Difference: Gender, Genre, and Scholarship on Sisera's Death.* Bloomington: Indiana University Press, 1988.

Baldwin, James M., ed. *Dictionary of Philosophy and Psychology.* New York: Macmillan, 1901–05.

Barande, I. "Das Verbrechen an Moses ersetzt den Todestrieb." *Jahrbuch der Psychanalyse* 21 (1987): 13–30.

Barclay, William. *Turning to God: A Study of Conversion in the Book of Acts and Today.* London: Epworth, 1963.

Barrett, William. *Death of the Soul: From Descartes to the Computer.* New York: Doubleday, 1986.

Barth, Hans Martin. "Gottes Wort ist dreifaltig: ein Beitrag zur Auseinandersetzung mit der 'archetypischen Hermeneutik' Eugen Drewermanns." *Theologische Literaturzeitung* 113 (1988): 244–54.

Barthes, Roland. "The Struggle with the Angel: Textual Analysis of Genesis 32:23–33." In *Structural Analysis and Biblical Exegesis: Interpretational Essays*, ed. Roland Barthes et al., 21–31. Pittsburgh: Pickwick, 1974.

Bartholinus, Caspar. *Manuductio ad veram Psychologiam e sacris literis.* Copenhagen: University of Copenhagen Press, 1618–19.

Bassett, R. L., K. Matthewson, and A. Galitis. "Recognizing the Person in Biblical Interpretation: An Empirical Study." *Journal of Psychology and Christianity* 12 (1993): 38–46.

Batey, Richard A. *Thank God I'm OK: The Gospel According to T.A.* Nashville: Abingdon, 1976.

Batson, C. Daniel and W. Larry Ventis. *The Religious Experience: A Social-Psychological Perspective.* New York: Oxford University Press, 1982.

Baxter, Andrew. *An Enquiry into the Nature of the Human Soul, Wherein the Immateriality of the Soul is Evinced from the Principles of Reason and Philosophy.* Reprint. Louisville: Lost Cause Press, 1961, London: James Bettenham, 1730.

Baxter, Steven S. "Some Thoughts on the Psychological Exegesis of Scripture." Unpublished manuscript, 1997.

Beaudoin, Suzanne, S. S. Ch. "Gospel Figures Show Their Shadows." *Human Development* IX (1, 1988): 6–12.

Bechtel, Lyn M. "Genesis 2.4b-3.24: A Myth about Human Maturation." *Journal for the Study of the Old Testament* 67 (1995): 3–26.

Beck, Johann Tobias. *Outlines of Biblical Psychology.* Trans. from 3d enlarged ed. of *Umriss der biblischen Seelenlehre.* Stuttgart: Belser, 1843. Edinburgh: T. & T. Clark, 1877.

Beit-Hallahmi, Benjamin. "Psychology of Religion 1880–1930: The Rise and Fall of a Psychological Movement." In *Current Perspectives in the Psychology of Religion*, ed. H. Newton Malony, 17–26. Grand Rapids: Eerdmans, 1977.

Beneke, Friedrich Eduard. *Lehrbuch der Psychologie*. Berlin: Druck u. Verlag von Ernst Siegfried Mittler, 1832.

Beneke, Friedrich Eduard. *Die Neue Psychologie: Erläuternde Aufsätze zur zweiten Auflage meines Lehrbuches der Psychologie als Naturwissenschaft*. Berlin: Posen u. Bromberg, 1845.

Bennet, E. A. *What Jung Really Said*. New York: Schocken, 1966.

Bennett, Boyce M. "Vision and Audition in Biblical Prophecy." *Parapsychology Review* 9 (1 1978): 1–12.

Benson, P. H. "New Testament Concepts for a Sociopsychological Model of Personality Development." In *Spiritual Well-Being: Sociological Perspectives*, ed. D. O. Moberg, 51–71. Washington, D.C.: University Press of America, 1979.

Berger, Klaus. *Historische Psychologie des Neuen Testaments*. Stuttgart: Verlag Katholisches Bibelwerk GmbH, 1991.

Berguer, G. *Some Aspects of the Life of Jesus: From the Psychological and Psycho-analytic Point of View*. Trans. Eleanor Stimson Brooks and Van Wyck Brooks. New York: Harcourt, Brace, 1923 [1920].

Berry, C. M. "Approaching the Integration of the Social Sciences and Biblical Theology." *Journal of Psychology and Theology* 8 (1980): 33–44.

Bettelheim, Bruno. *Freud and Man's Soul*. New York: Knopf, 1982.

The Bible and Culture Collective. *The Postmodern Bible*. New Haven: Yale University Press, 1995.

Bible and Culture Collective. "Psychoanalytic Criticism." In *The Postmodern Bible*, eds. Elizabeth A. Castelli, Stephen D. Moore, Gary Phillips, and Regina M. Schwartz. 187–224. New Haven: Yale University Press, 1995.

Bilotta, Vincent M., III. "An Experience of the Desert in the Gospel of Mark: A Psychotheological Reflection." *National Guild of Catholic Psychiatrists Bulletin* 28 (1982): 53–65.

Binet-Sanglé, Charles. "Le Prophète Elisée. Arch. di Anthropologia criminale." *Psichiatria e med. legale* 20 (1905): 136–41.

Bishop, J. G. "Psychological Insights in St. Paul's Mysticism." *Theology* 78 (1975): 318–24.

Blessing, Kamila. "Luke's Unjust Steward Viewed from the Window of Milton Erickson." Unpublished SBL paper, Washington, D. C., 1993.

_____. "Murray Bowen's Systems Psychodynamics as Hermeneutic." Unpublished SBL paper, Philadelphia, 1995.

Boisen, Anton. "What Did Jesus Think of Himself." *Journal of Bible and Religion* 20 (January 1952): 7–12.

Boivin, Michael J. "The Hebraic Model of the Person: Toward a Unified Psychological Science among Christian Helping Professionals." *Journal of Psychology and Theology* 19 (1991): 157–65.

Bolin, E. P., and G. M. Goldberg. "Behavioral Psychology and the Bible: General and Specific Considerations." *Journal of Psychology and Theology* 7 (3 1979): 167–75.

Bonaparte, Marie. "Eros, Saul de Tarse et Freud." *Revue Française de Psychanalyse* 21 (1957): 23–34.

Bond, Jesse Hickman. *Industrial Influence on the Psychology of Jesus. A Study of the Origin, Processes and Results of Psychological Conflict in His Ethical Struggle*. Boston: R. G. Gorman, 1925.

Bonnell, J. S. "The Demoniac of Gerasa. A Study in Modern Frustration." *Pastoral Psychology* (1956): 23ff.

Bookstaber, Philip David. *The Idea of the Development of the Soul in Medieval Jewish Philosophy*. Philadelphia: Maurice Jacobs, 1950.

Booth, Wayne C. *The Rhetoric of Fiction*. 2d ed. Chicago: University of Chicago Press, 1983.

Borg, Marcus. *Meeting Jesus Again For the First Time: The Historical Jesus and the Heart of Contemporary Faith*. San Francisco: HarperSanFrancisco, 1994.

Bousset, Wilhelm. *Kyrios Christos: Geschichte des Christusglaubens von den Anfangen des Christentums bis Irenaeus*. Göttingen: Vandenhoeck & Ruprecht, 1913.

Bower, Robert K., ed. *Biblical and Psychological Perspectives for Christian Counselors*. South Pasadena, Calif.: Publishers Services, 1974.

Boyarin, Daniel. "The Sea Resists: Midrash and the (Psycho)dynamics of Intertextuality." In *Intertextuality and the Reading of Midrash*, 93–104. Bloomington: Indiana University Press, 1990.

Boyd, Jeffrey H. *Reclaiming the Soul: The Search for Meaning in a Self-Centered Culture*. Cleveland, Ohio: Pilgrim, 1995.

Bregman, Lucy. "Symbolism/symbolizing." In *Dictionary of Pastoral Care and Counseling*, ed. R. Hunter. 1248–50. Nashville: Abingdon, 1990.

Brenner, Arthur B. "The Covenant with Abraham." *Psychoanalytic Review* 39 (1952): 34–52.

Brett, G. S. *A History of Psychology*. London: George Allen, 1912.

Brome, Vincent. *Jung: Man and Myth*. New York: Atheneum, 1981.

Broome, Edwin C. "Ezekiel's Abnormal Personality." *Journal of Biblical Literature* 65 (1946): 277–92.

Brown, C. *Jung's Hermeneutic of Doctrine: Its Theological Significance*. Chico, Calif.: Scholars Press, 1981.

Brown, Schuyler. "The Myth of Sophia." In *Jung and the Interpretation of the Bible*, ed. David L. Miller, 92–101. New York: Continuum, 1995.

_____. *Text and Psyche: Experiencing Scripture Today*. New York: Continuum, 1998.

Browning, Don. *Atonement and Psychotherapy*. Philadelphia: Westminster, 1966.

_____. *Religious Thought and the Modern Psychologies*. Philadelphia: Fortress Press, 1987.

Brunner, Emil. "Biblical Psychology." In *God and Man: Four Essays on the Nature of Personality*, 136–78. London: SCM Press, 1936.

Bruns, J. Edgar. "Depth-Psychology and the Fall: Jungian Interpretation of Gen 3." *Catholic Biblical Quarterly* 21 (1959): 78–82.

Bufford, Rodger K. "God and Behavior Mod: II. Some Reflections on Vos' Response." *Journal of Psychology and Theology* 6 (1978): 215–18.

_____. *The Human Reflex: Behavioral Psychology in Biblical Perspective*. New York: Harper & Row, 1982.

Bultmann, Rudolf. *Theology of the New Testament*. Trans. K. Grobel. New York: Charles Scribner's Sons, 1951.

Bundy, W. E. *The Psychic Health of Jesus*. New York: Macmillan, 1922.

Burton, Ernest de Witt. *Spirit, Soul, Flesh*. Chicago: University of Chicago Press, 1918.

Bush, George. *The Soul: An Enquiry into Scripture Psychology*. New York: Redfield, 1845.

Buss, Martin J. "Selfhood and Biblical Eschatology." *Zeitschrift für die alttestamentliche Wissenschaft* 100 (Supplement 1980): 214–22.

_____. "The Social Psychology of Prophecy." In *Prophecy: Essays Presented to Georg Fohrer on His Sixty-fifth Birthday*, ed. J. A. Emerton, 1–11. Berlin: Walter de Gruyter, 1980.

Cadbury, Henry. "Current Issues in New Testament Studies." *Harvard Divinity School Bulletin* 19 (1953): 49–64.

_____. "Motives of Biblical Scholarship." *Journal of Biblical Literature* 56 (1937): 1–16.

_____. "Mixed Motives in the Gospels." *Proceedings of the American Philosophical Society* 95 (1951): 117–24.

Caird, G. B. *The Language and Imagery of the Bible*. London: Duckworth, 1980.

Callan, Terrence. "Competition and Boasting: Toward a Psychological Portrait of Paul." *Studia Theologica: Scandinavian Journal of Theology* 40.2 (1986): 137–56.

_____. *Psychological Perspectives on the Life of Paul. An Application of the Methodology of Gerd Theissen*. Studies in the Bible and Early Christianity 22. Lewiston: Edwin Mellen, 1990.

Campbell, Joseph. *The Hero with a Thousand Faces*. New York: Pantheon, 1949.

Campbell, Joseph, ed. *The Portable Jung*. New York: Viking Press, 1971.

Capps, Donald. *Biblical Approaches to Pastoral Counseling*. Philadelphia: Westminster, 1981.

_____. "The Beatitudes and Erikson's Life Cycle Theory." *Pastoral Psychology* 33 (1985): 226–44.

_____. "The Bible's Role in Pastoral Care and Counseling: Four Basic Principles." *Journal of Psychology and Christianity* 3.4 (1984): 5–15.

_____. "Bible, Pastoral Use and Interpretation of." In *Dictionary of Pastoral Care and Counseling*, ed. R. Hunter, 82–85. Nashville: Abingdon, 1990.

_____. *The Child's Song: The Religious Abuse of Children*. Louisville: Westminster/John Knox, 1995.

Capps, Donald, and Richard K. Fenn, eds. *On Losing the Soul: Essays in the Social Psychology of Religion*. Albany, N.Y.: SUNY Press, 1995.

Carlson, David E. "Jesus' Style of Relation: The Search for a Biblical View of Counseling." *Journal of Psychology and Theology* 4.3 (1976): 181–92.

Carroll, M. P. "'Moses and Monotheism' Revisited: Freud's 'Personal Myth?'" *American Imago* 44 (1987): 15–35.

Carroll, Robert P. "Ancient Israelite Prophecy and Dissonance Theory." *Numen* 24 (1977): 135–51.

_____. "Prophecy and Dissonance: A Theoretical Approach to the Prophetic Tradition." *Zeitschrift für die alttestamentliche Wissenschaft* 92 (1, 1980): 108–19.

_____. *The Bible as a Problem for Christianity*. Valley Forge, Pa.: Trinity International Press, 1991.

Carter, John. "Toward a Biblical Model of Counseling." *Journal of Psychology and Theology* 8 (1980): 45–52.

_____. "Maturity, Psychological and Biblical." *Journal of Psychology and Theology* 2.2 (1974): 89–96.

Carus, Carl Gustav. *Psyche: Zur Entwicklungsgeschichte der Seele*. Pforzheim: Flammer u. Hoffmann, 1846.

Carus, Friedrich August. *Psychology of the Hebrews*. Leipzig: I. A. Barth u. P. G. Kummer, 1809.

Cassem, N. H. "Ezekiel's Psychotic Personality: Reservations on the Use of the Couch for Biblical Personalities." In *Word in the World*, ed. R. Clifford, 59–68. Cambridge, Mass.: Weston College Press, 1973.

Castelein, John D. "Glossolalia and the Psychology of the Self and Narcissism." *Journal of Religion and Health* 23 (Spring 1984): 47–62.

Cerling, Charles E., Jr. "Some Thoughts on a Biblical View of Anger: A Response." *Journal of Psychology and Theology* 2.1 (1974): 266–69.

Chambers, Oswald. *Biblical Psychology: A Series of Preliminary Studies*. 2d ed. London: Simpkin Marshall, 1900.

Chapman, Glenn H. "A Heuristic Correlation of Kohutian Psychology of the Self and Pauline Anthropology as a Resource for Pastoral Psychotherapy." D.Min. project, Western Theological Seminary, 1991.

Childs, Hal. "The Myth of the Historical Jesus and the Evolution of Consciousness: A Critique and Proposed Transformation of the Epistemology of John Dominic Crossan's Quest for the Historical Jesus from the Perspective of a Phenomenological Reading of C. G. Jung's Analytical Psychology." Ph.D. diss., Graduate Theological Union, 1997.

Chorisy, Maryse. "Quelques reflexions sur une psychologie de Cain." *Psyché* (1953): 88–95.

Churchill, Winston. *The Uncharted Way: The Psychology of the Gospel Doctrine.* Philadelphia: Dorrance, 1940.

Clark, David K. "Interpreting the Biblical Words for the Self." *Journal of Psychology and Theology* 18 (1990): 309–17.

Clements, R. D. "Physiological-psychological thought in Juan Luis Vives." *Journal of the History of the Behavioral Sciences* 3 (1967): 219–35.

Clouse, Bonnidell. "The Teachings of Jesus and Piaget's Concept of Mature Moral Judgment." *Journal of Psychology and Theology* 6 (1978): 175–82.

Coggins, R. J., and J. L. Houlden, eds. *A Dictionary of Biblical Interpretation.* Philadelphia: Trinity Press International, 1990.

Cohen, N. J. "Two That Are One: Sibling Rivalry in Genesis." *Judaism* 32 (1983): 331–42.

Cole, Dick T. "A Personality Sketch of Cain, the Son of Adam." *Journal of Psychology and Theology* 6 (1978): 37–39.

Coles, Robert. *The Spiritual Life of Children.* Boston: Houghton Mifflin, 1990.

Collins, Adela Yarbro. *Crisis and Catharsis: The Power of the Apocalypse.* Philadelphia: Westminster, 1984.

Cooper, Howard J. "Guilt and God, or 'Whatever Happened in the Garden?'" *Journal of Psychology and Judaism* 15 (Summer 1991): 75–88.

Corey, Michael Anthony. *Job, Jonah, and the Unconscious: A Psychological Interpretation of Evil and Spiritual Growth in the Old Testament.* Lanham, Md.: University Press of America, 1995.

Coriat, Isadore H. "Dreams and the Samson Myth." *Internationale Zeitschrift für Psychoanalyse* 2 (1914): 460–62.

Cousineau, Phil, ed. *Soul: An Archaeology: Readings from Socrates to Ray Charles.* San Francisco: HarperSanFrancisco, 1994.

Cowley, R. A. "The Concept of Guilt in the Writings of St. Paul in the Light of Contemporanean Psychotherapists." University of Bristol, 1973.

Cox, David. *Jung and St. Paul: A Study of the Doctrine of Justification by Faith and Its Relation to the Concept of Individuation.* New York: Association Press, 1959.

Crabb, Lawrence J. *Effective Biblical Counseling.* Grand Rapids, Mich.: Zondervan, 1977.

_____. "Biblical Authority and Christian Psychology." *Journal of Psychology and Theology* 9 (1981): 305–11.

Cranmer, David J., and Brian E. Eck. "God Said It: Psychology and Bibical Interpretation, How Text and Reader Interact Through the Glass Darkly." *Journal of Psychology and Theology* 22 (1994): 207–14.

Crawley, Alfred Ernest. *The Idea of the Soul.* London: A. & C. Black, 1909.

Crawshaw, William H. *The Indispensable Soul.* New York: Macmillan, 1931.

Crespy, Georges. "Exégèse et psychanalyse: Considérations aventureuses sur Romains 7:7–25." In *L'Évangile Hier: FS*, ed. P. E. Bonnard F. J. Leenhardt et al. Geneva: Éditions Labor et Fides, 1968.

Cross, F. L., and E. A. Livingstone, eds. *The Oxford Dictionary of the Christian Church*. 2d rev. ed. Oxford: Oxford University Press, 1990.

Crossan, John Dominic, ed. *Paul Ricoeur on Biblical Hermeneutics. Semeia* 4. Missoula: University of Montana, 1975.

_____. "Perspectives and Methods in Contemporary Biblical Criticism." *Biblical Research* 22 (1977): 39–49.

_____. "Who Killed Jesus? Crossan Responds to Brown." *Explorations* 10 (1, 1996): 2–4.

Crownfield, David, ed. *Body/Text: Julia Kristeva and the Study of Psychoanalysis and Religion*. Albany, N.Y.: SUNY Press, 1992.

Cunningham, A. "Psychoanalytic Approaches to Biblical Narrative (Genesis 1–4)." In *A Traditional Quest*, ed. D. Cohn-Sherbok. 113–32. Sheffield: JSOT, 1991.

Curtiss, Samuel Ives. *Franz Delitzsch: A Memorial Tribute*. Edinburgh: T. & T. Clark, 1891.

Dailey, Thomas F., OSFS. "The Wisdom of Job: Moral Maturity or Religious Reckoning?" Unpublished SBL paper, Philadelphia, 1995.

Dale, Patrick, and Allen Scult. *Rhetoric and Biblical Interpretation*. Bible and Literature Series 26. Sheffield: Almond, 1990.

Dales, Richard C. *The Problem of the Rational Soul in the Thirteenth Century*. Leiden: E. J. Brill, 1995.

Dallett, Janet. "Active Imagination in Practice." In *Jungian Analysis*, ed. M. Stein, 173–91. Boston: Shambala, 1984.

Darroch, Jane. "An Interpretation of the Personality of Jesus." *British Journal of Medical Psychology* 21 (1947): 75–79.

Daschke, Dereck M. "'Because of My Grief I Have Spoken:' The Psychology of Loss in 4 Ezra." Boston: Society of Biblical Literature, 1999.

Davies, Stevan L. *Jesus the Healer: Possession, Trance, and the Origins of Christianity*. New York: Continuum, 1995.

Davis, Thomas Kirby. *Mind and Spirit: A Study in Psychology*. Boston: Sherman, French & Co., 1914.

de Loosten, George (pseudonym) and [George Lomer]. *Jesus Christus vom Standpunkte des Psychiaters*. Bamberg: Handels-Druckerei, 1905.

de Vries, G. *Bijdrage tot de psychologie van Tertullianus*. Utrecht: Kemink en Zoon, 1929.

Deissmann, Adolf. "The Christ Mystic." In *The Writings of St. Paul*, ed. Wayne Meeks, 374–87. New York: Norton, 1972.

Delitzsch, Franz. *A System of Biblical Psychology* [= *System der biblischen Psychologie*. Leipzig: Dörffling & Franke, 1861; ET, Edinburgh: T. & T. Clark, 1869]. 2d ed. Trans. A. E. Wallis. Grand Rapids: Baker Book House, 1966.

Delorme, J. "Qu'est-ce qui fait courir les exégètes?" *Lumiere et Vie (Lyons)* 29 (1980): 77–89.

Derby, Josiah. "A Biblical Freudian Slip: II Samuel 12:6." *Jewish Bible Quarterly* 242 (1996): 107–11.

Deschenes, Paul, and Martha L. Rogers. "A Systems View of Jesus as a Change Agent." *Journal of Psychology and Theology* 9 (1981): 128–35.

Detweiler, Robert, and William G. Doty, eds. *The Daemonic Imagination: Biblical Text and Secular Story*. Vol. 60. AAR Studies in Religion. Atlanta: Scholars Press, 1990.

Dever, William. "Women's Popular Religion, Suppressed in the Bible, Now Revealed by Archaeology." *Biblical Archaeology Review* 17.2 (1991): 65.

Dewar, Lindsay. *The Holy Spirit and Modern Thought: An Inquiry into the Historical, Theological, and Psychological Aspects of the Christian Doctrine of the Holy Spirit.* London: Mowbray, 1959.

DiCenso, James J. "*Totem and Taboo* and the Constitutive Function of Symbolic Forms." *Journal of the American Academy of Religion* 64 (3 1996): 557–74.

Dolto, Françoise, and Gérard Sévérin. *The Jesus of Psychoanalysis: A Freudian Interpretation of the Gospel.* Trans. Helen R. Lane. New York: Doubleday, 1979.

Dourley, John P. *C. G. Jung and Paul Tillich—The Psyche as Sacrament.* Toronto: Inner Books, 1981.

_____. *The Illness That We Are: A Jungian Critique of Christianity.* Toronto: Inner City Books, 1984.

Drakeford, John W. *Psychology in Search of a Soul.* Nashville: Broadman Press, 1964.

Dreifuss, G. "The Figures of Satan and Abraham (In the Legends on Genesis 22, the Akedah)." *Journal of Analytic Psychology* 17 (1972): 166–78.

_____. "The Binding of Isaac (Genesis 22—The Akedah)." *Journal of Analytic Psychology* 20 (1975): 50–56.

Dreifuss, Gustav, and Judith Riemer. *Abraham: The Man and the Symbol: A Jungian Interpretation of the Biblical Story.* Trans. Greenwood, Naphtali. Wilmette, Ill.: Chiron, 1995.

Drewermann, Eugen. *Das Markusevangeliums, Erster Teil, Mk 1,1 bis 9,13.* Olten-Freiburg: Walter, 1987.

_____. *Das Markusevangeliums, Zweiter Teil.* Olten- Freiburg: Walter, 1988.

_____. *Das Matthäusevangeliums, Erster Teil, Mt 8,1—20,19. Bilder der Erfüllung.* Olten-Freiburg: Walter, 1992.

_____. *Das Matthäusevangeliums, Zweiter Teil, Mt 8,1—20,19. Bilder der Erfüllung.* Soluthurn-Düsseldorf: Walter, 1994.

_____. *Discovering the God Child Within: A Spiritual Psychology of the Infancy of Jesus.* New York: Crossroad, 1994.

_____. *Dying We Live: Meditations for Lent and Easter.* Maryknoll, N.Y.: Orbis, 1994.

_____. *Open Heavens: Meditations for Advent and Christmas.* Maryknoll, N.Y.: Orbis, 1994.

_____. *Psychoanalyse und Moraltheologie.* Mainz: Grünewald, 1982–84.

_____. *Strukturen des Bösen.* Paderborner Theologische Studien, München/Paderborn/Wien: Schöningh, 1981–82.

_____. *Tiefenpsychologie und Exegese: Die Wahrheit der Formen: Traum, Mythos, Märchen, Sage, und Legende.* Vol. 1. Olten/Freiburg: Walter, 1984a.

_____. *Tiefenpsychologie und Exegese: Die Wahrheit der Werke und der Worte: Wunder, Vision, Weissagung, Apokalypse, Geschichte, Gleichnis.* Vol. 2. Olten/Freiburg: Walter, 1984b.

Edinger, Edward. *The Bible and the Psyche: Individuation Symbolism in the Old Testament.* Toronto: Inner City Books, 1986.

_____. *The Christian Archetype: A Jungian Commentary on the Life of Christ.* Toronto: Inner City Books, 1987.

_____. *Transformation of the God-Image: An Elucidation of Jung's Answer to Job.* Toronto: Inner City Books, 1992.

Ehrenwald, Jan. "Scriptural Demonology and the Healing Miracles of the Bible." In *From Medicine Man to Freud*, ed. Jan Ehrenwald. New York: Dell, 1956.

Eichhorn, Herman. "Some Therapeutic Implications of the Crucifixion and Resurrection." *Pastoral Psychology* 13 (1962): 12–17.

Ellenberger, Henri. "The Unconscious Before Freud." *Bulletin of the Menninger Clinic* 21 (3 1957): 3–15.

_____. *The Discovery of the Unconscious: The History and Evolution of Dynamic Psychiatry.* New York: Basic Books, 1970.

Ellens, J. Harold. "Biblical Themes in Psychological Theory and Practice." In *Christian Counseling and Psychotherapy*, ed. D. G. Benner, 23–33. Grand Rapids: Baker, 1987.

_____. "Biblical Authority and Christian Psychology: II." *Journal of Psychology and Theology* 9 (1981): 318–25.

_____. "A Psychospiritual View of Sin." In *Counseling and the Human Predicament*, ed. L. Aden, 36–48. Grand Rapids: Baker, 1989.

_____. "The Bible and Psychology, an Interdisciplinary Pilgrimage." *Pastoral Psychology* 45 (3 1997): 193–208.

Ellis, Marc H. "Critical Thought and Messianic Trust: Reflections on a Jewish Theology of Liberation." In *The Future of Liberation Theology: Essays in Honor of Gustavo Gutierrez*, eds. Marc H. Ellis and Otto Maduro, 375–89. Maryknoll, N.Y.: Orbis, 1989.

Eltz-Hoffmann, Lieselotte v. "Biblisch Träume und ihre Deutung im Blickfeld der modernen Psychologies." *Wege zum Menschen* 12 (1960): 225–60.

Erikson, E. H. "The Galilean Sayings and the Sense of 'I.'" *Yale Review* 70 (1981): 321–62.

Eubanks, Larry Lee. "The Cathartic Effects of Irony in Jonah." Southern Baptist Theological Seminary, 1988.

Evans, C. S. "Mind." In *Dictionary of Pastoral Care and Counseling*, ed. Rodney J. Hunter. Nashville: Abingdon, 1990.

Evans, E. C. "Physiognomics in the Ancient World." *Transactions of the American Philosophical Society* 59 (1969): 5.

Exum, J. Cheryl, and Mark G. Brett. "Editorial Statement." *Biblical Interpretation* 1 (1993): i.

Exum, J. Cheryl, and David J. A. Clines, eds. *The New Literary Criticism and the Hebrew Bible.* Sheffield: Sheffield Academic Press, 1993.

Faur, J. "De-authorization of the Law: Paul and the Oedipal Model." In *Psychoanalysis and Religion*, eds. J. H. Smith and S. A. Handelman, 222–43. Baltimore: Johns Hopkins, 1990.

Felber, Jean. *Der Kainskomplex.* Wien/Innsbruck: 1956.

Felder, Cain Hope, ed. *Stony the Road We Trod: African American Biblical Interpretation.* Minneapolis: Fortress Press, 1991.

Feldman, Sandor S. "The Sin of Reuben, First-Born Son of Jacob." *Psychoanalysis and the Social Sciences* (1955): 282–87.

Feldman, Yael S. "'And Rebecca Loved Jacob,' but Freud Did Not." In *Freud and Forbidden Knowledge*, ed. P. Rudnytsky et al., 7–25. New York: New York University Press, 1994.

Feldmann, Arthur A. "Freud's 'Moses and Monotheism' and the Three Stages of Israelitish Religion." *Psychoanalysis and the Psychoanalytic Review* 31 (1944): 361–418.

Fenn, Richard K. "Introduction: Why the Soul?" In *On Losing the Soul: Essays in the Social Psychology of Religion*, eds. Donald Capps and Richard K. Fenn, 1–22. Albany, N.Y.: SUNY Press, 1995.

Festinger, L., H. W. Riecken, and S. Schachter. *Why Prophecy Fails: A Social and Psychological Study of a Modern Group that Predicted the Destruction of the World.* New York: Harper & Row, 1956.

Field, M. J. *Angels and Ministers of Grace: An Ethno-psychiatrist's Contribution to Biblical Criticism.* New York: Hill and Wang, 1972.

Finger, Hyman H. "Psychoanalytic Study of the Minor Prophet, Jonah." *Psychoanalytic Review* 41 (1954): 55–65.

Fiorenza, Elisabeth Schüssler. "The Ethics of Interpretation: De-Centering Biblical Scholarship." *JBL* 107 (1988): 3–17.

Fischer, H. *Gespaltener christliche Glaube: Eine psychoanalytische orientierte Religionskritik.* Hamburg: Reich, 1974.

Fish, S. *Is There a Text in This Class? The Authority of Interpretive Communities.* Cambridge, Mass.: Harvard University Press, 1980.

Fitzmyer, Joseph A., S. J. *Scripture, the Soul of Theology.* New York: Paulist, 1994.

Fletcher, M. Scott. *The Psychology of the New Testament.* 2d ed. New York: Hodder & Stoughton, 1912.

Fodor, A. "The Fall of Man in the Book of Genesis." *American Imago* 11 (1954): 201–31.

Ford, Richard. *The Parables of Jesus: Recovering the Art of Listening.* Minneapolis: Fortress Press, 1997.

Forster, Jonathan Langstaff. *Biblical Psychology.* London: Longmans, Green, 1873.

Fortune, R. F. "The Symbolism of the Serpent." *International Journal of Psychoanalysis* 7 (1926): 237–43.

Foster, James D., and Glenn T. Moran. "Piaget and Parables: The Convergence of Secular and Scriptural Views of Learning." *Journal of Psychology and Theology* 13 (Summer 1985): 97–103.

Fowler, Robert M. "Reader-Response Criticism: Figuring Mark's Reader." In *Mark and Method: New Approaches in Biblical Studies,* eds. Janice Capel Anderson and Stephen D. Moore, 50–83. Minneapolis: Fortress Press, 1992.

Franck, Rudolf. *Zur Frage nach der Psychotherapie Jesu.* Vol. 15. Arzt und Seelsorger, Schwerin: 1928.

Frankl, Viktor. *From Death Camp to Existentialism: A Psychiatrist's Path to a New Therappy.* Trans. Ilse Lasch. Boston: Beacon, 1959.

Frayn, Reginal Scott. *Revelation and the Unconscious.* London: Epworth, 1940.

Frei, Hans W. *The Eclipse of Biblical Narrative. A Study in Eighteenth and Nineteenth Century Hermeneutics.* New Haven: Yale University Press, 1974.

Freud, Sigmund. "'Great is Diana of the Ephesians.'" In *SE,* 342–44. 12. 1911b.

———. "Totem and Taboo." In *SE,* 1–161. 13. 1913.

———. "The *Moses* of Michelangelo." In *SE,* 211–36. 13. 1914a.

———. "The Future of an Illusion." In *SE,* 3–56. 21. 1927a.

———. *Moses and Monotheism.* Ger. orig. *Der Mann Moses und die monotheistische Religion: Drei Abhandlungen* ed., Vol. 23. Trans. Katherine Jones. *The Standard Edition,* ed. James Strachey. London: Hogarth, 1939.

———. *The Standard Edition of the Complete Psychological Works of Sigmund Freud.* James Strachey, ed. London: Hogarth Press and the Institute of Psychoanalysis, 1953–74.

———. "An Autobiographical Study." In *The Standard Edition,* ed. J. Strachey. 1–74. 20. London: Hogarth Press and the Institute of Psychoanalysis, 1959.

———. *Letters of Sigmund Freud.* Trans. T. Stern and J. Stern. E. L. Freud, ed. New York: Basic Books, 1960.

Freud, Sigmund, and C. G. Jung. *The Freud/Jung Letters: The Correspondence between Sigmund Freud and C. G. Jung.* Vol. 94. Trans. Ralph Manheim (Freud) and R. F. C. Hull (Jung). Bollingen Series, ed. William McGuire. Princeton: Princeton University Press, 1974.

Freud, Sigmund, and O. Pfister. *Psychoanalysis and Faith: The Letters of Sigmund Freud and Oskar Pfister*. Trans. E. Mosbacher. H. Meng and E. L. Freud, eds. New York: Basic Books, 1963.

Frey, Jorg. *Eugen Drewermann und die biblische Exegese: eine methodisch-kritische Analyse*. Tübingen: J.C.B. Mohr (P. Siebeck), 1995.

Froehlich, Karlfried, ed. *Biblical Interpretation in the Early Church*. Minneapolis: Fortress Press, 1984.

Fromm, Erich. *The Dogma of Christ and Other Essays on Religion, Psychology and Culture*. Orig. Ger. *Die Entwicklung des Christus Dogmas; eine psychoanalytische Studie zur sozial psychologischen Funktion er Religion* (Vienna: Internationaler psychoanalytischer Verlag, 1931). New York: Holt, Rinehart & Winston, 1931 [1963].

_____. *Sigmund Freud's Mission: An Analysis of His Personality and Mission*. New York: Harper & Row, 1959.

_____. *You Shall Be as Gods: A Radical Reinterpretation of the Old Testament and Its Tradition*. New York: Holt, Rinehart and Winston, 1966.

Fuller, Robert C. *Americans and the Unconscious*. New York: Oxford, 1986.

Gadamer, Hans-Georg. *Truth and Method*. New York: Seabury, 1975.

Gager, John. *Kingdom and Community: The Social World of Early Christianity*. Englewood Cliffs, N.J.: Prentice-Hall, 1975.

_____. "Some Notes on Paul's Conversion." *New Testament Studies* 27 (1981): 697–703.

Gaiser, Frederick J. "The Emergence of the Self in the Old Testament: A Study in Biblical Wellness." *Horizons in Biblical Theology* 14 (June 1992): 1–29.

Garfinkel, Stephen. "Another Model for Ezekiel's Abnormalities." *Journal of the Ancient Near Eastern Society* 19 (1989): 39–50.

Gaventa, Beverly. *From Darkness to Light: Aspects of Conversion in the New Testament*. Overtures to Biblical Theology. Philadelphia: Fortress Press, 1986.

Gay, Peter. *Freud: A Life for Our Time*. New York: Norton, 1988.

_____. *A Godless Jew: Freud, Atheism, and the Making of Psychoanalysis*. New Haven: Yale University Press, 1987.

Gelberman, J. E., and D. Kobak. "The Psalms as Psychological and Allegorical Poems." In *Poetry Therapy*, ed. Jack Leedy. Philadelphia: Lippincott, 1969.

Gibson, Dennis L. "Doubting Thomas, the Obsessive." *Journal of Psychology and Christianity* 4.2 (1985): 34–36.

Gill, Vincent E. "In the Father's House: Self-report Findings of Sexually Abused Daughters from Conservative Christian Homes." *Journal of Psychology and Theology* 16 (1988): 144–52.

Girard, René. *Violence and the Sacred*. Trans. Patrick Gregory. Baltimore/London: Johns Hopkins University Press, 1977.

Gladson, Jerry, and Ron Lucas. "Hebrew Wisdom and Psychotheological Dialogue." *Zygon*: 24 (1989): 357–76.

Gladson, Jerry A., and Charles Plott. "Unholy Wedlock? The Peril and Promise of Applying Psychology to the Bible." *Journal of Psychology and Christianity* 10 (Spring 1991): 54–64.

Gnilka, Joachim. "Psicologia des Profondo ed Esegesi." *Revista Biblica* 38 (1990): 3–12.

Goerres, A., and W. Kasper. *Tiefenpsychologische Deutung des Glaubens: Anfragen an Eugen Drewermann*. Freiburg [im Breisgau]: Herder, 1988.

Goettmann, Jacques. "L'arbre, L'homme et la Croix." *Bible et Vie Chrétienne* 35 (1960): 46–59.

Goitein, L. "The Importance of the Book of Job for Analytic Thought." *American Imago* 11 (1954): 407–15.

Goldbrunner, Josef. *Cure of Mind and Cure of Soul.* Trans. Stanley Godmann. New York: Pantheon Books, 1954.

Goldenberg, Naomi R. *Resurrecting the Body: Feminism, Religion, and Psychoanalysis* [previous title: *Returning Words to Flesh: Feminism, Psychoanalysis, and the Resurrection of the Body*]. New York: Crossroad, 1993.

Goodenough, Erwin R. *Jewish Symbols in the Greco-Roman Period.* Bollingen Series 37, New York: Pantheon, 1953–68.

_____. *Toward a Mature Faith.* Lanham, Md.: University Press of America, 1955.

_____. *The Psychology of Religious Experiences.* New York: Basic Books, 1965.

Goodnick, Benjamin. "The Oedipus Complex and Its Biblical Parallels." *Jewish Biblical Quarterly* 20 (Fall 1991): 24–34.

Gorman, F. H. "Ritual Studies and Biblical Studies: Assessment of the Past; Prospects for the Future." *Semeia* 67 (1994): 13–36.

Grässe, Johann Georg Theodor. *Bibliotheca Psychologica: Verzeichniss der Wichtigsten über das Wesen der Menschen und Thierseelen, und die Unsterblichkeitslehre handelnden Schriftsteller älterer und neuerer Zeit, in alphabetischer Ordnung zusammengestellt, und mit einter wissenschaftlichen Übersicht begleitet.* Leipzig: W. Engelmann, 1845.

Grant, Frederick C. *An Introduction to New Testament Thought.* New York: Abingdon, 1950.

_____. "Psychological Study of the Bible." In *Religions in Antiquity: Essays in Memory of Erwin Ramsdell Goodenough*, ed. Jacob Neusner. 107–24. Leiden: Brill, 1968.

Greenlee, L. F., Jr. "Kohut's Self Psychology and Theory of Narcissism: Some Implications Regarding the Fall and Restoration of Humanity." *Journal of Psychology and Theology* 14 (1986): 110–16.

Greer, Marie. "The Problem of Evil in Psychoanalysis: The Book of Job as a Defining Metaphor." Denver, Colo.: American Psychological Association, 1997.

Gregoire, Paul Edwin, Jr. "A Biblical Analysis of Behavior Therapy With Implications for its Use Within the Framework of Pastoral Counseling." Ed.D. diss., New Orleans Baptist Theological Seminary, 1996.

Grelot, Pierre. "L'exégèse Biblique au Carrefour." *Nouvelle Revue Theologique* 98 (1976): 481–511.

Greven, Philip. *Spare the Child: The Religious Roots of Punishment and the Psychological Impact of Physical Abuse.* New York: Knopf, 1990.

Griffin, David Ray. *Parapsychology, Philosophy and Spirituality: A Postmodern Explanation.* SUNY Series in Constructive Postmodern Thought. Albany, N.Y.: SUNY, 1997.

Grinberg, L. "Psychoanalytic Considerations on the Jewish Passover Totem Sacrifice and Meal." *American Imago* 19 (1962): 391–424.

Groff, Allen. "Biblical Psychology of Christian Experience." In *Conference on the Holy Spirit Digest in Springfield, Missouri*, ed. Gwen Jones. 244-51. Gospel Publishing House, 1983.

Gruber, L. "Moses: His Speech Impediment and Behavior Therapy." *Journal of Psychology and Judaism* 10 (1986): 5–13.

Gruender, Hubert. *Psychology without a Soul: A Criticism.* St. Louis: B. Herder, 1912.

Gubitz, Myron B. "Amalek: The Eternal Adversary." *Psychological Perspectives* 8 (1, 1977): 34–58.

Gunkel, H. *Die Wirkungen des Heiligen Geistes.* 2d ed. Göttingen: Vandenhoeck & Ruprecht, 1888.

Haas, H. F. *How to Psychoanalyze the Bible?* Orangeburg, S.C.: Haas Publication Committee, 1939.

Hackett, Charles D. "Psychoanalysis and Theology: Jacques Lacan and Paul." *Journal of Religion and Health* 21 (Fall 1982): 184–92.

Haley, Jay. *The Power Tactics of Jesus Christ*. New York: Avon, 1969.

Hall, Calvin, S., and Vernon J. Nordby. *A Primer of Jungian Psychology*. New York: Mentor Book, New American Library, 1973.

Hall, Calvin S. *A Primer of Freudian Psychology*. 25th Anniversary edition. New York: New American Library, 1979 [orig. 1954].

Hall, Granville Stanley. "The Jesus of History and of the Passion versus the Jesus of the Resurrection." *The American Journal of Religious Psychology and Education* 1 (1 1904): 30–64.

_____. "The Psychology of the Nativity." *Journal of Religious Psychology* 7 (1914): 421–65.

_____. *Jesus, the Christ, in the Light of Psychology*. Garden City, N.Y.: Doubleday, 1917.

Halperin, David J. *Seeking Ezekiel, Text and Psychology*. University Park: Pennsylvania State University Press, 1993.

Hamerton-Kelly, Robert G. "A Girardian Interpretation of Paul: Rivalry, Mimesis and Victimage in the Corinthian Correspondence." *Semeia* 33 (1985): 65–81.

_____. *Sacred Violence: Paul's Hermeneutic of the Cross*. Minneapolis: Fortress Press, 1992.

Handelman, Susan A. *The Slayers of Moses: The Emergence of Rabbinic Interpretation in Modern Literary Theory*. Albany, N.Y.: SUNY, 1983.

Harding, M. Esther. "The Cross as an Archetypal Symbol." In *Carl Jung and Christian Spirituality*, ed. Robert L. Moore. 1–15. New York: Paulist, 1988.

Hark, H. *Der Traum als Gottes vergessene Sprache: Symbolpsychologische Deutung biblischer und heutiger Träume*. Olten: Freiburg i. Brsg., 1982.

Harrington, Daniel. *Interpreting the New Testament*. Wilmington, Del.: Michael Glazier, 1979.

_____. "New and Old in Interpretation." *New Theology Review* 2 (1989): 39–49.

Harsch, Helmut. "Psychologische Interpretationen biblischer Texte?" In *Wege Zum Menschen: Festschrift für Adolf Köberle*, eds. U. Mann et al., 281–89. Göttingen: Vandenhoeck & Ruprecht, 1968.

_____. "Tiefenpsychologische Interpretation von John 2, 1–11." In *Versuche mehrdimensionaler Schriftauslegung: Bericht üker ein Gespräch*, eds. H. Harsch and G. Voss. 89–103. Stuttgart: KBW, 1972.

_____. "Tiefenpsychologisches zur Schriftauslegung." In *Versuche mehrdimensionaler Schriftauslegung*, eds. H. Harsch and G. Voss. 32–41. Stuttgart: Munich, 1972.

Harsch, Helmut, and Gerhard Voss, eds. *Versuche mehrdimensionaler Schriftauslegung*. Stuttgart: KBW Verlag, 1972.

Hart, Ray. *Unfinished Man and the Imagination*. New York: Herder and Herder, 1968.

Haughton, Rosemary. *The Liberated Heart*. New York: Seabury, 1974.

Häussermann, Friedrich. *Wortempfang und Symbol in der alttestamentlichen Prophetie: eine Untersuchung zur Psychologie des prophetischen Erlebnisses*. Beihefte zur Zeitschrift für die alttestamentliche Wissenschaft 58. Giessen: Töpelmann, 1932.

Hayes, John H., ed. *Dictionary of Biblical Interpretation*. Nashville: Abingdon, 1999.

Healer, Carl T. *Freud and St. Paul*. Philadelphia: Dorrance, 1972.

Hein, David. "Crisis and Identity (Psychological Interpretation of Prodigal Son Parable)." *The Scottish Journal of Religious Studies* 1.2 (1980): 119–31.

Henderson, James. "Object Relations and the Doctrine of 'Original Sin.'" *International Review of Psycho-Analysis* 2 (1975): 107–20.

Henderson, J. L., and M. Oakes. *The Wisdom of the Serpent: The Myths of Death, Rebirth and Resurrection*. New York: Collier, 1963.

Hengel, Martin. "Aufgaben der neutestamentlichen Wissenschaft." *New Testament Studies* 40 (1994): 321–57.

Henry, Patrick. "Water, Bread, Wine: Patterns in Religion." In *New Directions in New Testament Study*, 203–24. Philadelphia: Westminster, 1979.

Heron, Laurence T. *ESP in the Bible*. Garden City, N.Y.: Doubleday, 1974.

Hill, Jill, and Rand Cheadle. *The Bible Tells Me So: Uses and Abuses of Holy Scripture*. New York: Doubleday, 1996.

Hillman, James. *Archetypal Psychology: A Brief Account*. Dallas, Texas: Spring Publications, 1983.

_____. *Insearch: Psychology and Religion*. New York: Scribner's, 1967.

Hirsch, Woolf. *Rabbinic Psychology: Beliefs about the Soul in Rabbinic Literature of the Talmudic Period*. London: Edward Goldston, 1947.

Hitchcock, A. W. *The Psychology of Jesus: a Study of the Development of His Self-Consciousness*. Boston: Pilgrim Press, 1907.

Hofmann, Wolfgang. "La plainte de Job. Essai d'une interpretation psychiatrique." *Psychologie Medicale* 21 (1989): 361–63.

Holland, Norman H. *A Reader's Guide to Psychoanalytic Psychology and Literature-and-Psychology*. New York: Oxford University Press, 1990.

_____. *Five Readers Reading*. New Haven, Conn.: Yale University Press, 1975.

Holman, Charles Thomas. *The Cure of Souls: A Sociopsychological Approach*. Chicago: University of Chicago Press, 1932.

Homans, Peter. "Psychology and Hermeneutics: Jung's Contribution." *Zygon* 4 (1969): 333–54.

_____. "Psychology and Hermeneutics: An Exploration of Basic Issues and Resources." *Journal of Religion* 55 (1975): 327–47.

Hopkins, Brooke. "Jesus and Object-Use: A Winnicottian Account of the Resurrection Myth." *International Review of Psycho-Analysis* 16 (1989): 93–100.

Hothersall, David. *History of Psychology*. 3d ed. New York: McGraw Hill, 1995.

Howard, J. K. "The Concept of the Soul in Psychology and Religion." *Journal of the American Scientific Affiliation* 24.4 (1972): 147–54.

Howes, Elizabeth Boyden. *Die Evangelien im Aspekt der Tiefenpsychologie*. Vol. 11. Lebendige Baustein, Zurich: Origo, 1968.

Howes, Elizabeth Boyden, and Sheila Moon. *The Choicemaker*. Philadelphia: Westminster, 1973.

Hughes, R. A. "The Cain Complex and the Apostle Paul." *Soundings* 65 (1982): 5–22.

Hunt, Morton. *The Story of Psychology*. New York: Doubleday Anchor Books, 1993.

Hunter, Rodney J., ed. *Dictionary of Pastoral Care and Counseling*. Nashville: Abingdon, 1990.

Hurding, Roger F. *The Tree of Healing: Psychological and Biblical Foundations for Counseling and Pastoral Care*. Grand Rapids: Zondervan, 1988.

Hurst, John Fletcher. "Psychology of the Bible." In *Literature of Theology: A Classified Bibliography of Theological and General Religious Literature*, 173–74. New York: Hunt and Eaton, 1896.

Hurt, K. F. "The Quest for the Psychological Jesus." *Unitarian Universalist Christian* 37 (1982): 21–31.

Hutchison, William R., and Hartmut Lehmann, eds. *Many Are Chosen: Divine Election and Western Nationalisms*. Minneapolis: Fortress Press, 1994.

Huth, Werner. "Tiefenpsychologie und Ichpsychologische Aspekte der Geschichte vom Turmbau zu Babel." In *Der Babylonische Turm*, ed. A. Rosenberg, 64–88. München: Kösel, 1975.

Iser, Wolfgang. *The Act of Reading: A Theory of Aesthetic Response*. Baltimore: Johns Hopkins University Press, 1978.

_____. "The Reading Process: A Phenomenological Approach." In *Reader Response Criticism: From Formalism to Post-Structuralism*, ed. Jane P. Tompkins, 50–69. Baltimore: Johns Hopkins University Press, 1980.

Ives, Charles Linnaeus. *The Bible Doctrine of the Soul, an Answer to the Question: Is the Popular Conception of the Soul that of Holy Scriptures?* Rev. ed., *The Bible Doctrine of the Soul, or, Man's Nature and Destiny as Revealed*. Philadelphia: Claxton, Ramsen, and Haffelfinger, 1878.

Jacobi, W. *Die Ekstase der alttestamentlichen Propheten*. Munich: J. F. Bergmann, 1920.

Jacobs, Alan. "Psychological Criticism: From the Imagination to Freud and Beyond." In *Leland Ryken*, ed. Clarence Walhout. Grand Rapids: Eerdmans, 1992.

James, William. *Principles of Psychology*. New York: Henry Holt, 1890.

_____. *The Varieties of Religious Experience*. New York: Longmans, Green, and Co., 1902 [1985].

James, William. *A Pluralistic Universe*. New York: E. P. Dutton, 1971.

Jauss, Hans Robert. "Literary History as a Challenge to Literary Theory." *New Literary History* 2 (1970): 7–37.

Jeanrond, Werner G. *Text and Interpretation as Categories of Theological Thinking*. Trans. Thomas J. Wilson. New York: Crossroad, 1988.

Jobling, David. "Transference and Tact in Biblical Studies: A Psychological Approach to Gerd Theissen's Psychological Aspects of Pauline Theology." *Studies in Religion/Sciences Religieuses* 22 (1993): 451–62.

Johnes, Barbara Horton. "Anger: Psychological and Biblical Perspectives." Colorado State University, 1990.

Johnson, Cedric B. *The Psychology of Biblical Interpretation*. Grand Rapids: Zondervan, 1983.

Johnson, Cedric B., and H. Newton Malony. *Christian Conversion: Biblical and Psychological Perspectives*. Rosemead Psychology Series, Grand Rapids: Zondervan, 1982.

Johnson, E. L. "A Place for the Bible within Psychological Science." *Journal of Psychology and Theology* 20 (1992): 346–55.

Johnson, Luke Timothy. *The Real Jesus: The Misguided Quest for the Historical Jesus and the Truth of the Traditional Gospels*. San Francisco: HarperSanFrancisco, 1997.

Johnson, Paul E. "Jesus as Psychologist." *Pastoral Psychology* (December 1951): 17–21.

Johnston, M. E. "Some Speculations on the Psychology of St. John's Gospel." *Theological Annual* 6 (1982): 89–121.

Joines, Karen Randolph. *Serpent Symbolism in the Old Testament*. Haddonfield, N.J.: Haddonfield House, 1974.

Jones, Ernest. "Eine psychoanalytische Studie über den Heiligen Geist." *Imago* 9 (1928): 58–72.

_____. *The Life and Work of Sigmund Freud*. 3 vols. New York: Basic Books, 1953, 1955, 1957.

Jones, Stanton L. "A Constructive Relationship for Religion with the Science and Profession of Psychology: Perhaps the Boldest Model Yet." *American Psychologist* (March 1994): 184–99.

Joyce, G. C. *The Inspiration of Prophecy: An Essay in the Psychology of Religion*. New York: Oxford University Press, 1910.

Joyce, Paul. "Lamentations and the Grief Process: A Psychological Reading." *Biblical Interpretation* 1 (1993): 304–20.

Jung, Carl Gustav. *Psychological Reflections: A New Anthology of His Writings, 1905–1961*. Vol. 31. Bollingen Series, eds. Jolande Jacobi and R. F. C. Hull. Princeton: Princeton University Press, 1953.

_____. "Answer to Job." In *The Collected Works of C. G. Jung*, eds. Gerhard Adler et al., 355–470. Vol. 11. Princeton: Princeton University Press, 1953–78.

_____. *The Collected Works of C. G. Jung*. Vol. 20. Bollingen Series, eds. Gerhard Adler, et al. Princeton: Princeton UniversityPress, 1953–78.

_____. "Psychology and Literature." In *The Collected Works of C. G. Jung*, eds. Gerhard Adler et al., 84–105. 15. Princeton: Princeton University Press, 1953–78.

_____. "Freud and Jung: Contrasts." In *Collected Works*, eds. Herbert Read, Michael Fordham, and Gerhard Adler, 333–40, Pars. 768–84. 4. London: Routledge & Kegan Paul, 1961 [1929].

_____. *Memories, Dreams, Reflections*. New York: Pantheon, 1963.

_____. "Approaching the Unconscious." In *Man and His Symbols*, New York: Doubleday, 1964.

_____. *C. G. Jung Letters, I: 1905–1950*. Trans. R. F. C. Hull. Bollingen Series 95:1, eds. Gerhard Adler and Aniela Jaffé. Princeton: Princeton University Press, 1973.

_____. *C. G. Jung Letters, 2: 1951–1961*. Trans. R. F. C. Hull. Bollingen Series 95:2, eds. Gerhard Adler and Aniela Jaffé. Princeton: Princeton University Press, 1975.

_____. *The Visions Seminar*. Vol. 1. Zurich: Spring Publications, 1976.

_____. *C. G. Jung Speaking: Interviews and Encounters*. Bollingen Series 47, eds. William McGuire and R. F. C. Hull. Princeton: Princeton University Press, 1977.

_____. *The Zofingia Lectures*. ed. W. McGuire. Princeton: Princeton University Press, 1983.

Kanter, Felix. *Die Psychoanalyse in der Bibel. Hickl's Illustrierter Jüdischer Volkskalender für das Jahr 5688*. Brünn: Jüdischer Buch- und Kunst-Verlag, 1927/28.

Kaplan, Jacob Hyman. "Psychology of Prophecy: A Study of the Prophetic Mind as Manifested by the Ancient Hebrew Prophets." *American Journal of Religious Psychology and Education* (1906): 169–203.

Kaplan, Kalman J. "Jonah and Narcissus: Self-integration versus Self-destruction in Human Development." *Studies in Formative Spirituality* 8 (1987): 33–54.

Karrer, Martin. "Psychoanalyse und Auslegung: Erwagungen nach der Studie Hartmut Raguses ber Psychoanalyse und biblische Interpretation." *Evangelische Theologie* 54 (1994): 467–76.

Kassel, Maria. *Biblische Urbilder Tiefenpsychologische Auslegung nach C. G. Jung*. Vol. 147. Munich: Pfeiffer-Werkbücher, 1982.

_____. *Sei, der du werden sollst. Tiefenpsychologische Impulse aus der Bibel*. Vol. 157. Munich: Pfeiffer Werkbücher, 1982.

Katz, R. L. "A Psychoanalytic Comment on Job 3:25." *Hebrew Union College Annual* 29 (1958): 377–83.

Kaufman, Gordon. *The Theological Imagination: Constructing the Concept of God*. Philadelphia: Westminster, 1981.

Kelsey, Morton. *Dreams: The Dark Speech of the Spirit*. New York: Doubleday, 1968.

_____. *Healing and Christianity in Ancient Thought and Modern Times*. New York: Harper & Row, 1976.

Keyser, Leander Sylvester. *A Handbook of Christian Psychology*. Burlington, Iowa: The Lutheran Literary Board, 1928.

Kille, D. Andrew. "Word and Psyche: The Psychology of Religion and the Bible." *Paradigms* 7.2 (1992): 11–19.

_____. "Jacob—A Study in Individuation." In *Jung and the Interpretation of the Bible*, ed. David L. Miller., 40–54. New York: Continuum, 1995.

Kille, D. Andrew. "Psychological Biblical Criticism: Genesis 3 as a Test Case." Ph.D. diss., Graduate Theological Union, 1997.

King, J. R. "The Parables of Jesus: A Social Psychological Approach." *Journal of Psychology and Theology* 19 (1991): 257–67.

Klein, D. B. *Jewish Origins of the Psychoanalytic Movement.* New York: Praeger, 1981.

Klein, Walter C. *The Psychological Pattern of Old Testament Prophecy.* Evanston: Seabury-Western Theological Seminary, 1956.

Kluger, Rivkah Schärf. *Satan in the Old Testament.* Trans. H. Nagel. Studies in Jungian Thought, Evanston: Northwestern University Press, 1967.

_____. *Psyche and Bible: Three Old Testament Themes.* New York: Spring Publication, 1974.

_____. *Psyche in Scripture: "The Idea of the Chosen People" and Other Essays.* Toronto: Inner City Books, 1995.

Knapp, Bettina. *Manna and Mystery: A Jungian Approach to Hebrew Myth and Legend.* Evanston, Ill.: Chiron, 1995.

Knight, Christopher. "Hysteria and Myth: The Psychology of the Resurrection Appearances." *Modern Churchman* 31.2 (1989): 38–42.

Köberle, Justus. *Natur und Geist: nach der Auffassung des Alten Testaments: eine Untersuchung zur historischen Psychologie.* München: C. H. Beck, 1901.

Kogan, I. M. "Weltuntergangserlebnis und Wiedergeburtsphantasie bei einem Schizophrenen." *Internationale Zeitschrift für Psychoanalyse* 18 (1932): 86–104.

König, Eduard. "Die Sexualität im Hohenlied und ihre Grenze." *Zeitschrift für Sexualwissenschaft* 9 (1922): 1–4.

_____. *Sexuelle und verwandte modernste Bibeldeutungen.* Langensalza: Hermann Beyer u. Söhne, 1922.

Körtner, U. H. J. "Zurück zum vierfachen Schriftsinn? Tiefenpsychologie und geistliche Exegese." *Theologische Beiträge (Wuppertal)* 23.5 (1992): 249–65.

Kottayarikil, Cyriac. *Sigmund Freud on Religion and Morality: A Challenge to Christianity.* Vol. 3. Personation and Psychotherapy. Innsbruck: Resch, 1977.

Kretschmer, Wolfgang. *Psychologische Weisheit der Bibel.* Bern: Francke Verlag, 1955.

Kristeva, Julia. *In the Beginning Was Love: Psychoanalysis and Faith.* Trans. Arthur Goldhammer. New York: Columbia University Press, 1987.

Krondorfer, Björn, ed. *Body and Bible: Interpreting and Experiencing Biblical Narratives.* Philadelphia: Trinity Press International, 1992.

Kühlewein, Johannes. "Gotteserfahrung und Reifungsgeschichte in der Jakob-Esau-Erzählung." In *Werden und Wirken des Alten Testaments: Festschrift für Claus Westermann zum 70. Geburtstag,* ed. Rainier Albertz et al. Göttingen: Vandenhoeck & Ruprecht, 1980.

Kühn, Rolf. "Paradox und Dereflexion: Anregungen der Logotherapie V. E. Frankls für Religionsphilosophie und- psychologie." In *Archiv für Religionspsychologie,* ed. K. Krenn et al., 138–53. 1988.

Kühnholz, W. "Sexualität—Eine uralte Geschichte (Gen 3)." In *Doppeldeutlich: Tiefendimensionen biblischer Texte,* ed. Y. Spiegel, 35–43. Munich: Kaiser Verlag, 1978.

Kümmel, Werner Georg. *The New Testament: The History of the Investigation of Its Problems.* Trans. S. McLean Gilmour and Howard C. Kee. Nashville: Abingdon, 1972.

Kunkel, Fritz. *Creation Continues: A Psychological Interpretation of the First Gospel.* 2d ed. Eds. Elizabeth Kunkel and Ruth Spafford Morris. New York: Scribner's Son, 1946 [1973].

Kutz, Ilan. "Samson's Complex: The Compulsion to Re-enact Betrayal and Rage." *British Journal of Medical Psychology* 62.2 (1989): 123–34.

L'Heureux, Conrad E. *Life Journey and the Old Testament: An Experiential Approach to the Bible and Personal Transformation*. New York: Paulist, 1986.

LaBarre, W. *They Shall Take Up Serpents: Psychology of the Southern Snake-Handling Cult*. Minneapolis: University of Minnesota Press, 1962.

Lacocque, A., and P.-E. Lacocque. *Jonah: A Psycho-Religious Approach to the Prophet*. Columbia, S.C.: University of South Carolina Press, 1990.

Laidlaw, John. *The Bible Doctrine of Man, or, The Anthropology and Psychology of Scripture*. 7th Series of the Cunningham Lectures. Edinburgh: T. & T. Clark, 1879.

Laidlaw, John. "Psychology of the New Life." In *The Bible Doctrine of Man*, 263–66. Edinburgh: T. & T. Clark, 1879.

Lang, Bernhard. "Israelitische Prophetie und Rollenpsychologie." In *Neue Ansätze in der Religionswissenschaft*, eds. B. Gladigow and H. Kippenberg, 175–97. München: Kösel, 1983.

_____. *Eugen Drewermann, interprète de la Bible*. Paris: Cerf, 1994.

Lang, Lewis Wyatt. *Christ's Psychology of the Kingdom: A Study in Modern Psychology of the System of Jesus in the Gospels*. London: Group Publications, 1937.

Lapointe, F. H. "Origin and Evolution of the Term 'Psychology.'" *American Psychologist* 25 (1970): 640–46.

_____. "Who Originated the Term 'Psychology'?" *Journal of the History of the Behavioral Sciences* 8 (1972): 328–35.

Laughlin, Henry P. "King David's Anger." *Psychoanalytic Quarterly* 23 (1954): 87–95.

Laver, A. B. "Precursors of Psychology in Ancient Egypt." *Journal of the History of the Behavioral Sciences* 8 (1972): 181–95.

Leahey, Thomas Hardy. *A History of Psychology: Main Currents in Psychological Thought*. 2d ed. Englewood Cliffs, N.J.: Prentice-Hall, 1987.

Leavy, Stanley A. *In the Image of God: A Psychoanalytic View*. New Haven: Yale University Press, 1988.

Leiner, Martin. *Psychologie und Exegese: Grundfragen einer textpsychologischen Exegese des Neuen Testaments*. Gütersloh: Chr. Kaiser, 1995.

Lemonick, Michael D., J. Madeleine Nash, Alice Park, and James Willwerth. "In Search of the Mind: Glimpses of the Brain." *Time* 146 (3 1995): 44–52.

Lerner, Michael. "Cruelty Is not Destiny: Abraham and the Psychodynamics of Childhood." *Tikkun* 2 (1994): 124–45.

Leslie, Robert C. *Jesus and Logotherapy: The Ministry of Jesus as Interpreted Through the Psychotherapy of Viktor Frankl*. [reprinted as *Jesus as Counselor* (Nashville: Abingdon Press, Festival Book, 1982)] Nashville: Abingdon, 1965.

Levin, A. J. "Oedipus and Samson. The Neglected Hero-Child." *International Journal of Psycho-Analysis* 38 (1957): 105–16.

Levy, Ludwig. "Die Sexualsymbolik der Bibel und des Talmud." *Zeitschrift für Sexualwissenschaft* 1 (1914): 273–79; 318–26.

_____. "Die Sexualsymbolik des Ackerbaus in Bibel und Talmud." *Zeitschrift für Sexualwissenschaft* (1915): 437–44.

_____. "Sexualsymbolik in der Simsonsage." *Zeitschrift für Sexual wissenschaft* 3 (1916): 256–71.

_____. "Sexual symbolik in der biblischen Paradiesgeschichte." *Imago* 5 (1917–19): 16–30.

_____. "Die Kastration in der Bibel." *Imago* 6 (1920): 393–97.

Lewin, Isaac. "The Psychological Theory of Dreams in the Bible." *Journal of Psychology and Judaism* 7.2 (1983): 73–88.

Lindauer, M. S. *The Psychological Study of Literature: Limitations, Possibilities, and Accomplishments*. Chicago: Nelson-Hall, 1974.

Lowry, Richard. *The Evolution of Psychological Theory: A Critical History of Concepts and Presuppositions.* 2d ed. New York: Aldine, 1982.

Lubbers, Egbert. "Mirror of the Self: Psychology of the New Testament Self." *Interpretation* 6 (1952): 290–300.

Lubomirski, M. "Per un Metodo in Esegesi: Gerd Theissen, Psychologische Aspekte Paulinischer Theologie." *Gregorianum* 72 (1991): 747–55.

Lucker, Erwin L. "Themes of Self in the Judeo-Christian Scriptures and in the Personality Theories of Freud, Rogers and Skinner." U. S. International University, 1980.

Lüdemann, Gerd. *Texte und Träume: Ein Gang durch das Markusevangelium in Auseinandersetzung mit Eugen Drewermann.* Bensheimer Hefte 71. Göttingen: Vandenhoeck & Ruprecht, 1992.

_____. *The Unholy in Holy Scripture: The Dark Side of the Bible.* Louisville: Westminster/John Knox, 1997.

Luz, Ulrich. *Matthew in History: Interpretation, Influence, and Effects.* Minneapolis: Fortress Press, 1994.

Lynch, Thomas H. "Corroboration of Jungian Psychology in the Biblical Story of Abraham." *Psychotherapy: Theory, Research and Practice* 8 (4 1971): 315–18.

Maas, Jeannette P. "A Psychological Assessment of Job." *Pacific Journal of Theology* 2 (1989): 55–68.

Mahoney, Michael J. *Human Change Processes: The Scientific Foundations of Psychotherapy.* New York: HarperCollins, 1991.

Malony, H. Newton. "G. Stanley Hall's Theory of Conversion." *Journal of Psychology and Christianity* 3.3 (1984): 2–8.

Malony, H. Newton, and A. A. Lovekin. *Glossolalia: Behavioral Science Perspectives on Speaking in Tongues.* New York: Oxford University Press, 1985.

Malony, H. Newton, and Samuel Southard, eds. *Handbook of Religious Conversion.* Birmingham, Ala.: Religious Education Press, 1992.

Malony, H. Newton, and Bernard Spilka, eds. *Religion in Psychodynamic Perspective: The Contributions of Paul W. Pruyser.* New York: Oxford University Press, 1991.

March, Hans. *Die Psychotherapie Jesu.* Arzt und Seelsorger. Vol. 15. Schwerin: 1928.

Marotti, A. F. "Countertransference, the Communication Process, and the Dimensions of Psychoanalytic Criticism." *Critical Inquiry* 4 (1978): 471–89.

Martin, Bernice. "Whose Soul Is It Anyway?" In *On Losing the Soul: Essays in the Social Psychology of Religion,* eds. Donald Capps and Richard K. Fenn, 69–96. Albany, N.Y.: SUNY Press, 1995.

Martin, David. "Bedeviled." In *On Losing the Soul: Essays in the Social Psychology of Religion,* eds. Donald Capps and Richard K. Fenn, 39–68. Albany, N.Y.: SUNY Press, 1995.

Matto, Michele. *The Twelve Steps in the Bible.* Mahwah, N.J.: Paulist, 1991.

Mazor, Yair. "Genesis 22: The Ideological Rhetoric and the Psychological Composition." *Biblica* 67 (1986): 81–88.

McArthur, John F., Jr., and Wayne A. Mack. *Introduction to Biblical Counseling.* Irving, Tex.: Word, 1994.

McCasland, S. Vernon. *By the Finger of God. Demon Possessions and Exorcism in Early Christianity in Light of Modern Views of Mental Illness.* New York: Macmillan, 1951.

McCrossan, Charles Wesley. *The Mind Science of Christ Jesus: A Treatise on Christian Psychology Showing the Power of Suggestion and Revealing the Secrets of Mental and Spiritual Healing.* Santa Cruz: Sentinel Publishing Co., 1913.

McDargh, John. *Psychoanalytic Object Relations Theory and the Study of Religion: On Faith and the Imaging of God.* Lanham, Md.: University Press of America, 1983.

McGann, Diarmuid. "Jung and Scripture." *New Catholic World* 227 (Mar/Apr 1984): 60–63.

_____. *The Journeying Self: The Gospel of Mark Through a Jungian Perspective*. New York: Paulist, 1985.

McGann, Diarmuid. *Journeying Within Transcendence: A Jungian Perspective on the Gospel of John*. New York: Paulist, 1988.

McGinn, Bernard. *Antichrist: Two Thousand Years of the Human Fascination with Evil*. Dunmore, Pa.: Torch, 1994.

McGuire, W., ed. *The Freud/Jung Letters: The Correspondence between Sigmund Freud and C. G. Jung*. Princeton, N.J.: Princeton University, 1974.

McGuire, W., and R. F. C. Hull, eds. *C. G. Jung Speaking: Interviews and Encounters*. Vol. 97. Bollingen Series. Princeton, N.J.: Princeton University, 1977.

McKenzie, Steven L., and Stephen R. Haynes, eds. *To Each Its Own Meaning: An Introduction to Biblical Criticisms and Their Application*. Louisville: Westminster/John Knox, 1993.

McKnight, Edgar. *The Bible and the Reader: An Introduction to Literary Criticism*. Philadelphia: Fortress Press, 1985.

McMinn, M. R., and G. N. McMinn. "Complete Yet Inadequate: the Role of Learned Helplessness and Self-attribution from the Writings of Paul." *Journal of Psychology and Theology* 11 (1983): 303–10.

Meeks, Wayne A., ed. *The Writings of St. Paul*. New York: Norton, 1972.

Meier, L. "Jacob and His Four Wives." *Journal of Psychology and Judaism* 16 (1 1992): 45–71.

Meissner, William. W. *Psychoanalysis and Religious Experience*. New Haven: Yale University Press, 1984.

_____. *Thy Kingdom Come: Psychoanalytic Perspectives on the Messiah and the Millennium*. New York: Sheed & Ward, 1996.

Menninger, Karl. *Whatever Became of Sin?* New York: Hawthorn, 1973.

Merkur, Dan. "The Prophecies of Jeremiah." *American Imago* 42.1 (1985): 1–37.

_____. "Prophetic Initiation in Israel and Judah." In *The Psychoanalytic Study of Society*, eds. L. Bryce Boyer and Simon A. Grolnick, 37–67. 12. Hillsdale, N.J.: Analytic Press, 1988.

_____. "The Visionary Practices of Jewish Apocalyptists." In *The Psychoanalytic Study of Society*, eds. L. Bryce Boyer and Simon A. Grolnick, 119–48. 14. Hillsdale, N.J.: Analytic Press, 1989.

_____. "Freud and Hasidism." In *The Psychoanalytic Study of Society*, eds. L. Bryce Boyer, Ruth M. Boyer, and Howard F. Stein, 335–47. 19. Hillsdale, N.J.: Analytic Press, 1994.

Mertelmann, Volker. "Jesus von Nazareth und die christlichen Symbole unter dem Aspekt tiefenpsychologischer Überlegungen." *Wege zum Menschen* 23 (1971): 22–24.

Meurs, Van. *Jungian Literary Criticism: 1920–1980: An Annotated, Critical Bibliography of Works in English*. Metuchen, N.J.: Scarecrow, 1988.

Meyer, Stephen G. "The Psalms and Personal Counseling." *Journal of Psychology and Theology* 2.1 (1974): 26–30.

Meyerson, O. G., and L. Stoller. "A Psychoanalytic Interpretation of the Crucifixion." *Psychoanalysis and the Psychoanalytic Review* 48 (1962): 117–18.

Micklem, Edward Romilly. *Miracles and the New Psychology: A Study of the Healing Miracles of the New Testament*. New York: Oxford University Press, 1922.

Miell, David K. "Psychological Interpretation." In *A Dictionary of Biblical Interpretation*. Ed. R. J. Coggins and J. L. Houlden, 571–72. London: SCM Press, 1990.

Miles, Jack. "Jesus Before He Could Talk." *New York Times Magazine* (December 24, 1995): 28–33.

Miller, Alice. "The Mistreated Child in the Lamentations of Jeremiah." In *Breaking Down the Wall of Silence: The Liberating Experience of Facing Painful Truth,* 114–26. New York: Penguin, 1991.

Miller, David L. *Christs: Meditations on Archetypal Images in Christian Theology.* New York: Seabury, 1981.

_____. "Biblical Imagery and Psychological Likeness." In *Jung and the Interpretation of the Bible,* ed. David L. Miller, 102–12. New York: Continuum, 1995.

Miller, John W. *Jesus at Thirty: A Psychological and Historical Portrait.* Minneapolis: Fortress Press, 1997.

Mills, W. E., ed. *Speaking in Tongues: A Guide to Research on Glossalalia.* Grand Rapids: Eerdmans, 1986.

Mitchell, Clark. "Counseling from the Gospel of John." In *Johannine Studies,* ed. J. Priest, 148–70. Malibu, Calif.: Pepperdine University Press, 1989.

Monchy, S. J. R. de. "Adam-Cain-Oedipus." *American Imago* 19 (1962): 3–17.

Moore, Robert L. "Pauline Theology and the Return of the Repressed: Depth Psychology and Early Christian Thought." *Zygon* 13 (1978): 158–68.

Moore, Stephen D. "Psychoanalytic Criticism." In *The Postmodern Bible,* eds. Elizabeth A. Castelli, Stephen D. Moore, Gary Phillips, and Regina M. Schwartz, 187–224. New Haven: Yale University Press, 1995.

Morrow, William. "Toxic Religion and the Daughters of Job." Unpublished SBL paper, New Orleans, 1996.

Motet, Dan. "Kohlberg's Theory of Moral Development and the Christian Faith." *Journal of Psychology and Theology* 6.1 (1978): 18–21.

Moxon, C. "Epileptic Traits in Paulus of Tarsus." *Psychoanalytic Review* 9 (1922): 60–66.

Mudge, Lewis S. "Paul Ricoeur on Biblical Interpretation." In *Essays on Biblical Interpretation,* ed. Lewis S. Mudge, 1–40. Philadelphia: Fortress Press, 1980.

Muller, R. A. "Soul." In *Dictionary of Pastoral Care and Counseling,* ed. R. Hunter, 1201–3. Nashville: Abingdon, 1990.

Mumford, D. B. "Emotional Distress in the Hebrew Bible: Somatic or Psychological?" *British Journal of Psychiatry* 160 (1992): 92–97.

Murray, David J. *A History of Western Psychology.* Englewood Cliffs, N.J.: Prentice-Hall, 1983.

Murray, H. G. "Psychoanalysts Catch Job." *Christian Century* 46 (1929): 514–15.

Natoli, J. *Psychocriticism: An Annotated Bibliogrphy.* Westport, Conn.: Greenwood Press, 1984.

Neumann, Erich. *Depth Psychology and a New Ethic.* Trans. Eugene Rolfe. New York: Harper Torchbooks, 1973 [1948].

Newheart, Michael Willett. "Johannine Symbolism." In *Jung and the Interpretation of the Bible,* ed. David L. Miller, 71–91. New York: Continuum, 1995.

_____. "Toward a Psycho-Literary Reading of the Fourth Gospel." In *"What Is John?": Readers and Readings of the Fourth Gospel,* ed. Fernando F. Segovia. Atlanta: Scholars Press, 1996.

Nicole, Albert. *Judas the Betrayer: A Psychological Study of Judas Iscariot.* Trans. from French. Grand Rapids: Baker, 1924/1957.

Nida, Eugene A. "Implications of Contemporary Linguistics for Biblical Scholarship." *Journal of Biblical Literature* 91.1 (1972): 73–89.

Niederland, William G. "Jacob's Dream. With Some Remarks on Ladder and River Symbolism." *Journal of the Hillside Hospital* 3 (1954): 73–98.

Niederwimmer, Kurt. "Tiefenpsychologie und Exegese." In *Perspektiven der Pastoralpsychologie*, ed. Richard Riess. Göttingen: Vandenhoeck & Ruprecht, 1974.

North, Robert. "David's Rise: Sacral, Military, or Psychiatric." *Biblica* 63 (1982): 524–44.

Oates, Wayne. E. "The Diagnostic Use of the Bible: What a Man Sees in the Bible Is a Projection of His Inner Self." *Pastoral Psychology* 1 (1950): 43–46.

_____. *The Bible in Pastoral Care*. Philadelphia: Westminster, 1953.

_____. *Temptation. A Biblical and Psychological Approach*. Louisville: Westminster/Knox, 1991.

O'Connor, T. "Psychological Health According to Karen Horney Compared with the Moral Theme in the Pauline Writings." Pontificiae Univ. S. Thomae de Urbe; Dallas, Texas, 1976.

Oglesby, William B., Jr. *Biblical Themes for Pastoral Care*. Nashville: Abingdon, 1980.

Oliviera, W. I. de. "El simbolisme de la Torre de Babel. La confución de lenguas y la disociación esquizofrenica." *Revista de Psicoanálisis* 8 (1951): 359–61.

Olshausen, Hermann. "Olshausen's New Testament Psychology." *Methodist Review* 41 (April 1859): 254–65.

Ong, W. "The Psychodynamics of Oral Memory and Narrative: Some Implications for Biblical Studies." In *The Pedagogy of God's Image: Essays on Symbol and the Religious Imagination*, ed. R. Masson. Chico, Calif.: Scholars Press, 1982.

Outler, Albert. *Psychotherapy and the Christian Message*. New York: Harper & Bro., 1954.

Paine, Martyn. *Physiology of the Soul and Instinct as Distinguished from Materialism; with supplementary Demonstrations of the Divine Communication of the Narratives of Creation and the Flood*. New York: Harper & Brothers, 1868.

Parcells, Frank C., and Nathan P. Segel. "Oedipus and the Prodigal Son." *Psychoanalytic Quarterly* 28 (1955): 213–27.

Patrick, Dale, and Allen Scult. *Rhetoric and Biblical Interpretation*. Bible and Literature Series 26. Sheffield: Almond, 1990.

Patte, Daniel. *Ethics of Biblical Interpretation: A Reevaluation*. Louisville: Westminster/John Knox, 1995.

Patte, Daniel, and Aline Patte. *Structural Exegesis: From Theory to Practice*. Minneapolis: Fortress Press, 1978.

Paul, Robert A. *Moses and Civilization: Freud and the Judeo-Christian Master Narrative*. New Haven: Yale University Press, 1996.

Pedersen, John E. "Some Thoughts on a Biblical View of Anger." *Journal of Psychology and Theology* 2.3 (1974): 210–15.

Penn-Lewis, Jessie. *Soul and Spirit: A Glimpse into Bible Psychology. Together with Papers on "Soul Force" Versus "Spirit Force" from the Overcome*. Leicester: The Overcome Book Room, 1900.

Perry, Michael. "Psi in the Bible." *Parapsychology Review* 10.3 (1979): 9–14.

Peters, R. S., ed. *Brett's History of Psychology*. Cambridge: Massachusetts Institute of Technology, 1974.

Peters, R. S., and C. A. Mace. "Psychology." In *The Encyclopedia of Philosophy*, ed. Paul Edwards. Vol. 7, 1–27. New York: Macmillan, 1967.

Petersen, Norman. "'Point of View' in Mark's Narrative." *Semeia* 12 (1978): 97–121.

Petrén, Erik. *En psykolog läser Bibeln*. Stockholm: 1966.

Pfister, Oskar. "Die Entwicklung des Apostels Paulus. Eine religionsgeschichtliche und psychologische Skizze." *Imago* 6 (1920): 243–90.

_____. "The Illusion of a Future: A Friendly Discussion with Prof. Dr. Sigmund Freud." In *Affirming the Soul*, ed. Jeffrey H. Boyd, 177–216. Cheshire, Conn.: Soul Research Institute, 1928 [1994].

_____. "Neutestamentliche Seelsorge und psychoanalytische Therapie." *Imago* 20 (1943): 425–43.

Pfister, Oskar, and Sigmund Freud. *Psychoanalysis and Faith: The Letters of Sigmund Freud and Oskar Pfister*. Trans. Eric Mosbacher. Eds. Heinrich Meng and Ernst A. Freud. New York: Basic Books, 1963.

Pfrimmer, Théo. *Sigmund Freud, Lecteur de la Bible*. Protestant Faculty, University of Strasbourg, 1981.

Philipson, M. *Outline of a Jungian Aesthetics*. Evanston, Ill.: Northwestern University Press, 1963.

Philp, H. L. *Freud and Religious Belief*. New York: Pitman, 1956.

Pilch, John J. "Psychological and Psychoanalytical Approaches to Interpreting the Bible in Social-Scientific Context." *Biblical Theology Bulletin* 27 (1997): 112–16.

Porter, Noah. *The Human Intellect with an Introduction upon Psychology and the Soul*. New York: Scribner's, 1868.

Povah, John Walter. *The New Psychology and the Bible; A Lecture Delivered at a Vacation School for Old Testament Study, at King's Colleges Hostel, September, 1924*. London and New York: Longmans, Green & Co., 1924.

_____. *The New Psychology and the Hebrew Prophets*. London and New York: Longmans, Green & Co., 1925.

_____. *The Old Testament and Modern Problems in Psychology*. New York: Longmans, Green & Co., 1926.

Powers, Robert L. "Religion: Adler's View." In *International Encyclopedia of Psychiatry, Psychology, Psychoanalysis, and Neurology*, ed. Benjamin B. Wolman. 427–29. Vol. 9. New York: Van Nostrand Reinhold Company, 1976.

Powlinson, David A. "Which Presuppositions: Secular Psychology and the Categories of Biblical Thought." *Journal of Psychology and Theology* 12 (1984): 270–78.

Pregeant, Russell. *Engaging the New Testament: An Interdisciplinary Introduction*. Minneapolis: Fortress Press, 1995.

Pruyser, Paul. "Nathan and David. A Psychological Footnote." *Pastoral Psychology* 13 (1962): 14–18.

_____. "The Seamy Side of Current Religious Beliefs." In *Religion in Psychodynamic Perspective: the Contributions of Paul M. Pruyser*, eds. H. N. Maloney and B. Spilka, 47–65. New York: Oxford University Press, 1991 (1977).

_____. *Between Belief and Unbelief*. New York: Harper & Row, 1974.

_____. *The Play of the Imagination: Toward a Psychoanalysis of Culture*. New York: International Universities Press, 1983.

Quasten, Johannes. *Patrology*. Vol. 1: *The Beginnings of Patristic Literature*. Westminster, Md.: Newman Press, 1950.

_____. *Patrology*. Vol. 2: *The Ante-Nicene Literature After Irenaeus*. Westminster, Md.: Newman Press, 1953.

_____. *Patrology*. Vol. 3: *The Golden Age of Greek Patristic Literature From the Council of Nicaea to the Council of Chalcedon*. Utrecht: Spectrum, 1966.

_____. *Patrology*. Vol. 4: *The Golden Age of Latin Patristic Literature From the Council of Nicea to the Council of Chalcedon*. Trans. Placid Solari, OSB. ed. Angelo di Beraardino. Utrecht: Spectrum, 1988.

Quispel, Gilles. "On Jungian Interpretation of Apocalyptic Myth and Symbols." In *The Secret Book of Revelation*. New York: McGraw-Hill, 1979.

Raguse, H. "Der Oedipus-Komplex und die depressive Position: Psychoanalytische Reflexionen zur Wirkungsgeschichte des 12. Kapitels der Apokalypse des Johannes." *Zeitschrift für Psychoanalytische Theorie und Praxis* 7 (1992): 126–44.

Rank, Otto. *Seelenglaube und Psychologie; eine prinzipielle Untersuchung über Ursprung, Entwicklung und Wesen des Seelischen.* Leipzig: F. Deuticke, 1930. English: *Psychology and the Soul.* Trans. William D. Turner. Philadelphia: University of Pennsylvania Press, 1950.

Rashkow, Ilona N. *The Phallacy of Genesis: A Feminist-Psychoanalytic Approach.* Literary Currents in Biblical Interpretation. Louisville: Westminster/John Knox Press, 1993.

_____. "Daughters and Fathers in Genesis . . . Or, What is Wrong with This Picture?" In *The New Literary Criticism and the Hebrew Bible*, eds. Cheryl Exum and David J. A. Clines, 250–66. Sheffield: Sheffield Academic Press, 1995.

Rauch, Friedrich August. *Psychology; or, A View of the Human Soul: Including Anthropology.* New York: M. W. Dodd, 1840.

Raychaudhuri, Arun Kumar. "Jesus Christ and Sree Krisna. A Psychoanalytic Study." *American Imago* 14 (1957): 389–405.

Raymond, George Lansing. *The Psychology of Inspiration: An Attempt to Distinguish Religious from Scientific Truth and to Harmonize Christianity with Modern Thought.* New York: Funk & Wagnall's, 1907.

Rebell, Walter. *Gehorsam und Unabhängigkeit. Eine sozialpsychologische Studie zu Paulus.* Munich: Chr. Kaiser, 1986.

_____. "Psychologische Bibelauslegung." *Bibel und Kirche* 44 (1989): 111–17.

Reed, Thomas Anthony. "An Analysis of Christ's Behavior toward Simon Peter in Matthew's Gospel following the Contemporary Cognitive-Behavioral Model of Reality Therapy." Univ. of San Francisco, 1985.

Reider, Norman. "Medieval Oedipal Legends about Judas." *Psychoanalytic Quarterly* 29 (1960): 515–27.

Reik, Theodor. "Psychoanalytische Studien zur Bibel exegesis, I: Jakobs Kampf." *Imago* 5 (1917–19): 325–53.

_____. "Unbewusste Faktoren in der wissenschaftlichen Bibelarbeit." *Imago* 5 (1917–19): 358–63.

_____. "Das Kainszeichen. Ein psychoanalytischer Beitrag zur Bibelerkärung." *Imago* 5 (1917–19): 31–42.

_____. "Die Sünde der Volkzählung." *Imago* 5 (1919): 350–54.

_____. "Psychoanalytische Studien zur Bibelexegese I: Jakobs Kampf." *Imago* 5 (1919): 325–53.

_____. "Psychoanalytic Studies of Biblical Exegesis." In *Dogma and Compulsion: Psychoanalytic Studies of Religion and Myths*, 229–75. New York: International Universities, 1951.

_____. *Myth and Guilt.* New York: George Braziller, 1957.

_____. *Mystery on the Mountain: The Drama of the Sinai Revelation.* New York: Harper, 1959.

_____. *The Creation of Woman: A Psychoanalytic Inquiry into the Myth of Eve.* New York: Braziller, 1960.

_____. *The Temptation.* New York: George Braziller, 1961.

_____. *Pagan Rites in Judaism.* New York: Farrar, Straus, 1964.

Renik, O. "The Biblical Book of Job: Advice to Clinicians." *Psychoanalytic Quarterly* 60 (1991): 596–606.

Reynierse, J. H. "Behavior Therapy and Job's Recovery." *Journal of Psychology and Theology* 3 (1975): 187–94.

_____. "A Behavioristic Analysis of the Book of Job." *Journal of Psychology and Theology* 3 (1975): 75–81.

Ricoeur, Paul. *Freud and Philosophy: An Essay on Interpretation*. Trans. Denis Savage. New Haven: Yale University Press, 1970.

_____. "Philosophical Hermeneutics and Theological Hermeneutics." *Studies in Religion/Sciences religeuses* 5 (1975): 14–33.

_____. *Essays on Biblical Interpretation*, ed. Lewis S. Mudge. Philadelphia: Fortress Press, 1980.

Riess, Richard. "Psychogische Erwägungen zur Perikope von der Versuchung Jesu." *Wege dem Mesnchen* 22 (1970): 275–81.

Roback, Abraham Aron. "Freudian Psychology and Jewish Commentators of the Bible." *Jewish Forum* 1 (1918): 528–33.

Roberts, W. H. "A Psychological Study of the Growing Jesus." *Open Court* 45 (1931): 243–55.

Robinson, H. Wheeler. "Hebrew Psychology in Relation to Pauline Anthropology." In *Mansfield College Essays*. London: Hodder & Stoughton, 1926.

_____. *The Christian Doctrine of Man*. Edinburgh: T. & T. Clark, 1911.

_____. *Inspiration and Revelation in the Old Testament*. Oxford: Clarendon Press, 1946.

_____. "The Psychology of Inspiration." In *Inspiration and Revelation in the Old Testament*. Oxford: Clarendon, 1946.

Rodenbough, Jeannette G. "The Healing Journey: The Use of Biblical Narrative in the Grief Process." Columbia Theological Seminary, 1993.

Roffey, John W. "Genesis 3: A Foray into Psychology and Biblical Theology." *Colloquium: The Australian and New Zealand Theological Review* (1987): 48–56.

Rogers, Carl R. *On Becoming a Person*. Boston: Houghton Mifflin, 1961.

Rogers, M. L. "Some Biblical Families Examined from a Systems Perspective." *Journal of Psychology and Theology* 7 (1979): 251–58.

Róheim, Géza. "The Covenant of Abraham." *International Journal of Psycho-Analysis* 20 (1939): 452–59.

Róheim, Géza. "The Divine Child." *Journal of Clinical Psychopathology* 9 (1948): 309–23.

_____. "The Garden of Eden." *Psychoanalytic Review* 27 (1940): 1–26; 177–99.

_____. "The Passage of the Red Sea." *Man* 23 (1923): 152–55.

_____. "Passover and Initiation." *Man* 23 (1923): 178.

Rollins, Wayne G. *Jung and the Bible*. Atlanta: John Knox, 1983.

_____. "Jung's Challenge to Biblical Hermeneutics." In *Jung's Challenge to Contemporary Religion*, eds. Murray Stein and Robert L. Moore, 107–25. Peru, Ill.: Chiron, 1987.

_____. "Psychology, Hermeneutics, and the Bible." In *Jung and the Interpretation of the Bible*, ed. David L. Miller, 9–39. New York: Continuum, 1995.

_____. "Rationale and Agenda for a Psychological-Critical Approach to the Bible and Its Interpretation." In *Biblical and Humane*, eds. David Barr, Linda Bennett Elder, and Elizabeth Struthers Malbon, 153–72. Atlanta: Scholars Press, 1996.

_____. "The Bible and Psychology: New Directions in Biblical Scholarship." *Pastoral Psychology* 145:3 (1997): 163–79.

Roos, Magnus Friedrich. *Fundamenta Psychologiae ex sacra Scriptura sic collecta ut dicta eius de anima eiusque facultatibus agentia collecta, digesta atque explicata sint*. Tübingen: Lud. Friedr. Fuessi, 1769.

Rosenberg, Stuart E. *More Loves Than One: The Bible Confronts Psychiatry*. New York: Thomas Nelson, 1963.

Rosenblatt, Naomi H., and Joshua Horwitz. *Wrestling with Angels*. New York: Delacorte, 1995.

Rosenzweig, Efraim M. "Historische und psychoanalytische Bemerkungen über Volk und Land Israel mit besonderer Berücksichtigung des Deuteronomiums." In *Psychoanalytische Interpretationen biblischer Texte*, ed. Yorick, Spiegel. 185–99. Munich: Chr. Kaiser, 1972 [1939].

Rosenzweig, Saul. *Freud, Jung, and Hall the King-Maker: The Historic Expedition to America (1909)*. Seattle: Hogrefe & Huber, 1992.

Ross, D. G. *Stanley Hall: The Psychologist as Prophet*. Chicago: University of Chicago Press, 1972.

Rozell, Jack V. "Implications of the New Testament Concept of Conscience." In *Biblical and Psychological Perspectives for Christian Counselors*, ed. R. Bower, 151–209. South Pasadena, Calif.: Publishers Series, 1974.

Rubenstein, Richard. *My Brother Paul*. New York: Harper & Row, 1972.

Sales, Michel, S. J. "Possibilités et limites d'une lecture psychanalytique de la Bible." *Nouvelle Revue Theologique (Tournai)* 101 (1979): 699–723.

Sall, Millard J. "Demon Possession or Psychopathology? A Clinical Differentiation." *Journal of Psychology and Theology* 4.4 (4 1976): 286–90.

Sanday, William. "Christologies Ancient and Modern." In *Christology and Personality*, ed. William Sanday. New York: Oxford University Press, 1911.

_____. *Christology and Personality*. New York: Oxford University Press, 1911.

_____. *Personality in Christ and in Ourselves*. Oxford: Clarendon, 1911.

Sanford, John, ed. *Fritz Kunkel: Selected Writings*. Mahwah, N.J.: Paulist, 1984.

_____. *Dreams: God's Forgotten Language*. Philadelphia: Lippincott, 1968.

_____. *Healing and Wholeness*. New York: Paulist, 1977.

_____. *The Kingdom Within*. Philadelphia: Lippincott, 1970.

_____. "Jesus, Paul, and Depth Psychology." *Religious Education* 68 (1973): 673–89.

_____. *The Man Who Wrestled with God: Light from the Old Testament on the Psychology of Individuation*. King of Prussia, Pa.: Religious Publishing Co., 1974 [1981, republished by Paulist, Ramsey, N.J.].

_____. *King Saul, The Tragic Hero: A Study in Individuation*. New York: Paulist, 1985.

_____. *Mystical Christianity: A Psychological Commentary on the Gospel of John*. New York: Crossroad, 1993.

Saunders, Kenneth James. *Adventures of the Christian Soul: Being Chapters in the Psychology of Religion*. Cambridge: University Press, 1916.

Sauv, John R. "Joshua: A Story of Individuation." *Journal of Religion and Health* 31 (Winter 1992): 265–71.

Schaer, Hans. *Religion and the Cure of Souls in Jung's Psychology*. [Orig. Ger. *Religion und Seele in der Psychologie C. G. Jungs* (Zurich: Rascher Verlag, 1946)] Trans. R. F. C. Hull. Bollingen Series 21. New York: Pantheon, 1950.

Schärf, Rivkah. "Die Gestalt des Satans im Alten Testament." In *Symbolik des Geistes: Studien über psychische Phänomenologie*, ed. C. G. Jung. 151–319. Zürich: Rascher, 1953.

Scharfenberg, Joachim. "Existentiale und tiefenpsychologische Interpretationene biblischer Text." *Wege zum Menschen* 23 (1971): 1–8.

_____. *Sigmund Freud and His Critique of Religion*. Trans. O. C. Dean, Jr. Philadelphia: Fortress Press, 1988.

Schendler, David. "Judas, Oedipus, and Various Saints." *Psychoanalysis* 2 (1954): 41–46.

Schimmel, Sol. "Job and the Psychology of Suffering and Doubt." *Journal of Psychology and Judaism* 11 (1987): 239–49.

Schindler, Walter. "Depth Psychology and Dream Interpretation in the Bible." *International Journal of Sexology* 8 (1954): 77–82.

Schlamm, Leon. "The Bible and Jungian Depth Psychology." In *Using the Bible Today*, ed. D. Cohn-Sherbok, 76–86. London: Belew, 1991.

Schleiermacher, F. D. E. *Hermeneutics: The Handwritten Manuscripts by F. D. E. Schleiermacher*. Trans. James Duke. Heidelberg: Carl Winter, 1830 [1974].

Schlossmann, Howard H. "Circumcision as Defense. A Study in Psychoanalysis and Religion." *Psychoanalytic Quarterly* 35 (1966): 340–56.

Schmitt, John J. "Yahweh's Foundling: Psychological Reflections on Ezekiel 16." Unpublished SBL paper, Chicago, 1994.

Schmucker, Samuel Simon. *Psychology, or, Elements of a New System of Mental Philosophy on the Basis on Consciousness and Common Sense. Designed for Colleges and Academies*. New York: Harper & Brothers, 1842.

Schnackenburg, Rudolf. "Exegese und Tiefenpsychologie." In *Tiefenpsychologische Deutung des Glaubens*, eds. A. Görres and W. Kaspr, 26–48. Freiburg [im Breisgau]: Herder, 1988.

Schneider, Carl. "Psychologische Exegese." *Zeitschrift für systematische Theologie* 10 (1932/33): 126ff.

Schneiders, Sandra M. *The Revelatory Text: Interpreting the New Testament as Sacred Scripture*. San Francisco: HarperSanFrancisco, 1991.

Schökel, Luis Alonso, S. J. "The Psychology of Inspiration." In *The Bible in Its Literary Milieu*, eds. John Maier and Vincent Tollers, 24–56. Grand Rapids: Eerdmans, 1967.

Schüling, H. *Bibliographische Handbuch zur Geschichte der Psychologie des 16. Jahrhunderts*. Hildesheim: Georg Olms, 1967.

Schutter, William L. "Philo's Psychology of Prophetic Inspiration and Romans 10:20." In *Society of Biblical Literature: 1989 Seminar Papers*, ed. D. Lull, 624–33, 1989.

Schweitzer, Albert. *The Psychiatric Study of Jesus: Exposition and Criticism*. Trans. Charles R. Joy. Boston: Beacon, 1948 [1913].

Scott, Stephen Carter. "A Biblical Analysis of Reality Therapy: A Comparison of the Nature of Mankind in Genesis 1–11 and in Reality Therapy." M.A. thesis, Pacific Lutheran University, 1982.

Scroggs, Robin. *Paul for a New Day*. Philadelphia: Fortress Press, 1977.

_____. "The Heuristic Value of a Psychoanalytic Model in the Interpretation of Pauline Theology." *Zygon* 13 (1978): 136–57.

_____. "Psychology as a Tool to Interpret the Text: Emerging Trends in Biblical Thought." *Christian Century* (March 24, 1982): 335–38.

_____. *New Testament Essays for Today*. Minneapolis: Fortress Press, 1993.

Segovia, Fernando F. "Towards a New Direction in Johannine Scholarship: The Fourth Gospel from a Literary Perspective." *Semeia* 53 (1991).

_____. "The Significance of Social Location in Reading John's Story." *Interpretation* 49 (4 1995): 370–78.

Segovia, Fernando F., and Mary Ann Tolbert, eds. *Reading From This Place: Volume 2: Social Location and Biblical Interpretation in Global Perspective*. Minneapolis: Fortress Press, 1995.

Segal, Alan F. "Paul's Conversion: Psychological Study." In *Paul the Convert: The Apostolate and Apostasy of Paul the Pharisee*, 285–300. New Haven: Yale University Press, 1990.

Segal, Robert A., ed. *Theories of Myth: From Ancient Israel and Greece to Freud, Jung, Campbell, and Lévi-Strauss*. Hamden, Conn.: Garland, 1966.

Seierstad, Ivar P. *Die Offenbarungserlebnisse der Propheten Amos, Jesaja und Jeremia: eine Untersuchung der Erlebnisvorgänge unter besonderer Berücksichtingung ihrer religiös-sittlichen Art und Auswirkung.* Oslo: Jacob Dybwad, 1946.

Seiler, G. F. *Animadversiones ad psychologiam sacram.* 1778–87.

Shepard, Richard G. "Biblical Progression as Moral Development: The Analogy and Its Implications." *Journal of Psychology and Theology* 22 (1994): 182–86.

Shepperson, Vance L. "Jacob's Journey: From Narcissism Toward Wholeness." *Journal of Psychology and Theology* 12 (1984): 178–87.

Shevrin, Howard, and Scott Dickman. "The Psychological Unconscious: A Necessary Assumption for All Psychological Theory." *American Psychologist* 35 (1980): 421–34.

Shiryon, Michael. "The Stories of Exodus as Metaphors for Psychotherapy." *Journal of Psychology and Judaism* 16 (1992): 235–44.

_____. "Joshua—The Underestimated Leader: The Use of Psychology in the Book of Joshua." *Journal of Psychology and Judaism* 19 (1995): 205–25.

Shulman, Dennis G. "A Psychoanalytic Perspective on Abraham's Binding of Isaac: Implications for Who We Are and How We Change." Denver, Colo.: unpublished American Psychological Association paper, 1997.

Sigal, L. "The Feminine Divine in the Book of Esther: A Psychoanalytic Study." In *The Bible in Light of Cuneiform Literature: Scripture in Context III*, eds. B. W. Jones and G. L. Mattingly, 381–411. Lewiston: Mellen, 1990.

Simon, Theodor. *Die Psychologie des Apostels Paulus.* Göttingen: Vandenhoeck & Ruprecht, 1897.

Sladeck, P. "Kehret um! (Mark 1:15): Die Umkehrforderung des Evangeliums im Lichte einer christlichen Tiefenpsychogie." *Ordens-Korrespondenz* 15 (1974): 173–84.

Sloan, Bobby Neil. "Guilt: A New Testament Exegesis with Implications for Psychotherapy." Dekalb, Ill.: Northern Illinois University Press, 1988.

Slusser, Gerald H. *From Jung to Jesus: Myth and Consciousness in the New Testament.* Atlanta: John Knox, 1986.

Smith, Wilfred Cantwell. "The Study of Religion and the Study of the Bible." *Journal of the American Academy of Religion* 39 (1971): 131–40.

_____. *What Is Scripture? A Comparative Approach.* Minneapolis: Fortress Press, 1993.

Snell, James H. "A Study of the Relationship between the Teachings of Jesus in the Book of Matthew and Existential Psychology as Represented by Rollo May." D. Ed. diss., University of Northern Colorado, 1978.

Sparkman, Collys F. "Satan and His Ancestor from a Psychological Standpoint." *Journal of Religion and Psychology* 5 (1912): 52–86; 163–94.

Spiegel, Yorick. "Psychoanalyse und analytische Psychologie—Instrument der Exegese?" *Psychoanalytische Interpretationen biblischer Texte*, ed. Yorick Spiegel. Munich: Chr. Kaiser, 1972.

_____. *Psychoanalytische Interpretationen biblischer Texte.* Munich: Chr. Kaiser, 1972.

_____. *Doppeldeutlich: Tiefendimensionen biblischer Texte.* Munich: Chr. Kaiser, 1978.

Stahlke, P. "Jungian Archetypes and the Personality of Jesus in the Synoptics." *Journal of Psychology and Theology* 18 (1990): 174–78.

Stalker, James. *Christian Psychology.* New York and London: Hodder & Stoughton, 1914.

Stegemann, Ekkehard W. "Aspekte Psychoanalytischer Auslegung der Johannesoffenbarung." *Evangelische Theologie* 54 (1994): 452–66.

Stein, Calvert. "Psychotherapy in the Bible." *Journal of the American Academy of Psychiatry and Neurology* 1 (2–3 1976): 67–70.

Stein, Dominique. "Is a Psycho-Analytic Reading of the Bible Possible?" In *Conflicting Ways of Interpreting the Bible*, eds. Hans Küng and J. Moltmann, 24–32. New York: Seabury, 1980.

_____. *Lectures psychanalytiques de la Bible*. Paris: Editions du Cerg, 1985.

_____. "Une lecture psychanalytique de la Bible." *Revue des Sciences Philosophiques et Théologiques* 72 (1988): 95–108.

Stein, Franz. "Die Bedeutung der Namen in der Bibel." *Zeischrift für Psychoanalytische Pädagogik* 2 (1927): 9–93.

Stein, Murray, and Robert Moore, eds. *Jung's Challenge to Contemporary Religion*. Wilmette, Ill.: Chiron, 1987.

Stendahl, Krister. "The Apostle Paul and the Introspective Conscience of the West." *Harvard Theological Review* 56 (1963): 199–215.

Steven, George. *The Psychology of the Christian Soul*. New York and London: Hodder & Stoughton, 1911.

Steyn, J. "Some Psycholinguistic Factors Involved in the Discourses Analysis of Ancient Texts." *Theologia Evangelica* 17.2 (1984): 51–65.

Stibbe, Mark W. G. "Structuralism." In *A Dictionary of Biblical Interpretation*, ed. R. J. Coggins and J. L. Houlden, 650–55. Nashville: Abingdon, 1990.

Storfer, Adolf Josef. *Marias jungfräuliche Mutterschaft. Ein völkerpsychologisches Fragment über Sexualsymbolik*. Berlin: 1914.

Story, A. Vaughn. "Bible Study with Principles of Neuropsychology and Neurolinguistic Programming to Help Envision and Experience Ministry in the Holy Spirit." D. Min. project, Perkins School of Theology, 1990.

Stramara, Daniel F., O.S.B. "The Inward Journey: Towards a Biblical Christian Psychology." *The Pecos Benedictine* (September 1988): 2,7.

Streeter, B. H. *The Four Gospels*. London: Macmillan, 1936.

Strehlow, Barbara. "Ansatzpunkt tiefenpsychologischer Interpretationen biblischer Text bei Sigmund Freud." *Wege zum Menschen* 23 (1971): 16–21.

Strozier, Charles. *Apocalypse: On the Psychology of Fundamentalism in America*. Boston: Beacon, 1996.

Suggs, R. P., ed. *Jungian Literary Criticism*. Evanston: Northwestern University Press, 1992.

Sullender, R. Scott. *Grief and Growth: Perspectives from Life-Span Psychology and Pauline Theology*. New York: Paulist, 1985.

Sunden, Hjalmar. "Der psychologische Aspekt in der Rechfertigung durch den Glauben." *Kerygma und Dogma* 32.2 (1986): 120–31.

Swinburne, R. *The Evolution of the Soul*. Oxford: Clarendon, 1986.

Tan, Siang-Yang. "Cognitive-behavior Therapy: a Biblical Approach and Critique." *Journal of Psychology and Theology* 15 (1987): 103–12.

Tarachow, Sidney. "St. Paul and Early Christianity: A Psychoanalytic Study." In *Psychoanalysis and the Social Sciences*, ed. G. Roheim et al., 1–5. New York: International Universities Press, 1947–58.

_____. "Judas, the Beloved Executioner." *Psychoanalytic Quarterly* 29 (1960): 528–54.

Tenzler, J. "Tiefenpsychologie und Wunderfrage." *Münchener Theologische Zeitschrift* 25 (1974): 118–37.

Terrien, Samuel. *The Magnificat: Musicians as Biblical Interpreters*. New York: Paulist, 1995.

Theissen, Gerd. *Biblical Faith: An Evolutionary Approach*. Philadelphia: Fortress Press, 1985.

_____. "Lokal-und Sozialkolorit in der Geschichte von der syrophönikischen Frau (Mk 7:24-30)." *Zeitschrift für die nuetestamentliche Wissenschaft* 75 (1984): 202-25.

_____. *Psychological Aspects of Pauline Theology*. Trans. John P. Galvin. Philadelphia: Fortress Press, 1987.

Thevenot, Xavier. "Emmaus, une nouvelle Genese: une lecture psychanalytique de Genese 2–3 et Luc 24:13–35." *Mélanges de Science Religieuse* 37 (1980): 3–18.

Thiselton, Anthony C. *New Horizons in Hermeneutics: The Theory and Practice of Transforming Bible Reading*. Grand Rapids: Zondervan, 1992.

Thomas, David Edward. "The Psychological Approach to the Study of Prophecy." University of Chicago, 1914.

Thompson, Stith. *Motif Index of Folk Literature*. Bloomington: Indiana University Press, 1955–58.

Thompson, W. *Christ and Consciousness, Exploring Christ's Contribution to Human Consciousness*. New York: Paulist, 1977.

Tisdale, John R. "Transpersonal Psychology and Jesus' Kingdom of God." *Journal of Humanistic Psychology* 34.3 (1994): 31–47.

Tolbert, Mary Ann. "Prodigal Son: An Essay in Literary Criticism from a Psychoanalytic Perspective." *Semeia* 9 (1977): 1–20.

_____. *Perspectives on the Parables: An Approach to Multiple Interpretations*. Philadelphia: Fortress Press, 1978.

_____. "When Resistance Becomes Repression: Mark 13:9–27 and the Poetics of Location." In *Readings from this Place: Social Location and Biblical Interpretation in Global Perspective*, eds. Fernando F. Segovia and Mary Ann Tolbert, 331–46. 2. Minneapolis: Fortress Press, 1995.

Trible, Phyllis. *Texts of Terror: Literary-Feminist Readings of Biblical Narratives*. Overtures to Biblical Theology. Philadelphia: Fortress Press, 1984.

Tweedie, Donald. *Logotherapy and the Christian Faith*. Grand Rapids: Baker, 1961.

Twelftree, Graham. *Jesus the Exorcist*. Peabody, Mass.: Hendrickson, 1994.

Ulanov, Ann Belford. *The Wisdom of the Psyche*. Cambridge, Mass.: Cowley, 1988.

_____. "The Christian Fear of the Psyche." In *Picturing God*, Cambridge, Mass.: Cowley, 1986.

Ulanov, Ann Belford, and Barry Ulanov. *Religion and the Unconscious*. Philadelphia: Westminster, 1975.

_____. *Primary Speech: A Psychology of Prayer*. Atlanta: John Knox, 1982.

Uleyn, A. "A Psychoanalytic Approach to Mark's Gospel." *Lumen Vitae* 32 (1977): 479–92.

_____. "The Possessed Man of Gerasa: A Psychoanalytic Interpretation of Reader Reactions." In *Current Issues in Psychology of Religion*, eds. J. Belzen and J. Lans, 90–96. Amsterdam: Rodopi, 1986.

Underwood, Ralph L. "Scripture: The Substance of Pastoral Care." *Quarterly Review* 11 (Winter 1991): 33–46.

_____. *Pastoral Care and the Means of Grace*. Minneapolis: Fortress Press, 1993.

_____. "Primordial Texts: An Object Relations Approach to Biblical Hermeneutics." *Pastoral Psychology* 45.3 (1997): 181–92.

Van de Kemp, Hendrika. "Origin and Evolution of the Term 'Psychology': Addenda." *American Psychologist* 35 (1980): 774.

_____. "A Note on the Term 'Psychology' in English Titles: Predecessors of Rauch." *Journal of the History of the Behavioral Sciences* 19 (1983): 185.

_____. "'Concerning the Soul' [early writings]." In *Psychology and Theology in Western Thought, 1672–1965: A Historical and Annotated Bibliography*, 41ff. Millwood, N.Y.: Kraus International Publications, 1984.

_____. "'Psychologies of Jesus.'" In *Psychology and Theology in Western Thought, 1672–1965: A Historical and Annotated Bibliography. Bibliographies in the History of Psychology and Psychiatry* A Series, 69–73. Millwood, N.Y.: Kraus International Publications, 1984.

_____. "Dangers of Psychologism: The Place of God in Psychology." *Journal of Psychology and Theology* 14 (1986): 97–109.

Van der Post, Laurens. *Jung and the Story of Our Time*. New York: Vintage Books, 1977.

Van der Wolk, P. C. "Zur Psychologie des Rauchopfers." *Imago* 7 (1921): 131–41.

Van Kaam, Adrian. *The Woman at the Well*. Denville, N.J.: Dimension Books, 1976.

Van Praag, H. M. "The Downfall of King Saul: The Neurobiological Consequences of Losing Hope." *Judaism* 35 (1986): 414–28.

Vergote, Antoine. *The Religious Man: A Psychological Study of Religious Attitudes*. Trans. M.-B. Said. Dayton, Ohio: Pflaum, 1969.

_____. "Apport des données psychanalytique à l'exégese: vie, loi et clivage du moi dans l'epître aux Romains 7." In *Exégèse et Herméneutique*, ed. Xavier Leon-Dufour. 109–47. Paris: Seuil, 1971.

_____. "Psychanalyse et interprétation biblique." In *Supplément au Dictionnaire de la Bible*, eds. H. Cazelles and A. Feuillet., cols. 252–60. Vol. 9. Paris: Letouzey et Ané, 1973–75.

Via, Dan O. "The Prodigal Son: A Jungian Reading." In *Society of Biblical Literature: 1975 Papers*, ed. George MacRae, 219–32. Vol. 2. Missoula: Scholars Press, 1975.

Vitz, Paul C. *Sigmund Freud's Christian Unconscious*. New York: Guilford Press, 1988.

Vogels, W. "The Spiritual Growth of Job: A Psychological Approach to the Book of Job." *Biblical Theology Bulletin* 11 (1981): 77–80.

_____. "The Inner Development of Job: One More Look at Psychology and the Book of Job." *Science et Esprit* 35 (1983): 227–30.

Von Franz, Marie-Louise. *The Psychological Meaning of Redemption Motifs in Fairytales*. Toronto: Inner City Books, 1980.

Vonck, P. "The Crippling Victory: The Story of Jacob's Struggle at the River Jabbok (Genesis 32: 23–33)." *African Ecclesial Review* 26 (1984): 75–87.

Wachinger, Lorenz. "Spiegelung und dunkles Wort: Tiefenpsychologische Schriftauslegung—am Beispiel des Ps 91 (90)." In *Liturgie und Dichtung, II*, eds. H. Becker and R. Kaczynski, 335–57. St. Ottilien: Eos, 1983.

Wahl, Herbert. "Empathie und Text: das selbstpsychologische Modell interaktiver Texthermeneutik." *Theologische Quartalschrift* 169.3 (1989): 201–22.

Wall, Ernest A. "The Kerygma's Psychology and Human Distress." *Journal of Psychology and Theology* 1.4 (1973): 48–56.

Waller, George. *The Biblical View of the Soul*. London and New York: Longmans, Green & Co., 1904.

Wallwork, Ernest. "Thou Shalt Love Thy Neighbor as Thyself: The Freudian Critique." *Journal of Religious Ethics* 7 (1982): 264–319.

_____. "Ethics After Freud." *Criterion* 32.1 (1993): 24–32.

Walsh, J. A. "The Dream of Joseph: A Jungian Interpretation." *Journal of Psychology and Theology* 11 (1983): 20–27.

Ward, Colleen A., and Michael Beaubrun H. "The psychodynamics of demon possession." *Journal of the Scientific Study of Religion* 19 (1980): 201–7.

Warrior, Robert. "Canaanites, Cowboys, and Indians: Deliverance, Conquest, and Liberation Theology Today." *Christianity and Crisis* 29 (1989): 261–65.

Watt, Trevor. "Joseph's Dreams." In *Jung and the Interpretation of the Bible*, ed. David L. Miller, 55–70. New York: Continuum, 1995.

Watts, Richard E. "Biblical Agape as a Model of Social Interest." *Individual Psychology: Journal of Adlerian Theory, Research and Practice* 48:1 (1992): 35–40.

Weems, Renita. *Battered Love: Marriage, Sex, and Violence in the Hebrew Prophets.* Minneapolis: Fortress Press, 1995.

Wehr, Gerhard. *Portrait of Jung: An Illustrated Biography.* Trans. W. A. Hargreaves. New York: Herder & Herder, 1971.

_____. "The Task of Depth Psychological Biblical Interpretation." *Analytische Psychologie* 1.5 (1974): 48–54.

_____. *Jung: A Biography.* Trans. David M. Weeks. Boston: Shambala, 1988.

Weinberg, Joel. "Der Mensch im Weltbild des Chronisten: seine Psyche." *Vetus Testamentum* 33 (July 1983): 298–316.

Weiss, Abner. "Jacob's Struggle: A Psycho-Existential Exegesis." *Journal of Psychology and Judaism* 18 (Spring 1994): 19–31.

Weiss, Samuel A. "The Biblical Story of Ruth. Analytic Implications of the Hebrew Masoretic Text." *American Imago* 16 (1959): 195–209.

Wellisch, E. *Isaac and Oedipus. A Study in Biblical Psychology of the Sacrifice of Isaac, the Akedah.* London: Routledge and Kegan Paul, 1954.

Wernik, Uri. "Frustrated Beliefs and Early Christianity: A Psychological Enquiry into the Gospels of the New Testament." *Numen* 22 (1975): 96–130.

Westman, Heinz. *The Springs of Creativity: The Bible and the Creative Process of the Psyche.* Peru, Ill.: Chiron, 1961.

_____. *The Structure of Biblical Myths: The Ontogenesis of the Psyche.* Dallas, Tex.: Spring, 1983.

White, Hugh. *Narration and Discourse in the Book of Genesis.* Cambridge: Cambridge University Press, 1991.

Whyte, Lancelot Law. "Unconscious." In *The Encyclopedia of Philosophy*, ed. Paul Edwards. 185–89. New York: Macmillan, 1967.

_____. *The Unconscious Before Freud.* London and New York: Julian Friedmann Publishers and St. Martin's Press, 1978.

Widengren, George. *Literary and Psychological Aspects of the Hebrew Prophets.* Uppsala: Lundequistska, 1948.

Wiggins, James. *Religion as Story.* New York: Harper & Row, 1976.

Wilder, Amos. "Myth and Dream in Christian Scripture." In *Myths, Dreams, and Religion*, ed. Joseph Campbell, 67–90. New York: Dutton, 1970.

Wiles, Maurice, and Mark Santer, eds. *Documents in Early Christian Thought.* New York: Cambridge University Press, 1975.

Willett, Michael. *Wisdom Christology in the Fourth Gospel.* Lewiston: Mellen Research University Press, 1992.

Williams, James G. *The Bible, Violence, and the Sacred: Liberation from the Myth of Sanctioned Violence.* Valley Forge, Pa.: Trinity Press International, 1995.

Wilson, R. W. "Psychology, Western." In *Dictionary of Pastoral Care and Counseling*, ed. Rodney J. Hunter. 995–98. Nashville: Abingdon, 1990.

Wimberly, Edward P. *Using Scripture in Pastoral Counseling.* Nashville: Abingdon, 1994.

Wink, Walter. *The Bible in Human Transformation: Toward a New Paradigm for Biblical Study.* Philadelphia: Fortress Press, 1973.

_____. *The Dangers of Psychologizing in the Use of Psychoanalytic Insights in Biblical Studies.* Unpublished SBL paper, Washington D. C., 1974.

_____. *Engaging the Powers.* Minneapolis: Fortress Press, 1992.

_____. *Naming the Powers: The Language of Power in the New Testament.* Philadelphia: Fortress Press, 1984.

_____. "On Wrestling with God: Using Psychological Insights in Biblical Study." *Religion in Life* 47 (1978): 136–47.

_____. "On Psychologizing." In *Transforming Bible Study: A Leader's Guide*, 163–65. 2d rev. ed. Nashville: Abingdon, 1989.

_____. *Transforming Bible Study: A Leader's Guide*. 2d rev. ed., Nashville: Abingdon, 1980.

_____. *Unmasking the Powers: The Invisible Forces that Determine Human Existence*. Philadelphia: Fortress, 1986.

Winnicott, D. W. *Playing and Reality*. London: Tavistock, 1971.

Wise, Carroll A. *Psychiatry and the Bible*. New York: Harper & Row, 1956.

Wittels, Fritz. "Psychoanalysis and History. The Nibelungs and the Bible." *Psychoanalytic Quarterly* 15 (1946): 88–103.

Wittmann, E. C., and C. R. Bollmann. *Bible Therapy: How the Bible Solves Your Problems: A Guide to God's Word*. New York: Simon & Schuster, 1977.

Wohlgelernter, D. K. "Goal Directedness: Understanding the Development of the Book of Job." *Individual Psychology: Journal of Adlerian Theory, Research and Practice* 44 (1988): 296–306.

Wolff, Hanna. *Jesus the Therapist*. Oak Park, Ill.: Meyer Stone Books, 1987. [Ger. ed., *Jesus als Psychotherapeut. Jesu Menschenbehandlung als Modell moderner Psychotherapie* (Stuttgart: Radius-Verlag, 1978)],

Wolff, Werner. *Changing Concepts of the Bible: A Psychological Analysis of Its Words, Symbols, and Beliefs*. New York: Hermitage, 1951.

Wood, F. B. "A Neuropsychological Commentary on Biblical Faith." In *Civil Religion and Transcendent Experience*, ed. R. Wood, 129–35. Macon, Ga: Mercer University Press, 1988.

Wright, Elizabeth. *Psychoanalytic Criticism: Theory and Practice*. 2d ed. New York: Methuen, 1987.

Wright, Emily Dudley. *The Psychology of Christ*. New York: Cochrane, 1909.

Wright, Jerry R. "Symbols for the Christ in the Gospel of John and the Archetypal Self in the Psychology of Carl Gustav Jung." Columbia Theological Seminar, 1991.

Wuellner, Wilhelm H., and Robert C. Leslie. *The Surprising Gospel: Intriguing Psychological Insights from the New Testament*. Nashville: Abingdon, 1984.

Wulff, David. *Psychology of Religion: Classic and Contemporary Views*. New York: John Wiley and Sons, 1991.

Young, Allan. "Psychiatry and Self in Bible and Talmud: The Example of Posttraumatic Stress Disorder and Enemy *herem*." *Koroth* 9 (1988): 194–210.

Young, Frances. *The Art of Performance. Towards a Theology of Holy Scripture*. London: Darton, Longman, and Todd, 1990.

Yungblut, John R. *Rediscovering the Christ*. New York: Seabury, 1974.

Zabriskie, Colleen. "A Psychological Analysis of Biblical Interpretations Pertaining to Women." *Journal of Psychology and Theology* 4 (1976): 304–12.

Zeligs, Dorothy. "Psychological Factors in the Teaching of Biblical Stories." *Jewish Eduction* 22 (1951/53): 24–28.

_____. *Psychoanalysis and the Bible: A Study in Depth of Seven Leaders*. New York: Bloch, 1974.

_____. *Moses: A Psychodynamic Study*. New York: Human Sciences Press, 1986.

Zimmermann, Frank. "The Book of Ecclesiastes in the Light of Some Psychoanalytic Observations." *American Imago* (1948): 301–5.

_____. "Origin and Significance of the Jewish Rite of Circumcision." *Psychoanalysis and the Psychoanalytic Review* 38 (1951): 103–12.

Index of Modern Authors

Index of Biblical and Psychological Subjects